PSYCHOLOGY IN BUSINESS

THEORY AND APPLICATIONS

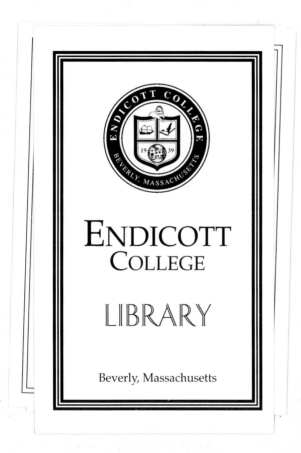

PSYCHOLOGY IN BUSINESS
Theory and Applications

Eugene F. McKenna
M.Sc., Ph.D., A.C.I.S., A.B.Ps.S.
North East London Polytechnic

LAWRENCE ERLBAUM ASSOCIATES, PUBLISHERS
London   Hillsdale, New Jersey

Lawrence Erlbaum Associates Ltd., Publishers
Chancery House
319 City Road
London EC1V 1LJ

British Library Cataloguing in Publication Data

McKenna, Eugene F.
  Psychology in business: theory and applications.
  1. Psychology 2. Management
  3. Organizational behaviour
  I. Title
  150' .24658   BF121

ISBN 0-86377-041-X
ISBN 0-86377-042-8 Pbk

Typeset by CK Typesetters Ltd., Sutton.
Printed and bound by A. Wheaton & Co. Ltd., Exeter.

Contents

FOREWORD

There have been repeated calls for business and management studies to become more relevant. Some see this as requiring less attention to the theories of contributory disciplines in favour of greater concentration on the ways in which excellent organizations are managed in practice. Business students and members of executive programmes in fact often experience difficulty in seeing how conceptual and theoretical material bears upon the practical circumstances they have known or can envisage.

Business and management education is, however, an investment for the future. It cannot develop its clients' capacities for coping with the changed world ahead simply by reference to what succeeds today. Students must be provided with an intellectual apparatus that will help them to make sense of new situations. This is precisely what sound theories should enable them to do, and is the reason why Kurt Lewin, the pioneering social psychologist, once stated that "there is nothing so practical as a good theory."

The reality is that we all resort constantly to the theories we carry around in our heads, and have to do so if we are to avoid going back to first base every time we make a decision. However, our own theories may not be too well informed. They may be based on the quite narrow combination of individual common sense and necessarily limited experience. Home-grown theories can therefore lead to inappropriate actions. The fact that countries such as Britain which have less well-educated managements also tend to display relatively poor business performance reinforces the point. Successful management requires trained and informed minds.

Business and management studies therefore become particularly relevant when they demonstrate how soundly based bodies of knowledge can, through the economical language of concepts and theoretical propositions, enlighten an understanding of practical problems. From such understanding flows the capacity to deal with those problems. Eugene McKenna in his book performs this extremely relevant service by elucidating the contributions which the discipline of psychology can offer to the world of business.

Business students, particularly those intending to specialize in popular subjects such as accounting and marketing, often fail to see the point of studying psychology. Eugene McKenna succeeds in making the point convincingly. What he achieves in this book serves to demonstrate that much of the problem lies in the fact that the links between psychology and business practice have not been brought out adequately by previous authors.

Textbooks on psychology provide a sound and comprehensive treatment, but they are generally directed at the student of the discipline itself. They contain plenty on rats, monkeys, and flashing lights, but little or nothing on the world of business and management. The teacher, or more likely the student, is left to make the linkages. Texts on organizational behaviour do refer to the practical sphere, but they are usually limited in their coverage of the range of contributions that psychology can offer. They are not particularly concerned to provide an insight into psychological perspectives and methods, yet this intellectual apparatus is precisely the item of value. For it is the portable resource which students can carry away with them and transfer from one situation to another, from present to future.

Psychology in Business takes the reader through the mainstream areas of psychology. It describes the theories and models which have been developed, and assesses both their contributions and limitations. Each chapter takes care to demonstrate the relevance of this material for business situations with particular reference to accounting and marketing. The author also gives special attention to the currently extremely significant subjects of new technology, health and safety at work, and stress. The book is clearly written and well organized, and strives to allow nothing to stand between the reader's appreciation of psychology and the way it informs very practical problems.

Eugene McKenna has drawn upon his wide knowledge and working experience to produce what I believe will be seen as a pioneering book. It builds bridges between psychology and other structured areas of study such as accounting, and between psychology and areas of practice such as advertising. It answers the call for relevance without compromising the integrity of its subject.

Professor John Child
ESRC Work Organization Research Centre
University of Aston in Birmingham

PREFACE

A quick glance at the syllabi on behavioural science for diploma and degree courses in business and management studies at both the undergraduate and postgraduate levels, and at the professional level, will convince the reader of the importance of the study of psychology. Practice varies with regard to how psychology is presented; it can be taught as a separate subject, alternatively it can form a major part of a programme in organizational behaviour or behavioural science at the foundation or intermediate stage of a course.

At this stage of the course, psychological topics tend to be categorized by traditional areas of study (e.g., personality, perception, groups, leadership, etc.). It is later in the course, in the main, that the focus changes to themes and issues, when more than one social science discipline may be introduced as explanatory mechanisms.

The main emphasis of this book is the study of the individual and the group—the realm of social psychology. It is not uncommon for students who study behavioural science on business and management courses, and relevant professional courses in such areas as personnel, marketing, accounting, production, and health and safety, to complain about the lack of relevance and applicability of the subject. Being aware of this, I felt a basic textbook on psychology was needed which would introduce the reader to a wider range of issues in psychology than that found in the "psychology section" of conventional textbooks on organizational behaviour, and which would be applied more to the business context than is usual in standard introductory textbooks on psychology.

To meet this perceived need I wrote this text in a style likely to engage the interest of the student, drawing on numerous real-life examples and research studies relevant to the world of business which are so often absent from comparable texts. In addition, I felt it necessary to capture the spirit of the comparatively recent development in business and management education, namely the integration, or linking, of disciplines and subject areas. Consequently, in this textbook you will find numerous links between psychology and other subjects in the business and management studies curricula.

In a sense I tried to establish links, and to build bridges, between psychology and the other subjects in order to foster a more relevant applied perspective and to provide a useful foundation for more advanced integration later in the course. This was assisted by a search of the literature outside mainstream psychology; for example, the literature on the psychological aspects of accounting, marketing, personnel, and safety at work, etc., was used to obtain suitable empirical and practical applications of the psychological concepts.

My major objective has been to produce a text which would introduce the basic concepts and principles in social psychology clearly with emphasis on their relevance and applications, but at the same time not to over-popularize the subject.

The text requires no previous study of psychology. Despite its suitability for use on degree, diploma, and professional courses, it can profitably be used by business managers on short non-examination courses.

Each chapter has a brief introduction, which maps out the area to be covered, a summary, and a list of review questions. Although each chapter is self-contained, the reader will find a number of cross references to other topics in the book. The final chapter is unlike the rest; it focuses on the hazards and stressful conditions which feature in organizational life.

The impact of new technology is considered in more than one setting in the body of the text.

Finally, I hope to have realized my objective in writing this book; and I hope the reader finds his or her excursion through it a pleasant and rewarding experience.

Acknowledgements

This book owes its existence to a number of beneficial influences arising from many sources. In particular, my thanks to those mentioned below who reviewed earlier drafts of the manuscript and made valuable comments and suggestions, that were seriously considered with a view to improving the quality of the final draft.

Bernard Barry, Cranfield School of Management
Tony Chapman, Cranfield School of Management
Andrew Lock, Kingston Polytechnic
Peter Ribeaux, Middlesex Polytechnic

Dedication
To Alison, Geraldine, and Graham

Introduction:
Perspectives and Enquiry

The study of psychology provides valuable knowledge and insights that help us to understand the behaviour of people in business organizations and settings. As a consequence, the manager is equipped with pertinent information about human behaviour when faced with human problems in a business and management context. The contribution that psychology has made to the solution of many human problems encountered in business is significant. It has resulted in better management of human resources, improved methods of personnel selection, appraisal and training, improved morale and efficiency of operations, a reduction in accident rates and better working conditions.

Despite these claims to success, it should be stated that psychology is not a panacea for all the human problems associated with business. For example, there are occasions when the outcome of the application of personnel selection techniques is less than perfect. Likewise, a programme to raise the level of morale in a company may, for a variety of reasons, fail to meet the expectations of the management, even though the results provide grounds for optimism.

In the study of human behaviour the psychologist is concerned with a repertoire of behaviour that is both observable (e.g. walking and talking) and unobservable (e.g. feeling and thinking). Animal behaviour has also captured the interest of the psychologist.

DIFFERENT PERSPECTIVES IN PSYCHOLOGY

The development of psychological thought has been influenced by the different traditions associated with the study of behaviour. These traditions are often referred to as "perspectives" or "models of man." The major perspectives could be classified as the *psychoanalytical*, the *behaviourist* and the *phenomenological* approaches. The *psychoanalytical* approach, initiated by Freud, ignores or shows little interest in certain areas of contemporary psychology (e.g. attitudes, perception, learning) because of a prime preoccupation with providing help for neurotic patients. This approach, which is discussed in Chapter 1, provided a major impetus to the early development of modern psychology. In psychoanalysis the therapist takes note of what the patient has to say and perceives emotional reactions and signs of resistance to the treatment. In a discussion with the patient the therapist interprets the information emanating from the analysis session. The central thrust of this approach is that man's behaviour can be investigated in a non-experimental way, that behaviour is determined by some unconscious force, and that behavioural difficulties or abnormalities in adult life spring from childhood.

Behaviourism is the approach to psychology that is confined to what is objective, observable and measurable. This approach advocated a scientific means of studying behaviour in carefully controlled conditions, and featured prominently in psychology until the 1950s. The use of animals in many behaviourist experiments may be influenced partly by the fact that they are less complicated than humans, with a lower propensity to rely on previous experience when faced with a stimulus. Behaviourism, which is discussed in Chapter 4, provided psychology with a number of valuable experimental methods.

However, the preoccupation with behaviour that can be observed and objectively measured has obvious weaknesses. These are primarily associated with the neglect of the processing capacity of the human brain. Factors such as subjective feelings, expectations, plans and thought processes are ruled out because they do not lend themselves to scientific analysis in the same way that observable behaviour does. In a sense behaviourism may be viewed as a mechanistic view of man, with the emphasis on the inputs and outputs from the "machine" but with little regard to the functioning of the internal mechanics.

The final approach, *phenomenology*, amounts to a humanistic reaction to behaviourism. In this approach the emphasis is essentially on man's experience rather than his behaviour. For instance, even though on occasions we all share common perceptions, each person perceives the world in his own distinctive way. Our unique perceptions, and action strategies based on them, tend to determine what we are and how we react. In the process the individual utilizes previous experience, needs, expectations and attitudes. This approach to psychology is adopted throughout the book where a cognitive view of man is acknowledged.

Among the issues discussed in the main chapters of the book are: personality profiles; job satisfaction and motivation; perception and communication; learning and training; decision-making; employee attitudes and morale; social interactions of people in groups and teamwork; supervision and leadership; the impact of modern technology; and pressures and hazards at work. Explanations of these and other issues dealt with in the book come from the different perspectives in psychology identified above. Since the various chapters draw heavily on empirical or research evidence in psychology, it seems appropriate to acknowledge the methods used in psychological enquiry.

METHODS OF PSYCHOLOGICAL ENQUIRY

Knowledge about human behaviour can be obtained in part through experience, and it is possible to derive some useful insights by this means. However, insight into human behaviour derived from experience has its limitations, simply because our perceptions of the behaviour of others are not always reliable, partly due to the influence exerted by our attitudes and values. In addition, our observations may be based on a limited and possibly unrepresentative sample which does not provide an adequate basis for generalization about human behaviour. By contrast, research provides an approach for obtaining information about many dimensions of behaviour that cannot be acquired through experience alone. When psychologists conduct research into various aspects of behaviour they try to apply the scientific method. Scientific enquiry is based on the assumption that events and phenomena are *caused*. So a major objective of psychological research is to determine what factors cause people to behave in a particular way. But achieving this objective is extraordinarily difficult because psychologists, unlike physical scientists, have to deal with unpredictable material. Subjects lie, lack self-insight, give socially approved responses, and try to satisfy the needs of the experimenter as they see them.

In reality a great deal of psychological research at the empirical level is concerned with identifying relationships between events and phenomena, and the question of why people behave in a given manner often remains unanswered. However, the identification of relationships can be productive in increasing our knowledge and insight. For instance, a strong relationship between management style and a low level of morale among subordinates might not tell us what particular aspects of management style cause the problems. But it does allow us to focus more clearly on the source of the difficulties.

Research psychologists in the course of their work evaluate claims, impressions, ideas and theories and search for real and valid evidence to test and generate ideas about relationships between circumstances and behaviour. As more empirical information about behaviour is accumulated, hypotheses or speculations about certain aspects of behaviour are developed. This can be done in a systematic and controlled way. The aim is to discover general explanations or theories. In building theories the researcher is engaged in explaining, understanding, predicting and controlling phenomena.

As research data accumulates and theories are confirmed, laws and principles are put forward. Although in certain areas of psychology it has been possible to create an impressive collection of empirical evidence that has some theoretical credibility or a resemblance to the ingredients of a cause-and-effect relationship, much of the research in business psychology is at the empirical stage with modest developments in the theoretical sphere.

In order to ensure that the findings of psychological research are as objective, reliable and quantifiable as possible, the characteristics of the scientific method are adopted. These include: definition and control of the variables used in the research study; data analysis; replication; and hypothesis testing.

Variables used in research are referred to as "independent" and "dependent" variables. The independent variable is the factor that is varied—e.g., the level of illumination in a particular task is physically controlled by the experimenter. This could then be related to a measurable dependent variable, such as the number of units of production. In other circumstances the dependent variable could be classified rather than measured. For example, the subject's behaviour (dependent variable) in response to a variation in experimental conditions of stress (independent variable) might be classified as belonging to one of the following categories: (1) remains calm; (2) loses composure; (3) loses self-control. Such classifications should be made in a reliable manner, sometimes by more than one observer.

Apart from the control of the independent variable by the experimenter, it is also necessary to control extraneous variables to prevent a contaminating effect. For instance, in assessing the significance of training techniques to employee performance, it would be necessary to ensure that factors other than training methods did not significantly influence the results. Contaminating factors in this case could be educational background, intelligence, age, and experience. In some cases extraneous variables cannot be foreseen, but it must be recognized that extraneous variables can have a contaminating effect on results, leading to incorrect conclusions.

The requirement to come forward with operational definitions of variables or phenomena that can be subjected to empirical testing is prompted by the desire to bring precision into the meaning of concepts used in research. Ambiguities could otherwise arise. In experimental conditions raw data, often in quantitative form, is collected and summarized, and usually subjected to statistical analysis. Descriptive statistics, as the term implies, are concerned with describing phenomena in statistical terms, e.g., a key characteristic of a sample of managers, such as the average weekly hours spent at work.

Inferential statistics are concerned with drawing inferences from the analysis of the data. In measuring the strength of the association between two variables, the question of statistical significance arises. Is the relationship significant or not significant, or is it due to chance? The psychologist uses inferential statistics to make inferences about general events or populations from observations of samples and to convey to us some idea of the confidence we can have in those inferences.

Replication arises when an experiment is repeated. We expect to come up with the same result if the study is repeated, otherwise our explanations and descriptions are unreliable. The notion of reliability and validity is discussed in the section on *Attitude Measurement* in Chapter 6. A final characteristic of the scientific method is hypothesis testing. The research starts with the formulation of hypotheses, preceded by a search of the literature. Research evidence is then related to the hypotheses, resulting in their acceptance or rejection—Karl Popper is of the view that science proceeds by refuting hypotheses. The researcher then comes up with new observations that challenge new hypotheses.

Different branches of psychology use different techniques when applying the scientific method. For instance, in certain branches of social psychology (e.g., attitudes) questionnaires are used. Reinforcement schedules, referred to in Chapter 4, can be used in operant conditioning (part of learning theory). Electrodes that stimulate the brain are the preserve of physiological psychology. The important thing to bear in mind is that the technique used should be appropriate to the research problem in hand.

Different settings are used to carry out psychological research. An experiment can be carried out under controlled conditions in a laboratory or work situation where the independent variable is under the control of the experimenter. For example, there is an account of the systematic manipulation of the independent variable to demonstrate a causal effect on the dependent variable in the discussion of operant conditioning in Chapter 4. Here the frequency of dispensation of food pellets to the pigeon in Skinner's experiment is varied because the experimenter thinks this will cause changes in behaviour. In another case the experimenter may introduce different types of incentive schemes and assess the impact they make on the individual's performance.

Another approach is the study of human behaviour in a real-life setting. For example, the researcher collects data on identical groups of workers engaged in the same task but working under different styles of supervision. Their job performance under different supervisory conditions could then be compared. However, it might prove difficult to create groups which are identical in terms of age, sex, skill, length of service and so on.

Survey research methods, using both interviews and questionnaires, are frequently used in real-life settings. When various attributes of a particular population are collected this is referred to as a *descriptive* survey. When causal relationships or associations (e.g., the relationship between systems of executive reward and motivation) are explored, surveys are *explanatory* in nature. The two types of survey can be interrelated. In the section on *Attitude Measurement* in Chapter 6 there is a discussion of scales used in attitude surveys.

The major advantage of surveys is that comparable data from a number of respondents can be obtained and patterns in the data can be explored. The major disadvantages are that we may over-simplify behaviour, and that by placing such a heavy reliance on the subject's verbal report the research is exposed to certain weaknesses. These could include shortcomings in the memory of the subject as well as biased viewpoints. In addition, the subject is free to withhold critical information.

Memories, thoughts and feelings (non-observable data) can be inferred from observing behaviour and from self-reporting by the individual. Sometimes the psychologist uses observation to corroborate the evidence in a self-report. For example, the subject's statements about his or her active involvement in the life of the organization could be validated by observing the nature and extent of that involvement.

Observation, as a method of investigation, can be used in a variety of ways. It lends itself to the development of insights which could subsequently lead to hypothesis formation and it may facilitate the interpretation of data obtained by other techniques. It can be used where subjects (e.g., infants or animals) cannot provide verbal reports. Likewise, it could be suitable where people do not like being interviewed or having to fill in questionnaire forms, or where they might distort the answers.

The psychologist engaged in observation can record the behaviour of individuals and groups as it occurs, although the recording of observations during the actual process of observation can prove difficult. If keeping a record follows the act of observation, the question to ask is how soon after the event does one make the record. Without the benefit of an action play-back facility, it is difficult to check the accuracy of one's perceptions. Not all behaviour can be observed, because of the subject's need for privacy in certain circumstances, and it is important to acknowledge the possibility that people may alter their behaviour if they know they are being watched. The observer has to guard against bias stemming from personal prejudice, and must try to maintain objectivity when relationships develop between the observer and other members of the group.

In the light of the above observations it is imperative that an observation episode is planned and executed in a systematic and rigorous way. Observation can be structured or unstructured, and it is helpful if there are two or more observers so that they can compare notes and check bias. Unstructured observation often takes the form of participant observation and is often used in exploratory investigations. A participant observer could be, knowingly or unknowingly, a member of the group he or she is observing. Participant observation can also be carried out in secret, e.g., an experimenter may pose as a convert in a religious sect. A participant observer involved in the life of a group is more strategically placed to understand the complexities and subtleties of behaviour and its meaning than the psychologist applying standardized questionnaires or creating artificial and restrictive laboratory situations. However, field work is a time-consuming exercise. In structured observation, the observer knows in advance what behaviour is relevant to the research objectives. A specific plan can be devised to collect and record observations with the opportunity to exercise more precision and control. Although the well-trained observer may produce very reliable results, some of the subtleties detected in unstructured observation may be lost in structured observation.

1 PERSONALITY

1 Personality

Personality, a complex topic comprising a number of perspectives, has been studied by psychologists from many different angles; definitions of the concept of personality reflect this state of affairs.

This chapter opens with a definition of personality, followed by an examination of the approaches used by researchers to study the subject.

Next, there is an analysis of the psycho-analytical perspective, and a brief description of projective tests. The latter, which have an indirect relationship with psychoanalysis, are used in consumer motivation research and are complementary to role playing and visualization.

There follows a discussion of a number of other perspectives on personality, some more important than others. These can be classified as follows: traits, types, interpersonal, behavioural, social, and cognitive. Psychographics is an approach used in consumer behaviour research. All of the perspectives above provide valuable insights which illuminate our understanding of the personality factor. The discussion is illustrated, where appropriate, with examples relevant to the business context.

DEFINITION

Repeatedly, we evaluate the people we meet in everyday life. We make subjective assessments of their behaviour. We note their personal appearance and their mannerisms. We listen to what they have to say and watch what they do in different settings. We use this information to make a subjective judgement of the "personality" of the person concerned. This process elicits descriptions of personality traits such as boring, cautious, rigid, uninspiring; or alternatively, lively, innovative, imaginative, and so on. The definitions which follow capture what is generally meant by personality.

Personality consists of the physical, mental, moral and social qualities of the individual. These qualities are dynamic and integrated: they can be observed by other people in everyday life. Personality is comprised of the individual's natural and acquired impulses, habits, interests, sentiments, ideals, opinions, and beliefs as they are projected to the outside world. Personality consists of "those relatively stable and enduring aspects of the individual which distinguish him from other people and at the same time form the basis of our predictions concerning his future behaviour."[1]

Just as there are many definitions of personality, so there are many theories of personality.

RESEARCH APPROACHES

There are two fundamental approaches to the study of personality. One is the idiographic approach, and the other, the nomothetic.

Idiographic Approach

The researcher adopting this approach operates in the belief that the individual is not just a collection of separate traits, but is a well-integrated organism. The individual reacts as a system to various situations, with past experiences and future intentions contributing to present behaviour.

Allport constructed an idiographic portrait of a woman named Jenny, by using the 301 letters she had written over a period of 11 years, and by examining them from a number of different perspectives.[2]

This emphasis on a very intensive study of individual cases is said to capture the wholeness and the uniqueness of the personality as it functions in the many and the diverse situations found day-to-day. The approach tries to capture the essence of the total personality.

This approach is often criticized because it does not lend itself easily to scientific measurement, and because there are difficulties in extrapolating from the particular—the single or few cases—to people in general. This problem could be overcome by studying many more individual cases, but it would prove very costly.

Nomothetic Approach

The main objective of the nomothetic approach is the isolation of one or more of the variables of personality. This is done by measuring the variables scientifically under controlled conditions, using a sufficiently large test sample. It is hoped that the relationship between traits and behaviour is generalizable and repeatable in other samples of people at other times. This approach is fundamentally opposed to the idiographic approach. There follows an example of a nomothetically based empirical study.[3]

In the study subjects were asked to state their feelings about aggression

TABLE 1.1
Variables in Hetherington and Wray's (1964)
Nomothetic Study

Criteria No.	Aggression	Desire for Social Approval
I	High	High
II	High	Low
III	Low	High
IV	Low	Low

and social approval on questionnaires. Each subject was presented with photographed cartoons expressing aggression, and was asked to evaluate what they saw on a scale ranging from extremely funny to extremely un-funny. Their responses were then classified according to the four criteria illustrated in Table 1.1. The researchers assumed that if the cartoons were viewed as funny the subject found little difficulty in condoning aggression. If the opposite was the case, they assumed that aggression was disapproved of, or perhaps was considered a delicate subject.

In an attempt to evaluate the disinhibiting effect of alcohol on the ac-ceptance and expression of aggression following exposure to the cartoons, half the subjects were given alcoholic drink. Those subjects who did not take alcoholic drink and who were classified in accordance with Criterion I in Table 1.1, were more disturbed by the cartoons and rated them 'much less funny' than those subjects who were fitted into Criterion II. The subjects who took alcoholic drink, and who were also classified in accordance with Criterion I in Table 1.1, perceived the cartoons as being funny. They had a high need for social approval, but it appears that the alcohol diluted this strong desire and permitted them enjoyment of the aggressive humour which would otherwise have been disturbing. Those subjects who took alcoholic drink and were classified in accordance with Criterion II acted in a similar way to their counterparts who did not take alcoholic drink.

The researchers contend that subjects classified as low in aggression did not have much of an impulse to express aggression, whether or not they had taken alcoholic drink. Subjects classified in accordance with Criterion I—high in aggression and high in desire for social approval—have strong aggressive impulses, but they repress these impulses because of their strong desire for social approval. It would be interesting to know whether social approval diminishes in importance under the influence of alcohol, or whether alcohol reduces the fear of social disapproval of an aggressive act.

The final comment on the weaknesses of the two approaches to the study of personality must be reserved for somebody who has made a close study of personality: Lazarus makes the point that the idiographic approach is too global and does not possess valued scientific features such as controlled observation, precision of measurement or repeatability.[4] Neither does he believe that the nomothetic approach is the correct one for distortions arise in any analysis when component parts are studied in isolation and when there is a failure to examine the full range of reactions to the variety of life's circumstances.

PSYCHO-ANALYTICAL PERSPECTIVE

Freud's greatest contribution to our understanding of human behaviour was probably his recognition of the power the unconscious has in directing that behaviour.[5]

Levels of Awareness

Freud classified awareness into three levels—*conscious*, *preconscious*, and *unconscious*. That of which one is aware, is in the *conscious* mind. As I write this section, I am fully aware of what I am doing. But I am not aware of a great deal of information which, if required, could be brought to the level of awareness. For example, I could recall the broad details of the way I spent each day of my holiday with the children last year once I had put my mind to it. All such material is said to be *preconscious*—in the sense that it is not presently in awareness but, with some effort, can be recalled. The third level of awareness—the *unconscious* mind—is about that which we are totally unaware of, and therefore it cannot normally be brought into awareness. The material in the unconscious mind comprises drives, desires, urges, some memories and deep-rooted moral standards.

It follows that the individual can be motivated by forces in the unconscious mind of which he or she is unaware. For example, one may hear reference to an individual's behaviour as being "entirely out of character" and difficult to explain, or we recognize a person's behaviour as being due to a strange impulse—these are examples of a lack of insight into forces that are motivating the individual. Psycho-therapy or hypnosis could be used to gain a clearer understanding of the unconscious factors that motivate behaviour.

Structure of Personality

Freud conceived the structure of personality as being comprised of three parts with different functions. These are the *id*, *ego*, and *superego*.

1. Id.   The *id* is the biological basis of personality. It consists of the inherited characteristics of the individual and can be viewed as a collection of instinctive desires, urges or needs all demanding immediate gratification. It is concerned with trying to maintain a balance between forces within the person, which produce conflict and tension. The *id* finds these conflicts difficult to accept and is therefore keen to reduce them.

The *id* tends to be irrational and impulsive; it adheres to the pleasure principle. That is, it invites and accepts pleasure and tries to avoid displeasure. It has no values, no right or wrong, no moral standards and no consideration for other people.

The *id* is cut off from the external world and, because it is frequently kept in check by the *ego*, it is forced to fantasize in order to relieve tension. The main force energizing the *id* is the *libido*.

The *libido*, which is sexual in nature, is also concerned with self-preservation. Sex is interpreted widely by Freud. Pleasurable sensations applied to any bodily function, as well as feelings such as tenderness, friendship and satisfaction at work, could fall within the definition of sex. After analyzing the dreams of battle-shocked soldiers, Freud concluded that aggression as well as sex might be an important instinct separate from the *libido*. This was called the *death instinct*, and if operationalized could result in masochism, self-injury and suicide in extreme cases.

2. Ego.   The new-born child has no *ego*. Exposed to grim realities—cold, thirst, noise, etc.—which can produce anxiety, and powerless to be rid of these disturbing situations, help is only forthcoming from those close to the child. It is the confluence of forces in the environment acting on the surface of the *id* that contributes to the formation of a separate mental process called the *ego*. The internal part of the *id* will still remain latent as the external part of the *id* is transformed into the *pre-conscious ego*. The *infantile ego* is only dimly aware of the external world and tends to be narcissistic—as its needs are met, so it is happy. Objects responsible for the gratification of its needs come from outside. Hunger, for instance, is satisfied by its mother's milk or a substitute. When the infant is free from such discomforts as pressure in the bowels and bladder, irritation of the skin, and extremes of temperature, it falls asleep.

As the child grows up he or she becomes less narcissistic and begins to recognize the omnipotence of the outer world which satisfies his or her needs. There are times when external reality may be perceived as overwhelming and results in fantasies. The *ego* gradually becomes able to protect the growing child from the internal threats from the *id*, as well as the external threats; in fact, it is the main mental force controlling behaviour in the well-adjusted adult. The *ego* pursues pleasure; it seeks to avoid unpleasant situations. Unlike the *id*, which is intent on the immediate gratification of instinctual urges, the *ego* is capable of logical reasoning and learning by experience. It clings to the task of self-preservation and postpones or suppresses demands made by the instincts when it feels that meeting these demands would be to the disadvantage of the organism. But there are times when it considers it appropriate to meet these instinctual demands. It is rational in its perspective in the sense that it weighs up situations realistically, taking into consideration such factors as special abilities, aptitudes, temperament, limitations and the prevailing circumstances.

There are times when the *ego* is caught off balance and impulses from the *id* reach the level of consciousness in disguised forms. The psychotherapist is then offered scope to place interpretations on behaviour such as slips of the tongue, jokes and so on. In sleep the *ego* severs contact with the external world permitting the *id* to express itself. This should not have any adverse repercussions because the *ego* controls the movement of the organism. Wishes that are warded off when awake now take the stage and expose themselves in dreams, often in symbolic form. The interpretation of dreams is a well known approach in psycho-analysis. Anxiety is said to develop when the *ego* is experiencing difficulty facing the demands of the *id*.

3. Superego. The *superego* is a new mental process which develops as a result of the weakness of the *infantile ego*. Eventually it represents the standards and ethical values acquired from parents and society in general. Initially, however, it represents the "voice of the parents" and their moral standards, as perceived by the child. It may be childish and irrational, imposing rigid restrictions which persist into adulthood without much consideration for the changed circumstances. The *superego* is mostly unconscious, thus if the *ego* does not live up to its expectations conflict develops.

When there is conflict the aggressive forces stored in the *superego* turn against the *ego* with accusations, creating feelings of depression and guilt.

Depression is self-directed aggression. The manic depressive oscillates between the joy and happiness resulting from the approving *superego*, and the tortures resulting from the feelings of guilt and depression when the *superego* becomes sadistic. At a less severe level, the disapproval of the *superego* is evident when the individual claims to feel bad about something he or she has or has not done, and is troubled by his or her conscience. When somebody feels proud of something they have done, self-congratulation comes into play, no doubt with the approval of the *superego*. As the individual gets older, the *superego* gradually draws away from the infantile images of the parent; it becomes more impersonal and more related to the objective social and ethical standards to which the individual subscribes. An individual's *superego* in the course of its development takes over from parent substitutes, such as teachers, admired figures in public life or high social ideals.

Defence Mechanisms

The interaction of the three aspects of personality structure produces constant strife. "Id, the psychic powerhouse, a lawless mob of instinctual urges, demands release; superego, the harsh unbending moralist, demands total inhibition of these urges; ego, the rational decision-maker, has to try to keep the peace between these two forces and to take into account the demands of external reality."[6] It is argued that the *ego* needs reinforcements to function adequately. These are called *ego defence mechanisms* and they shed light on our understanding of the behaviour of people.

Consisting of at least five major strategies, they are designed to protect the *ego* from the excessive demands of the *id* and the *superego* and to cope with the external reality. Each strategy is illustrated by simple examples.

1. Repression.   This is the mechanism whereby the *ego* protects itself from damage or discomfort by denying the existence of a potential threat from within. Distressing feelings and memories are unconsciously removed from the level of awareness. The individual may repress sexual or aggressive desires which would adversely affect the stability of the self. Likewise, the individual may repress painful memories which if recalled would make him or her feel bad. Repression can create problems when the repressed desire or memory becomes so strong that it makes its way into the level of consciousness, perhaps through dreams or some form of anxiety.

By contrast SUPPRESSION amounts to the conscious control of desires, fantasies, wishes or memories. Suppression appears to be a healthier form of defence, for in suppressing a desire a conscious decision is made that, for the time being at least, it will not find expression in its present form.

2 Projection.   This is a mechanism whereby feelings which create acute discomfort are projected on to an object or another person. In this case the disturbing emotions can be blamed on the other person.

The manager who continually interprets other employees' behaviour as conspiratorial or politically inspired might have such tendencies. A student who has a strong desire to cheat in an examination, but somehow cannot go through with it, might become suspicious of other students and unjustifiably accuse them of cheating.

3. Fixation.   This is the mechanism whereby the *ego* is protected by not proceeding from a particular stage of personality development. So if a child experiences a lot of anxiety about asserting its independence and moving away from being dependent on its parents, the *ego* refuses to accept the challenge to develop. As far as this characteristic is concerned, it tends to become fixated at an immature level.

4. Regression.   This is the mechanism whereby the *ego* reverts to an earlier form of behaviour when confronted by a threat. For example, an employee facing a frustrating situation at work may burst into tears or sulk. This form of coping behaviour may well have been successful when dealing with threats of a lower magnitude earlier in life. The child experiencing major difficulties at school may play truant, and as an adult, may adopt similar behaviour when confronting major problems at work.

5. *Reaction Formation.*   This is the mechanism whereby the *ego* copes with undesirable impulses or desires by developing a pattern of behaviour which is the direct opposite of these impulses or desires. An employee who harbours deep anti-social feelings towards people may develop pleasant mannerisms and good social skills in dealings with colleagues at work as a means of keeping his or her feelings in check. If an occasion arises when this mechanism fails to function properly, colleagues will be shocked by this individual's outburst of hostility.

Defence mechanisms are entirely unconscious and the person is unaware of using them. When used successfully, they become a normal feature of coping behaviour whereby the individual can resolve personal conflicts. They also play a crucial part in the development of characteristics of personality. If used unsuccessfully, the *ego* cannot cope and neurosis or psychosis may result.

Personality Development

Freud subscribed to the view that there were three stages of sexual development during infancy.The stages are associated with libidinous satisfaction derived from a preoccupation with different parts of the body.

The infant derives pleasure at first from its mouth—sucking its mother's breast or an inferior substitute such as sucking its thumb—followed by pleasure from the anus and finally pleasure from the genitals. If conflicts are not resolved at any one of these stages, the person may become fixated at that stage, producing a profound effect on character.

The first stage is the oral stage and it lasts for a year. During this period in which the infant is highly dependent upon others for its survival, the *libido* manifests itself through sucking and chewing. Early oral pleasures are perpetuated when the adult indulges in, for example, excessive smoking, eating and kissing, and the chewing of gum. If a person fails to negotiate this stage successfully, and develops an oral fixation, this could lead to adult behaviour such as dependency (as in the original feeding situation), immaturity, optimism or pessimism, sadism, oral aggression (the need to bite), and a suspicious nature.

In the second year of life the anus becomes the focal point for libidinous satisfaction. The infant is intensely interested in the bowel movements and obtains satisfaction from this process. The child establishes that the control of the bowel movements is something with which the parents are obviously concerned. During the anal stage toilet training takes place, and the way this is handled can have significant effects on later developments. If the person becomes fixated at this stage, this can affect adult behaviour and is reflected in such characteristics as stinginess, obstinacy, obsessionality, sadism and orderliness. These characteristics are said to be associated with the early pleasure derived from the excretion and the retention of faeces.

Around the age of three the child's interest moves towards a preoccu-pation with the genitals. The main focus is the exploration and manipulation of the genitals, and this is known as the phallic stage. The little boy develops feelings of sexual attraction towards his mother and at the same time feelings of jealousy or resentment are directed against his father who he looks upon as a rival for the mother's affection.

This phenomenon is known as the Oedipus complex. In Greek mytho-logy Oedipus Rex, a character from a play by Sophocles, killed his father and married his mother without knowing the identity of either. The Oedipus complex comes to an end in the fourth or fifth year, brought about by the boy's fear that his illicit desires might be punished by the father with castra-tion.

The position of the little girl is unclear, although penis envy is attributed to her. This comes about when the little girl recognizes the alleged inferior nature of her sexual organ in relation to the masculine one. She develops an envious desire to be like the boy and turns her attention towards her father.

Her attachment to her father is crystallized in the Electra complex. Again, in Greek mythology, Electra connives at the death of her mother, Clytemnestra, who murdered her father, Agamemnon.

The boy resolves the Oedipal conflict by modelling himself on his father and repressing his incestuous urges; the girl, on the other hand, resolves the Electra conflict by the recognition that she might lose the love of her mother if she realized her illicit desires. Unsuccessful resolution of these conflicts for both sexes can lead to major problems in adulthood, particularly problems of sexual identification and neurotic tendencies. Those fixated at this stage of development are said to display characteristics such as extreme self-love, excessive ambition, exhibitionism and bragging.

After the phallic stage comes the latency period which lasts until adoles-cence during which time sexual impulses are inhibited and satisfying re-lationships are developed.

Freud has been criticized for the prime emphasis he placed on sexual desires. Lazarus puts an interesting interpretation on the Oedipus complex. He maintains that the Oedipus complex could be better understood in terms of social relations within the family. "The boy might come to fear the father not because he literally expects castration, or because of sexual urges toward the mother, but because the father controls power within the family, part-icularly in the Viennese society of the late 1800s. Also the girl might envy the boy, not literally for his penis, but because in most societies girls are usually considered subordinate to boys."[4]

Psycho-analytical theory sees the origin of personality in the conflicts between the *id*, *ego* and *superego* and in the way in which the conflicts are resolved at each stage of development. Adult behaviour is said to be related to the success, or otherwise, of negotiating the various stages of development. Some of Freud's followers, notably Jung and Adler, felt that it was unsatisfactory to emphasize persistently the sexual roots of neurosis to the exclusion of other factors.

Adler was of the view that human behaviour can be explained in terms of a struggle for power in order to overcome feelings of mental or physical inferiority.[7] This contribution was of significant benefit to psycho-analysis because it recognized that non-sexual factors could also lead to conflict, and that neurosis is a disorder of the total personality.

In modern developments in the mainstream of psycho-analysis, the *ego* receives increasing attention, and the influence people have on each other receives a high priority. The quality of the mother-child relationship is a critical interpersonal influence because it is the base of subsequent personal relationships.[8]

Freud's greatest contribution is not the detail of his theory of personality but his systematic approach to the study of personality and the emphasis on the part played by unconscious forces and previous experience on behaviour.[9]

If one were to apply Freudian analysis to the behaviour of consumers, one might conclude that the marketeer must recognize that products and advertisements appeal to unconscious as well as conscious motives, and that the symbolism inherent in the design of products and advertisements, especially if it contains sexual implications, can have an effect opposite to that intended. For example, if an advertisement is sexually explicit, it could offend the *superego* and therefore lose its impact. In the promotion of an aftershave lotion for men, an explicit sexual theme may be projected through packaging and advertising with the intention of appealing to the *id*. The product could be made acceptable to the *superego* by projecting a subsequent image of the consumer in a more sober social setting. The *ego* could very well be satisfied with this outcome.[10]

Psycho-analytical theories of personality, such as Freud's, are often criticized by other psychologists for their lack of a satisfactory definition of their key concepts, for their lack of scientific rigour, and the fact that the theories either do not generate testable predictions about human behaviour or, when predictions are made, that they do not work out in practice.

PROJECTIVE TESTS

An appropriate way to assess personality based on unconscious processes is to use assessment methods that include face-to-face analysis and projective techniques. These methods are expensive and time-consuming to administer and they do not lead to quantifiable results. However, they are used as a framework for motivational research in studies of consumer behaviour. The ideas of Freud were the inspiration behind projective techniques, but the relationship between psycho-analytic theory and projective techniques is merely indirect.

Projective techniques require a person to respond to ambiguous or unstructured situations as a means of exploring unconscious impulses and motives. Subjects are unaware of the purpose of the test; consequently the *ego's* defences are off guard, and unconscious forces emerge in disguised form. It is the job of the assessor to interpret these responses. Two well known projective tests are examined below.

Rorschach Test

The Rorschach test consists of a series of ten ink-blots or formless shapes, in which one half is the mirror image of the other. An ink-blot, similar to the one used in the test, is shown in Fig.1.1.

The subject is asked to say what the blot resembles. The abnormal personality is likely to perceive gruesome or horrific images in the blots, and this may be indicative of serious conflicts which are still unresolved. The normal personality sees more tranquil images.

FIG. 1.1   An ink blot.

Thematic Apperception Test

The Thematic Apperception Test (TAT) consists of twenty pictures of varying degrees of clarity. An example of a straightforward scene would be a boy reading at a desk. The subject examines each picture and then tells a story about the scene portrayed, including what led up to the scene, the current situation and what is likely to happen in the future. The responses are analyzed and recurrent themes mentioned in the stories are particularly noted. A subject who harbours intense hostility may read hostility in one form or another, such as severe conflict or death, into the stories. In motivation research in the field of marketing a similar test to the one described above was used.[11] In a cigar survey a cartoon was used portraying a man coming home from work who announces to his wife, "I've decided to take up smoking cigars, dear." The respondent is asked to fill in the wife's response.

Tests of this type are carried out in the belief that a person may attribute to another person an opinion that he or she holds but is unwilling to express. In order to get around the expression of a direct personal view, a question may be worded in the third person. For example, instead of "what are the health hazards attached to cigarette smoking?," respondents are presented with the following statement: "Some people who smoke cigarettes may suffer from ill-health at some stage in their life." and then asked "I wonder if you can guess what adverse effects of cigarette smoking they are referring to?"

Whereas some psychologists find projective tests useful in providing initial clinical insights, others are sceptical of their value in assessing unconscious processes and believe that subjects can quite easily fake the tests.[12]

ROLE PLAYING OR VISUALIZATION

Apart from the use of projective tests in consumer motivation research, role playing or visualization techniques have been used to create personality descriptions of consumers.

A study was conducted in the USA into the consumption of instant coffee at a time when instant coffee was not widely used.[13] Direct questioning of housewives revealed that they did not like its flavour.

Subsequently, the housewives were given two shopping-lists covering a number of items and asked to describe the personality of the woman who bought the groceries. The main distinguishing feature between the two lists was that one shopping list—A—contained Nescafé instant coffee and the other list—B—had ground coffee. The results showed that 48% of the women shown list A said the shopper was lazy and did not plan well, but less than 12% of the women shown list B arrived at that conclusion. The shopper was perceived as a spendthrift by 12% of the women shown list A, but none of the women shown list B expressed that view. Again, 16% of the women shown list A said the shopper was not a good wife, but none of the women shown list B expressed that view.

By the addition of a pie-mix to the two shopping-lists, and by using two new samples of housewives, the personality descriptions of the shopper using the B list became closer to those of the shopper using the A list. Was it the inclusion of a prepared food item that evoked a stereotyped personality description?

The original sample was divided into users and non-users of instant coffee, as the result of a pantry check. Significant differences were found between the two groups of housewives, as illustrated in Table 1.2.

The shopping-list study was repeated eighteen years later. No significant differences were found between the characteristics attributed by the subjects to the ground coffee vs. the instant coffee user. However, a fairly

TABLE 1.2
Haire's Analysis of Shopper Profiles (1950)

Descriptions of Shoppers	Instant Coffee Users %	Instant Coffee Non-Users %
Shopper is economical	70	18
Shopper is a good housewife (plans well and cares for the family)	29	0
Shopper cannot cook/does not like cooking	16	55
Shopper is lazy	19	39

large number of subjects felt that the instant coffee shopper was a busy, active person in contrast to the shopper preferring ground coffee, who was seen as dull, unadventuresome and not very elegant.[14] A Canadian replication of the original shopping-list study concluded with the assertion that the original findings still hold true with a sample of French-Canadians in a middle class surburb of Montreal.[15]

These studies highlight role playing or visualization, and though the association between personality stereotypes and consumer behaviour is interesting it cannot be conclusive.

People might find it difficult or impossible to come up with an authentic personality description from a shopping-list. In order not to disappoint the interviewer, or to give what is expected, they co-operate. We never know the depth or strength of the personality stereotype.[11]

TRAIT PERSPECTIVE

An important means of studying personality is the trait perspective. A trait is an individual characteristic in thought, feeling, and action, either inherited or acquired, and refers to tendencies to act or react in certain ways.[16] The possession of a particular trait, for example, anxiety, does not imply that the person will always be anxious, rather, it suggests that the person is disposed to react with anxiety in given situations.

Traits can be placed in particular categories. MOTIVE traits refer to goals which guide the behaviour of the individual; for example, a person may possess a recognizable trait related to achievement. ABILITY traits refer to the individual's general and specific capability and skill; for example, in this category cognitive traits such as knowing, perceiving and reasoning would be included. TEMPERAMENT traits would include optimism, depression and various energetic tendencies. STYLISTIC traits refer to gestures and styles of behaving unrelated to specific tactics to achieve a particular goal.

Traits contain two basic dimensions. One is the manner in which the trait manifests itself at the surface—for example, the display of aggressive behaviour—the other is where the trait exists below the surface, and the observer has to infer the nature of the quality. Such a quality could be a belief held by the individual or, again, his or her power of self-control. In distinguishing between people, the use of a rich vocabulary of traits can help enormously. Each individual's traits may be considered unique. For example, one person's loyalty and the way he or she expresses it, will differ from another person's loyalty. Likewise the way traits are organized in the individual's total personality can be considered distinctive.[17]

Allport's Categories

Allport puts traits into three categories—CARDINAL, CENTRAL, and SECONDARY. A cardinal trait refers to some predominant characteristic, for example, a determined stance taken by a politician on a number of issues. One can have five to ten central traits—for example, intelligence, a sense of humour, compassion, sensitivity, honesty—which distinguish one individual from another. Finally, secondary traits are weak or peripheral and are relatively unimportant in characterizing a person or their lifestyle. Allport emphasizes that traits are not independent entities within a person; they are an interdependent set of attributes which come together to produce an effect on behaviour.

The following example illustrates this point. Many traits contribute to the total performance of a person telling a joke or a story at a party. Motive traits, such as entertaining others or showing-off, are evident, and stylistic traits, such as being bashful, boring or delightfully entertaining, are also reflected. In essence, the entertainer's traits combine to form a coherent cluster. This leads to Allport's concept of the self *(proprium)*, a concept which embraces distinctive and important personal characteristics, such as self-image, self-esteem, rational thinker or alternatively irrational, or impetuous.

Cattell's 16 PF Test

Cattell is another influential trait theorist.[18] His approach was to reduce systematically the list of personality traits to a small manageable number by using a statistical method called factor analysis. The attraction of this method is that it enables complex data to be quantified and reduced to a more manageable form, though the total research process in which factor analysis is used contains some intuitive judgement.

The following example illustrates Cattell's approach. We are concerned with measuring the ability of a group of students to do four activities:(1), use calculus; (2), understand physics; (3), play football; and (4), skate on ice. We would expect those who do well in mathematics also to do well in physics, but not necessarily to do well in sport. Though we are unlikely to use factor analysis in this situation, if it were used it would reveal two factors or

SOURCE traits underlying the above activities, namely mathematical and scientific ability and ability in sport. The source traits affect the pattern of behaviour which is visible to the observer.

The observable behavioural patterns are called SURFACE traits. At work or college a cluster of surface traits—e.g., possession of a large vocabulary, an understanding of accounting and quantitative methods, and a knowledge of business history—may be observed in the behaviour of the individual. These surface traits could be underpinned by at least three independent source traits—education, intelligence and a studious temperament. Through various forms of tests, inter-correlations of personality variables, and the use of observational data, Cattell chose sixteen personality factors which are said to represent source traits. These are shown in Table 1.3.

The source traits are the backbone of the enduring aspects of behaviour, and it is through their interaction that the more readily observed surface traits of an individual are determined. These surface traits happen to coincide with descriptions of personality in everyday use. The factors on the 16 Personality Factor Questionnaire used to measure personality are relatively independent and are not correlated significantly among themselves. So a person's score on any one of these factors should not influence their score on another, though there may be some weak correlations.

When further analysis is carried out, Cattell arrived at second-order factors, of which anxiety is one. The second-order factors are said to influ-

TABLE 1.3
Factors in Cattell's 16 PF Questionnaire

Low Score Description	Factor	High Score Description
Reserved, detached, critical	A	Outgoing, warm-hearted
Less intelligent, concrete thinking	B	More intelligent, abstract thinking
Affected by feelings, easily upset	C	Emotionally stable, faces reality
Humble, mild, accommodating	E	Assertive, aggressive, stubborn
Sober, prudent, serious	F	Happy-go-lucky, impulsive, lively
Expedient, disregards rules	G	Conscientious, persevering
Shy, restrained, timid	H	Venturesome, socially bold
Tough-minded, self-reliant	I	Tender-minded, clinging
Trusting, adaptable	L	Suspicious, self-opinionated
Practical, careful	M	Imaginative
Forthright, natural	N	Shrewd, calculating
Self-assured, confident	O	Apprehensive, self-reproaching
Conservative	Q1	Experimenting, liberal
Group-dependent	Q2	Self-sufficient
Undisciplined self-conflict	Q3	Controlled, socially precise
Relaxed, tranquil	Q4	Tense, frustrated

Source: Catell, R. B. (1974). How good is the modern questionnaire? General principles for evaluation. *Journal of Personality Assessment, 38,* 115–129.

ence behaviour only through the source traits or primary factors. The primary factors are considered to be more accurate than the second-order factors in describing and predicting behaviour.

Though source traits are said to be enduring aspects of personality, there are circumstances in one's life when predictions of behaviour on the basis of traits alone can be misleading. For example, a person who is suffering from fatigue or who is frightened or under the influence of drugs may indulge in unexpected behaviour. Cattell recognizes that environmental and hereditary factors interact and influence the source traits to different degrees. The validity of the 16 PF test has been questioned[19], but a more recent version of the questionnaire has been considered by Cattell to be an improvement on earlier versions.[20] The major criticisms of Cattell's theory are said to be that the assumptions governing factor analysis force us to oversimplify personality.[8]

Nevertheless a number of researchers have used the 16 PF questionnaire with managers. The 16 PF instrument comprises 187 questions presented in a forced choice format. For each question three answers are given—agree, uncertain and disagree. The instructions discourage the excessive use of the 'uncertain' response. In this type of process there is always a danger that respondents may distort their true position on various issues by unwittingly giving an inaccurate response or giving a socially acceptable response. However, this danger may be minimized in a supportive climate

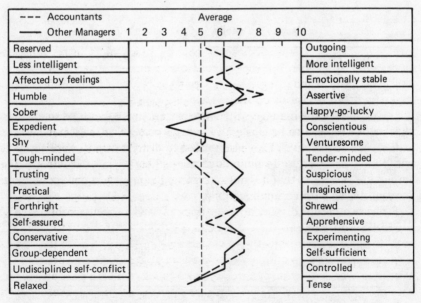

FIG. 1.2 Personality profiles of accountants and managers using Cattell's 16 PF test.

where questionnaires are completed anonymously. A study of 400 managers and accountants attending different courses at the Ashridge Management College was undertaken using the 16 PF test.[21] Their personality profiles appear in Fig 1.2.

The researcher makes the point that the profiles in Fig. 1.2 refer to the people who participated in the study, and that there is no implication that accountants or managers in general should be like this or that this constitutes the profile of successful accountants or managers, although one cannot rule out this possibility. The following characteristics were shared by both accountants and managers.

1. Tendency Towards Assertiveness and Shrewdness.   This would be reflected in a tendency to be self-assured, dominant, independent-minded, bold in approach, hard, stern, hostile, solemn, tough-minded and authoritarian. Also, there would be a tendency to be polished and experienced.

2. Tendency Towards Experimenting.   This would be reflected in a tendency to be interested in intellectual matters and fundamental issues. There was also a tendency to take issue with old or new ideas, to be better informed with less of an inclination to moralize but more of an inclination to experiment generally in life.

3. Tendency Towards Relaxation.   This would be reflected in a tendency to be calm, relaxed, composed and satisfied.

However, there were differences between the accountants and managers. The accountants showed a tendency to be tough-minded and self-sufficient, that is they were more likely to be practical, realistic, independent, and responsible, but they were also uncultured, sometimes phlegmatic, hard, cynical and smug. They tended to be resolute with a preference to make and take decisions on their own.

By contrast, the managers tended to be more expedient and suspicious, that is they tended to be unsteady, lacking perseverence, sometimes impatient and obstructive. They also tended to distrust others, were prone to self-doubt, and were self-opinionated and deliberate in their actions. The researcher maintains that it is not surprising that managers and accountants have problems with communication.

The two groups display different approaches to solving problems. The managers would like to solve problems quickly, are prepared to bend the rules to achieve their objectives, and are also more prepared to take risks. The accountants, who offer services to the managers, are quite prepared to take time over problems, but are not prepared to bend the rules and in any case prefer to go it alone. Since both are assertive, conflict is likely to develop. The researcher feels that certain personality types choose accounting as a career and she is of the view that anybody who proposes to study and qualify in accounting needs to be able to pay great attention to detail, and have patience, good concentration, a good memory, and an ability to handle figures. These characteristics are said to be compatible with the qualities identified in the profile of the accountant's personality, as illustrated in Fig.1.2.

In another study a sample of 603 middle managers representing a wide range of managerial jobs completed the 16 PF questionnaire when attending a course at the Henley Administrative Staff College.[22] The profiles emerging from this exercise, and attributable to the different occupational groups, are as follows:

Accountants tend to be more critical and aloof than the average manager. They are more precise and objective, but are somewhat rigid in their attitudes. They share with bankers a lower level of competitiveness than other managers.

Sales managers generally displayed an extravert nature—outgoing, adaptive, attentive, with a competitive nature. They tended to be cheerful, talkative, enthusiastic, adventurous, sociable, friendly, impulsive, carefree, unconventional.

Engineers, like accountants, tend to be more critical and aloof than other managers. They also tend to be introspective and less communicative than other managers, and show a tendency towards slowness and caution. They are more tough-minded than other managers, unsentimental, self-reliant, responsible and capable of keeping to the point. They tend to be conventional and are concerned with objectivity and immediate practicalities, rather than indulging in far-fetched imaginative ideas.

Production managers, like engineers, are tough-minded and conventional, but are more assertive and feel free to participate in and to criticize group behaviour.

Research and Development managers, like accountants and engineers, tend to be critical, aloof and tough-minded. They are brighter and more alert than other managers, but are more restrained and socially inhibited. As a result, they are likely to minimize personal contact with others. Though they may have feelings of inferiority and feel threats from the environment, they are more radical in their thinking than other managers. They tend to be well informed and inclined to experiment with solutions to problems. Likewise, they are receptive to change and new ideas and are inclined towards analytical thought.

Personnel managers tend to be more outgoing and adaptable than other managers and prefer occupations that deal with people. They are more sensitive and tender-minded, less realistic and tolerant of the rougher aspects of life, and more cultured. They tend to fuss more in group or committee meetings, slowing down the process of decision-taking. They tend to be more imaginative than other managers and are more concerned with introspection and the inner life—an important characteristic for anyone involved in planning and looking beyond immediate needs. Though they may be somewhat impractical, careless and lacking in self-control to a limited extent, they display a romantic liking for travel and new experiences.

A group of researchers in Australia created a profile of the Australian manager after using the 16 PF instrument with 475 managers. Having engaged in international comparisons they arrived at the following tentative conclusion.[23] The analysis of the data suggested that: "Australian and British managers are less extravert than U.S. managers. Australian and U.S. managers have lower scores on intelligence than British managers. Australian managers tend to be more dominating and assertive than British or U.S. managers. Australian managers appear more imaginative and less practical than British or U.S. managers. Australian and British managers are more forthright and less shrewd than U.S. managers. Australian managers are more self-sufficient than British or U.S. managers."

These studies are illustrative of a research process designed to identify personality traits. The results could profitably be used by a psychologist particularly in a counselling situation. In this sense profiles could be used in management development to foster self-awareness and assist in planning self-development but it would appear unwise to use them for selection purposes because of the possibility that a respondent may distort the results.

Other Tests

Examples of other tests used to measure personality traits are the Thurstone and Edwards schedules. The Thurstone Temperament Schedule attempts to measure personality traits on seven dimensions. A high score on each dimension would reflect the following characteristics.

1. Active. The person is likely to be in a rush, probably speaking, walking, driving, working and eating at a fast rate when it is unnecessary to do so.

2. Vigorous. The person usually enjoys physical activity requiring a lot of energy, is active in sport and outdoor occupations and engages in work requiring the use of the hands or tools.

3. Impulsive. The person is usually happy-go-lucky, likes to take chances and make quick decisions.

4. Dominant. The person has the capacity for taking initiatives and assuming responsibility, and probably takes satisfaction from organizing social activities, persuading others and promoting new ventures.

5. Stable. The person is likely to remain calm in a crisis, is able to disregard distractions while studying or working and is not irritated if interrupted when concentrating.

6. *Sociable.* The person usually enjoys the company of others, makes friends easily, is sympathetic, cooperative and agreeable in relations with others.

7. *Reflective.* The person indulges in meditative thinking, enjoys dealing with theoretical rather than practical problems, and prefers to work alone with material requiring accuracy and fine detail.

Using the above personality test or inventory, a researcher concluded that the traits "active" and "impulsive" were associated with the ownership of convertible cars, while the traits "stable" and "sociable" applied to owners of standard and compact cars.[24]

The Edwards Personal Preference Schedule was used to measure the relative strength of fifteen needs, such as achievement, affiliation, dominance, sex, deference or compliance, in relation to particular purchases.[25] Personality profiles varied between groups on the basis of demographic factors such as age, sex, income, size of town or city, and region. When the profiles were related to purchases of various products (e.g., cars, cigarettes, cosmetics and paper towels) certain relationships emerged.

An illustrative finding was the relationship between personality and cigarette smoking. Heavy smokers scored high on sex, aggression and achievement, and low on order, deference, and compliance. Smokers of filter cigarettes scored high on dominance, change, and achievement, and low on aggression, autonomy, and need for independence. If one were to take this type of study seriously, it would be natural to attempt to direct an appropriate sales message to the most prominent needs. In this study a mail order advertisement written around an appeal for change brought in twice as many returns from the group scoring high on the need for change than from the group scoring low on this need.[11]

Another study singled out the role of achievement as a personality trait. Subjects scoring high on the need for achievement appeared to favour products that might be referred to as virile and masculine—boating equipment, skis, lawn mowers. On the other hand, male subjects scoring low on the need for achievement tended to favour products that might be thought of as meticulous or fastidious—automatic dishwashers, headache remedies, mouthwashes, electric toothbrushes, deodorants.[26]

The trait approach to personality has been used extensively in research into consumer behaviour but the results have been generally disappointing. However, this approach has contributed to the development of psychographics, a topic that will be discussed later.

Further Observations

Other observations of personal characteristics of accountants, which are not based on personality inventories or tests, indicate that the accountant is cold or impersonal, and conservative.[27] This is said to be particularly so for accountants with a professional accounting background.[28] In a study of the role of management accountants it was concluded that caution, risk aversion, conservatism, preference for well-tried procedures and a lack of knowledge of other functions tended to undermine the effectiveness of their service to managers.[29] This conclusion can be substantiated by the findings of another study. Financial managers were part of a group of managers with the least mental flexibility, the most closed minds and the most conservative attitude when it came to challenging formal authority and procedures.[30]

By contrast, attention could be focused on the desirable qualities of interviewers involved in the selection process.[31] It is suggested that the interviewer should be able to demonstrate counselling skills.[32] In addition, it is said that capable interviewers possess characteristics which are not highly valued in a social sense—timidity, anxiety and insecurity—and that people with these qualities feel the most need to subject others to assessment.[33]

TYPE PERSPECTIVE

When a person shares a pattern of traits with a large group of people he or she is said to belong to a personality type.

The best known typology in ancient Greece was that of Hippocrates in the fifth century BC. He theorized that the body contained four fluids or humours—yellow bile, black bile, high blood pressure, and phlegm. In AD 180 Galen allocated temperaments to the four humours to show how physical conditions in the form of internal abnormalities could affect patterns of behaviour. These relationships are depicted in Table 1.4.

Recently an American business consultant generalized on the basis of

TABLE 1.4
The Four Humours

Humours	Temperaments	Behaviour
Yellow Bile	Choleric	Active but changeable mood; rapid thinking; highly strung; easily provoked; strong emotions.
Black Bile	Melancholic	Pessimistic; tendency towards ill-founded fears; resistance to provocation; strong emotions once aroused.
High Blood Pressure	Sanguine	Cheerful; easy going and supremely confident; weak emotions though easily aroused.
Excess Phlegm	Phlegmatic	Sluggish; supremely calm; slow thinking; resistant to provocation; weak emotions even when aroused.

his experience of personality testing and came to the following conclusion. He maintained that personality types in business roughly correspond with the classical temperaments identified above.

> A *People Catalyst* (Choleric) type thrives on involvement with those around him, and sees service to mankind as a life goal. A *Hard Charger* (Melancholic) is the executive who believes in tradition, follows rules, and sees a prescribed way of doing things. The *Fast Track* (Sanguine) executive sees risk in terms of challenge. He can turn on to special projects at the exclusion of all else. He is particularly good at pulling things and people together. The *Power Broker* (Phlegmatic) executive is innovative and resourceful, and is especially good at motivating others.[34]

Probably the best known modern physical typology is that of Sheldon.[35] Working from the photographs of 4000 college students he defined physical types similar to those which appear in Fig.1.3.

Eysenck's Typology

A prominent type theorist is Eysenck.[36] In his work he stresses the second-order factors or types, as opposed to traits, in the personality of the individual. Take, for example, the personality type known as Extraversion. It is expressed in the form of a hierarchical organization in Fig.1.4.

Eysenck shares Cattell's view that biological factors are involved in the determination of personality, but unlike Cattell much of Eysenck's early work grew out of his interest in abnormal psychology and psychiatry. Eysenck related his own research to the ancient typology referred to in Table 1.4 and found a fairly good relationship with the original theory, as shown in Fig.1.5.

It was in his original study of 700 neurotic soldiers that Eysenck found that factor analysis of 39 items of personal data, including personality

(a)   (b)   (c)

FIG. 1.3   Sheldon's physical typology. (a) Endomorphic: Soft round body, stocky but not exactly fat. Large trunk, thick neck and relatively short legs. Generally relaxed in temperament, loves comfort, sociable and affectionate. (b) Mesomorphic: Well endowed with bone and muscle—the Greek God type of body build. The temperament is assertive, noisy, aggressive, and energetic. (c) Ectomorphic: A fragile body build, with a temperament which is inhibited in actions, over-restrained, and socially withdrawn, with an inferiority complex.

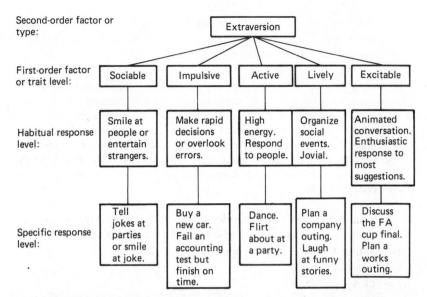

FIG 1.4 Eysenck's structure of personality as related to extraversion. Adapted from: Eysenck, H. J. (1967) *The biological basis of personality*. Courtesy of Charles C. Thomas, Publisher, Springfield, Illinois.

ratings, resulted in the establishment of two basic dimensions of personality—Extraversion/Introversion and Neuroticism/Stability.[37] This structure of personality was substantiated by further research with a large number of subjects. In a later investigation with psychiatric patients, Eysenck established a third dimension of personality, unrelated to Extraversion and Neuroticism, which he called Psychoticism. It should be noted that these dimensions of personality relate to the extreme ends of a continuum, and only very few people would fall into these categories. With regard to Extraversion, for example, most people would fall somewhere in between, – they would be neither very extraverted nor very introverted.

According to Eysenck, the typical extravert is sociable, likes parties, has many friends, needs people to converse with, but does not like reading or studying alone. Extraverts need excitement, take chances, are often adventurous, act on the spur of the moment, and are generally impulsive individuals. They are fond of practical jokes, always have a ready answer and generally like change. They are carefree, optimistic and like to laugh and be merry. They prefer to keep moving and remain active, tend to be aggressive and lose their temper quickly. Altogether their feelings are not kept under tight control and they are not always reliable.

The typical introvert is a quiet, retiring person, introspective, and fond of books rather than people. Introverts are reserved and distant except with intimate friends. They tend to plan ahead, take precautions, and distrust any

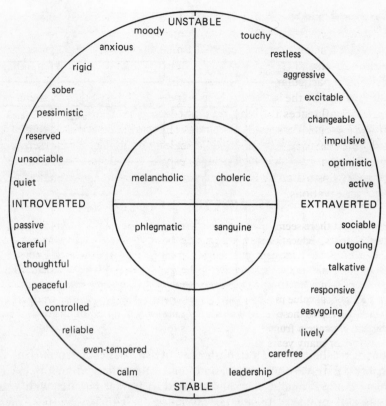

FIG. 1.5   Eysenck's typology of personality. From: Eysenck, H. J. (1947) *Dimensions of personality*. London: Routledge and Kegan Paul. Reproduced by permission of Curtis Brown Ltd. Copyright H. J. Eysenck.

impulse of the moment. They do not like excitement, take matters of everyday life with proper seriousness, and like a well-ordered approach to life. They keep their feelings under close control, seldom behave in an aggressive way, and do not lose their temper easily. They are reliable, somewhat pessimistic, and place great value on ethical standards.[38]

The Neuroticism dimension is akin to the idea of emotional instability. Individuals who fall into the extreme end of the neuroticism dimension tend to be more prone to worries and anxieties, and more easily upset. They are also likely to complain of headaches, and experience sleeping or eating difficulties. Although they may be more likely to develop neurotic disorder under stressful conditions, in practice the frequency of such events is low and most individuals function adequately in their family, work and social life. Most of Eysenck's research and theory has been concerned with the Extraversion and Neuroticism dimensions, and until recently the Psychoticism dimension received less attention. The Psychoticism dimension in its extreme form would be concerned with states such as obsessions, phobias, hysteria, acute depression and schizophrenia.

Eysenck's concept of personality embraces the view that an individual inherits a particular type of nervous system which predisposes him or her to develop in a particular way. However, the final form personality takes will be determined by the biological basis of personality as well as by the various socializing influences the individual encounters in everyday life.[39]

The Eysenck Personality Inventory (EPI) is the device used to measure the dimensions of personality, and lie scale items are included to screen out respondents making socially desirable responses. In evaluating the model of personality postulated by Eysenck, two clinical psychologists make the following observations.

> At present there seems to be little justification for Eysenck's suggestions that psychiatrists, educationalists, or parole boards should base their recommendations for treatment, teaching or probation on measures of Extraversion, Neuroticism or Psychoticism. The questionnaires which Eysenck has developed may continue to be useful tools for personality investigators but their practical value in relation to groups or individuals remains to be demonstrated. Despite these reservations, the main body of Eysenck's theory seems certain to prove a fruitful source of ideas for investigation in the field of personality for many years to come.[8]

Personality Types and Accidents

As long ago as 1926 researchers were interested in the relationship between personality, particularly accident-proneness, and accident rates.[40] Accident-proneness was defined as a personal idiosyncrasy predisposing the individual who possesses it to a relatively high accident rate. Although aware of the weaknesses of the tests used, the researchers concluded that variations in accident liability are not solely determined by external factors or by chance, but are due in a significant way to measurable individual differences. A relationship was found between accidents and aesthetokinetic coordination; the latter refers to the way the individual uses the hand and arm in response to stimuli recorded and interpreted by the sense organs. Poor integration and nervous instability could lead to accidents. There was a slight indication that the accident-prone are industrially inefficient and more liable to report sick, and consequently react unfavourably to their work environment, but this needed to be confirmed.

In more recent studies the concept of accident-proneness appears to be elusive. It is suggested that the accident-prone personality can be described variously as aggressive, hostile or overactive, but no permanent or stable personality trait of the accident-prone person can be identified.[41] It is also suggested that the propensity to accidental injury increased at certain times—e.g. in conditions of poor vision, fatigue, alcoholic use, and where certain hazards or stressors exist in the environment. But these conditions may be of a temporary nature.[42] The young and inexperienced could also be vulnerable to accidents, but likewise this could be a temporary state, just as it could be for a person going through a bad patch of ill-health or stress. Sometimes people are defined as accident-prone if they are not as good as their peers in recognizing hazardous situations. It may be more sensible to suggest that it is only at certain times that a person's accident liability increases.

An HM Principal Inspector of Factories, Accident Prevention Advisory Unit in the U.K., had this to say about accident-proneness:

Accident-proneness as a concept has little use in practical accident prevention. The concept itself is ill-defined, no stable personality characteristics that can be identified with accident-proneness have been discovered. So therefore, nothing can be done to identify individuals who may be accident-prone in order to treat them or to remove them from areas of greatest risk. Alternative explanations must be found for persons experiencing multiple accidents. . . . Rather than focusing on accident-proneness we should concentrate on the elimination of risk and provide education to assist employees to cope with unforeseen hazard situations.[43]

Notwithstanding what has been said above, a study conducted in South Africa concluded that accident-prone pilots were more neurotic (emotionally unstable) and more extraverted (impulsive) than those who were less accident-prone. In Canada, taxi drivers with a high frequency of accidents were said to have had more disturbed childhoods, to have been more frequently absent without leave while in the forces, and to have displayed more aggression than those who had a low frequency of accidents.[44] Studies conducted among male workers in British industry suggest a highly significant relationship between accidents and extraversion but no direct relationship between accidents and neuroticism.[45]

A brief examination of other typologies of personality follows.

Jung's Typology

Jung, a prominent psychologist whose work preceded that of Eysenck, identifies two broad categories—extravert and introvert. An extravert is outward-looking, responds better to facts and is more scientific than philosophical. An extravert is subjective, philosophical, a day-dreamer and the artistic type. Jung entered the domain of traits when he classified personality by primary characteristics. This approach concentrates on the information processing characteristics of the individual.[46] These characteristics can be viewed as being located at the ends of the orthogonal axes shown in Fig.1.6.

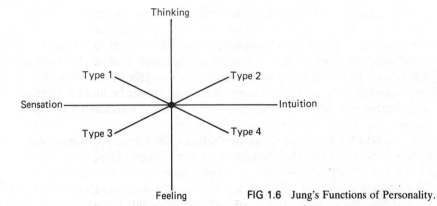

FIG 1.6   Jung's Functions of Personality.

A type 1 person (sensation-thinking) is cold, analytic, lives for the present, is interested primarily in facts, and extremely practical. A type 4 person (intuition-feeling) is the opposite of type 1, and is emotional, sociable, takes a broad view, and is prone to hypothesizing more than others. A type 2 person is rational, analytic, takes a broad view, and is sociable. The opposite (type 3) is factual, wishes to grasp tangible things, but is emotional.

Jung's functions of personality have been applied to the problem of the implementation of management science techiques. Managers who exhibit sensation-thinking characteristics are said to be more willing to construct and accept management science techniques — e.g. linear programming — than are managers who are predominantly endowed with intuition-feeling characteristics. Yet many top-level executives are of the latter type. The manager with the intuition-feeling characteristics is said to be more able to implement change and innovation within an organization if he or she is convinced of the usefulness of the management science techniques.[47]

Allport's Typology
A typology propounded by Allport et al. has the following characteristics:
Theoretical—pursuit of knowledge;
Aesthetic—striving towards art and natural beauty;
Social—pursuit of humanitarian goals;
Political—pursuit of power;
Religious—spiritual pursuits;
Economic—pursuit of material possessions.[48]

The characteristic which features most prominently in an individual is the determining factor of personality. In a study of managers in diverse cultures and countries, a questionnaire was used bearing some similarities to the typology mentioned above. The results of the study indicate that different values and cultures pose different problems with respect to interaction between people.[49]

PSYCHOGRAPHICS

Given the weak predictive relationship between personality variables and buyer behaviour, researchers in consumer behaviour have used alternative approaches. Psychographics, which incorporates lifestyles or patterns of behaviour adopted by consumers, is one such approach. To gather psychographic data a distinctive technique is used by which consumers are classified by activity, interest and opinion (AIO). Researchers assemble a large number of items similar to those found in standardized personality and interest inventories. The responses derived from the administration of these inventories are correlated with the buying of products or exposure to the advertising media.

This type of technique measures activities in terms of how people spend their time at work and leisure, their interests expressed as what they consider important in their immediate surroundings, their opinions on social issues, on institutions, and on themselves. Finally, basic facts such as their age, income and where they live may be added. Colonel Sander's Kentucky Fried Chicken was originally advertised in a folksy, homely, small town way. Then it was established that it was heavily consumed by young housewives with an AIO profile that reflected a more contemporary image. The advertising and packaging of the product were changed to reflect these findings.[50]

INTERPERSONAL PERSPECTIVE

Psycho-analysis, trait and type theory attempt to analyze personality in terms of dimensions or insights previously developed by researchers in the field. Interpersonal approaches focus instead on how individuals perceive themselves and their environment, and how a subjective view is matched against objective reality. In effect, individuals try to make sense out of their experience.

The personality theories of Rogers and Kelly are prime examples of the interpersonal approach. Though these theories were developed from the fields of counselling and psychotherapy they are not concerned with the hidden meanings of an individual's behaviour, as in psycho-analysis. The individual is considered to be in the best position to make statements about him or herself, and these form the basis for therapy.

Self-concept

The important factor in Rogers' theory is the concept of the self.[51] The self in this context comprises the pattern of perception, feelings, attitudes and values which the individual considers to be unique to him or herself. Rogers also refers to the "ideal self" which is the individual as he or she would like to be. In the well-adjusted individual the difference between the self and the ideal self would not be significant. But where there is a discrepancy between the self and actual experience, imbalance arises and this can result in tension and maladjustment.

However, when the individual is aware of the state of imbalance he or she may change his or her behaviour to bring it into line with his or her self-concept, or alternatively modify that self-concept. When the experiences are clearly perceived as too threatening to the individual's self-concept, they may be repressed. Rogers speaks of defence mechanisms—e.g. repression—in much the same way as Freud, as a means of maintaining the integrity of the self. He also mentions the importance of different forms of positive gestures in the shaping of the self-concept.[52] These would include approval, sympathy, love and respect from others, though the conditions to be satisfied before acquiring these benefits could put a lot of pressure on the individual and may elicit defence mechanisms.

For example, if the parents value scholastic achievement, the child is likely to develop a self-concept which emphasizes academic achievement. But if the child's performance at school does not match this ideal, an *ego-defensive* strategy may have to be used. This could take the form of ignoring actual experience. The problem with this is that, as more and more experiences are not allowed to reach the level of awareness, the self can sever contact with reality and the individual becomes increasingly maladjusted. The neurotic individual is placed in a position of heavy reliance on defence mechanisms because of a significant mismatch between actual experience and self-concept.

It is important that the therapist who uses Rogers' ideas is neither directive nor disinterested, but is client-centred. Understanding the client's own view of him or herself necessitates an exploration of his or her total experience. The desired result is constructive change to facilitate greater self-fulfilment of the client. Important conditions for the success of client-centred therapy appear to be the provision of adequate levels of empathy, genuineness, warmth on the part of the therapist, and an environment suitable for self-exploration by the client of feelings, values, fears, and relationships.

A particular criticism of Rogers' theory is that it focuses too much on the cognitive dimensions of personality, to the relative neglect of unconscious processes. Also, the use of self-reports can prove unreliable because the client may be unduly influenced by what the therapist expects from the encounter and may be prone to make socially desirable responses to the therapist. In addition, it can be argued that the client does not have perfect insight into his or her own condition.[8]

There is some support for the self-concept in studies of consumer behaviour. It appears that consumers prefer brands which relate both to their self-perceptions and to subjective images of brands. In one study the relationship between consumers' self-images and product images in nineteen product categories—e.g. club membership, coffee, beer, and wine—was investigated. It was found that the preferences of consumers were positively related either to self-image or to ideal self-image.[53] In another study consumers of cars perceived themselves as having characteristics similar to owners of their particular make of car, and saw themselves as possessing a self-concept different from consumers of a competing make.[54] The words used to describe the owners of the different makes of car are illustrated in Table 1.5.

TABLE 1.5
Self-image of Car Owners

Volkswagon Owners	Pontiac GTO Owners
Thrifty	Status-conscious
Sensible	Flashy
Creative	Fashionable
Individualistic	Adventurous
Practical	Interested in opposite sex
Conservative	Sporty
Economical	Style-conscious
Quality-conscious	Pleasure-seeking

Personal Construct Theory

According to Kelly, a psychological theory should be about understanding a person's behaviour with a view to predicting future actions. Humans are seen as scientists who are trying to make sense out of their world. They are continually testing assumptions about various things with reference to experience and evidence. There is no absolute truth or objective reality, but humans can use "constructs" to interpret situations in order to improve their understanding and ability to predict future events. So a construct is a way of predicting future happenings, and it is only useful if predictions are fairly accurate.[55] If the construct "dishonest" is applied to a person, then a prediction is made about how that person is expected to behave in a position where, for example, he or she handles a lot of money.

When using constructs, we are concerned with two opposite poles—beautiful/ugly, honest/dishonest, good/bad, warm/cold, intelligent/stupid, and so on. Constructs arise when a person construes two persons or objects as having a characteristic in common, which is different from that associated with a third person or object. Some constructs are more general than others. For example, the construct "beautiful/ugly" may apply to nearly everything in the world, while the construct "intelligent/stupid" may

TABLE 1.6
Hierarchy of Constructs

Happier	vs.	Unhappier
↑		↑
Closer personal relationships	vs.	Poorer personal relationships
↑		↑
More accepted by people	vs.	Not so well accepted by people
↑		↑
Makes a good first impression	vs.	Makes a poor first impression
↑		↑
Well dressed	vs.	Badly dressed

fit only humans or mammals. Each construct will have its own hierarchy. This is illustrated in Table 1.6.[56]

In this example, a person was asked whether he would prefer to see himself as well dressed or badly dressed, and replied that he would like to see himself as well dressed. When asked why, he replied that it was in order to make a good first impression on people. The question "Why?" was repeatedly asked after each reply until the person reached the ceiling of the hierarchy. When asked why he wanted to be happier, he gave no direct response, other than saying it was what life was about. Some constructs are classified as superordinate (superior) and are related to a number of subordinate or peripheral constructs. The superordinate constructs, which are really stable, are considered to be core constructs and give the person a sense of identity and continuity.

If a person can only state one pole of a construct, the other pole is said to be submerged. For example, if a person uses "intelligent" to describe people, the existence of the opposite pole "stupid" is implied even though it is not used. So if it is asserted that somebody is intelligent, this implies a contrast. To have abstracted the idea of intelligent, a person must be aware of several intelligent people, and at least one stupid person. Thus, at one moment, the person's construct is intelligent versus stupid.

Normally people revise their constructs in the light of experience. If predictions based on a construct are continually wrong, this could give rise to a revision of the appropriate construct. Constructs, then, may change over time, particularly where they are flexible enough to accommodate new events, although others are relatively inflexible in that they rarely allow new events to be accepted. Constructs which are closely correlated with others are called "tight" constructs, and predictions do not vary. For example, "This is a library, therefore it contains books." When constructs are "loose," it is possible to make a number of predictions in similar circumstances—in the same way that, for example, a track-suit could be used for a variety of sporting activities at a given venue. Generally, constructs should not be too tightly or too loosely organized. Each individual has his or her own personal construct system, and its structure and organization constitutes that individual's personality.

Important Factors in Personal Construct Theory. Anxiety, threat, hostility and aggression are important factors in Kelly's Personal Construct Theory. Anxiety is said to arise when the person is aware that perceived events cannot be construed within the construct system. An accountant who cannot figure out how to write a management report may experience anxiety. The anxiety arises when the accountant recognizes that the challenge with which he or she is presented lies outside the orbit of his or her construct system. The real cause of the anxiety is the realization that the construct system is inadequate to cope with the situation.

Threat is an awareness of an imminent major change in the person's core construct. An academic construes him or herself to be an able scholar. However, over the years his or her research and scholarly achievements are patchy and his or her publications are negligible. Therefore, he or she has to reappraise his or her role and finds the experience threatening.

Hostility arises when there is a realization that there is mismatch between a construct and its prediction. A senior manager recruits an accountant to provide a management accounting service to the organization. However, the accountant prefers to operate as a financial accountant. The hostile senior manager does not change his or her view of the accountant. Instead he or she offers inducements and incentives so that the accountant may gravitate towards the provision of a management accounting service.

Another response that is possible when constructs are not working is aggression. A sales representative considers him or herself to be first rate in a large group of companies. He or she attends a sales convention organized by the group and encounters other sales representatives with excellent track records. He or she finds it difficult to keep up with them, and his or her response is aggression.

It is obvious that Kelly's definitions of anxiety, threat, hostility, and aggression are not quite the same as the conventional definitions of these terms. He has nothing to say about the development of the person, and pays little attention to how the individual comes to construe events. It is as if all that matters is how the individual sees the world at a given moment.

Rep Test. The Role Construct Repertory Test (Rep Test) is a method used to arrive at the basic constructs which a person uses and the interrelationship between them. The test is based on the premise that a construct can be measured by first noting the similarities and contrasts among events.

For example, a person is asked to list a series of people or events that are regarded as important—e.g. lecturers, friends, relatives, marriage, purchase of a house. Once the list is prepared, the person is asked, in the case of people, to give the name of someone who can be classified as a lecturer, friend and relative. The person receives three cards, each card bearing one of the names he or she has given. The person is asked to say in what way two of them are alike but different from the third name. This procedure is repeated with different cards until an adequate number of constructs has been elicited. A simple example of the elicitation of a construct is as follows.

Counsellor: List three people you most admire.

Client: My friend, my relative and my tutor.

Counsellor: How are two of these people alike but yet different from the third person?

Client: My friend and my relative are outgoing, but my tutor is introverted.

Repertory Grid.   A method developed from the Rep Test is called the Repertory Grid, and has been used in a variety of settings, including management selection and development. This method allows the investigator to use a number of different types of element. An element could be the title of a job or a name. Constructs may be elicited, or alternatively provided, by the investigator. In the above example the construct "outgoing" was elicited by the counsellor. In Table 1.7 the constructs provided may be considered critical, in terms of personality characteristics, in an industrial environment. The elements (names of executives) are listed as single and paired combinations; the pair share the same constructs.

TABLE 1.7
Elements and Constructs in a Repertory Grid

Elements		Constructs
Research scientist	⎫ (Pair)	Innovative
Head of Department	⎭	Optimistic
Production manager	(Single)	Favours status quo Pessimistic

In this process more constructs could be elicited until constructs are either repeated or the subjects cannot give any more constructs. Other elements in triad form in the domain of executive personality characteristics could be elicited, and this in turn would lead to the elicitation of more constructs. The final list of elements and constructs will then be used to produce a grid with the elements along the top and the constructs down the side. The

	Manager	Workers in general	Senior union official	Person W	Top management	Person Y	Government	Person X	Person Z	Junior supervisors	Welfare	Person V	Person U	Staff in general	Managers' staff association
Powerful															
Leaders															
National															
Elected															
Takes management view															
High ranking															
Have control															
Responsible															
Takes workers' view															
Employed by organisation															
Impersonal															
Cooperative															
Takes decisions															
Militant															
Communicative															
Good															

5 = definitely yes
4 = yes
3 = uncertain
2 = no
1 = definitely no

FIG 1.7   A Repertory Grid. From: Smith, M. (1978) Using repertory grids to evaluate training. *Personnel Management,* February, 36-37.

subject is then asked to grade each element on each construct using either a five or seven-point scale. The grid shown in Fig.1.7 is a simplified represent-ation of constructs and elements after being reduced in number following a consensus process. The grid was the outcome of an elicitation process with a group of supervisors attending a short course at an educational establish-ment.[57] To assist with the processing of the grid data, statistical computer packages can be used as a prelude to the interpretation of the outcome of the exercise.

BEHAVIOURAL PERSPECTIVE

Though there is no single behavioural position, there is a significant view that the main source of behaviour can be found in the individual's environ-ment, and not within the person. Though genetic inheritance is not discoun-ted, the feeling is that reference to traits, psycho-analysis and the physiologi-cal basis of behaviour is not particularly illuminating. It is maintained that a person's development and behaviour is primarily influenced by what happens to him or her from childhood onwards and by the learning that takes place. Therefore, the environment is said to exert a powerful influence in terms of behavioural change. A major authority who expounded this view is Skinner.[58] His views on conditioning and reinforcement are more fully reported in the discussion on learning in Chapter 4.

Reinforcement

A behavioural or social learning approach can be illustrated with reference to reinforcement in child training. When the child conforms to certain stan-dards it may receive parental reinforcement in the form of a reward such as an expression of pleasure, a smile, praise, a pat on the head, and so on. The parent has the capacity to shape the child's response. When the child emits an inborn social response—a smile—it becomes part of the child's repertoire of responses when it is reinforced.

In the development of language intermittent reinforcement may also be applied. For example, the mother is positively encouraging the development of language when periodically all meaningful language sounds emitted by the child are reinforced. The reinforcer could simply be the expression of delight on the mother's face. However, if the mother does not reinforce or reward the early crude attempts to pronounce words, this could give rise to a delay in the learning of language. But equally, understanding a child's crude utterances too readily and quickly may encourage late talking. Sometimes it is difficult to establish the reinforcers associated with the child's behaviour. For example, the motives for stealing or lying may be connected with the values of the child's peer group and this is something which lies outside the control of the parents.

Negative and non-reinforcement are also strategies at the disposal of parents. Negative reinforcement takes the form of punishment and may be appropriately applied in certain circumstances: for example, a child with insufficient road sense is corrected.

Punishment which inflicts pain should be avoided. It may inhibit rather than stamp out undesirable behaviour. It may also lead to delinquency, block the flow of communication and create resentment. Non-reinforcement can take the form of a threat to withdraw approval, or alternatively actually withdrawing approval, and can be effective when there is a good relationship between the parent and the child. With non-reinforcement the child's response is likely to become extinct, and further training may be needed to reinstate it.

Imitation

Do we always have to experience happenings personally or directly in order to learn? According to Bandura, much learning takes place when we observe what other people do and note the consequences of their behaviour.[59] The child may imitate the mannerisms of its father, the intonation and favourite phrases of its mother, and the same accent as members of its peer group. Words which are imitated may be used without perfect understanding. Imitation is encouraged where the child observes its role model—e.g. the parent—being rewarded for engaging in a certain work or leisure activity. Likewise, the child finds imitation easy when it is specifically rewarded for copying a role model. Of course, the child could imitate a "deviant" parent but, if the parent is punished for the deviancy, then there is less likelihood of the child copying the parent.

Socialization

The child learns the significance of a number of roles in society. There is the realization that one has to conform to rules, but equally to learn the contradictions inherent in the complex system of rules; in fact parents may not be able to help in resolving this difficulty. There is the realization that there are times for competition, and times for cooperation. Bending the rules may be permissible in order to win, but one expects to be penalized if one is caught cheating. One learns to control aggressive and other impulses. The notion of right and wrong (conscience) is transmitted in a variety of ways and is often developed fortuitously. For example, a child taking money from the father's wallet is stealing, but taking a slice of cake off the table without permission is bad manners. Not very long ago it was more acceptable for the young man to sow his wild oats. The young girl, however, was expected to preserve her virginity. One finds here a pragmatic acceptance of prostitution but a moral rejection of it. During early socialization a number of values are internalized (adopted); these subsequently regulate behaviour without the need for the imposition of control in the form of punishment.

Learning to be male and female is also part of the socialization process. Boys are often expected to be rough and tough and to play football or rugby and not to cry. They are also expected to be assertive and certainly not encouraged to play with dolls. The non-conformist boy is frequently called a cissy. The little boy is more likely to use his fists in an aggressive encounter. The little girl is expected to play with dolls and be quiet, gentle and decorous, and to take up a pastime such as ballet. The non-conformist girl is called a tomboy. However, in today's society this stereotyping is being challenged, and roles are changing.

The work of Mead in primitive societies highlights the effect of child rearing practices on subsequent adult behaviour.[60] For example, child rearing practices in the Tchambuli tribe produced males who played stereotyped female roles. The men were domesticated, looked after the children, attended to the household needs, curled their hair and adorned themselves with flowers. The women were unadorned, had their heads shaven, did the hunting and generally engaged in masculine pursuits. However, it was the men who were the warriors. Perhaps the male is temperamentally more suited to the performance of aggressive acts, although in the animal world the female can be aggressive when protecting her young.

A behavioural approach to personality has been criticized because it is said to present an oversimplified view of human behaviour, but particularly because it does not pay sufficient attention to the importance of cognitive processes.[8]

Situational Variables

To complement a behavioural approach, reference is made to the potency of situational variables and how they are selected and evaluated.[61] The same situation can elicit a different response in different individuals, and different situations can elicit similar responses in one individual. The way the person selects information and evaluates it can have a profound effect on his or her response to a particular stimulus. Of course previous learning of an appropriate nature also has a part to play in this process. In the following example one accountant has a situational advantage over the other.

A balance sheet depicting the financial position of a company is presented to two accountants. One accountant has a particular insight into the quality of the senior management of the company and the state of its market. The other has no such knowledge apart from a superficial understanding of the internal affairs of the company. In these circumstances it is highly likely that the balance sheet will be interpreted differently by the two accountants. In other circumstances we would normally be confident that the two accountants would produce an identical response to a particular stimulus. If they encountered a red traffic light whilst driving in separate cars, for example, one would expect them to stop their cars. Situations alone do not determine behaviour.

PB-C

An INTERACTIONIST perspective takes into account both the situation and the personality characteristics of the individual. People bring something of themselves to situations that they encounter in everyday life; these personal characteristics vary from one person to another. Therefore, every situation interacts with personality and is interpreted and analyzed with reference to the unique set of past experiences, learning and the biological qualities of each individual.[62] To close this chapter, some outstanding topics that deal with the social and cognitive approaches to personality are discussed.

SOCIAL CONTEXT

Some psychoanalysts, who revised Freud's doctrine of instinctual and sexual motives in human behaviour, began to stress the role of social context in the determination of behaviour. As mentioned earlier, Adler stressed humans' striving for superiority in order to compensate for feelings of inferiority.[7] According to Fromm, humans have a compelling need to belong, and seek ways of relating to others and escaping from freedom, but in the process conflict and anxiety can be encountered.[63]

It would appear that certain advertisements contain messages which can be related to the above concepts. The purchaser of a unique car is told he or she will feel superior, and only distinctive and discriminating buyers purchase a particular brand of perfume! Likewise, the consumer is told that loneliness will be dispelled once membership of a particular club is obtained.

Horney felt that the way to appreciate the individual's conflicts was to understand how personality is shaped by the texture of society.[64] In a highly competitive culture the child feels helpless, alone and insecure because of being dependent on adults. The child develops ways of coping with the basic anxiety generated by these forces. Each way of coping involves a different strategy:

1. Moving toward people—protecting oneself by gestures of affection, dependency and submission (Compliant).

2. Moving against people—protecting oneself through aggression, hostility and attack (Aggressive).

3. Moving away from people—protecting oneself by isolation and withdrawal (Detached).

Compliant people are likely to conform to social norms, to subordinate themselves to the wishes of others and will tend to avoid conflict. Likewise, they are unlikely to be assertive or to seek power.

Aggressive people want to excel and manipulate others by securing power over them. They need to confirm their self-image because of uncertainty about their talents.

Detached people place emotional distance between themselves and others, place a high value on freedom from obligations, like their independence and self-sufficiency, and prefer to use their intellect more than their feelings.

A measure of personality (based on Horney's model), which has not been used to any significant extent, has been used in connection with the behaviour of consumers. This measure, which needs refinement and development, sets out to gauge a person's interpersonal orientation.[65] The results indicate that people of different personality types tend to use different products and brands. The compliant types prefer well-know brand names, and are heavy users of mouthwash and toilet soaps. The aggressive types (males) tend to use a razor rather than an electric shaver; they are heavy users of cologne and after-shave lotion and buy Old Spice deodorant and Van Heusen shirts. The detached types seem to be least aware of brands.

COGNITIVE PERSPECTIVE

An early behavioural theorist, Rotter, developed the notion of internal-external control of reinforcement.[66]

Internal-External Locus of Control
Because of its strong cognitive emphasis, this is considered to be a dimension of personality. Internal-External (I-E) is not a typology. Rather it is a continuum: a person can fall anywhere along that continuum from external at one end to internal at the other. Most people are clustered somewhere in the middle. People differ in their attitude to control. Certain people (externals) feel that the outcome of their efforts is controlled by forces and events external to themselves, such as chance, fate, and powerful figures in authority; while others (internals) are convinced that control is an internal matter related to their own efforts and talents.

Internals will be confident that they can bring about changes in their own behaviour and environment, whereas externals feel somewhat powerless to bring about change. With regard to home security, internals are likely to take certain precautions, such as installing burglar alarms, mortice locks and bright outside lights, if such action discourages intruders. Externals are much less likely to take such precautions if they believe that a person determined to break into the house will always find a way regardless of deterrents.

Internals and externals view reward or reinforcement differently. If internals receive positive reinforcement after a particular behavioural act, this will increase the likelihood of that behaviour occurring again; negative reinforcement will have the opposite effect. Externals are more likely to believe that positive reinforcement following a particular behavioural act was a matter of pure luck, and so there is little point in repeating that behaviour in the future. Faced with a problem, internals expect that defining the situation as one in which personal efforts will make a difference will help them to resolve the problem. On the other hand, externals will operate with the expectation that chance or other uncontrollable factors are critical, and they will behave accordingly.

The person builds up expectations about the relationship between behaviour and its consequences, and expectancy will be either strengthened or reduced depending on the similarity or otherwise of that behaviour in the future to its consequences. In this way the person distinguishes behaviour that brings about predictable results from behaviour that does not. The executive will develop a relatively stable set of expectancies regarding the control of his or her behaviour at committee meetings, in terms of results or success either due to his or her own actions, or to some other factor.

Expectancy also manifests itself in the following illustration. I consider it necessary to have an extension built to my house. Following various enquiries I approach a particular building contractor to discuss the costs of such a project. I will have certain expectations about a satisfactory outcome if the contract is given to this builder: These expectations could be based on my previous experience of doing business with him. But if I had no previous experience of his work, then my expectation that using him would result in satisfactory work could depend on other factors.

I could rely on the recommendation of somebody I know who had a similar extension built by the builder in question and was most pleased with the outcome. Likewise I may be able to inspect similar projects undertaken by the builder, with the help of an expert. Of course I could be optimistic about the venture and this could be reflected in a general expectancy that the contract will work out well. If, however, I am a distrusting person, this will lower my expectancy that doing business with the builder will be a productive exercise. If I am an external in disposition, the expectancy that commissioning work on the extension will lead to a positive outcome could be dampened.

Externals are likely to be compliant and conforming individuals, prone to persuasion and ready to accept information from others. Because they expect that they cannot control the consequences of their own behaviour, they are more willing to place reliance on others. Internals seem to have greater confidence in their own competence and they appear to be more independent. They prefer to be in control, and consequently resist any efforts on the part of others to manipulate them. The most fundamental difference between internals and externals lies in the way they seek knowledge about their environment. The internals, unlike the externals, realize that they are in control of the reinforcement or reward that follows their behaviour, and put greater effort into obtaining information about their environment.[62] Apparently secretarial staff, who were classified as externals, were found to be more reluctant to use word processing equipment, whereas their non-external peers displayed natural curiosity about the potential of the equipment.[67]

A questionnaire, referred to as the I-E scale, has been developed by Rotter and is used to measure the orientation of internals and externals.[68] The questionnaire consists of 29 items. Each item consists of two statements. The subject is asked to select the statement that is closest to his or her belief. The following statements bear some similarity to statements on the I-E scale:

1. (a) Many people can be described as victims of circumstance.
   (b) What happens to other people is pretty much of their own making.
2. (a) Much of what happens to me is probably a matter of luck.
   (b) What happens to me is my own doing.
3. (a) It is foolish to think one can really change another person's basic attitudes.
   (b) When I am right I can convince others.

The concept of the internal-external locus of control has generated a fair amount of research in recent years. The validity of the I-E scale has been questioned, particularly on the grounds that it is socially desirable to be portrayed as an internal. It is suggested that some people fake the test in order to project a favourable image.[8]

Field Dependency-Independency

This concept was developed following experiments on perception. A field-dependent person tends to be strongly influenced by the background or surroundings of a particular stimulus. A field-independent person is not so influenced and can differentiate more easily between parts of the stimulus and its surroundings.[69] This concept was extended to embrace cognitive style, and as a consequence entered the domain of personality.

The field-independent person has the capacity to interpret events in a detailed organized way, and has a clearer view of the constituent parts of the objects or situations encountered. He or she has a clearer view of his or her own beliefs, needs, and characteristics, and of the ways in which they differ from those of other people. In one study, subjects had their cognitive style tested prior to being set a task involving the use of a computer program and a set of data to answer a series of questions. It was concluded that cognitive style was significantly related to the number of correct answers. It is interesting to note that field-independent individuals performed particularly well.[70]

The field-dependent person tends to be susceptible to social influences and relies less on his or her own judgement. He or she cannot always see how the individual parts fit into the total picture, and finds it difficult to differentiate between them and to relate his or her own beliefs, needs, and characteristics. Likewise, he or she finds it difficult to see a clear distinction between the latter characteristics and those of a similar nature possessed by others.

SUMMARY

Having defined what we mean by personality, two basic approaches to the study of personality were introduced. These are referred to as the idiographic and nomothetic approaches. There followed an analysis of a number of perspectives on personality, starting with the psycho-analytical. This draws heavily on the contribution of Freud and was discussed with reference to levels of awareness; personality structure (*id, ego* and *superego*); defence mechanisms (repression, projection, fixation, regression and reaction formation); and finally personality development.

Projective tests, designed to assess personality based on unconscious processes, were said to be only indirectly related to psychoanalysis. Two well known projective tests are the Rorschach test and the Thematic Apperception test. These tests, though subject to certain weaknesses, can be used in consumer motivation research. In addition, role playing and visualization techniques used to create personality descriptions of consumers were mentioned.

The next major perspective on personality discussed was trait theory. Different categories of traits, including Allport's category, were described. Cattell was identified as an influential trait theorist. He drew a distinction between source traits and surface traits. His 16 PF personality test represents source traits. The outcome of personality testing, using the 16 PF, was stated with reference to a managerial and executive population. Other tests mentioned, which can be used to measure personality traits, were the Thurstone Temperament Schedule and the Edwards Personal Preference Schedule. It was suggested that the trait approach to personality has weaknesses, particularly in research into consumer behaviour and when used for the selection of people for jobs. There appears to be a natural tendency to refer to the desirable or undesirable personal characteristics of occupational groups, quite independent of formal personality tests.

When a person shares a pattern of traits with a large group of people he or she is said to belong to a personality type. Types, as a perspective on personality, were discussed initially with reference to the theory of the four humours and Sheldon's physical typology. This was followed by a brief examination of the typologies advanced by the influential psychologists, Jung and Allport. The major part of the discussion was devoted to the important contribution made by another influential psychologist, Eysenck. The relationship between personality types and accidents was explored, and psychographics as a technique in consumer research designed to compensate for the weaknesses of the trait and type approaches was briefly acknowledged.

An interpersonal perspective on personality, suitably illustrated, focused on how individuals perceived themselves and their environment, and how a subjective view is matched against objective reality. The notion of the Self-concept (Rogers) and Personal Construct Theory (Kelly) were introduced. The important factors in Personal Construct Theory were noted, and examples of the use of the repertory grid, which is derived from Kelly's theory, were given.

A behavioural perspective on personality, primarily concerned with reinforcement, imitation and socialization recognized that a person's development and behaviour is primarily influenced by happenings from childhood onwards and by the learning that takes place. The weakness of the behavioural approach was accepted, and the relevance of a situational emphasis to complement it was noted. An interactionist approach was said to be more realistic because it recognized both the situation and personality characteristics.

Finally, the social context, as a determining influence on behaviour, and a cognitive perspective on personality were acknowledged. The latter consists of the internal-external locus of control and field dependency-independency.

QUESTIONS

1. What is meant by the term "Personality"?
2. Distinguish between the idiographic and nomothetic approaches to the study of personality.
3. Examine the potential of Freudian analysis in any business context.
4. Identify the differences between projective tests and role playing or visualization, and comment on the usefulness of these techniques in the field of marketing.
5. Define a trait, giving examples of different categories of traits.
6. What significance is attached to trait and type analysis in an employment setting?
7. Is there any scientific basis for the suggestion that certain people are accident-prone?
8. Why do marketeers use psychographics?
9. What is the relationship between Personal Construct Theory and the Repertory Grid?
10. Discuss the difference between reinforcement and socialization in the context of a behavioural perspective on personality.
11. Define the following terms.
    (a) interactionist view;
    (b) compliant strategy;
    (c) internal-external locus of control;
    (d) field dependency-independency.

REFERENCES

1. Wright, D.S., Taylor, A., Davies, D.R., Sluckin, W., Lee, S.G.M. & Reason, J.T. (1970) *Introducing Psychology. An Experimental Approach.* London: Penguin.
2. Allport, G.W. (1965) *Letters from Jenny.* New York: Harcourt, Brace & World.
3. Hetherington, E.M. & Wray, N.P. (1964) Aggression, need for social approval and humour preferences. *Journal of Abnormal and Social Psychology*, 68, 685–689.
4. Lazarus, R.S. (1971) *Personality.* Englewood Cliffs: Prentice-Hall.
5. Freud, S. (1938) *The Basic Writings of Sigmund Freud.* New York: Modern Library.
6. Mackay, K. (1973) *An Introduction to Psychology.* London: Macmillan.
7. Brown, J.A.C. (1961) *Freud and the Post–Freudians.* Harmondsworth: Penguin.
8. Peck, D. & Whitlow, D. (1975) *Approaches to Personality Theory.* London: Methuen.
9. Robertson, I.T. & Cooper, C.L. (1983) *Human Behaviour in Organisations.* Plymouth: Macdonald and Evans.
10. Williams, K.C. (1981) *Behavioural Aspects of Marketing.* London: Heinemann.
11. Anastasi, A. (1979) *Fields of Applied Psychology.* Tokyo: McGraw-Hill.
12. Holmes, D.S. (1974) The conscious control of thematic projection. *Journal of Consulting and Clinical Psychology*, 42, 323–329.
13. Haire, M. (1950) Projective techniques in market research. *Journal of Marketing*, 14, 649–656.
14. Webster, F.E. & Von Pechmann, F. (1970) A replication of the shopping list study. *Journal of Marketing*, 34, 61–77.
15. Lane, G.S. & Watson, G.L. (1975) A Canadian replication of Mason Haire's shopping list study. *Journal of the Academy of Marketing Science*, 13, Spring, 48.
16. Drever, J. (1964) *A Dictionary of Psychology.* Harmondsworth: Penguin.
17. Allport, G.W. (1961) *Pattern and Growth in Personality.* New York: Holt, Rinehart & Winston.
18. Cattell, R.B. (1965) *The Scientific Analysis of Personality.* Harmondsworth: Penguin.
19. Howarth, E. & Browne, A. (1971) An item factor analysis of the 16 PF. *Personality*, 2, 117–139.
20. Cattell, R.B. (1974) How good is the modern questionnaire? General principles for evaluation. *Journal of Personality Assessment*, 38, 115–129.
21. Barden, V. (1970) Yes, the accountants are different. (Report of a study at The Ashridge Management College.) *Accountancy Age, 16 October*, 15.
22. Hartston, W.R. & Mottram, R.D. (1976) *Personality Profiles of Managers: A Study of Occupational Differences.* Cambridge: Industrial Training Research Unit.
23. Barry, B. & Dowling, P. (1984) *Towards an Australian Management Style: A Study of the Personality Characteristics and Management Style of Australian Managers.* Victoria: The Australian Institute of Management.
24. Westfall, R. (1962) Psychological factors in predicting product choice. *Journal of Marketing*, 26, 34–40.
25. Koponen, A. (1960) Personality characteristics of purchasers. *Journal of Advertising Research*, 1, 6–12.
26. Landon, E.L. (1972) A sex-role explanation of purchase intention differences of consumers who are high and low in need for achievement. *Association for Consumer Research, Proceedings of Third Annual Conference* (Ed. M. Venkatesan) 1–8.
27. De Coster, D.T. & Rhode, J.G. (1971) The accountant's stereotype: real and imagined, deserved or unwarranted. *The Accounting Review*, 46, 651–662.
28. Lawler, E.E. & Rhode, J.G. (1976) *Information and Control in Organizations.* Santa-Monica, California: Goodyear.
29. Hopper, T. (1978) *Role Conflicts of Management Accountants in the Context of their*

Structural Relationship to Production. M.Phil. Thesis (Unpublished). University of Aston in Birmingham.

30. Child, J. & Ellis, A. (1973) Predictors of variation in management roles. *Human Relations, 26,* 227–250.

31. Lewis, C. (1984) What's new in selection. *Personnel Management, January,* 14–16.

32. Lewis, C. (1980) Investigating the employment interview: a consideration of counselling skills. *Journal of Occupational Psychology, 53,* 111–116.

33. Bayne, R. & Fletcher, C. (1983) Selecting the selectors. *Personnel Management, June.*

34. Leigh, J. (1985) Executives and the personality factor. *Sky, 4, May,* 34–38.

35. Sheldon, W.H. (1954) *A Guide for Somatotyping the Adult Male at All Ages.* New York: Harper.

36. Eysenck, H.J. (1953) *The Structure of Human Personality.* London: Methuen.

37. Eysenck, H.J. (1947) *Dimensions of Personality.* London: Routledge & Kegan Paul.

38. Eysenck, H.J. (1965) *Fact and Fiction in Psychology.* Harmondsworth: Penguin.

39. Eysenck, H.J. (1967) *The Biological Basis of Behaviour.* Springfield, Ill: C.C. Thomas.

40. Farmer, E. & Chambers, E.G. (1926) *A Psychological Study of Individual Differences in Accident Rates.* Report No. 38, Industrial Fatigue Research Board, Medical Research Council, 1–46.

41. Haddon, W., Suchman, E. & Klein, D. (1964) *Accident Research: Its Methods and Approaches.* New York: Harper & Row.

42. Hirschfield, A. & Behan, R. (1963) Etiological considerations of industrial injuries. *Journal of the American Medical Association, October.*

43. Lindsey, F. (1980) Accident proneness–does it exist? *Occupational Safety and Health, 10, February,* 8–9.

44. Feldman, M.P. (1971) *Psychology in the Industrial Environment.* London: Butterworths.

45. Craske, S. (1968) A study of the relation between personality and accident history. *British Journal of Medical Psychology, 41,* 399–404.

46. Jung, C.G. (1965) Analytical Psychology. In W. Sahakian (Ed.), *Psychology of Personality: Readings in Theory.* Chicago: Rand McNally.

47. Mitroff, I., et al. (1974) On managing science in the systems age: two schemes for the study of science as a whole systems phenomenon. *Interfaces, 4,* 50.

48. Allport, G.W., Vernon, P.E. & Lindzey, G. (1960) *A Study of Values: A Scale for Measuring the Dominant Interests in Personality.* Boston: Houghton Mifflin.

49. England, G.W. & Lee, R. (1974) The relationship between managerial values and managerial success in the U.S., Japan, India and Australia. *Journal of Applied Psychology, 59,* 411–419.

50. Wells, W.D. & Tigert, D.J. (1971) Activities, interests and opinions. *Journal of Advertising Research, 11,* 27–35.

51. Rogers, C.R. (1951) *Client-Centred Therapy.* Boston: Houghton Mifflin.

52. Rogers, C.R. (1959) A theory of therapy, personality and interpersonal relationships as developed in the client-centred framework. In S. Koch (Ed.) *Psychology: A Study of a Science, Vol.3.* New York: McGraw-Hill.

53. Landon, E.L. (1974) Self-concept, ideal self-concept and consumer purchase intentions. *Journal of Consumer Research, 1.*

54. Grubb, E.L. & Hupp, G. (1968) Perception of self, generalized stereotypes and brand selection. *Journal of Marketing Research 5,* 58–63.

55. Kelly, G.A. (1955) *The Psychology of Personal Constructs.* New York: W.W.Norton.

56. Bannister, D. (1970) *Perspectives in Personal Construct Theory.* New York: Academic Press, 56.

57. Smith, M. (1978) Using Repertory Grids to evaluate training. *Personnel Management, February,* 36–37.

58. Skinner, B.F. (1974) *About Behaviourism*. London: Jonathan Cape.
59. Bandura, A. (1969) *Principles of Behaviour Modification*. London: Holt, Rinehart & Winston.
60. Mead, M. (1935) *Sex and Temperament in Three Primitive Societies*. New York: William Morrow.
61. Mischel, W. (1973) Toward a cognitive social learning reconceptualization of personality. *Psychological Review, 80*, 252–283.
62. Phares, E.J. (1984) *Introduction to Personality*. Columbus, Ohio: Charles E. Merrill Publishing Co.
63. Fromm, E. (1941) *Escape from Freedom*. New York: Rinehart.
64. Horney, K.B. (1945) *Our Inner Conflicts*. New York: W.W.Norton.
65. Cohen, J.B. (1967) An interpersonal orientation to the study of consumer behaviour. *Journal of Marketing Research, 4*, 270–278.
66. Rotter, J.B. (1954) *Social Learning and Clinical Psychology*. Englewood Cliffs: Prentice–Hall.
67. Arndt, S., Feltes, J. & Hanak, J. (1983) Secretarial attitudes towards word processors as a function of familiarity and locus of control. *Behaviour and Information Technology, 2*, 17–22.
68. Rotter, J.B. (1966) Generalized expectancies for internal versus external control of reinforcement. *Psychological Monographs, 8*, (1, Whole No. 609).
69. Witkin, H.A. (1965) Psychological differentiation and forms of pathology. *Journal of Abnormal and Social Psychology, 70*, 317–336.
70. Egly, D.G. (1982) Cognitive style, categorization and vocational effects on performance of *REL. DATABASE* users. *SIGSOC Bulletin, 13*, 91–97.

2 MOTIVATION

2 Motivation

The opening section of this chapter is devoted to a definition of the concept of motivation. This is followed by an analysis of factors that contribute to a state of arousal in motivated behaviour. Next is a brief description of frustration followed by an identification of situations likely to contribute to monotony and boredom at work—a condition likely to affect the motivation of the employee. Rest pauses may be used to counteract the worst effects of monotony and fatigue.

The major theories of job satisfaction and motivation are considered at length and there is reference to job design and the role of new technology. The discussion is brought to a close with an examination of a cognitive theory of motivation with particular application to budgeting and management control.

DEFINITION

The question of motivation arises when we ask why people behave in a certain way. When a person is motivated he or she is responding to conditions operating within and outside of him or herself. Motivation is frequently studied with reference to needs, motives, drives, and goals or incentives.

Needs
Needs can be classified as, for example, physiological, security or safety, social, and *ego* or esteem needs. It is possible to have a need and do nothing about it, but equally a pressing need can give rise to a specific pattern of behaviour.

Motives
Motives consist of inner states that energize, activate, and direct the behaviour of the individual as he or she strives to attain a goal or acquire an

incentive. A single motive may produce many effects, while a single effect may have several motives.

For example, a person's purchase of a cake mix may be influenced by a craving for sweet things, pride in his or her ability as a cook, and a need for social approval from family or guests.

Motives can act in concert or vary in intensity, and are related to needs and goals or incentives. Motives can serve as a means by which consumers evaluate competing products. This can be seen when a car buyer, motivated by convenience, may be attracted to a model with electronic windows, central door locking and electronic speed control in preference to a similar car without these facilities.

Drives

The concept of drive is an important feature of many theories of motivation and is linked with theories of learning, such as Hull's theory (see Chapter 4).

An individual is said to be in a state of drive when he or she adopts a pattern of behaviour in order to achieve a particular goal. For example, a hungry person, who is obviously preoccupied with satisfying a physiological need, behaves (a state of drive) in such a way as to indicate that he or she is in search of food or nourishment (a goal or incentive). When the person obtains sufficient nourishment the behaviour (the drive) subsides for the time being. The stronger the drive the greater the level of arousal experienced by the individual. A raised level of arousal implies increased awareness, energy and speed and can be effective in the performance of well-learned mental and physical skills. On the other hand, a lower level of arousal is more suited for tasks of a really complex nature.

The thalamus and reticular formation (both areas of the brain) exert influence on the arousal mechanism. The thalamus is the focal point of excitement and depression, pleasure and pain. The function of the reticular formation is to increase or decrease the level of arousal, and apart from filtering information it decides what should be passed on to the higher brain and what should be rejected. Obviously a high priority would be given to information that alerts us to a potential danger.

There follows an illustration of arousal in the motivation process. A person suddenly realizes that what appears to be a harmless cow in a field turns out to be an angry bull about to charge. There is a high level of motivation to escape, and information is registered in the hypothalamus (an organ with an important central control function), which directs two processes simultaneously. One process is the reticular formation which transmits a message electrically through the sympathetic nervous system to the various parts of the body; the other is the pituitary gland which, under the control of the hypothalamus, transmits chemically through the adrenal medulla which secretes adrenalin.

The nervous system and chemical processes together prepare the body for effective speedy action by increasing the blood supply to the brain and muscles and decreasing the blood supply to the digestive system; by increasing the heart beat and rate of breathing; by alerting relevant parts of the brain to ensure that the necessary skill (to run) is properly performed; and finally, directing the movement of the body by monitoring the bull's movements, the condition of the ground, where the gate is located and so on.

It is through the co-ordination of all these processes that the person escapes. After these processes are complete, the level of arousal drops and the person enters a state of relative calm with the help of the parasympathetic nervous system. The emotion of fear, which activated flight, featured prominently in the above cycle of events. Anger is also an emotion that is considered in the context of motivation, and produces a physiological change in the form of a greater production of nor-adrenalin, resulting in a "fight" response.

Goals or Incentives

Goals or incentives satisfy or reduce the behaviour associated with the drive. For example, the eating of food by the hungry person could lead to a reduction or elimination of the hunger drive.

In the field of safety various incentive programmes have been designed to motivate people to meet good safety standards. Tangible rewards, such as jewellery, gifts and plaques, as opposed to cash, for meeting safety targets, are more common in the U.S. Something like a pin is said to provide a symbol of achievement, it is visible to others and it provides a lasting memento of the occasion which justified recognition. It is often suggested that the key to a successful safety incentive programme is to make safety a group activity, for in so doing peer pressure is used to reinforce safe work habits.

AROUSAL STIMULI

The stimuli which influence states of arousal are illustrated using examples drawn from marketing and accounting. Sandwiched between the wants and needs of the consumer and the product or service advertised by a company is the appeal of the product of service.

Appeal

The appeal is the message contained in, for example, an advertisement. Consumer studies conducted for a sweet manufacturer established that eating sweets was associated with completing a job that the sweet eater considered disagreeable—a form of reward for doing an unpleasant or tough job. The company switched its advertising slogan in two test markets from "smooth, rich, creamy coated chocolates, everybody likes them" to "make that tough job easier, you deserve our chocolates," with a consequent increase in sales.[1]

Appeals in advertising can either be positive or negative. They are positive when a pleasant situation follows the use of the product, and negative when an unpleasant situation may occur if the product is not used. An example of a negative appeal is a message on the label of a garment containing an assurance that the cloth will not shrink if a particular washing detergent is used. The way a negative appeal is presented is crucial, for if the situation presented is too unpleasant, as in the case of a detailed picture of a serious accident, people could turn away completely from the advertisement. With negative appeals the emphasis is placed on the action the individual may take to avoid the unpleasant situation; it is escaping from fear that reinforces learning, rather than being confronted by fear itself.

Feeling Tone

The feeling a product generates is also worthy of note. This is referred to as a feeling tone.

In a house-to-house survey of hosiery preferences in one city, four identical samples of hosiery were presented to housewives. Some of the samples contained a card which had been immersed in a faint perfume; and though awareness of the scent was not altogether evident, the perfume created a pleasant feeling towards the product, with significant results in consumer choice.[2]

In an advertisement for soup, pictures of the glowing health of happy children or the warmth and comfort of a hot bowl of soup on a blustery day could generate certain feelings about the product.

Companies deliberately change the image and appeal of a product in the hope of influencing the motivational disposition of consumers. The brand image of Marlboro cigarettes was originally elegant and somewhat feminine. The company adopted a strategy to change the image of the product by conducting an advertising campaign in which ranchers, hunters and other sturdy outdoor types, often displaying tattoo-marks, were seen smoking Marlboro cigarettes.

Brand names and trade marks are sometimes chosen to strengthen the desired brand image. The story of Green Giant peas is a good example of this strategy.[3] A small company in Minnesota, called the Minnesota Valley Canning Company, marketed extra large peas grown from a particular seed. The company selected the brand name Green Giant and pictures of a smiling green giant were used in the packaging and all product advertisements. The company extended the use of the green giant brand to some of its other canned products, such as corn. Because the symbol was both popular and effective, the company changed its name to the Green Giant Company. This is an example of transforming a successful brand image into a corporate image. Usually the reverse is the case, for example, when a company such as BP or ICI uses the corporate image to promote the public acceptability of a product.

Colour and Print Type

Colours in an advertisement can capture our attention, portray realism and may arouse feelings about an object. From common experience red is associated with danger, fire and blood, blue with cool rivers and lakes, and orange/yellow with sunlight and comfortable warmth.

Printing types and other graphic elements also have significant motivational implications. When reading a book, poor legibility of type may decrease speed and accuracy of reading, and increase visual fatigue. In an advertisement poor legibility reduces the motivation to read further, and the ensuing frustration may become associated with the product. Various print types, and the layout of printed matter have to be considered in order to ensure good legibility.[4] Unfamiliar type and arrangement tends to slow down reading. A passage set completely in capitals rather than capitals and lower case, for example, can have an adverse effect on reading speed. At the same time, capitals are suitable for a message which will be read from a distance, for example, on a billboard or road sign.

The fastest reading rate and the fewest eye fixations were found to be associated with black print on a white background. Other good combinations of colour were green on white, blue on white and black on yellow.[4] Bad combinations were red on green and black on purple, which could slow down reading by more than 50%.

Because of emotional reactions and associations aroused by different types of print, brand names may use particular typefaces to convey certain qualities—old English or elaborate types, for example, might be used to create a genteel or aristocratic impression.

Sounds and Imagery

When devising brand names or selecting appropriate words for advertising copy, feeling tones aroused by different sounds should be considered. Meaningful associations in a phonetic sense should be explored when choosing a brand name, likewise ease of pronunciation is important because difficult pronunciation can arouse arouse annoyance and hostility. The makers of Suchard Chocolates printed on the wrappers of each chocolate the slogan—Say Soo Shard—because consumers were finding it difficult to pronounce the name. Eventually the company adopted a live trademark—an attractive little girl known as "Sue Shard"—who was featured in all advertisements and radio commercials and made personal appearances.[5]

Imagery is evoked by language, and a factually correct statement about a product could generate imagery that is unappetizing. For example, "Evaporated milk makes a fine curd in the stomach and is therefore more digestible than regular milk."[4]

Accounting Data as Stimuli

Accounting information is a stimulus to a particular pattern of behaviour in business and to this extent it creates a state of arousal. In effect, it triggers off a drive when it provides the decision-maker with the financial information necessary to formulate and implement a strategy regarding a particular goal. Though the accounting information stimulates the drive, it is the motive behind the decision-maker's goal which provides the drive in the first place. Of interest to the accountant in his or her assessment of the relative usefulness and relevance of accounting information, is the nature of the decision-maker's motives and goals, and the effect accounting information has on the drive state of the recipient. Like any other desired information, accounting information serves to alleviate a state of anxiety by increasing knowledge and minimizing the uncertainty facing decision-makers within the system.

How useful is financial accounting information as a stimulus or motivating force in the making and taking of investment decisions and actions? The relationship between published information with regard to earnings expectations and subsequent share price movements for selected companies was examined in order to see which financial data confirmed or conflicted with the investor's own expectations and in turn influenced the price of shares through decisions to buy or sell.[6] It was concluded that accounting data constituted a small part of the total information used by investors for this type of decision, and that there was little correlation between published data expectations and subsequent share price movements.

Certain users of financial accounting information (financial analysts, financial executives and bankers) were asked how useful and relevant they felt current cost and price level adjusted accounting information to be. All the groups sampled felt that both types of accounting information were useful, although the financial executives were the least enthusiastic about the relevance of the information.[7]

In a similar survey shareholders, bankers and financial analysts were asked to express their views on the usefulness of current cost accounting information and it was found to be generally regarded as a useful addition to the historic cost information. Only a small number of respondents would want current cost information as a complete replacement for historical cost information.[8]

In a laboratory experiment, accounting students played the role of investment analysts in a business game.[9] The researchers tried to assess the relative usefulness of items of accounting information by measuring the demand for particular items of information that could be purchased for money, and then went on to assess the effects of these items of information on the subjects' forecasts of price movements and the investment decisions that followed. One might view this study as artificial; however, the major finding of any significance was that information related to the industry was more widely used than individual company information and that accounting information was useful in the making of investment decisions. The above studies indicate that certain types and items of accounting information have a better motivating effect than others. It is therefore necessary to highlight relevancy in the provision of accounting information.

FRUSTRATION

There are occasions when the individual is in a motivated state in order to achieve a particular goal which will satisfy a deficient need—for example, the hungry person is seeking food or the ambitious employee is seeking a more challenging job. But when an obstacle is placed in the individual's pathway to the achievement of the goal (such as being caught up in a traffic jam preventing a job applicant from attending a selection interview), this can give rise to feelings of frustration and produce either positive or negative reactions. A positive reaction comes about when the person tries to resolve the difficulty in a constructive manner. For example, in the face of opposition to the implementation of a certain part of safety policy, the safety practitioner might decide to engage in more consultation with those who object to the scheme. It is also conceivable that the frustrating event makes the individual divert his or her energies into the achievement of alternative goals. In the lives of individuals over the centuries, frustrating events could have been responsible for significant personal accomplishments.

However, frustration can generate various forms of destructive behaviour. The individual may engage in physical or verbal aggression or regress to an earlier form of behaviour when, for example, a display of temper achieved the desired result. There are other circumstances when the individual reacts to frustrating situations in the same way irrespective of the magnitude of the event, and as a result the reaction may be totally inappropriate in given circumstances (i.e., shouting or making caustic remarks irrespective of the degree of magnitude of the frustrating event). Some individuals show a tendency to give up and withdraw from the situation, whereas others find the atmosphere surrounding the obstacle to the achievement of the goal unsettling and repress the experience to the unconscious mind.

MONOTONY AND BOREDOM

Monotony and boredom are associated with problems of motivation and as such are risk factors in safety at work. Boredom can be caused by a number of factors, and is particularly a problem in mass production industries.

Lack of Variety and Challenge

Lack of variety and the absence of challenge due to the short job cycle, which is a result of keeping the number of operations to a minimum, causes boredom. A comment by an assembly line worker in a car plant a number of years ago highlights this problem:

> The job gets so sickening—day in day out plugging in ignition wires. I get through one motor, turn around and there's another staring me in the face. It is sickening.[10]

Accidents apparently occur when employees perform repetitive tasks by instinct rather than thinking about what they are doing.

Loss of Skill and Independence

Another source of boredom is the lack of opportunity to exercise skill or to act independently. This arises when the work is subdivided and simplified to such an extent that the person feels there is little scope to exercise ingenuity or initiative. As a result the individual's contribution seems to be negligible. For some people the challenge of the job is important, and when they experience an inadequate sense of accomplishment they feel dissatisfied.

But it should be noted that some people prefer to daydream and this is more likely to be possible in a job that does not offer much of a challenge, in fact in a job that is likely to require only surface attention. However, having pride in one's work and involvement in the efficient execution of one's duties, is a good way of avoiding most accidents.

Pace of Work

Another factor contributing to boredom is the inability to control the pace of work, particularly on an assembly line where a machine determines how fast somebody will work. The relentless rhythm of the assembly line makes natural pacing difficult or impossible, although the worker may have some opportunity to vary the pace of work by bank building. Probably most people want a varied work pace, but some prefer to be machine-paced because they find that there is no need to pay attention to how fast they work, and that in these circumstances there is little interference from the foreman. Eventually they accept the rhythm of movement imposed on them.

Workers try to alleviate boredom in a number of ways. They might try to make a game out of work by varying the speed of the production line and setting their own sub–targets. If the noise is not too loud, they might engage in conversation, or they might make frequent visits to the cloakroom. Another outlet might be gambling and horseplay, and the ultimate tactic would be to go absent, or leave the organization. There may also be attempts to change work practices, and active resistance to management initiatives could be mounted.

Repetitive Work

The safety implications of highly repetitive work, which is monotonous and boring, need restating.

The prospect of dozing close to a vat of molten lead is not a pleasant thought. Apart from lead poisoning, there is the risk of drowning! Likewise there is the danger of the nodding heads of drowsy workers hitting projecting parts of machinery after lunch. How can boredom be combated? Canned music could be used as a means of keeping people at least partially awake. Another method is to startle workers into instant wakefulness by an occasional announcement over the loud speakers, though this should be done with due care. The taped music could be switched off in mid-bar, followed by a 30-second pause to give the sleeper time to wake up, and then an announcement made in a clear-toned urgent voice that, "In a few moments there will be a special announcement."

Items likely to scare people should be avoided, but the announcement should have some interest. An item of low interest would be the dangers of smoking in the toilet, whereas an item of strong interest would be news of a works outing, or the latest score in a major football contest. News related to work should be confined to relevant items such as proposed pay increases or a visit by a factory inspector. Controversial subjects should be avoided.

In recent times the advent of the industrial robot and automatic handling systems has had the effect of eliminating repetitive, tedious and often unpleasant tasks. At Volvo, automatic welding lines replaced manual jigs and manual welding lines, freeing men from hard and tedious work where absenteeism and labour turnover was high. Likewise, the use of paint-spraying robots can eliminate unhealthy and monotonous jobs. The automation of work processes involving asbestos, lead based products or intensive dust creation is welcome on health grounds. At the same time such developments amount to deskilling of jobs, and create other problems in turn.

REST PAUSES

The effect of a rest pause is particularly beneficial in repetitive work of a monotonous nature. Heavy muscular work, tasks which require close concentration, and operations involving a continuous standing or sitting posture are also suitable cases for the introduction of rest pauses. The speed of operations at work is another factor to be considered in relation to rest pauses. Work conditions which require a working rate in excess of the natural rhythm of the body are likely to lead to fatigue, and if they cannot be avoided at least their effects should be alleviated by suitable rest pauses.

Because of complaints about fatigue among operators of VDU equipment, it is suggested that regular rest pauses should be provided for employees who frequently use VDUs.[11]

Ideally continuous work at a VDU should be interrupted by occasional movement or by spells of alternative work. Otherwise it is recommended that mid-morning and mid-afternoon breaks of 10 to 15 minutes are taken away from the equipment. The maximum continuous work period at a VDU should not exceed two hours, and there should be no more than seven hours' viewing in any one day.[12]

The following are examples of union agreements on rest pauses.[11] In an agreement between APEX and International Harvester it was recommended that a maximum of one hour's continuous work at a VDU should be followed by a minimum break of 10 minutes. Another agreement between the same union and Coventry Climax recommended rest pauses at regular intervals to total not less than 60 minutes in a normal working day.

Apart from scheduled rest pauses, the unscheduled rest pause is a feature of repetitive tasks when the worker decides for him or herself to have a break. At other times workers experience a lapse of attention (an involuntary rest pause) and this can give rise to mistakes and accidents. It is said that just before a rest pause inhibition sets in—central nervous fatigue—and this undermines to some extent what has previously been learnt, leading to a lower level of performance. Several minutes after the rest pause, disinhibition and consolidation occur to restore performance to the customary level, which reflects what the employee has learnt about the job to date.

JOB SATISFACTION AND JOB DESIGN

One particular view of motivation suggests that people strive toward realizing their inner potential (self-actualization) and may suffer some personal disadvantage in doing so. For example, the adolescent may feel it necessary to leave the comfort of the parental home in order to assert his or her independence. Likewise, there are occasions when a person forfeits comfort and security in order to support an unpopular principle or cause. These are examples of a person's desire to satisfy a pressing need. Maslow identified a hierarchy of needs ranging from the most primitive, which humans share with the lower forms of life, to those associated with the higher forms of life.[13]

Hierarchy of Needs

The hierarchy of needs is represented in pyramidal form in Fig.2.1.
The foot of the pyramid represents the most basic needs. The individual strives to move upwards through the hierarchy. Maslow observed that "man is a wanting animal and rarely reaches a state of complete satisfaction except

FIG. 2.1   Maslow's hierarchy of needs.

for a short time. As one desire is satisfied, another pops up to take its place."
Thus only if the lower needs are satisfied will the higher needs appear.

With respect to some PHYSIOLOGICAL needs, there are certain automatic responses to internal imbalances in the human body. A self-correcting
mechanism ensures that the level of sugar remains constant in the blood
stream (except in diabetics). We are motivated to drink lots of liquid after
eating salty foods. When our body temperature becomes too high, we per-
spire and are motivated to remove a garment or open a window. A feature of
physiological needs is that they have to be satisfied regularly; consumption
of products related to these needs is high, and apart from the emphasis in an
advertising message on the convenience factor of certain foodstuffs, the nutritional value may also be acknowledged.

SAFETY needs include physical security, emotional security, job security, a modestly comfortable and predictable routine, and a desire for fair
treatment and justice at work. The need for security could motivate the car
buyer to emphasize safety features, such as child-proof locks, head restraints
and a collapsible steering wheel, when making a choice. The need for security could also be manifest when the individual is convinced that a signalling
system is necessary for his or her future security; as a result, he or she is
motivated to install a smoke detector in the house. Security needs could be
aroused at work when there is uncertainty about continued employment
with the company. Likewise, the threat of health and safety hazards could
arouse safety needs.

Higher than safety needs come AFFILIATION needs. These include social
contacts, belonging to a group, friendship and love. Social motivation is also
described as dependency (submissive behaviour aimed at an authority

figure), dominance, personal relationships (both platonic and sexual) and aggression.[14] It can find expression in the following way. In order to avoid a feeling of inferiority among others, a consumer may be attracted to the use of a mouth wash to counteract bad breath. Others may purchase goods that meet with the social approval of other people. Shoppers may be more inclined to rely on a friendly sales assistant for information and advice. Social needs act as important motivators of behaviour when the individual has a need to belong to a group at work, which, for example, offers the opportunity to develop meaningful associations with colleagues, to give and receive friendship, understanding and compassion, and to be accepted by colleagues.

The consequences of not satisfying needs, such as security and social needs, could be various forms of undesirable behaviour—resistance to change, resistance to budget pressures, antagonism and an unwillingness to cooperate—designed to defeat the achievement of organizational goals.

The next level in the hierarchy of needs is ESTEEM, divided into self-esteem and esteem from others. Self-esteem includes the need for self-respect and self-confidence, the need to achieve something worthwhile as a result of job performance, the need to be fairly independent at work, the need to acquire technical knowledge about one's job and perform one's duties in a competent manner.

A message in an advertisement could stimulate the need to attain a feeling of self-esteem. In an advertisement for an Audi Sports car a female engineer proclaims, "I pick the car and my husband picks the colour."

Esteem from others includes the need for recognition as a result of efficient and effective job performance, the need to be appreciated by colleagues for one's overall contribution at work and the need to establish a reputation and status in the organization. The desire for power would probably belong to the category of esteem needs. Argyle recognizes self-image as an essential part of esteem motivation, and there is a tendency to develop attitudes and beliefs towards the self which are consistent and integrated.[14] The person could be motivated to get others to accept and respect the self-image, and perhaps avoid people or alternatively try to change their attitudes if they are not prepared to do so.

SELF-ACTUALIZATION, at the apex of the pyramid, implies self-fulfilment derived from achievement following the successful accomplishment of, for example, a demanding and challenging assignment at work. The sequence of events in climbing the hierarchy of needs is that the gratification of the higher needs follow gratification of the lower needs, and it is often asserted that in western industrialized society the lower needs are reasonably well satisfied for most people most of the time. Since needs which are gratified are no longer determinants of behaviour, it follows that the higher needs assume importance for many people in our culture. This should be borne in mind by those responsible for the design of control systems in organizations.

People seem to have different priorities when it comes to specifying the most important human needs at a particular time. Maslow maintains that if a person has a history of chronic deprivation at a particular need level—e.g., an individual cannot find a job that adequately utilizes his or her abilities—this person is likely to be very sensitive to that particular need. On the other hand, where people have previously experienced adequate and consistent gratification of a lower need, they can become relatively unconcerned about subsequent deprivations of that need because their focus has shifted to higher need gratification—the artists' preoccupation with their work pushes problems of subsistence to one side.

How does the accountant fit into this scheme of things? A study conducted in the U.S., in which the subjects were 269 Certified Public Accountants employed in large and small public accounting firms, provides some interesting insights.[15] Overall the accountants employed in the smaller firms reported less satisfaction of the social, security and self-actualization needs than those employed in the larger firms. For the purposes of this study physiological needs were not considered. Instead they were replaced by AUTONOMY needs. Autonomy needs are concerned with the opportunity for independent thought and action, authority in one's position and the opportunity to participate in setting work goals.

In addition to the size of the firm, the researchers considered the level at which the accountant operated within the firm. They found that partners and principals in the large firms felt that they experienced more opportunity for personal growth, development, self-fulfilment and accomplishment—self-actualization—than did their counterparts in the small firms. Partners and principals in the larger firms also indicated that the job security need is the most satisfied need, followed by self-actualization, social, autonomy, and esteem needs in that order.

The satisfaction enjoyed by partners and principals in the smaller firms assumed a different pattern. They perceived autonomy—opportunity for independent thought and action, authority in position and opportunity to participate in goal-setting—as the need most satisfied, with lesser degrees of satisfaction, in descending order of importance, attached to social, security, esteem, and self-actualization needs. Below the level of partner and principal, the need satisfaction of managers and supervisors, employed in both the large and small firms, did not differ in any significant way, and are in line with the findings of other studies of managerial motivation which show that the higher level needs—autonomy, esteem and self-actualization—are the least satisfied in practice.

So partners and principals are out of step in this respect. In the larger firms their self-actualization needs are well satisfied, and in the smaller firms their autonomy needs are well satisfied.

A sample of 1900 managers rated several needs similar to the ones identified by Maslow—security, social, esteem, autonomy and self-actualization—in terms of the importance and level of satisfaction associated with each need. It was found that highly satisfied needs were seen as relatively unimportant, and vice versa. There was an exception as far as self-actualization needs were concerned; they appeared to remain constant, irrespective of how satisfied people felt about them. The self-actualization needs lost importance only if lower level needs were deprived.[16]

In a study based on the success of managerial trainees over a five-year period in the American Telephone & Telegraph Company, Maslow's concept was also subjected to an empirical test. The successful group—success being measured in terms of fifth year income—reported the highest satisfaction of achievement, esteem and self-actualization needs.[17]

If one were to accept and generalize on the basis of the findings from the study of Certified Public Accountants reported above, one might suggest to the go-ahead professional accountant to seek employment in the larger firm when in need of self-actualization—when opportunities for growth and development and feelings of self-fulfilment and accomplishment are sought. On the other hand, if the ambitious professional accountant values the opportunity to exercise a high degree of autonomy in the form of an opportunity for independent thought and action, authority in his or her position and opportunity to participate in goal-setting, then the smaller firm is the better option.

Apart from the needs which form part of the hierarchy of needs, Maslow acknowledges other needs, for example, desire for beautiful things could be classified as an aesthetic need. Satisfaction of this need would come from beautiful or attractive surroundings. A person sitting in a room with a crookedly hung picture on the wall may go through the motions of straightening it. Maslow acknowledges that not all behaviour is motivated, at least in the sense of need gratification—seeking what is lacking and needed. Though behaviour may not be motivated, it is certainly determined. For example, expressive behaviour could simply be an expression of personality, e.g., a smile on the face may be brought about by an association of ideas or some external stimulus.

The assumptions behind the hierarchy of needs have been criticized as mystical and value-laden, since they flirt so continuously with the evaluation of people in terms of normative judgements of high and low, advanced and primitive, good and bad.[18] Nevertheless, Maslow's theory has made a significant impact on the development and application of theories of motivation based on "human needs."

Dual-Factor Theory
The work of Herzberg is consistent with Maslow's theory. His dual-factor

TABLE 2.1
Dual-Factor Theory

Motivators	Hygiene Factors
Achievement	Company Policy and Administration
Recognition	Supervision
Work itself	Salary
Responsibility	Inter-personal Relations
Advancement	Working Conditions
Growth	Status
	Security

theory is based on considerable empirical evidence and is built on the principle that people are motivated towards what makes them feel good, and away from what makes them feel bad.[19] Herzberg's research identifies motivators as factors producing good feelings in the work situation; these are listed in Table 2.1. By contrast he suggests that hygiene factors, also listed in Table 2.1, arouse bad feelings in the work situation.

Hygiene factors are clearly concerned with the work environment rather than the work itself. They differ significantly from motivators in as much as they "can only prevent illness but not bring about good health." In other words, lack of adequate "job hygiene" will cause dissatisfaction, but its presence will not of itself cause satisfaction; it is the motivators that do this. The absence of the motivators will not cause dissatisfaction, assuming the job hygiene factors are adequate, but there will be no positive motivation. It is axiomatic in Herzberg's approach that job satisfaction and job dissatisfaction are not opposites. The opposite of job satisfaction is not job dissatisfaction, it is no job satisfaction—the opposite of job dissatisfaction is lack of job dissatisfaction. This is illustrated in Table 2.2.

TABLE 2.2
Herzberg's View of Factors Contributing to Job Satisfaction and Dissatisfaction

Adequate ◀ ——————— **Motivators** ——————▶ Inadequate
(Satisfaction)   (No satisfaction)

Adequate ◀ ——————— **Hygiene factors** ——————▶ Inadequate
(No dissatisfaction)   (Dissatisfaction)

Adopting Herzberg's approach a manager should build motivators into the job so as to positively promote job satisfaction; in order to minimize dissatisfaction, hygiene factors should be improved.

In the motivation of sales representatives the following motivators and hygiene factors might be considered. With regard to motivators, they could be given responsibility for making decisions, such as negotiating prices and terms subject to certain conditions; involved in setting their own sales targets; given responsibility for planning their own time and journeys. The organization could ensure that as much relevant information as possible is available to the salesforce, and that feedback of information from the salesforce is acted upon and seen to be acted upon.

The hygiene factors associated with material reward are likely to receive emphasis. Salary, commission, bonuses, promotions and competitions are rewards which could be related to the achievement of sales objectives. These objectives could include sales volume, expense control, profitability of sales volume and new account development. Incentive schemes could be devised for a pre-determined period aimed at, for example, the movement of old models from retailers' inventories before the launch of a new product. A system of "prize points" could be used, which would be linked to specific performance targets, allowing each representative to compete against him or herself. This might be used to raise the level of a representative's performance. As an alternative to money, which may be swallowed up in household expenditure, merchandise incentives—such as holidays abroad, video recorders, etc.—may create greater excitement, with lower tax implications. From the organization's point of view it is important that extra effort flows from the incentives given, and that the costs of providing the incentives are less than the extra sales revenue.

The provision of an efficient administrative back-up service and good working relationships with colleagues are hygiene factors worthy of mention. In a study of the motivation of sales executives in two major companies in the U.K., it was concluded that those who held the most favourable attitudes derived satisfaction from the motivators—the job itself, achievement, and scope for development.[20] However, if the motivators were in any way restricted, social relationships, security, and other "hygiene" benefits arose as factors promoting satisfaction. Particular hygiene factors—communication and budgetary control systems—aroused dissatisfaction in the more enthusiastic groups.

Theory X and Y

Whilst advocating a similar position to that advanced by Herzberg, McGregor postulates two views of humans—theory X and Y.

Theory X is the belief that people are naturally lazy and unwilling to work and must be bribed, frightened or manipulated if they are to put forth any effort at all.

This is contrasted with an optimistic perspective of people—theory Y. This view is likely to be held by a manager who believes in providing "motivators" as motivational devices. A theory Y view states that work is as natural as play; the capacity to assume responsibility for directing one's own efforts is widely, not narrowly, distributed in the population, and if people are passive, indolent, and irresponsible on the job, it is because of their experiences in organizations and not generally because of some inherent human weakness. McGregor would subscribe to the theory Y view in the belief that there are more people than is generally believed able and willing to make a constructive contribution towards the solution of organizational problems.[21]

Job Enrichment

Earlier it was suggested by Herzberg that motivators are critical factors residing in the job. Towards the provision of motivators he prescribes various methods of job enrichment. This is an approach to job design that attempts to make tasks more intrinsically interesting, involving, and rewarding; it involves both vertical and horizontal loading. Vertical loading entails injecting more important and challenging duties into the job, whereas horizontal loading is akin to job enlargement—increasing the number or diversity of task activities—and job rotation, i.e., moving people back and forth among different tasks.

The underlying belief in Herzberg's approach is that increased job satisfaction is an important source of motivation and will lead to better performance because of its association with increased productivity and reduced turnover, absenteeism and tardiness.

Criticisms of the Dual-Factor Theory

There is research evidence which is not entirely compatible with the findings of Herzberg. A study by Wernimont replicated Herzberg's investigations, using 50 accountants and 82 engineers, and the results suggest that either "motivators" or "hygiene" factors can cause both satisfied and dissatisfied feelings about the job.[22] Although this result conflicts significantly with the claims of Herzberg that hygiene factors contribute most to dissatisfaction with the job, the Wernimont study agrees with him that motivators are important determinants of satisfied feelings about the job.

It is suggested that it is *dissatisfaction*, rather than *satisfaction*—as in the Herzberg model— that is tied up with performance.[23] When dissatisfied, the employee will search for alternative courses of action to alleviate this condition. He or she will take into account, and strike a balance between, the expected worth of the reward for action and his or her own level of aspiration.

The findings of a study of the motivation of senior business executives employed by a large public company in the U.K., show that financial reward assumes a position of significant importance as a motivating force.[24] A sample of 2246 executives was divided into the following six motivational groups: Material Reward; Leadership; Variety and Challenge; Job Interest or Vocation; Comfortable, Secure Life among Friends; Status and Prestige. The group of executives who displayed a strong drive for material reward was the largest of any of the six groups, accounting for 25% of the total sample. "They rated highly such rewards as money in terms of spending power, fringe benefits affording tax advantages or opportunities to accumulate capital, ... Relatively unimportant to these people, on the other hand, were opportunities for plenty of free time, having congenial colleagues and a job with a high degree of intellectual or vocational interest."

Besides adequate motivators and hygiene factors, the nature of the expectations that the employee brings to the work situation must be considered.[22] People approach their jobs with a desire and expectation to have an interest in their work, to be recognized for their efforts, to feel a sense of achievement, to receive a particular level of remuneration, to have congenial colleagues and so on. Lack of attainment or frustration of any of these needs cause people to be dissatisfied with their jobs.

The relationship the individual has with work can be viewed from two angles—input and output. The individual's education, intelligence, training, status, health, appearance, etc., may be conceived as his or her input. The output can be thought of in terms of rewards which can be intrinsic or extrinsic; intrinsic in the sense of deriving satisfaction from completing the job to one's standards; extrinsic in the sense of financial reward. A mismatch of the input and output factors would therefore have significant implications for the level of satisfaction, irrespective of the distinction between motivators and hygiene factors.

A feature of the dual-factor theory of motivation propounded by Herzberg is the association of the motivators with job satisfaction.

The prescribing of job enrichment is the logical extension to this line of thinking. But a pertinent question to ask is whether every category of worker responds positively to job enrichment—in terms of more challenging work, etc. There is convincing evidence to suggest that the answer is "no." For workers of one cultural background, jobs characterized as varied, complex and demanding were associated with low job satisfaction; this is out of step with the motivator/hygiene concept. In a similar vein it is maintained that individual differences must be accepted; job enlargement as a means to enriching jobs may produce benefits for certain individuals—for example, white collar and supervisory workers and non-alienated blue collar workers. Other workers may not welcome an opportunity to become more involved in their work and to participate more in decision-making.[25,26] A large group of technicians in both high- and low-satisfaction groups mentioned hygiene factors more frequently than motivator factors as determinants of both job satisfaction and dissatisfaction.[27] At Luton in the U.K. researchers found that workers sought jobs voluntarily on the assembly line, and they had previously given up jobs elsewhere offering interest, status, responsibility and the opportunity to use their ability and skill.[28] Further criticisms of Herzberg's theory have been raised and these are based on evidence derived from a review of roughly 40 studies related to Herzberg's dual–factor theory of motivation.[29] These are:

1. Methodological weaknesses—since Herzberg asks subjects to "think of a time when you felt exceptionally good or exceptionally bad about your job" and relate what happened, people are likely to respond in such a way as to take credit for satisfactory happenings, but they will blame failure on the environment in order to protect their self-image. This accounts for the hygiene/motivator equation.

2. Because the respondents' statements are evaluated and interpreted by a rater or experimenter under uncontrolled conditions, the outcome could be contaminated as a result of the evaluation method used.

3. Herzberg's measure would not pick up a situation where a person dislikes a part of the job, but overall is satisfied with the job.

4. The theory is not consistent with previous findings in research on satisfaction and productivity.

The Job Characteristics Model

A more recent approach to job enrichment, which has not been extensively evaluated, is propounded by Hackman and Oldham.[30] The authors focus on what they call the five core characteristics of a job.

1. Skill Variety. This focuses on the extent to which a job requires a number of different skills and talents. The job of a personnel specialist would receive a high score on this dimension, whereas the job of an operator on a production assembly line would receive a low score.

2. Task Identity. This focuses on the extent to which the job requires the performance of a whole unit, which is identifiable with a visible outcome. The job of a carpenter, who constructs a piece of furniture from raw material, would receive a high score on this dimension, whereas an operator who solders wires on to a piece of equipment would receive a low score.

3. Task Significance. This focuses on the extent to which the job makes a significant impact on the lives and work of other people inside and outside the organization. The job of a surgeon in a hospital would receive a high score on this dimension, whereas the job of a filing clerk would receive a low score.

4. Autonomy. This can be viewed as the degree of freedom, discretion, and independence which a job possesses at both the planning and execution stages. The job of a polytechnic or university lecturer would receive a high score on this dimension, whereas the job of an accounts clerk, who is closely supervised, would receive a low score.

5. *Feedback from the Job.* This focuses on the extent to which direct and unambiguous information about the effectiveness of the job holder's performance is available whilst he or she is engaged in carrying out the activities of the job. The airline pilot receives information on the progress of the flight from the instrument panel in the cockpit and from ground control. The pilot's job would receive a high score on this dimension, whereas the job of a sales representative, who may have to wait some time to establish the effectiveness of his or her performance, would receive a low score.

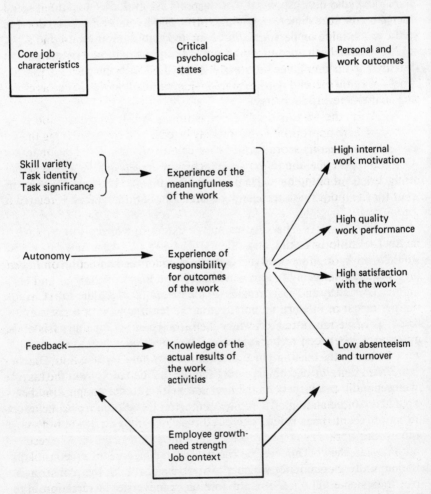

FIG. 2.2   The job characteristics model. From: Hackman, J. R. (1977) *Work Design.* In J. R. Hackman & J. L. Suttle (Eds.), *Improving Life at Work.* Santa Monica, Cal.: Scott, Foresman.

The five characteristics are given a numerical value and are then combined into a single index called the Motivating Potential Score (MPS).

$$\text{MPS} = \frac{\left[\begin{array}{c}\text{Skill} \\ \text{Variety}\end{array} \times \begin{array}{c}\text{Task} \\ \text{Identity}\end{array} \times \begin{array}{c}\text{Task} \\ \text{Significance}\end{array}\right]}{3} \times \text{Autonomy} \times \text{Feedback}$$

The Job Diagnostic Survey, filled out by the job holder, is used to measure the five core characteristics so as to arrive at the MPS calculation. For job enrichment to work, three factors have to be considered: (1) employee growth; (2) need strength; and (3) current job context. The individual who desires growth will respond positively to a job that scores highly on the core dimensions—high MPS. But the individual who does not place much value on personal growth or accomplishment would find a high MPS situation both uncomfortable and a source of anxiety. It is also suggested that if an employee is grossly dissatisfied with contextual job factors—pay, job security or supervision—job enrichment will not be as effective as if the reverse was true.

Finally, the MPS is used to assess the extent to which the job is enriched. Where appropriate, the job may be enriched by redesigning the job so as to increase its score on the core characteristics. The Hackman and Oldham theoretical model of job enrichment depicted in Fig.2.2 is sufficiently new for it not to have received a thorough test. However, there is support for the model with respect to satisfaction, but not when it is related to productivity.[31]

New Technology and Jobs

In the section on *Monotony and Boredom*, under the subsection on *Repetitive Work,* the effects of modern technology in displacing labour and eliminating unhealthy and monotonous jobs were briefly considered. In Chapter 8, the impact of modern technology on the management process is examined. Here we return to the former theme and continue the analysis of the relationship between technology and jobs.

Over two decades ago in a study of the effects of automation, Blauner concluded that, instead of increasing feelings of alienation from the task, as was generally the view at that time, automation in the chemical industry actually reduced alienation.[32] In an attempt to explain Blauner's conclusions in more recent times it was suggested that the subjects in his study were blue-collar workers who performed fragmented manual work. As a result of automation, they became semi-skilled white-collar workers responsible for the monitoring of complete segments of work. Therefore, the consequence of the implementation of the automation process was the creation of enriched jobs; and it was not surprising to discover that alienation assumed a position of minor significance.[33]

A valid question to ask is whether the same outcome would arise if computers were introduced into traditional white-collar jobs. Apparently, it depends upon the type of white-collar employment under consideration. When clerical workers have an involvement with the computer, which amounts to keying-in data and the retrieval of information, then it is said that the computer system restricts the employees' personal control over their work, with predictable results.[34]

A similar finding was reported in a study of managerial staff in the production function after a production and scheduling computer system was introduced into three assembly plants of an electronics company. The computer system contributed to changes in the content of the jobs of production planners and resulted in a loss of discretion and greater control of their work. The same applied to all managers who were involved with the computer system. They all felt constrained by policies, plans and procedures, and were more dependent on the work of others than ever before.[35]

In the two studies cited above there was evidence of alienation springing from white-collar employment—managerial and clerical staff—as a result of the implementation of computer systems. However, other evidence relating to white-collar employment seems to indicate that computer systems produce the opposite effect in particular circumstances. For example, specialists in computing and those in certain managerial positions are at an advantage when they can control the periods of time in which they use the computer. Also, in many cases the computer can enlarge the jobs of the users.[36] Other evidence showed that the introduction of computers generated more varied, interesting, responsible, and productive work.[37]

Some positive and negative features of computerized information systems have been identified.[38] The positive features are:

1. Responsibility shifts to the person most suited to carry out the task. For example, the author or journalist keys in information to the computer, and corrects the script or document. This process, together with a freer flow of information between individuals, blurs somewhat the traditional organizational roles. Also, the changes in the direction in which information flows tend to create new social groups with their own particular phraseology.

2. The shifts in resources, and the changing roles, lead to enlarged jobs in a qualitative sense—more varied tasks when in contact with others—for secretarial and support staff.

3. An increase in communication results from the rapid turn round of messages due to electronic mail systems.

The negative features are:

1. The need for increased security measures can seriously disrupt working practices.

2. An unhealthy identification with and a personal attachment to an electronic work station may give rise to minor behavioural disturbances. (Issues connected with this are discussed in Chapter 9.)

The debate on the impact of technology on jobs and organizational systems is likely to continue for a long time, simply because the rate of change in this field is quite significant. There is now a view that the traditional status of technology as a variable determining various aspects of organization structure, which obviously includes jobs, is in question. What appears to be critical currently is the impact of decisions to select the technological equipment, the capability of the latter and the way it is used. In addition, the influence of cultural and political forces within the organization with respect to the use of the technology, and the way key staff control computerized systems, are considerations that have to be borne in mind.[39]

There is a suggestion that the human and organizational implications surrounding the adoption of computer technologies are often pushed aside or given insufficient attention, even though these are intimately tied up with the success of technical change.[40] A further suggestion from this source is that work should be organized around the technology, and that one should recognize that the choices an organization has to make to accommodate the new technology are often not given serious consideration. In fact, the physical layout of the workplace and organizational structures created by past decisions are too easily accepted, and insufficient attention is given to the exploration of new ways and means to build the infrastructure of work around computing technology.

COGNITIVE PROCESSES

The cognitive approach to motivation is primarily concerned with the desire of individuals to produce an effect on their environment and in the process to develop certain skills. We learn about visual forms, how to grasp and let go of objects and co-ordinate the hands and the eyes. Constancy—which is explained in Chapter 3—facilitates the stabilization of our perception, and we develop a cognitive map to guide and structure our behaviour. Individuals in their relationship with the environment like to be active, to explore, to manipulate, to control, to create, and to accomplish things.[41] Likewise, young children like to hold, rattle and pull toys apart. Monkeys became more skilled with practice at manipulating mechanical devices placed outside their cages.[42]

A cognitive theory of motivation recognizes that many aspects of motivation arise when people are fully aware of their motives and actions, and of the risks involved, and make plans guided by their expectations. We find a number of instances where people engage in purposeful behaviour in which they set a course of action right at the beginning, recognize the obstacles on the way to achieving their plans and finally overcome the obstacles and feel satisfied with their performance. It appears that the greater the sense of self-control attained, the greater the level of success in carrying out both short and long term plans. In experiments connected with studying the level of aspiration—something within our reach—the setting of goals has received particular attention. We are more likely to be motivated by realistic goals where we recognize the possibility of failure.[43] Group influence can be an important factor when it comes to fixing the level of aspiration. If one's performance in an activity is better than the average for the group, this may lead to a lowering of the level of aspirations next time round. But equally, if one establishes that one's performance is worse than that of somebody whose standing in the group is low, this could give rise to an upward shift in the level of aspiration.[44] If achievement falls far below the aspiration level, the aspiration level may be subsequently reduced until the disparity is slight.[45] Equilibrium is said to occur when the aspiration level exceeds achievement by a small amount.

Cognitive Theory and Budgeting

Budgets and cost standards are said to motivate employees by acting as goals or incentives, and a fair amount of research evidence focuses on the motivational effects of budget standards or targets of varying degrees of tightness.[46,47] Good standards of performance have been associated with high levels of aspiration.[48] The performance implications of different levels of budget difficulty were analyzed using the following procedures. Goals were set at a normal level (capable of being achieved 50% of the time), and at a difficult level (capable of being achieved 25% of the time). When compared with normal goals, difficult goals gave rise to either good or bad performance. When good performance followed the difficult goal, this goal had become an aspiration level. So where the difficult goal was seen as a challenge (as was the case with high achievers and younger performers), actual performance was better than target. In this situation results were in excess of the aspiration level. Where bad performance followed the difficult goal, the budgetee obviously viewed the achievement of the goal as being impossible, failed to set an aspiration level, and began to show withdrawal symptoms.[48] Variation in levels of aspiration appears to be a function of success or failure. It is maintained that success raises the level of aspiration and failure lowers it, and that failure has a more varied effect on level of aspiration than has success.

Movements in levels of aspiration are to some extent influenced by changes in a person's confidence in his or her ability to achieve the goal.[45] Past budget performance is likely to affect the level at which future budget targets are set. Managers felt it to be in their interest to agree lower rather than higher budget targets, striking a balance between present job security and increasing future income.[49] These managers, whose track record may be either impressive or wanting, were quite subtle in the manner in which they tried to influence forecasts in order to win short or long term approval or personal benefits.

Another study tested the effect on performance of varying degrees of tightness in the budget.[46] As the budget gets tighter, the employee is motivated and aspires to higher levels of aspiration with results lower than the aspiration level. At this stage the budget target is not achieved. Beyond this stage both levels of aspiration and results fall because the budgetee no longer believes that it is possible to achieve the budget target. This can create negative motivation resulting in a deterioration in performance. Similar findings are reported in a study conducted in the U.K.[50] As can be seen in Fig.2.3, the budget level which motivates the best performance is unlikely to be achieved most of the time, but a budget which is usually achieved will motivate only at a lower level of performance. In other studies it was concluded that the best performance was achieved in situations where budget targets were clearly understood, and where they were tight but attainable.[51,52] Department meetings were found to be useful in facilitating the adoption of budget targets as the manager's personal goals. But cultural, organizational, and personality factors all affect an individual manager's reaction to a budget standard.[50]

We have already seen how success or failure in meeting budget targets gives rise to variations in levels of aspiration, and how past performance in relation to the budget can affect future budget levels. When the budgetees were able to bargain on a budget standard, they presented biased informa-

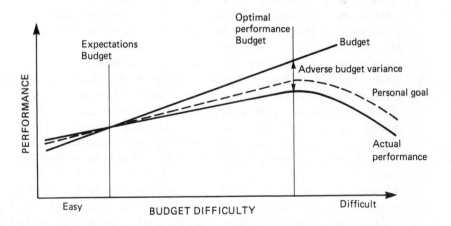

FIG. 2.3 The effect of budget difficulty on performance. From: Otley, D. T. (1977). Behavioural aspects of budgeting. *Accountants Digest ICAEW, 49* Summer.

tion so as to secure the best personal advantage; this would normally manifest itself in a lower rather than higher budget standard. The budgetees (managers) tried to strike a balance between two objectives—present job security and increasing future income.[49] For example, one manager may disappoint a superior now because of the conservative budget he or she has adopted for the coming budget period, hoping to win the superior's approval when he or she achieves the budget at the end of the budget period. Another manager may feel he or she has little reputation left because of poor past budget performance, but submits an almost unreal forecast (excessively high) so as to win approval now. At the end of the budget period he or she will have to live with the unfavourable consequences of this action. Yet another manager has a high standing with his or her superior because of good past performances, and decides to aim for an easier budget target for the coming budget period, an action which will receive acclaim later when the budget is met. His or her record can quite easily absorb the present disappointment on the part of the superior. Of course there are also circumstances when genuine over or under-estimation occurs and this may arise when sales are subject to fluctuation. When sales are rising there is a tendency to under-estimate budgeted sales.[53]

Achievement Motivation

A person with a motive to achieve tends to define his or her goals in accordance with some standard of excellence. McClelland believes that a society's overall economic performance will be high if the average level of the need to achieve is high in the population (e.g. U.S.).[54] He cites evidence to the effect that in any society the amount of achievement imagery in its children's literature—a reflection of the values society places on achievement—is a fairly good predictor of economic growth in that country for the following twenty years. Apparently, parental expectations and rewards are important conditioning influences on the performances of children high in the need to achieve. The need to achieve (N.Ach) can be modified through a training programme which supports the view that learning is an important agent in motivation. McClelland developed a method for measuring achievement motivation whereby unconscious projections of the individual's fantasy were analyzed.

Entrepreneurs are said to be high in N.Ach but distinguished scientists are not. Perhaps in the latter case, because of long periods without feedback on progress and working on tasks with low success probabilities, this is understandable. High achievers can flourish if the tasks given to them are challenging but feasible, where they have a sense of control over what they accomplish, and where they are receiving regular feedback on how well they are doing.

High achievers prefer to work on their own where they have control over the outcome of action; they do not like situations where there are no standards to measure their performance by, or where the task is too difficult or too easy. Money is looked upon more as a symbol of achievement rather than an intrinsic motivating factor. The desire for success appears to be the major motivating force; the fear of failure is said to depress $N.Ach$ causing a person to shy clear of achievement-type tasks. Women are said to feel differently about achievement and score lower than men in the tests; the assertion is made that many women have a fear of success because high achievement is seen as being incompatible with traditional notions of femininity and female roles.[55] Perhaps the situation is different today!

McClelland has devised programmes to arouse $N.Ach$ in executives by helping the individual to develop self-insight and cultivate the appropriate outlook. Most organizational conditions would appear not to be compatible with the needs of the high achiever, since managers, particularly in large organizations, frequently cannot act alone. However, an association between achievement motivation and budgetary control has been emphasized—"the most sophisticated budgetary system may be of little practical consequence if it fails to elicit the achievement motivations of a significant number of managers and employees."[56]

Need for Power

A system has been devised for arriving at a need for power profile ($N.Pow$) in a similar manner to that adopted by McClelland with $N.Ach$.[57] McClelland, having closely studied the relationship of $N.Pow$ to style of management and performance, concludes that for managers in large organizations, rather than for entrepreneurs, $N.Pow$ is more important for effectiveness than $N.Ach$.[58] $N.Pow$ is a motive that involves other people, whereas $N.Ach$ can exclude other people. Since managers in large organizations frequently cannot act alone, they have to depend on influencing others for their success. For this reason McClelland believes that $N.Pow$ is related to success in the exercise of managerial leadership. People might feel uncomfortable about being told that they are high in $N.Pow$ because of the traditional association between seeking power and suppression, exploitation and tyranny. McClelland expresses some observations about those high in $N.Pow$, and suggests two types of groups.

1. At the fantasy level the first group projects itself in terms of sexual exploitation and the use of physical aggression. They tend to act as impulsive tough guys behaving in accordance with their fantasies.

2. At the fantasy level the second group projects itself in a more conventional form, such as winning in a competitive game or election. The members of this group prefer to seek "institutionalized power" with its established environment and rules, and they seek posts of responsibility in organizations and have a capacity for creating a good work climate.[59]

Unlike the need for achievement, the need for power is a motive that involves other people in the organization and is closely linked with management styles.

One group of managers high in the need for power has been identified by McClelland as being competitive, with management potential, in search of responsibility and institutional power.[59] Power is often associated with prestige, status, social eminence or superiority, and it can affect an individual's self-concept. Sometimes managers who exercise control in organizations are looked up to with respect because they occupy positions of power, although they might feel uncomfortable if they were told they were high in the need for power because of the traditional link between seeking power and its negative associations referred to above (e.g. suppression, exploitation and tyranny). It may be argued as a general proposition that members of an organization may prefer to exercise influence than to be powerless, and it is conceivable that managers and workers are much more likely to feel that they have too little, rather than enough or too much, authority in their work.

Certain psychological satisfactions are likely to be derived from the exercise of power, and certain managers get enormous pleasure and satisfaction from influencing the work situation in a way that is compatible with their own interests. There is further discussion of power in Chapter 8.

In some respects the rationale for certain organizational controls may be embedded in the psyche of the manager. But it is all too easy to become preoccupied with the rewards accompanying power and forget its more unpalatable side. Managers in their role of exercising control can suffer frustration and serious tension as a result of a number of organizational demands. Some of these have been identified as extra responsibility, commitment, loyalty and the burdens of taking decisions.[60]

Expectancy Theory

A recognizable development within the cognitive theory of motivation is the emergence of expectancy theory. This theory expounds the view that we choose among alternative behaviours, i.e., we anticipate the possible outcome of various actions, we place a weighting or value on each possible outcome, assessing the probability that each outcome will be the result of an alternative action; and finally, the course of action that maximizes our expected value will be chosen. Vroom put forward a well-known formulation of expectancy theory, and this is depicted in Fig.2.4.[61]

It is possible to quantify valence, expectancy and instrumentality. If we multiply each of the first-level outcomes by the expectancy (probability) that an outcome will follow action, and add up the results, we arrive at the strength of motivation to elect for a particular course of action. The preference for a first-level outcome depends upon how effective this outcome is in

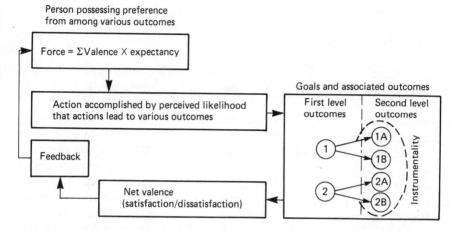

FIG. 2.4 Vroom's expectancy model. Adapted from: Vroom, V. H. (1964) *Work and motivation*. New York: John Wiley & Sons.

KEY: *Valence:* strength of preference for a particular outcome – can be positive (desired) or negative (not desired); *Outcome:* that which results from action; *First-level Outcome:* immediate effect of one's actions, e.g., a "job well done" – this is normally what the organization is looking for; *Second level Outcome:* that which results from the first-level outcome, e.g., a job well done may eventually lead to a promotion; *Expectancy* probability that certain piece of behaviour (i.e., certain level of effort in the job) will give rise to a particular first level outcome (i.e., improved performance); *Instrumentality:* strength of the causal relationship between the first level-outcomes and the second-level outcomes (e.g., a strong causal relationship would exist if increased effort had a beneficial effect for the employee, such as a pay increase.

bringing about a second-level outcome which is valued. We can expect the person to choose a pattern of behaviour that has a high motivational force attached to it. Expectancy theory, therefore, postulates that if the above process was followed, a person's choice of behaviour would approximate the model's prediction.

Porter and Lawler place expectancy theory firmly in an organizational context, with practical ramifications.[62] They also put forward the view that the strength of motivation is dependent upon the person's perceived probability that it will lead to a desired outcome. Their model is illustrated in Fig. 2.5.

The factors that affect the amount of effort somebody puts into their work are the value they place on the outcome which they hope will materialize as a result of their efforts and the probability that reward will follow the effort. Porter and Lawler are in agreement with Vroom when they propose that the probability that effort will lead to acceptable performance should be multiplied by the strength of the causal relationship between first-level and second-level outcomes (instrumentality)—the good performance/reward equation.

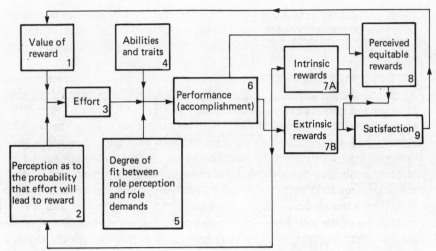

FIG. 2.5   Porter and Lawler's expectancy model. From: Porter, L. W. & Lawler, E. E. (1968) *Managerial attitudes and performance*. Homewood, Ill.: R. D. Irwin Inc.

But effort is not the only consideration; a person's abilities and traits will also have an effect on performance, as well as the person's perception of his or her organizational role. Based on research evidence, it is concluded that successful managers perceive their roles as requiring the display of inner-directed personality traits, i.e., forcefulness, imagination, independence, self-confidence, decisiveness. Other things being equal, these managers are expected to perform better. The same cannot be said of the managers who perceive their roles as requiring the display of other-directed traits, i.e., co-operation, adaptability, caution, agreeableness and tactfulness.[62] These managers are considered less effective as measured by peer ratings, supervisor ratings and promotions.

The next thing to consider is the relationship between performance and rewards. Rewards are comprised of two types: intrinsic—feeling of challenge, achievement, success—and extrinsic—organizational rewards such as pay, promotion, fringe benefits, etc. Satisfaction should come about if the receipt of both intrinsic and extrinsic rewards is the consequence of performance; but the level of satisfaction depends on how near the rewards are to what the person perceives as equitable for the services rendered. The closer the fit between actual rewards and perceived equitable rewards, the greater the level of satisfaction experienced.

The feedback loop between satisfaction and reward indicates that rewards associated with higher order needs (intrinsic rewards) assume greater importance as the individual receives more rewards for his or her effort. Apparently the more intrinsic rewards the individual receives the better this is from the point of view of higher future effort. The emphasis on intrinsic rewards reminds one of Herzberg's motivators; but unlike Herzberg's model where satisfaction precedes performance, the Porter and Lawler model shows performance leading to satisfaction with rewards and perceived equity serving as intervening variables. But note the weight given to extrinsic rewards, such as pay, in the Porter and Lawler model.

Reverting to Fig.2.5, the feedback loop between intrinsic/extrinsic rewards and the perceived probability that effort will lead to reward suggests that, if good performance is rewarded, the perceived likelihood that effort leads to reward will grow stronger. The message conveyed by the work of Porter and Lawler is that not only should jobs be designed or redesigned (job enrichment) so that they pose challenge, variety and autonomy—i.e., intrinsic qualities—but also extrinsic rewards, such as pay, should be provided and equated with perceived equitable rewards. In addition, there should be a match between the employees' traits and abilities and the requirements of the job. This has already been recognized elsewhere. For example, where workers' abilities and experience correspond closely to those required by their jobs, job satisfaction is said to have a high positive relationship with job performance, while in those situations where there is inconsistency the relationship is likely to be progressively lower.[63]

The Porter and Lawler model has not been extensively tested as yet, but the authors have amassed some evidence which is consistent with the model. The message conveyed by this work is as follows.

1. One should endeavour to relate employees' traits and abilities to the job and ensure that employees have accurate role perceptions. This action is likely to contribute to a high level of effort.

2. Jobs should be designed so that they pose challenge, variety and autonomy (intrinsic qualities), but also ensure that extrinsic rewards, such as pay, are equated with perceived equitable rewards.

Porter and Lawler maintain that some employees with relatively low performance are dissatisfied with the rewards received, and they attribute this condition to the belief that low performers tend subjectively to overrate their performance relative to that of high performers.

Expectancy Theory and Management Control

It is now proposed to place the Porter and Lawler model in the context of a management control system.

Standards of Performance. Performance standards reflect managements' expectations of what constitutes successful performance, with an implicit understanding that appropriate extrinsic rewards will follow. It is accepted that recognition will be forthcoming if actual performance reaches the standards laid down. Whilst the individual is engaged in subjectively assessing the rewards associated with meeting standards of performance, it would be beneficial if he had access to knowledge or was aware of the set of rewards associated with effective performance. The subordinate's expectancy of future extrinsic satisfaction or utility associated with meeting standards can be affected by the degree to which the manager has recognized past achievements. In fact it is likely that there could be revision of the expectancy that the meeting of standards gives rise to extrinsic rewards if management have been inconsistent in providing rewards related to performance.

The significance of deviations from past performance standards is important when perceiving the difficulties inherent in achieving standards, and expectations may have to be adjusted accordingly. Apart from the satisfaction derived from achieving standards, there are likely to be occasions when people derive satisfaction from having activities structured and ambiguities minimized along the path to the attainment of goals. The above interpretation of an expectancy approach to control, places much emphasis on the superior and subordinate relationship and the provision of extrinsic rewards, but it does not detract in any way from the potency of intrinsic rewards in this process.

Measurement of Performance.   The process leading up to performance evaluation (performance measurement), for the purpose of reward, has been the subject of close scrutiny, particularly in the context of management accounting. Confidence in the measuring aspect of a control system is likely to be undermined if the individual feels that some aspects of his or her performance should be measured but are not.[64] Confidence could also be diluted if the measurement includes items that the individual feels are misleading indicators. There may be, for example, situations where accounting measures of performance are inadequate in conditions of uncertainty or ambiguity surrounding the performance of the task.[65]

It is also suggested that greater trust is vested in measurements where subjective elements—i.e., the superior's informal notion of what constitutes good performance—are minimized or eliminated. In a study of the information needs of managers it was found that a significant amount of control data was not used because it related to events outside the province of the manager, it was too detailed or not detailed enough and it arrived too late.[66]

There are other criticisms of management accountants operating in the budgeting process because of their failure to present information in an easily understandable form relevant to the manager's responsibilities, and their reluctance to ensure accuracy and realism of the information by sufficient managerial involvement in the determination of the manager's needs.[67]

Because of the difficulty of measuring non-monetary aspects of performance, the accounting system usually restricts itself to reporting on financial performance. But therein lies a danger in that managers may be motivated to emphasize things that can be measured to the neglect of those that cannot. It is of course possible to create a composite measure of performance, incorporating non–financial measures, but then the priorities and the value system of senior management may be ingrained in the weighting each dimension receives. For this very reason it may be considered unacceptable, apart from the difficulty of translating it into numerical form.

Frequently in practice attention is focused on significant deviations from standards, as opposed to the meeting of standards. In such a system it is generally the unfavourable deviation requiring corrective action that activates a response, whereas it requires exceptional success to attract management's attention and recognition. This type of system may be viewed by subordinates as negative rather than positive, with an emphasis on failure. The consequences may be defensiveness, over-cautious behaviour and other dysfunctional effects.[68]

Employees may be motivated to distort measurements used for policing purposes so as to present a favourable impression of their performance.[69] The motivation to distort the measurements is to a large extent removed, according to Likert, if measurements are supportive and used for self-guidance rather than for policing purposes. In many situations in organizations it is difficult to measure a person's contribution to a set of results, because frequently tasks are interdependent and efforts are joint or interpersonal, where an individual may have only partial control over the outcome of a group's activities. In addition, external disturbances or chance events can invalidate to some extent the performance of even the most skilled operator.

However, it is suggested that one should separate performance evaluation for the purposes of reward from control measures, otherwise there might be an inclination to distort information and set easy standards to secure personal advantage.[70] This is particularly so when significant rewards which are valued—e.g., enhanced promotion prospects, status and salary bonuses—are tied to the attainment of budgetary targets. In such circumstances managers will be highly motivated to attain such targets and many will report performance at or near the target levels. This would be achieved by bargaining for easier targets in the discussions of budgets, particularly in conditions where estimates and judgements are difficult to validate. Likewise, figures could be adjusted to make short-term results look better, not to mention the falsification of reported information. Therefore, if measures of performance are imperfect, putting too much stress on the attainment of budgets which are linked to rewards can produce a range of undesirable consequences.[71]

Rewards.   The adequacy of the intrinsic rewards is a function of the role the individual occupies; these rewards originate from within the individual in the form of psychological satisfactions. However, management has some influence in the determination of intrinsic rewards since it can create organizational conditions within which opportunities exist for the exercise of self-control. Perhaps management's influence is even more pronounced in the provision of extrinsic rewards—e.g., pay, promotion, etc—to reinforce performance. But it is claimed, quite emphatically, that for differential extrinsic rewards to be effective in motivating performance a number of conditions must be present.[64] These are:

1. The organization can offer important rewards.
2. Rewards can be varied widely depending on the individual's current performance.
3. Meaningful performance appraisal sessions can take place between superiors and subordinates.
4. Performance can be measured objectively, including all relevant measurable items.
5. It must be possible to publicize how rewards are given.
6. Superiors are willing and able to explain and support the reward system in discussions with their subordinates.
7. Trust is high.
8. The plan will not cause negative outcomes to be tied to performance.

The condition which refers to objectivity in performance measurement would be difficult to meet, but this would hardly invalidate the effectiveness of a scheme that satisfies most of the conditions. Rewards are also discussed in connection with the concept of reinforcement in Chapter 4.

Finally, the equitable nature of reward is important. We are all inclined to compare each other's inputs (e.g. education, experience, effort, skill) and outputs (e.g. salary, increases in salary, fringe benefits, promotion), consciously or otherwise, and if we perceive our input as justifying a larger output or if, on a comparative basis, we feel we are unfairly treated, feelings of inequity can arise.[72] Perhaps some of us would also feel uncomfortable if we were overcompensated. A feeling of inequity could influence the level of satisfaction and the amount of effort put into a job — for example, the quantity and quality of the dissatisfied individual's production could be adversely affected, and the sense of inequality may lead to an increase in absenteeism or voluntary resignation. In practice it may be difficult to select a person or persons to act as a comparative model, or to evaluate one's own inputs and outputs, or those of others.[73]

SUMMARY

The concept of motivation consists of needs, motives, drives, and goals or incentives. Level of arousal, which is related to a drive, is an important feature of the motivated state. Various examples of arousal stimuli in marketing and accounting were given. Frustration, which can produce either positive or negative reactions, can obstruct the attainment of the goals of the individual, and as such is an important ingredient in the motivational process.

Monotony and boredom, brought about by conditions such as a lack of variety and challenge in the job, lack of opportunity to exercise skill and to act independently, highly repetitive work, and an inability to control the pace of work, can have a demotivating effect. Particularly in the area of production, the safety implications of highly repetitive work should be noted. Various measures to mitigate the effects of boredom were suggested. Rest pauses have particular relevance when considering work of a repetitive or monotonous nature.

Theories of motivation—the hierarchy of needs, the dual-factor theory, theory X and Y, and the job characteristics model—were considered with reference to job satisfaction, job enrichment and job design. The methodological weaknesses of the research underpinning Herzberg's dual-factor theory were noted. Illustrations of the motivation of sales representatives, accountants and business executives were given. The likely impact of new technology on jobs was introduced.

A cognitive theory of motivation was discussed with particular reference to the budgeting process. The cognitive perspective incorporates levels of aspiration, achievement and power motivation and expectancy theory. The Porter and Lawler expectancy model was discussed and applied to planning and control processes within an organizational framework.

QUESTIONS

1. Illustrate what is meant by needs, motives, drives, goals or incentives.
2. Distinguish between feeling tone and appeal when considering the motivational disposition of the consumer.
3. How important is accounting data as arousal stimuli?
4. In what circumstances is frustration likely to generate destructive behaviour?
5. What causes boredom among workers in a factory, and what steps can be taken to reduce it?
6. Why are rest pauses necessary in modern office conditions?
7. Examine the theory which underpins job enrichment schemes.
8. Discuss the motivational significance of budget targets.
9. In what way does expectancy theory illuminate our understanding of the process of management control?

REFERENCES

1. Yoell, W.W. (1952) Make your advertising themes match consumer behaviour. *Printers Ink, 238(12),* 82–87.

2. Laird, D.A. (1932) How the consumer estimates quality by subconscious sensory impression. *Journal of Applied Psychology, 16,* 241–246.

3. Crawford, J.W. (1960) *Advertising: Communications From Management.* Boston: Allyn and Bacon.

4. Anastasi, A. (1979) *Fields of Applied Psychology, (2nd Edition).* Tokyo: McGraw-Hill.

5. Grube, C.S. (1947) How the public learned to pronounce "Suchard". *Advertising and Selling, October,* 68.

6. Benston, G.R. (1967) Published corporate accounting data and stock prices. *Empirical Research in Accounting: Selected Studies,* 1–54.

7. Estes, R.W. (1968) An assessment of the usefulness of current cost and price-level information by financial statement users. *Journal of Accounting Research, Autumn,* 200–207.

8. Brenner, V.C. (1970) Financial statement users' views on the desirability of reporting current cost information. *Journal of Accounting Research, Autumn,* 159–166.

9. Pankoff, L.D. & Virgil, R.L. (1970) Some preliminary findings from a laboratory experiment on the usefulness of financial accounting information to security analysts. *Empirical Research in Accounting: Selected Studies,* 1–61.

10. Strauss, G. & Sayles, L.R. (1960) *Personnel: The Human Problems of Management.* Englewood Cliffs, NJ: Prentice-Hall.

11. Manos, J. (1980) Stressless use of VDUs. *Health and Safety at Work, August,* 34–36.

12. Anderson, D. (1980) VDUs—eyestrain or eyewash? *Health and Safety at Work, August,* 36–39.

13. Maslow, A.H. (1954) *Motivation and Personality.* New York: Harper & Row.

14. Argyle, M. (1968) *The Psychology of Interpersonal Behaviour.* Harmondsworth: Penguin.

15. Strawser, R.H., Ivancevich, J.M. & Lyon H.L. (1969) A note on the job satisfaction of accountants in large and small CPA firms. *Journal of Accounting Research, Vol.7 No.2,* Autumn, 339–345.

16. Alderfer, C.P. (1972) *Existence, Relatedness and Growth: Human Needs in Organizational Settings.* New York: Free Press.

17. Hall, D.T. & Nougaim, K.E. (1968) An examination of Maslow's need hierarchy in an organizational setting. *Organizational Behaviour and Human Performance, 3,* 12–35.

18. Lazarus, R.S. (1971) *Personality.* Englewood Cliffs, NJ: Prentice-Hall.

19. Herzberg, F. (1966) *Work and the Nature of Man.* London: Staples Press.

20. Smith, G.P. (1967) The motivation of sales executives. *Ashridge Papers in Management Studies, No.2 Autumn.* Ashridge Management College, Berkhamsted.

21. McGregor, D. (1960) *The Human Side of Enterprise.* New York: McGraw-Hill.

22. Wernimont, P. (1966) Intrinsic and extrinsic factors in job satisfaction. *Journal of Applied Psychology, 50,* 1, 41–50.

23. March, J.G. & Simon, H.A. (1958) *Organizations.* New York: Wiley.

24. McDougall, C. (1973) How well do you reward your managers? *Personnel Management, March,* 38–43.

25. Turner, A.N. & Lawrence P.R. (1965) *Industrial Jobs and the Worker.* Boston: Harvard University.

26. Hulin, C.L. & Blood, M.R. (1968) Job enlargement, individual differences and workers responses. *Psychological Bulletin, 69,* 1, 41–55.

27. Hinrichs, J.R. & Mischkind, L.A. (1967) Empirical and theoretical limitations of the two-factor hypothesis of job satisfaction. *Journal of Applied Psychology, 51*, 2, 191–200.

28. Goldthorpe, J.H., Lockwood, D., Bechhofer, F. & Platt, J. (1970) *The Affluent Worker: Industrial Attitudes and Behaviour.* Cambridge: Cambridge University Press.

29. House, R.J. & Wigdor, L.A. (1967) Herzberg's dual-factor theory of job satisfaction and motivation: a review of the evidence and a criticism. *Personnel Psychology, 20*, 4, 369–389.

30. Hackman, J.R. & Oldham, G.R. (1975) Development of the job diagnostic survey. *Journal of Applied Psychology, 60*, 2, 159–170.

31. Umstot, D.D., Bell, C.H. & Mitchell, T.R. (1976) Effects of job enrichment and task goals on satisfaction and productivity: implications for job design. *Journal of Applied Psychology, 61*, 4, 379–394.

32. Blauner, R. (1964) *Alienation and Freedom.* Chicago: University of Chicago Press.

33. Crawley, R. & Spurgeon, P. (1979) Computer assistance and the air traffic controller's job satisfaction. In R.G. Sell & P. Shipley (Eds.), *Satisfaction in Work Design: Ergonomics and Other Approaches.* London: Taylor and Francis.

34. Mumford, E. & Banks, O. (1967) *The Computer and the Clerk.* London: Routledge & Kegan Paul.

35. Bjorn-Anderson, N. & Pedersen, P.H. (1977) Computer systems as a vehicle for changes in the management structure. *ISRG Working Paper No. 77-3,* Copenhagen.

36. Kling, R. & Scacchi, W. (1980) Computing as social action: the social dynamics of computing in complex organizations. *Advances in Computers, 19*, 249–347.

37. Oborne, D.J. (1985) *Computers at Work: A Behavioural Approach.* Chichester: John Wiley and Sons.

38. Strassman, P.A. (1982) Overview of strategic aspects of information management. *Office: Technology and People, 1*, 71–89.

39. Child, J. (1984) New technology and developments in management organization. *Omega, 12*, 3, 211–23.

40. Buchanan, D.A. & Huczynski, A.A. (1985) *Organizational Behaviour—An Introductory Text.* London: Prentice-Hall International.

41. White, R.W. (1960) Competence and psychosexual stages of development. In M.R. Jones (Ed.) *Nebraska Symposium on Motivation* 97–141, Lincoln: University of Nebraska Press.

42. Harlow, H.F. (1953) Mice, monkeys, men and motives. *Psychological Review, 60*, 23–32.

43. Atkinson, J.W. (1964) *An Introduction to Motivation.* New Jersey: Van Nostrand.

44. Lewin, K. (1964) The psychology of a successful figure. In H.S. Leavitt & L.R. Pondy (Eds.), *Readings in Managerial Psychology*, Chicago: University of Chicago Press, 25–31.

45. Child, I.L. & Whiting, J.W.M. (1954) Determinants of level of aspiration: evidence from everyday life. In H. Brand (Ed.), *The Study of Personality.* New York: Wiley.

46. Hofestede, G.H. (1968) *The Game of Budget Control.* London: Tavistock.

47. Stedry, A.C. (1960) *Budget Control and Cost Behaviour.* Englewood Cliffs, NJ: Prentice-Hall.

48. Stedry, A.C. & Kay, E. (1964) *The Effects Of Goal Difficulty On Performance: A Field Experiment.* MIT: Sloan School of Management.

49. Lowe, E.A. & Shaw, R.W. (1968) An analysis of managerial biasing: evidence from a company's budgeting process. *Journal of Management Studies, V*, October, 304–315.

50. Otley, D.T. (1977) Behavioural aspects of budgeting. *Accountants Digest ICAEW, No. 49*, Summer.

51. Kenis, I. (1977) Effects of budgetary goal characteristics on managerial attitudes and performance. *The Accounting Review,* October, 707–721.

52. Merchant, K.A. (1981) The design of the corporate budgeting system: influences on managerial behaviour and performance. *The Accounting Review, October,* 813–829.

53. Lowe, E.A. & Shaw, R.W. (1970) The accuracy of short-term business forecasting: an analysis of a firm's sales budgeting. *Journal of Industrial Economics, 18,* 275–289.

54. McClelland, D.C. (1967) *The Achieving Society.* New York: The Free Press.

55. Horner, M.S. (1970) Femininity and successful achievement: a basic inconsistency. In Y. Bardwich et al (Eds.), *Feminine, Personality and Conflict.* Belmont, Calif.: Brooks and Cole Publishing.

56. Hopwood, A. (1974) *Accounting and Human Behaviour.* London: Haymarket.

57. Veroff, J. (1953) Development and validation of a projective measure of power motivation. *Journal of Abnormal and Social Psychology, 55,* 1–8.

58. McClelland, D.C. (1970) The two faces of power. *Journal of International Affairs, 24,* 1, 29–47.

59. McClelland, D.C. (1975) Good guys make bum bosses. *Psychology Today, December,* 69–70.

60. Tannenbaum, A.S. (1962) Control in organizations: individual adjustment and organizational performance. *Administrative Science Quarterly, 7,* 236–257.

61. Vroom, V.H. (1964) *Work and Motivation.* New York: Wiley.

62. Porter, L.W. & Lawler E.E. (1968) *Managerial Attitudes and Performance.* Homewood, Ill: R.D. Irwin.

63. Carlson, R.E. (1969) Degree of job fit as a moderator of the relationship between job performance and job satisfaction. *Personnel Psychology, 22,* 159–170.

64. Porter, L.W., Lawler, E.E. & Hackman, J.R. (1975) *Behaviour in Organisations.* New York: McGraw-Hill.

65. Hirst, M.K. (1981) Accounting information and the evaluation of subordinate performance: a situational approach. *The Accounting Review, October,* 771–784.

66. Beresford Dew, R. & Gee, K.P. (1973) *Management Control and Information.* London: Macmillan.

67. Hopper, T. (1978) *Role Conflicts of Management Accountants in the Context of Their Structural Relationship to Production.* Unpublished M.Phil. thesis. University of Aston in Birmingham.

68. Sayles, L.R. & Chandler, M.K. (1971) *Managing Large Systems: Organizations for the Future.* New York: Harper & Row.

69. Likert, R. (1961) *New Patterns of Management.* New York: McGraw-Hill.

70. Ross, I.C. (1957) *Role specialisation in Supervision,* Unpublished Ph.d. thesis. Columbia University.

71. Otley, D.T. (1982) Budgets and managerial motivation. *Journal of General Management, 8,* 1, Autumn, 26–42.

72. Adams, J.S. (1963) Towards an understanding of inequity. *Journal of Abnormal and Social Psychology, 67,* 422–36.

73. Robbins, S. P. (1983). *Organizational Behavior: Concepts, Controversies, and Applications* (2nd Edn.). Englewood Cliffs, NJ: Prentice-Hall.

3 PERCEPTION AND COMMUNICATION

3 Perception and Communication

The process of perception is an important activity in the life of the individual. Our environment is littered with numerous stimuli trying to attract our attention. The quality of our perception depends on the way we organize, process and interpret the stimuli or information reaching our senses. When we interpret a situation or event, we are then in a position to respond. The sequence of events depicted here will act as a framework for the discussion on perception in this chapter.

Stimulus→Attention→Organization→
Interpretation→Response

As an extension of Interpretation, person perception is discussed, and given the importance of perception in communication the final section is devoted to an examination of communication processes.

STIMULUS

Before any information can be registered it has to be sensed and this is accomplished through the senses. The eventual response can be an intentional reaction to the stimulus received and processed, but equally it could be a reflex response which is generally outside the control of the person. When focusing on a stimulus and how it is perceived, there are a number of philosophical views to consider, though this is beyond the scope of this text. However, one such view may be briefly acknowledged. The phenomomenologists are of the view that it is the way we cognitively construe or interpret the stimuli reaching our senses that determines our responses. So what we perceive as reality is a reconstruction of what is in our environment. This reconstruction involves adding information and ignoring parts of the information coming our way; the information added or ignored will depend

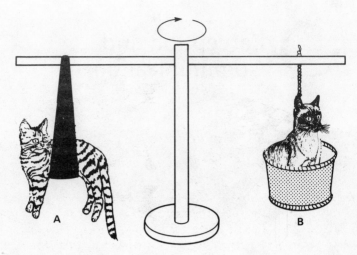

FIG. 3.1   The active kitten (A) and the passive kitten (B). Source: Held, R. & Hein, A. (1963) Movement-produced stimulation in the development of visually guided behavior. *Journal of Comparative and Physiological Psychology, 5,* 56, 872-876.

not only on the experience, education, personality and training of the perceiver, but also on the purpose for which the information is to be used. For example, the accounts of a company are to a greater or lesser extent a reconstruction of the economic reality of the business, though there are, of course, problems in finding a suitable unit of measurement and the most appropriate method of presentation.[1]

The question is also asked whether perception is innate or learned. It is suggested that normal perception is to some extent learned. In one experimental study kittens were brought up in the dark except during the period when the experiment was in progress.[2] One kitten was strapped into a basket and carried around by an active partner in a rotating arm during the experimental periods (see Fig.3.1). The active kitten had the superior view and developed normal perception while the passive kitten remained effectively blind. In another experiment young animals and human infants were exposed to a visual cliff (see Fig.3.2).[3] This is a patterned area with a steep drop in the middle, which is covered by glass to prevent a fall over the cliff. Both the animals and the human infants behaved in the same way by avoiding the deep side. The results of this experiment would suggest that perception is either innate or learned at a very early stage in the development of the animal or human.

The Senses
We rely on the senses in order to experience the world around us and to adapt to our environment. Normal stimuli impinging on our senses are taken

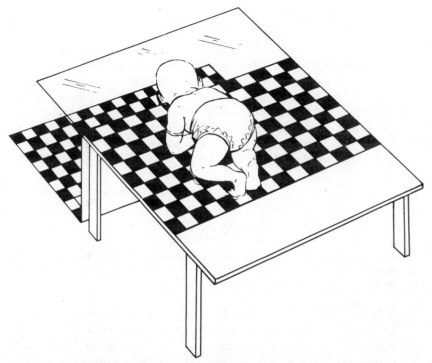

FIG. 3.2 The visual cliff. Source: Gibson, E.J. (1969) *Principles of perceptual learning and development*. New York: Appleton-Century-Crofts.

for granted, and it is when we find ourselves in a situation of sensory isolation that we positively yearn for stimuli from the outside world. When deprived of sensory stimulation, people suffer from disorientation, confusion and emotional disturbance and are vulnerable to persuasion and pressure. Also in these circumstances people engage in warding-off depression by dwelling on past experiences.

Man possesses at least 10 sensory channels — vision, hearing, taste, smell, touch, warmth, cold, pain, kinesthesis and vestibular. Each sense provides a channel through which information received from the world is transmitted to the brain. For each sense receptor at the surface of the body there are nerves which connect it to the brain and certain areas of the central nervous system; these nerves are made up of a bundle of neurons which are responsible for transmitting information by electrical impulses. Because there are different channels through which qualitatively different information flows, each type of information has its own pathway to the brain, but perception through the different senses can be integrated. This is illustrated when we simultaneously hear the lecturer speak, feel the hardness of the chair we are seated on and feel uncomfortably hot because of the high temperature of the room.

Vision. Vision is perhaps the most important and most often-used sense, and it has been suggested that we obtain three-quarters of our information about the world through sight.

The physical stimulation necessary for vision is electromagnetic energy, in the wavelength range between 380 to 780 nanometers (a nanometer is a millionth of a millimetre). All creatures see approximately the same wave band of electromagnetic energy as light, but there are some differences. For example, humans are blind to ultra-violet light, but honey-bees and ants can see it. Likewise, humans cannot perceive infra-red radiation either by vision or touch because it lies between light and heat, but rattlesnakes are sensitive to it.

The eye encodes the information it receives as electromagnetic radiation (light) into a form that the human nervous system can use. The retina at the back of the eye transforms the light energy into electro-chemical energy; this manifests itself as an impulse in the group of nerves running from the eye to the brain (called the optic nerve). The nerve impulses are received by the brain, translated and identified, and the body's reaction to the information is then determined by nerve impulses from the brain to the muscles powering the actions of different parts of the body — legs, arms, hands, and so on.

As well as the wavelength of the light, the intensity of the light determines what we can or cannot see. The human eye is sensitive to light intensities ranging from a low of 5–10 lux to a high of 100,000 lux (a lux is one lumen per square metre of surface). Different tasks require different levels of illumination — imagine, for example, the amount of visual detail required to drive a car, with all the complex and changing visual information involved. A driver would, however, tolerate a much lower level of illumination when travelling at 20 mph than at 60 mph, as he or she would have more time in which to resolve dimly seen objects and distances.

When specifying an optimum light level in the workplace (i.e., finding a light level that provides sufficient illumination without causing glare), it is important to consider the nature of the tasks being performed, and also to take account of individual differences. For instance, the performance of people with abnormal vision — e.g., partial sight defect — can be greatly improved by brighter illumination.

The sensory receptors in the eye are divided into two types: the rods and the cones. The cones perceive different wavelengths of light — i.e., they are sensitive to different colours. The cones are clustered near the centre of the retina. The rods are distributed around the perimeter of the retina, and cannot distinguish between different colours, but are much more sensitive to very low levels of light. Apparently the primates are the only mammals which can see in colour, but birds and a number of other animals have colour vision. One suggestion is that as most mammals are active at night, they are operating in low light levels; the colour receptors are either not functioning or not present. It has been proposed that mammals do in fact possess all the receptors needed to see colours, but that the process by which the brain recognizes the nerve impulses triggered by different colours has not evolved. This type of example highlights the importance of the two sides of visual perception — the physical equipment of the eye and the nervous system, and the psychological processes occurring in the brain to analyze and identify nerve impulses.

The choice of green for use in the early VDUs was probably due to the availability of green phospher. Red is a favoured choice for many displays where light-emitting diodes are used, for example, in electronic calculators. Red appears to be identified more frequently than any other colour of the same brightness as distinctive, and red numerals are far more legible than green ones.

A number of problems connected with abnormal colour vision have been found at places of work,[4] such as inefficiency, financial loss, personal embarrassment and danger. Mistakes in colour identification with unacceptable consequences that have occurred in the U.K. include: a day's production of colour-coded resistors had to be discarded; a crop of unripe tomatoes were picked too early; a buyer experienced difficulty in the selection of cured tobacco leaves; the wrong coloured thread was used in the weaving of a piece of carpet; a red entry was put in the place of a black one in an accountant's records; and a colour blind electrician received an electric shock from faulty wiring on a piece of equipment.

It is therefore important to consider the implications of employing people with defective colour perception. In Britain alone, roughly two million men and 150,000 women experience defective colour perception, though very few individuals are fully blind to colours.[4] Red, orange, green and brown pose the greatest difficulty for those with some degree of defective colour perception.

Light has to be evenly distributed, otherwise glare will result, causing discomfort, visual fatigue and accidents. Glare is caused by a marked contrast in brightness between two surfaces which has the effect of concentrating the light in one direction rather than diffusing it (e.g., the effect produced when light descends on shiny metal or glossy paper on a desk). It is advisable to darken the surroundings when vision is concentrated on a work surface in order to reduce visual strain. However, too great a contrast between the surroundings and the work area should be avoided.

Visual displays are important in providing the individual with pertinent information. There are several displays in a car which provide the driver with information. The windscreen is a kind of display — sometimes called a real-time display — from which the driver will obtain information through vision concerning the speed of the car on the road, and the position of other vehicles. Another display is the instrument panel which provides information about the internal functioning of the car as well as its relation to other parts of the car-road system. The design of the displays and controls will influence performance. If the driver cannot see the instrument panel, or cannot see through the windscreen, his or her performance will suffer.

Visual displays to show readings can assume different forms. In Fig.3.3 we have (a) a vertical dial, (b) a horizontal dial, (c) a semicircular design, (d) a round design, and (e) an open window design. The smallest percentage of errors in reading the information on display was obtained with the open window design — the dial moves but the pointer remains fixed. The area to scan is the smallest and this could be an important consideration when it comes to accuracy of reading. However, when the direction and rate of movement of the pointer is required, as for example when assessing the speed of a car in motion, the moving pointer is more suitable.[5] Auditory signals may complement visual ones when one is overwhelmed by visual displays. Even in circumstances where visual displays are not overwhelming, as, for example, when reading the speedometer of a car, it might be useful if an auditory signal was emitted whenever the speed exceeded the statutory limit.

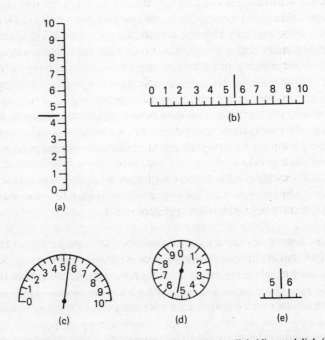

FIG. 3.3. (a) vertical dial; (b) horizontal dial; (c) semi-circular dial; (d) round dial; (e) open window dial. Source: Feldman, M. (1971) *Psychology in the Industrial Environment.* Sevenoaks: Butterworth.

Visual perception is an important consideration when a consumer is faced with making a decision, and product advertising and packaging are designed in order to provide visual cues. In packaging, for example, Dreft detergent proudly displays colour stripes with the words "colour safe," obviously appealing to the customer's natural desire to preserve the colour of the garment going into the wash. The appearance of the product is critical because it has to compete with other detergents in the same display position in the supermarket. Likewise expensive cosmetics are found in attractive packaging in order to project a glamorous image

Hearing. The physical stimulus for hearing is waves of pressure in the air. The sound waves vary in frequency (pitch, measured in Hz), intensity (loudness), and complexity (tonal quality). Sounds that human beings can hear range from low tones of 20 Hz to high ones of 20,000 Hz. At the low end of the sound range we feel vibration more than we hear sound. We hear best in the range 1000 to 4000 Hz. Many animals, including cats and dogs, can hear high-pitched sounds which we cannot hear, and cats have an upper limit of approximately 150,000 Hz. Frequency and intensity are both important in determining perceived loudness. Tonal quality enables us to distinguish different musical instruments and different voices. But there are other sounds which have little or no tonal quality, and we call these noises, for example, the hissing noise made by blowing air across a microphone. A violin tone, by contrast, has many strong harmonics. Loud noises are known to cause hearing loss; boiler-makers and footplate men have suffered impaired hearing because of loud noises.[5] Although people have the capacity to adapt to continuous loud noises, as happens in certain factories and at parties, the distracting noises are tolerated, but soon pose a psychological strain, leading to irritability and annoyance. Distraction, for whatever reason, causes errors. Of course not all sounds are unpleasant or distracting, and people involved in marketing a product or service recognize the advantages of pleasant sounds. For example, advertisers use jingles — catchy tunes which people can hum or whistle — as a major awareness technique to associate a certain tune with a certain product through repetition.

Other Senses. The senses of smell and taste are based on the recognition of chemicals by special receptor cells. Smell receptors are located in the roof of the nasal passages and taste receptors are located in the taste buds on the tongue, cheeks and throat. When chemicals which "smell" or "taste" come into contact with these cells, a nerve impulse is triggered and directed to the brain.

Whole industries have grown up around our perceptions of tastes and smells — many people regularly buy deodorant to suppress "unpleasant" smells, and perfume to make themselves smell attractive. Flavourings are added to many products to disguise unpleasant tastes. Our perception of what is a "good" taste or smell is strongly influenced by social and cultural considerations, and at the same time, we are more disposed to accept a product if it tastes or smells pleasant.

Receptors for four different senses are found in the skin: touch, warmth, cold, and pain. In the same way as smell and taste, our sense of touch is conditioned by social and cultural factors. We think of smooth baby's skin as "pleasant" and work-roughened or chapped skin as "unpleasant" to touch. These conditioned responses are both used and reinforced by advertising — for example, an advertisement for hand cream which promised to "leave the skin silky soft" would both appeal to our idea of soft skin as being pleasant, and reinforce the idea of soft skin being desirable.

Warmth and cold are felt when the receptors in the skin pick up even and continuous temperature changes. The pain receptors appear to be stimulated by tissue destruction — when cells are destroyed by touching a hot surface, for example, a nerve impulse is sent to the brain signalling "pain", which then initiates a series of quick responses, such as snatching the burnt limb away from the hot surface. Interestingly, it has been shown that loss of a limb can often result in the feeling of pain in the limb that is actually no longer there. It is as though we lack the right type of nerve receptors to tell us that a limb is missing, and so the pain signals are used instead.

Finally, the two remaining senses are kinesthesis and the vestibular sense. Kinesthesis is the sense of where one's limbs and body are in space — the way in which you can know where your hand or foot is, even in pitch darkness. The kinesthesis receptors are located throughout the muscles, tendons, and joints of the body. The vestibular sense is the sense of balance and movement, the receptors for which are located in the inner ear. This interlocking system of senses provides a network for registering stimuli both internal and external to an organism.

Sense receptors can be overloaded and cease to register stimuli — after a while a person wearing perfume can no longer smell it, for example, while others are still immediately aware of it. They are also affected by changes in the individual's surroundings, habits and circumstances. For example, it has been shown that confinement in an isolation chamber promotes an increased tolerance of pain.[5] Finally, the way environmental hazards affect our senses is discussed in Chapter 9.

ATTENTION (SELECTIVE PERCEPTION)

In everyday life, many stimuli vie for the attention of the individual. On commercial television the consumer is bombarded with a large number of messages. Likewise when one enters a chemist shop to buy razor blades, one is exposed to many products. The investor interested in the financial health of a company could in certain circumstances have a lot of information from which to choose. However, we cannot attend to all stimuli, so selectivity must be exercised. Selective perception amounts to picking out those stimuli that are most likely to be important and ignoring the others. Certain conventions govern selective perception, and are discussed with reference to external physical stimuli, absolute and differential thresholds, and the disposition of the perceiver.

External Physical Stimuli

Certain types of external physical stimuli attract our attention, such as size (e.g., large objects); repetition (e.g., events which occur repeatedly); position (e.g., position of an advertisement on a newspaper page); colour; and moving objects in a stationary setting. All of these stimuli have particular properties which cause us to focus attention on them. These stimuli are now discussed and subsequently general applications are explored.

1. Size.   In studying the effects of advertising, physical stimuli such as size, repetition, position and colour have been analysed.[6] Increasing the size of an advertisement will generally increase its readership — it encounters less competition from other advertisements on a newspaper or magazine page, but obviously there is limited scope for the enlargement of the advertisement. In a large advertisement there is an opportunity to include more illustrations and more text. Advertisements with a large proportion of unfilled background or "white space" tend to attract attention because of their novelty, stark simplicity and startling appearance.

2. Repetition.   Repetition is an important factor aimed at increasing the readership of an advertisement. For those readers who notice the advertisement on more than one occasion, the repeated exposure strengthens the initial impact of the advertisement. This was borne out in an experimental study when pairs of advertisements were exposed in a stereoscope for a short time. The subjects were young women, divided into an experimental group and a control group. The experimental group had much more contact with the advertisements, which dealt with brassières and girdles and included a picture of a model, than did the control group. The result was that the experimental group recalled these advertisements significantly more often than did the control group.[7] Constant repetition is said to produce familiarity, and if a brand is relatively risk-free with some incentive given at the point of sale (e.g., price discount), shoppers may purchase the product because of accumulated familiarity, even though they have not actively attended to the advertising message.[8]

3. Position.   The position of an advertisement within a magazine or newspaper is crucial. Placing an advertisement near a popular editorial feature gives it an advantage, particularly where the content of the advertisement bears some relationship to the editorial, for example, it is important to place advertisements for books on or near the book review pages. Such a location helps to select an interested audience and attract readers at a time when they are particularly receptive to the appeal of the product. It is claimed that placing advertisements on and inside the front cover, on page one and both on and inside the back cover of a magazine creates a significant readership advantage of between 30 and 64% over positions on the inside pages.[9] With respect to position within a page, it is suggested that the upper half of a page gets more attention than the lower half, and the left -hand side of the page gets more attention than the right.[10]

4. *Colour.*   Colour is often used as a device to attract attention and portray realism. In a mass of black and white a modicum of colour catches the eye. Where colour is still a novelty, as with newspapers, the addition of even a single colour to an advertisement will enhance its attention-getting value.

Colour can be used to emphasize the attractive features of a product or to create a suitable atmosphere — high technology products such as cameras are usually produced in black or metallic finishes, but recently some have been marketed with a less serious, more sporty image, in bright primary colours. Some products, such as motor cars, come in a variety of colours, but others, such as toothpaste, are limited in colour range. It would somehow seem incongruous to use black toothpaste.

Standards, based on psychological research, for the optimum use of colour in coding systems have been adopted by the British Standards Institution after collaboration with industry. There are colour codes to denote different types of fire extinguisher, for industrial and medical gas cylinders, for the hatched yellow lines at busy but dangerous crossroads, and for traffic signalling.

Colour can be used in the workplace for the enhancement of lighting effects, for creating pleasant surroundings and for putting across and reinforcing the safety message. When planning the colour scheme or décor for a room it is important to consider the use to which the room will be put. For repetitive and monotonous activities the overall décor could be made more stimulating by providing small areas of bright colours. A large working area can be divided into smaller identifiable segments by using different colour schemes complementing each other. Where mental concentration is a necessary feature of office life, the colour scheme should be light and non-intensive.

The effects of colours on the psychological state of the individual should also be considered, as some colours act as a stimulant while others act as a depressant. A dark blue ceiling may appear to be refreshing to begin with

TABLE 3.1
The Effects of Different Colours

Colour	Psychological Effect	Temperature Effect	Distance Effect
Violet	Aggressive & tiring	Cold	Very close
Blue	Restful	Cold	Further away
Brown	Exciting	Neutral	Claustrophobic
Green	Very restful	Cold–neutral	Further away
Yellow	Exciting	Very warm	Close
Orange	Exciting	Very warm	Very close
Red	Very stimulating	Warm	Close

but in time the apparent coldness may become an irritant. Various effects are attributed to different colours and these are shown in Table 3.1.[11]

5. *Movement.* Movement, or the illusion of movement, may also be used to capture attention. People are attracted by neon lighting and by billboards with rotating bars that carry a different message on each surface.

Other Applications of Physical Stimuli
A number of the stimuli identified in the previous section could be incorporated in the following examples.

1. *Notices and Warnings.* Employees must be alerted to dangerous equipment, areas, processes, etc. It is important to attract their attention to the hazards which are present and to inform and remind them of the safety precautions they should take. This is usually done with notices. Notices and warnings should be varied from time to time in order to attract fresh attention. Warnings are necessary in the following conditions, particularly on the factory floor: where a particular hazard cannot be "designed out" of a piece of equipment; where an operator cannot be removed physically from the potentially dangerous point of contact; and where effective guards cannot be installed. An employer has a legal duty in the U.K. to inform employees about hazards at work. Employees are more likely to cooperate in keeping rules made for their benefit if they appreciate the risks and the reasons for the precautions.

Warnings may be either dynamic or static. Dynamic warnings consist of warning lights and audible sounds, and static warnings consist of pictures, symbols and diagrams. These should be universally understood, they should convey *why* something is a hazard, how it arises from the use or misuse of a piece of equipment or process, and what to do if an injury should occur. They should be complete, allow for any literacy or language problems and be conspicious and capable of attracting attention. Warnings should be updated periodically, and redundancy should be built into the information provision process. Redundancy in this context is the injection of essentially the same information through two or more sense channels (e.g., vision and hearing).[12]

In the U.K. there are statutory safety regulations requiring that dangerous substances be supplied and conveyed in containers of sound construction carrying an appropriate warning label. Such labels would include pictorial symbols indicating the general hazards, such as "explosive," "highly inflammable," "toxic," or "corrosive," as well as important health and safety information. The justification for this legislation is that inadequately labelled or badly packed dangerous substances cause accidents and injury.

2. *Illustrations.*   Illustrations of a product are useful devices to attract attention. They could be attractive photographs of the product or pictures of various appertizing foods that can be prepared using the product, for example, a photograph of a cake along with the recipe for the cake could be used on packaging for flour. Illustrations serve to facilitate comprehension of ideas about the product, to arouse feelings about it and to help identify the product when the consumer is out shopping. Pictures of people generally rate highly in attention value, but there is evidence suggesting that when human models are used in a printed advertisement the appropriateness of the model for the product may influence judgements about product quality.[6,13] It is essential that the illustrated advertisement does not become an end in itself and detract attention from the product.

3. *Cues.*   Cues are physical stimuli that act as symbols, giving us an indication of what to expect and facilitating judgements. The names of supermarkets (e.g., Sainsbury), brand names (e.g., St. Michael), packaging and price are cues that convey the quality of the store or product and help us make our decision to buy. Judgements are also made about a company from cues such as the helpfulness of the staff, and the image of the company (e.g., Harrods). Perhaps when we confront a situation where there is an absence of cues about a store, greater reliance is placed on the assessment of the quality of service and product at the time of purchase. Sometimes reliance on a few cues could lead to stereotyping which might not be justified in particular circumstances. This might arise when someone calls at the door selling insurance or a product. Because of a negative stereotype of a door-to-door salesman, which could be totally unjustified in given circumstances, the customer withdraws from what might otherwise be a fruitful commercial encounter.

A trademark is a reduced cue, serving as a conditioned stimulus for the recall of the product and company name. It may symbolize some advantageous characteristic of the product — e.g., Long Life for milk. A trademark tends to evoke ideas and feelings associated with the product, either through previous advertising or through the customer's own contact with the product. When the trademark is a direct representation of the brand name of the product, as is the case with Kellogg's Corn Flakes, the association between the brand name and trademark is particularly easy to establish and the likelihood of confusion with other products or brands is minimized. Sometimes a brand name is so strongly identified with a product that it is used as a generic term, for example, Kleenex to denote any cleansing tissue. In circumstances such as these there is a danger of associating dissatisfaction with the original brand if the customer is dissatisfied with the purchase of an inferior brand.

4. *Financial Data.* Published accounting information is a stimulus attended to by the investor. However, there are other sources of information at the disposal of the investor apart from these, such as commentaries and tips in the financial press, government reports on the state of the economy, employers' and trade association reports, stock brokers' reports, merger reports, the latest inflation and balance of payments figures, and so on. The proposition that published accounts are only one of many sources of information is supported by at least one study.[14] The results of this study indicate that most movement in share prices took place in the twelve months preceding the announcement of profits, and that on average there was only a 10% change in the value of shares at the time the profits were announced.

The accountant's image may also be important as a stimulus. Where the accountant is seen as conservative in outlook the investor may adjust his or her judgement accordingly. There is a belief in some quarters that annual reports and accounts have become complex and cumbersome documents prepared by financial experts for financial experts, despite official exhortation to be realistic about the user's requirements.[15] Financial statements should be designed for users "who have limited authority, ability or resources to obtain information and who rely on financial statements" (Objectives of Financial Statements AICPA 1973). The clarity or ambiguity of accounting stimuli is discussed again under the headings of *Perceptual Organization* and *Interpretation*.

5. *Clarity.* In written official documents and forms, clarity is an important principle. It is very important, for example, for tax literature to be as clear as possible. In a comparatively recent annual report of the Inland Revenue in the U.K. it is stated that "good communications are crucial to our task of assessing and collecting the revenue due from the public efficiently and with a minimum of friction.... Like any other organization with millions of individual contacts with members of the public each year, we have to rely for the exchange of information largely on forms and standard printed mat-

erials."[16] The accuracy of tax returns is obviously related to the degree of difficulty experienced in comprehending tax forms and guides.

At the time of writing, the form P1 used by the Inland Revenue has changed colour; it is now white rather than blue although the titles and sub-titles are blue. There have been other improvements to form P1 and guide.[16] The format is much better, with much more space generally; the size of the print has been enlarged though perhaps it is still too small for elderly people to read; the number of introductory comments in the guide, in order to establish the right mental focus, have been increased; and there have been changes in wording, e.g., "correspondence" with the tax office has become "letters." Other revisions and changes have affected the tax guide associated with Forms 11 and 11P, and a start has been made on the revision of all the main explanatory leaflets and booklets. The above developments are indicative of a determination to strive for clarity in the presentation of a stimulus to the target audience.

Absolute and Differential Thresholds

Each sense receptor requires some minimum level of energy to excite it before perception is organized. The minimum level is called the "absolute threshold" — a point below which we never perceive energy. The absolute threshold for light is a flame from a candle seen at a distance of 30 miles on a dark clear night; for sound it is the tick of a watch under quiet conditions at a distance of 20 feet; for taste it is one teaspoon of sugar in two gallons of water; and for smell, it is one drop of perfume diffused into the entire volume of a three-room apartment.[17]

The differential threshold is the smallest amount by which two similar stimuli must be different in order to be perceived as different. People differ in both absolute and differential thresholds. For example, the professional wine taster can frequently distinguish between two bottles of wine that the amateur finds the same. In the production of paper the mixing foreman must ascertain exactly when the pulpy mixture is at the appropriate consistency for the type of paper required — an example of an acute differential threshold.[18]

The concepts of absolute and differential thresholds are important in the field of safety. The safety engineer and the design engineer must acquaint themselves with people's absolute and differential thresholds and allow for these when designing signals.

Thresholds need not only concern the physical stimuli of the real world. For example, in accounting the absolute threshold could be considered as the minimum level of information required by the individual to perceive the overall profitability or financial position of a business. An example of a differential threshold might be a discrepancy in figures detected in the course of a financial audit. To the experienced and competent auditor this discrepancy is serious enough to warrant further investigation, but to the inexperienced auditor the detection of the discrepancy may not signal a need for further action.

It has already been acknowledged that stimuli below the absolute threshold level cannot be perceived. However, on the basis of an experiment conducted in the autumn of 1957 in the U.S. it was thought that subliminal perception — perception below the absolute threshold level — existed in and affected buying behaviour.[10] The experiment was conducted by a commercial firm in a New Jersey cinema. The words "Eat Popcorn" and "Drink Coca-Cola" were flashed alternately on the screen every five seconds for 1/3000th of a second during the showing of the regular film. These stimuli were described as subliminal, and the firm claimed that over the six weeks this procedure was followed the sale of popcorn in the foyer rose by 57.5% and Coca-Cola by 18.1%. The report of these results aroused widespread public alarm, and this type of advertising was described as the "super soft-sell" and the "invisible sell." The claims made for these experiments could not be evaluated because of the refusal by the commercial firm to reveal the details of the experimental procedure and results. It should be noted that in situations like this one factors other than subliminal advertising may influence the results: for example, a high proportion of teenagers in the audience during this period, changes in the display of the two products and in the sales tactics, and the weather.[19]

Subliminal perception is not a mysterious technique for projecting ideas directly into the mind by evading the individual's conscious defences. There is no evidence to suggest that weak stimuli, that is stimuli below the absolute threshold level, exert more influence on behaviour than strong stimuli; in fact the reverse is the case. Also, as the stimulus becomes weaker, the probability of misperception becomes higher. With regard to subliminal stimuli, individual threshold differences must be considered because a word flashed across a cinema screen for a short period may have significance for one person because it falls above his or her absolute threshold, but not for another because it falls below the minimum level.

Sensory Adaptation.   Absolute and differential thresholds are known to fluctuate, and this fluctuation is referred to as sensory adaptation. When going from bright daylight into a darkened room the eyes will take up to 25 minutes to achieve an 80% adaptation; going the other way, from a darkened room into bright sunlight, a slightly quicker visual adaptation occurs. Some workers in the photographic industry spend a full working day in conditions of almost total darkness. Their dark-adaptation rate is faster, and they can achieve adaptation within 15 to 20 minutes.[20]

Sensory adaptation also takes the form of reduced awareness of the stimuli to which one is exposed on a continual basis. An example of this would be a worker becoming oblivious to the dangers of operating certain types of machinery and consequently risking an accident. However, there are other occasions when sensory adaptation can have beneficial consequences and result in better performance. This could arise when, for example, a person experiences a decrease in awareness of background noise, and by adapting to it ensures that it does not adversely affect performance.

Disposition of the Perceiver

Unlike the physical stimuli discussed at length above, there are other less quantifiable variables that are unique to the individual. These can be classified as the internal state of the person — e.g., personality, motivation, and previous learning — and affect the way people perceive. The disposition of the individual will be discussed with reference to the preparatory set, orientation, intensity of motives and familiarity of stimuli.

1. Preparatory Set.   The preparatory set basically refers to the range of things that, because of our internal state, we are almost programmed to see. Items outside the preparatory set are virtually ignored irrespective of what is contained in the stimuli to which we are exposed. The interest we have in certain things influences our attention. Perhaps more women are interested in advertisements for children's and babies' clothing than men, and the position could be reversed when attention focuses on cars and lawn mowers. Users of accounting information may take insufficient interest in financial data for a number of reasons, such as failure to meet their requirements because of the accountants' preoccupation with the techniques of accounting rather than the use to which accounting information is put.[21] In one study of the use of accounting control by middle managers it was found that a significant amount of the information prepared for control purposes was not properly used because it was considered not totally relevant, too detailed, not detailed enough, or too late.[22]

2. Orientation.   The particular orientation — the attitude adopted by the perceiver towards a set of physical stimuli based on interests, background, etc. — is also critical. This is borne out in the results of two studies.

In one study a group of students was presented with a set of numbers in the form of cost and revenue statements. Both statements were analyzed by all the students but there was a 10-week interval between the analysis of the two statements, with one half of the group working first on the revenue statements and the other half beginning with the cost statements. It was found that the context in which the students operated influenced their outlook; when analysing costs they tended to over-estimate costs, but under-estimated sales when analysing revenue. Perhaps people are somewhat conservative in outlook when engaged in information processing connected with money values. By over-estimating costs there will be a tendency to minimize losses, whereas by under-estimating sales the likelihood of overstating income is reduced.[23]

In the second study a group of managers drawn from a large manufacturing company participated while attending a management course. The managers came from different functional backgrounds (e.g., accounting, marketing and production), and they were asked to specify the major problem facing a company depicted in a case study that they had read. The majority of managers perceived the major problem as being related to their own area of specialization.[24]

3. Intensity of Motives. Perception is selectively affected by personal motives as we pay most attention to stimuli that appeal to fairly intense motives. Thus our perception may be distorted by our motivations. This point is emphasized in the following study. Ten-year-old children were asked to estimate the size of a coin in front of them by varying the size of a spot of light until they thought it was the same as a series of coins ranging from a penny to half a crown. It was found that the estimated size of every coin was larger than its true size. This type of over-estimation did not occur with a control group which tried to estimate the size of cardboard discs the same size as the coins. When the experiment was conducted among separate groups from both affluent and poor backgrounds, over-estimation was detected in both cases, but was more pronounced among children from the poorer background. Here we observe that perception is accentuated when valued objects are perceived.[25]

Where a stimulus is related to a need deficiency, our perception of that stimulus could be acute. The hungry person will display selectivity by tuning into food-related stimuli in his or her environment because of their association with the reduction of a need deficiency (hunger). Selective perception can also help us to cope with a threat. Here our value system assists us by ignoring messages, particularly mildly threatening ones, that tend to question our values and this could be achieved without conscious awareness.

The following study demonstrated how perception acts as a defence in certain circumstances.[26] Words were shown to subjects only briefly so that they found it impossible to recognize them. The period of display was then lengthened until recognition occurred. An electronic measure of emotion — the galvanic skin response (GSR) — was used to gauge the electrical resistance of the skin when an emotional reaction was aroused. The words were made up of eleven which were neutral and seven which were taboo (e.g., bitch, whore, rape). Each time a word was flashed the subject gave his or her opinion of what the word was. An emotional reaction (as gauged by GSR) occurred even in circumstances when taboo words were shown so briefly that recognition was not reported by the subjects. Taboo words had to be exposed for longer than neutral words before being read, as they were apparently more difficult to recognize. When the words were flashed very briefly, and the subjects guessed what the words were, it was found that neutral words were construed in a structurally similar sense — e.g., instead of recognizing the word "trade" as such, it was recognized as "trace" — but completely different words were substituted for taboo words. One might conclude that subjects suppress the reporting of taboo words even when they clearly perceive them, or that they have a higher threshold with respect to these words and are therefore not alerted to them; or that because these words appear less often in print than other words, they are less familiar and are recognized more slowly.

On the basis of this study one might accept that stimuli of a mildly threatening nature (e.g., a distasteful advertisement) tend to be ignored. Conversely, one may hypothesize that strongly threatening stimuli can capture our attention. We are protected from the distraction of mildly threatening stimuli, but alerted to the danger of strongly threatening stimuli.

4. *Familiarity of Stimuli.*   Experience of a particular stimulus, such as a particular piece of music, amidst a range of stimuli to which we may be indifferent attracts our attention. Alternatively, a novel or unfamiliar object amidst range of familiar ones, for instance, a strange face at a social event or a novel piece of accounting data in a stereotyped accounting report, produces a similar effect. Experience may also predispose us to discount the claims of the advertiser of a product; we do so on the basis of dissatisfaction experienced as a result of previously using that product. Previous learning creates a tendency to pay attention to familiar patterns, though this might bring about problems when we accept a stimulus which bears a similarity to a familiar stimulus–we see what we expect to see rather than what is.

PERCEPTUAL ORGANIZATION

Having focused our attention on relevant stimuli, the next step is to organize the information contained in the stimuli. This could be difficult in circumstances where the stimuli are ambiguous. Dots, lines and other shapes can have meaning for us; likewise we attribute meaning to sounds — a sound that emanates from within the home invites questions about where it is coming from and what it is.

Ambiguous Figures
When you first glance at the lines in Fig 3.4 you may conclude that they epitomize disorganization. You suddenly begin to realize that it is a drawing and could represent either a duck or a rabbit and then it fluctuates between both images. Likewise you see in Fig. 3.5 either a kneeling woman or a man's

FIG. 3.5   An ambiguous figure - a kneeling woman or a man's face. Source: Fisher, G.H. (1967) Preparation of ambiguous stimulus materials. *Perception and Psychophysics, 2,* 421-422.

FIG. 3.4   An ambiguous figure – a duck or a rabbit.

face, or perhaps both. With ambiguous figures there appears to be a need to create a whole image.

The concept of organization also arises when a series of musical notes is perceived as a tune. For example "Moon River" would be immediately recognized by those who had heard this song previously, whether it was sung by a soprano or a bass voice, although in each case the notes are different. It is the pattern of notes rather than the individual notes that is important.

Figure/Background
We rarely encounter ambiguity with three-dimensional objects in our normal visual world. But with two-dimensional objects we find it difficult to distinguish between background and figure. The figure/background stimuli are presented in Figs. 3.6 and 3.7. Two different pictures could be derived

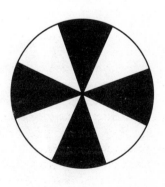

FIG. 3.6   An ambiguous figure – a vase or two profiles.

FIG. 3.7   A black or white cross.

FIG. 3.8   Multistable figures.

from Fig 3.6; at one moment we see a figure of a white vase against a black background, and the next moment we see two black profiles against a white background. In Fig. 3.7 we see either a black cross on a white background or a white cross on a black background.

The figure/background relationship is also found in senses other than vision. For example, when we listen to a symphony we perceive the melody or theme as a figure and the chords as background. Reversible figure/background relationships illustrate the "multistability" of our perceptual organization. This is shown in Fig. 3.8 where each image can be "organized" in different ways, generating different three-dimensional or two-dimensional figures. For example the image on the right of Fig 3.8 can be seen as a hexagon, with lines from the points converging at the centre, or as a cube tipped forward.

Gestalt Laws of Organization

A number of rules or laws governing the organization of perception, sometimes referred to as the "Gestalt Laws of Organization," follow:

1. Area   Where one part of an area depicting an ambiguous figure is smaller in size than the remainder it is more likely that the smaller area will be seen as a figure and the rest of the total area as background. If you glance at Fig. 3.9 (a), it is usual to see the small areas of white as the figure of a white cross and the large area of black as the background. By contrast, in Fig. 3.9 (b) a black cross set in a white background is more likely to be seen.

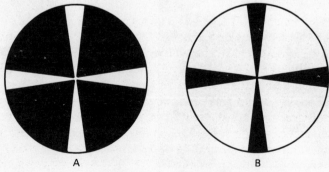

FIG. 3.9   Reversible figures.

2. Proximity. In Fig. 3.10 we see three pairs of vertical lines instead of six vertical lines. The law of proximity states that items which are close together in space or time tend to be perceived as forming an organized group, or belonging together. When one flicks through the pages of a book, small sections of text with headings stand out from the remainder of the text because of their distance from the previous section.

FIG 3.10   Groupings of vertical lines.

3. Similarity. In Fig. 3.11 (a) most people would see one triangle formed by the dots with the apex at the top, and another triangle formed by rings, i.e., with the apex at the bottom. The triangles are perceived in this way because the dots and rings look different and therefore are organized separately. In a textbook pictures and diagrams are instantly seen to be similar, and different from the body of the text. In Fig. 3.11 (b) we do not see a triangle, we see a hexagon or a six-pointed star because all the dots are the same. Grouping in accordance with similarity does not always occur. We see Fig. 3.11 (c) more easily as a six-pointed star than as one set of dots and another set of rings. In this illustration similarity is competing with the principle of symmetry or "good figure"; neither the circles nor the dots form a symmetrical pattern by themselves.

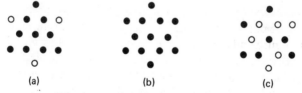

(a)   (b)   (c)

FIG. 3.11   Examples of perceptual grouping.

4. Continuation. There is a tendency to perceive a line that starts in a particular way as continuing in that way. For example, a line that starts off as a curve is seen continuing in a smooth curve course. Equally a straight line is seen as continuing on a straight course and if it changes direction it is seen to form an angle rather than a curve. Figure 3.12 illustrates the principle of continuation. We see the curved and straight lines as crossing each other and having dots in common, but it requires some effort on our part to perceive a straight line becoming a curved line at one of these intersecting points or junctions. A numerical illustration of continuation is shown when you are asked to specify a number to follow 4, 8, 12, 16. The most likely answer is 20 because of a tendency to follow a perceived pattern. But in fact any number would be good enough since you were not asked to maintain the pattern.

FIG. 3.12   Examples of perceptual continuity.

5. *Common Fate.*   This arises where elements which are seen as moving together take the shape of an organized group. The soldier in the jungle or wilderness who is perfectly camouflaged against his background is invisible until he moves; when he moves he becomes a figure and remains so while he is in motion. Two of the following circles share a common fate because they move in the same direction:

6. *Closure.*   We compensate for the missing portions of incomplete stimuli so that we can perceive a whole rather than a disorganized group. In Fig. 3.13 the left hand drawing is seen as a circle with gaps in it and the centre drawing as a square with gaps in it, rather than as disconnected lines. If these pictures were flashed very rapidly on to a screen, they might be perceived as complete pictures without gaps. The drawing on the extreme right will also be perceived as a form rather than disconnected lines (e.g., a man on horseback).

All of the principles discussed here also apply to perception using senses other than vision.

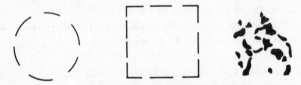

FIG. 3.13   Examples of Closure.

Applications

The principle of the gestalt psychologists that the "whole is more than the sum of its parts" is seen at work in the illustrations of perceptual organization shown here. The principle of organization is frequently applied in our daily life. When an advertisement for a product is viewed on commercial television, the soundtrack and visual stimuli complement each other and help the consumer to organize the message. Repetition of a message in an advertisement also contributes to perceptual organization.

For example, an advertisement for a new personal computer with a word processing facility at an attractive price is advertised in the colour supplement of a Sunday newspaper. This advertisement, which highlights the versatility and usefulness of the computer and associated software, as well as the price, is repeated over a period of time. Eventually, a consumer who has not responded to, or been aware of, initial exposures to the advertisement, sees the advantages of the computer and decides to buy one. Repetition has been instrumental in bringing about the organization of the consumer's perceptions.

In another case perceptual organization with respect to the features of a familiar product affects the consumer's decision when comparing that product with competing products. For example, a consumer of Maxwell House instant coffee will pick out this brand from among other brands on a shelf in a supermarket, without comparing each brand of coffee feature by feature. He or she has an organized overall perception of the product — cost, taste, etc.

People's ability to organize their perception of individual stimuli into a coherent whole can be affected by particular situations, or blocked by the poor presentation or masking of the stimuli themselves. For example, at an annual general meeting of a public company, private shareholders may feel uncomfortable in a large conference room or hall, and be disconcerted by the need to use microphones to make themselves heard. It is easy for people to mishear or misunderstand the information being presented, and to form an incorrect impression of what is being discussed or reported. When they try to quiz the senior management they may get to their feet, only to realize that they have not in fact been able to organize their thoughts and questions adequately, and are therefore easily fobbed off with evasions or bland assurances.

There is evidence to suggest that shareholders, particularly private shareholders, have difficulty in organizing their perception of annual reports and prefer alternative sources of information because they are written for the user with limited financial ability.[27] A further reference to this evidence is made in the next section on *Perceptual Interpretation*. Where does the blame lie for the problems experienced by shareholders? According to an academic accountant interested in the problems of language in financial reporting, the fault is in the accounting profession's unwillingness to use straightforward language to express essentially straightforward ideas and techniques. Though he acknowledges the need for technical language in every profession, it must not be a barrier to communicating with the public. Much of the accountancy profession's language is "bogus, existing only to impress the innocent and unwary; much of it is not essential, it cannot be justified on practical grounds and fulfils no purpose, except possibly to act as a kind of masonic glue between different members of the profession." All too frequently accountants are complacent and pay insufficient attention to the user with limited financial expertise who finds the language at best confusing and at worst incomprehensible.[28]

In the startling conclusion to a study of the information needs of middle managers in various companies, two researchers found what amounted to a language barrier between the producers and users of company information.[22] The managers questioned did not like the form in which the information was presented and also noted that it was not in the language of their discipline; they would have preferred language that had meaning to them — i.e., in terms of weights or volume or hours, and not the language of costs and standards of output so dear to the accountants.

Where an apparently simple statement such as "The accounts have been prepared on the historical cost basis of accounting" appears in the published accounts, are users with limited financial expertise expected to know what comprises the historical cost basis and its limitations? Are they expected to know what the alternative bases are? The words "basis" and "convention" are used interchangeably in published accounts, but is the average private shareholder to know that the word "basis" means the same as "convention" when these terms are applied to historical cost accounting? Unlike the average private shareholder, the experienced financial analyst would not find it difficult to grapple with the contents of the annual accounts, though he or she might be critical of the low informational content.[28]

With respect to accounting policies, a distinction can be made between two levels of technical language, high-level and low-level.[28] In Table 3.2 extracts from company reports, taking into account different accounting policy considerations, are sub-divided into high-level technical language on the left side and low-level technical language on the right. Companies using high-level technical language, which is probably the case with most companies, make no attempt to appeal to the lay person by putting the jargon into everyday speech or leaving out such language altogether. The illustrations of high-level technical language in Table 3.2, with the exception of the comment on Pilkington's Research and Development policy, are extremely complex from a technical accounting point of view, but paradoxically the informational content is negligible for those who *can* comprehend accounting technicalities — i.e., experienced financial analysts.

The information which appears under the heading of low-level technical information in Table 3.2 is much more helpful to the reader with limited financial expertise. An example of a genuine effort to explain the notions underpinning some of the figures in the accounts are the comments on depreciation policy by ICI and deferred tax by Beecham. Of course there is a danger that reports would be of little value to the qualified accountant or experienced user of published accounts if they were oversimplified. One authority asks why accountants should accept the risks entailed in simplification since small shareholders have certain options open to them to deal with the status quo; for example, they can educate themselves in the interpretation of accounts, they can seek expert advice or invest in mutual funds

TABLE 3.2
Illustrations of High-level and Low-Level Technical Language in Company Reports

Policy	High-level Technical Language	Low-level Technical Language
Basis of Consolidation: Goodwill	(i) "On the acquisition of a business, fair values are attributed to the net assets acquired. Goodwill arises where the price paid for a business exceeds the values attributable to such net assets. Goodwill associated with major acquisitions is capitalized and retained in the balance sheet unless it is determined that there is no continuing value, in which case the goodwill is written off to group profit, as an extraordinary item. Immaterial amounts arising each year on acquisition of minor businesses are also written off as extraordinary items." (*ICI 1977*) (ii) "Net goodwill arising from acquisitions is written off." (*Delta Metal 1977*)	"The results of subsidiaries are consolidated from their effective dates of acquisition. Where the cost of an acquisition is greater than the underlying net asset value at the date of acquisition a premium arises. Such premiums (referred to as goodwill) are shown as a deduction from ordinary shareholders' funds." (*Bowater 1977*)

COMMENT: *Note that there is no apparent correlation between brevity and low-level technicality. Delta's could not be briefer but as it stands, it is incomprehensible to the layperson. ICI's is riddled with subconcepts of continuing value, materiality and extraordinary items which compound the problem of understanding an already tortuous statement. Bowater, on the other hand, takes space to explain how goodwill arises and how it is accounted for, which leaves the reader fully aware that the shareholders are paying for it. It does not, however, explain what goodwill is.*

Policy	High-level Technical Language	Low-level Technical Language
Stock	"Stocks of oil and chemicals are valued at the lower of approximate group cost including overheads, using first-in first-out method and net realizable value. For purposes of valuation Petroleum Revenue Tax (PRT) is treated as a cost. Stocks of stores are stated at or below cost calculated mainly using the average method." (*BP 1977*)	"Stocks and work in progress are valued at the lower of cost and net realizable value. Cost includes all direct expenditure and works overhead expenditure incurred in bringing goods to their current state under normal operating conditions. The works overhead expenditure includes charges for depreciation, replacement and obsolescence of fixed assets but excludes research and development, distribution, selling, divisional and head office expenses." (*Pilkington 1977*)

(continued over)

TABLE 3.2 continued

Policy	High-level Technical Language	Low-level Technical Language

COMMENT: *The difference in the use of technical language should be clear, with BP parading the old warhorses of FIFO and average method in front of shareholders. While we include Pilkington under 'low-level' there is still much that could be done to make this type of fuller explanation even more meaningful. So far as we can determine from a survey of accounts no company takes the trouble to spell out to readers the crucial role stock valuation plays in profit determination; by doing so they could explain the convention of including the most conservative of valuations and therefore bring meaning to the phrase "lower of cost and net realizable value."*

Policy	High-level Technical Language	Low-level Technical Language
Depreciation	"Depreciation is charged on the straight-line basis over the effective lives of the assets except for: (i) Tonnage plants commissioned in the U.K. since 1 October 1969 where depreciation is calculated on an annuity basis over the life of the contract. (ii) Freehold land where no depreciation is charged. Straight-line depreciation rates vary according to the class of asset, but are typically: Freehold buildings 2% pa Leasehold land and buildings 2% pa (etc, etc)" (*BOC 1977*)	"The group's policy is to write off the book value of each fixed asset evenly over its estimated remaining lives of individual productive assets, taking account of commercial and technical obsolescence as well as normal wear and tear. Estimates of asset lives cannot be made with precision and in practice a range of possible lives exists. The group, recognizing to some extent the problem of continuing inflation, has, in its historical cost accounts, adopted lives at the lower end of the range . . ." (*ICI 1977*)

COMMENT: *Depreciation is not a difficult concept for the layperson to comprehend. Even though, notice the way that ICI has avoided the highly technical phrase straight-line basis (not to mention the annuity basis!) and it makes the adventurous, and truthful, remark about the imprecision of this accounting technique. How dare ICI blow the cover on the spurious note of accuracy the profession has spent so long injecting into accounts!*

Policy	High-level Technical Language	Low-level Technical Language
Research and development	(i) "Revenue expenditure on research and development is charged against profits of the year in which it is incurred and is not carried forward as an asset to be recouped out of future profits. Capital expenditure on research laboratories, equipment and plant is written off over its expected working life." (*Pilkington 1977*) (ii) "Research and development expenditure is written off in the year in which it is incurred	(i) "Expenditure on laboratory buildings and equipment is capitalized and written off in accordance with the group's depreciation policy. Other research and development expenditure is written off in the year in which it is incurred." (*Beecham 1977*) (ii) "Research and development expenditure is written off as incurred against profits of the year." (*Unigate 1977*)

(continued over)

TABLE 3.2 continued

Policy	High-level Technical Language	Low-level Technical Language
	except in so far as it is carried forward as an overhead recovery in the cost of data processing equipment held in fixed assets and finished goods inventory." (*ICL 1977*)	

COMMENT: *Apart from ICL's policy which is probably meaningless to the layperson, there is not much to choose between the other three; in other words we do not see the polarization in this policy as we have in the others. The reason for selecting Pilkington for the high-level category is because it draws the unnecessarily complex distinction between revenue and capital expenditures, a distinction which, at the margin, is far from clear even to accountants. Beecham, on the other hand, does not, even although their policy is identical to that of Pilkington. Unigate wins a mention because of its simplicity and because it actually specifies that the R & D is written off against profits, something Beecham takes for granted.*

Policy	High-level Technical Language	Low-level Technical Language
Deferred taxation	(i) "In the profit and loss account the taxation charge includes a deferred taxation sum calculated on the liability method, arising from deferral of all timing differences and stock relief. In the balance sheet the deferred taxation account also deals with recoverable advance corporation tax. That part of the total deferred liability that, in the opinion of the directors, is unlikely to have to be met in the foreseeable future is reclassified and included in the reserves." (*Woolworth 1978*). (ii) ". . . profits arising from disposals of assets where the gain has been 'rolled over' in accordance with the provisions of Section 33 Finance Act 1965." (*EMI 1977*).	"Fixed assets are, in many cases, written off for tax purposes more rapidly than for accounting purposes. There are also certain items of revenue, and of expense, which are not subject to tax or deductible for tax purposes in the year in which they are dealt with in the accounts. In addition there is tax relief for the appreciation in value of stocks held by U.K. companies. In order to avoid undue distortion, from one year to another, in the taxation charged against profits, the estimated taxation attributable to the net amount of these differences arising in each year, calculated at the rates of tax ruling for that year, is dealt with as deferred taxation." (*Beecham 1977*)

COMMENT: *This topic is extremely complex and Beecham has gone to considerable lengths to explain the circumstances surrounding the entries in the account. Without careful study of such an explanation a lay reader of accounts will never follow the highly technical "wonder from good old Woolies" in the left-hand column, which has all the appearance of an unprocessed crib from ED 19. But the pièce de résistance in technicality comes from the extract taken from EMI's deferred tax policy which assumes knowledge not only of accounting technique but fiscal statute!*

Source: Lothian, A. (1978) Bad language in financial reports. *Accountancy*, November, 42-46.

generally managed by experts. Oversimplification, apart from being prone to unreliability with the prospect of financial loss, would indeed be as great a misrepresentation of reality as is the current, generally inadequate, attempt by the accounting profession to present complex concepts, such as inflation.[29]

As we peruse Table 3.2, it is well to keep in mind a publication — *SSAP2 Disclosure of Accounting Policies* (Accounting Standards Committee) — aimed at the accounting profession, and to note what it has to say about accounting policies. "The accounting policies followed for dealing with items which are judged material or critical in determining profit and loss for the year and in stating the financial position should be disclosed by way of note to the accounts. The explanations should be clear, fair and as brief as possible." So as to introduce realism to the figures in the accounts "current cost" adjustments were advocated in the Hyde report (by the Accounting Standards Committee), though companies are not asked to explain to readers of the accounts why these adjustments are required or what effects they are likely to have, but some companies do.[28]

Shareholders are not alone in experiencing difficulties in organizing perception when at the receiving end of the output of a professional group. A report from the Royal Society, the foremost learned scientific association in the U.K., recently warned scientists to stop baffling the public with jargon and learn to communicate with ordinary people as a matter of urgency. The report goes on to say that the public should be helped to understand the scientific aspects of such issues as acid rain, nuclear power and matters connected within *in vitro* fertilization or animal experimentation, because of the importance of public opinion in influencing the country's decision-making process. Therefore, the language must be simple, free of jargon and intelligible to the general lay public.[30]

Constancy

One way in which people organize their world and make it more understandable is by emphasizing stability and constancy. Constancy refers to situations where we see objects as stable despite great changes in the stimuli reaching the sensory organs. An object remains constant despite variations in its size and this allows us to make an adjustment to the reality confronting us. The following are examples of perceptual constancies.

1. Size. The image on the retina of the eye produced by a nearer object is in fact bigger than that produced by a distant object, but we make allowances for that fact, i.e., we are not normally aware of a football player diminishing in size as he moves away from us into the penalty box. We have a remarkable ability to keep the observed size of things constant in spite of large fluctuations in their retinal image.

2. Shape.   The ability to maintain a constant shape in spite of different retinal images is called "shape constancy." Like size constancy, it acts to our advantage by keeping our world of perception orderly. Imagine the confusion you would experience if your car in a crowded car park was seen as a different object acccording to the different retinal images produced from the different viewing positions—front, side, back, etc.

3. Light.   Different object surfaces absorb different amounts of light. If a surface absorbs all the light that falls on it, it is seen as black, but if it reflects most of the light it is usually seen as white. We make unconscious inferences about the colour and brightness of familiar materials, because we have the advantage of experience of this type of phenomenon. Apparently, however, with unfamiliar materials, constancy still applies.

Constancy can also apply to the perception of people. In one study it was demonstrated that there was considerable stability in people's judgements of politicians before and after reading newspaper reports of the activity of the politician in question. However, it appears that constancy is strongest when there is no great discrepancy between the position of the politician, in terms of his or her behaviour, before and after the newspaper reports. Even where a marked discrepancy exists, some degree of constancy still remains.[31] A detailed account of "person perception" appears later in this chapter.

Visual Illusions
Under certain conditions constancy does not hold good, and what we see appears to be quite different from what we know to be true — these are illusions. Visual illusions are illustrated in Figs. 3.14, 3.15, 3.16, and 3.17.

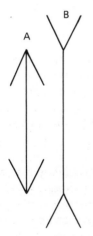

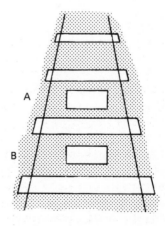

FIG. 3.14   The Müeller-Lyer Illusion.   FIG. 3.15   The Ponzo Illusion.

An illusion can be described as a reliable perceptual error; it is stable and not due to a hasty or careless exploration or processing of stimuli on our part. A widely discussed illusion is the Mueller–Lyer illusion as depicted in Fig. 3.14 (A & B).

Though the lines A and B in Fig. 3.14 are the same length, we see A as the shorter line. In Fig. 3.15 we see the two rectangles, A and B, as different even though they are the same size.

With regard to Figs 3.14 and 3.15, we can measure the lines A and B and likewise the rectangles A and B and establish that they *are* equal in length, yet we cannot, even consciously, make the necessary adjustments to *see* them as equal. It is suggested that the reason for many of the two-dimensional illusions is that we misinterpret them as three-dimensional figures which we expect to obey the laws of perspective.[32] For example, in Fig. 3.15 presumably we make some attempt at scaling sizes in accordance with their perceived distance.

The moon illusion is another illustration of the above principle. In Fig. 3.16 the moon seems to be much larger when it appears on the horizon then when it is high in the sky. But it is the same distance away from us in both cases and the image projected on to the retina is also the same in both cases. Nevertheless we still see the sizes as different.

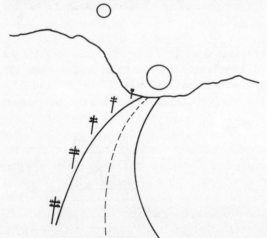

FIG 3.16   The moon illusion.

The Ames Room illusion depicted in Fig. 3.17 shows how the nearest woman in a room seems taller than the woman furthest away, even though both women are about the same size. How do these illusions occur, particularly since we have seen earlier how unconscious inference is introduced in order to maintain constancy? We may attempt to explain the moon illusion as follows. The moon at the horizon looks further away because of all the information we are given on distance from the intervening terrain.

FIG. 3.17   The Ames room. Photograph copyright © Eastern Counties Newspapers Ltd.
Used by permission.

Hence, when we see the moon in this position, we unconsciously "blow up"
the image to compensate for this increased distance.[33]

In much the same way we are fooled into believing that the two women
in the Ames Room in Fig. 3.17, who are the same size, are in a rectangularly
shaped room and that they are at the same distance from us. But the room is
not rectangular; the little woman is much further away than the big woman.
However, constancy is not maintained and our judgement of the relative size
of the two women is distorted because we have not allowed for distance.

Has the concept of the illusion any relevance to business? According to
an academic accountant, probably the most significant "illusion" in accounting today, although the number of investors who experience it is uncertain,
is the conception of profit.[1] Shareholders show an inability to change their
conception of profit when calculated on a current cost basis as opposed to a
historical cost basis, and thus do not appreciate from reading published accounts how much of the profit can be distributed while still providing for the
replacement of the assets. An illustration of this illusion for those with limited financial expertise, appears in Table 3.3.

Although the historical cost basis for calculating profit suggests that
£15,000 is available for distribution as dividends, this fails to take into ac-

TABLE 3.3
What is the Maximum Amount of Profit that
should be Distributed?

	£	£
Sales		110,000
Purchases	80,000	
Less:		
Closing stock	<u>20,000</u>	<u>60,000</u>
Gross profit		50,000
Less:		
Salaries	13,000	
Expenses	12,000	
Depreciation	<u>10,000</u>	<u>35,000</u>
Profit		<u>15,000</u>
Assets:		
Fixed assets at cost	110,000	
Less: Depreciation	<u>10,000</u>	100,000
Stock		20,000
Debtors		15,000
Cash		<u>5,000</u>
Capital		<u>140,000</u>

The replacement cost of –
Fixed assets £120,000
Stock   £ 25,000

Source: Thomas, A.   (1978) Some perceptual illusions in accounting. *Accountancy, 89,* 54-56.

count the replacement cost of assets. Furthermore, the measurement of profit is not an exact science and thus more than one concept of profit may be desirable. However, many investors find this enigmatic.

Illusions can also result from the variety of different accounting policies which are in use. The bases of depreciation, valuation of stock and treatment of development costs differ from company to company and may thus make comparisons misleading.

PERCEPTUAL INTERPRETATION

Having organized our perception, the next step before an appropriate response can be made is interpretation. Perceptual interpretation occurs when we relate stimuli to a cognitive context. The cognitive context consists of various thought processes, ideas and feelings about experiences and happenings in the world around us, which we have built up, based on our own life experiences. It is a primary determinant of perception and response, since it embraces such phenomena as our needs, goals, values, education and training, and accounts for the selectivity in perception that was referred to earlier. As a result the same objective stimulus or happening could be perceived differently by different people. For example, at the scene of an accident it is not unusual to come across conflicting eye-witness reports. Likewise, some people may think of soya in terms of animal feedstuff, while others see it as a cheap inferior meat substitute and still others as an economical meat substitute for human consumption.[8]

Perceptual Errors in Safety

Inaccurate interpretation of stimuli can be of crucial importance at particular moments. At the British Association for the Advancement of Science Conference in 1982 Professor Reason, a psychologist, having closely scrutinized the events leading up to the London (Moorgate) tube disaster of 1975, in which 42 people lost their lives and 74 were injured, challenged the suicide theory put forward at that time. The driver of the train failed to slow down as he approached Moorgate Station, and Professor Reason said that he must have mistaken the stretch of track between Old Street and Moorgate for the distance between Essex Road (the station before Old Street) and Old Street. The distance between Essex Road and Old Street Stations is longer than the distance between Old Street and Moorgate Stations. On the fateful trip, which was the third trip of that day, the driver may have been in a daydream and picked up cues marking the approach to Moorgate Station incorrectly. The lights on the approaching tunnel were turned off, and the cue — i.e., the absence of lights — led him to believe that he was travelling between Essex Road and Old Street Stations instead of between Old Street and Moorgate Stations.

Therefore, the need to slow down was less critical, and the driver continued in a state of reduced vigilance for several seconds. Otherwise, he would have been confronted by a barrage of signals on his arrival at Moorgate Station. When the signals suddenly registered, and the driver realized he had made a mistake, this could have induced a state of "freezing." This amounts to an extreme state of involuntary immobility and is compatible with the fact that the driver had his hands on the controls at the moment of impact. Even a man intent on suicide would automatically have raised his hands to protect his face.[34]

If this account of the circumstances leading up to the Moorgate tube disaster is credible, it highlights the problem of interpretation in perception and the devastating consequences that follow certain types of perceptual error.

Interpretation of Financial Reports

What sort of issues arise when examining the relevance of perceptual interpretation to accounting?

In evaluating a business the users of the annual report and accounts of a company emphasize one or more of the following perceptual categories: (1) profit; (2) growth in sales; (3) capital employed; (4) liquidity; (5) responsibility to employees or customers; (6) profile of the directors, and so on. Generally, the users of accounting information consist of the managers and employees of the company, investors, bankers, other lenders, customers and suppliers. They all have a common interest in the survival and profitability of the company and each group possesses its own particular needs with respect to the information required in order to enhance its bank of information on the health and prospects of the enterprise. Accounting information has an important contribution to make in filling the "knowledge gap" of the person receiving it (the perceiver). Users of accounting information are not really in a position to produce this information for their own use, since among other things they do not normally have the knowledge, skill, experience, resources, and time to do so.

Accountants produce this information on behalf of the user, and so they are entrusted with the task of selecting data and putting it into a form suitable for communication. Accountants are thus well-disposed to influence both what appears in accounting statements or reports and the quality of the information. Like everybody else accountants can only focus attention on a limited number of factors simultaneously and naturally are subject to limitations when observing economic activity. It is unlikely that they perceive all that should be recorded and reported, and that begs an important question: How much vital information is missed? Also, if too much or too little is reported, how will this affect the user's perception of the business?

Since accountants stand to influence the information user's behaviour, it is obviously highly desirable that they display honesty, credibility and reliability in the pursuit of the compilation and dissemination of accounting data. Credibility is a crucial characteristic and on it rests the standing of the information system and the accountants that operate it. The audit, which reports on an annual or more frequent basis, is one means of establishing credibility for the benefit of the user. It is intended to remove the natural uncertainty and anxiety felt about the credibility of accounting information. The internal or external audit is normally undertaken by accountants and in this capacity they exert some influence on the users' decisions by giving them confidence to use the accounting information.

There is, however, scope for the directors of a company to manipulate reported profits by selecting accounting policies that give them the opportunity to provide results that are in their own interest and not necessarily to the advantage of the shareholder. For example, many companies require their divisions to capitalize leases as being, in effect, debt capital; however, in the published accounts such leases are not capitalized, and this results in a favourable impression of the return on capital.[1] Audited accounts may not be regarded as the only source of valid information about a company on which to base decisions about buying and selling shares or whether or not to grant credit to a business. But the question of credibility for alternative sources of information remains. Perhaps a share tip in the *Sunday Times or Observer* may be perceived as having greater validity than one in the *News of The World.*

The interpretation of financial reports and statements appears to be problematic. In an analysis of footnotes which appear at the end of financial statements and reports, it was found that the messages in the footnotes were understood by only a limited number of people of high educational attainment.[35]

In a survey of 301 private shareholders in Scottish and Newcastle Breweries apparently 70% of those questioned doubted their ability to assess potential bankruptcy of the company on the basis of the way in which the information they receive is presented.[27] A mere 39% found accounting information relevant to their investment decisions, though the manner in which company reports were actually used in making investment decisions was not investigated. The term "current assets" had no meaning for 57% of respondents, and only 28% of respondents could give a reasonable definition of depreciation. The chairman's report was read by 52% of respondents, 39% of respondents read the profit and loss account thoroughly, but only 29% read the balance sheet thoroughly. According to 53% of respondents the reports should be less technical, written in layperson's language and summarized or, alternatively, they should be augmented by a simpler version. Most respondents merely glanced through the annual report, paying greatest attention to the chairman's summary of the main events of the year and his views on the prospects for the future. This study identified not only the severe difficulties encountered by private shareholders in interpreting financial statements, but also the fact that available financial information about companies is generally little used among the largest single important group of financial-report users.

It also suggests that reporting accountants are failing to communicate effectively with a large number of individuals and that existing financial reports have become documents which are prepared by accountants for accountants. The researchers believe that the communication gap between companies and their private shareholders is so serious that the accountancy profession must give attention to a number of suggestions. These are that existing statements should be simplified, terms used in financial reports should be defined, reported financial results should be commented on and explained, and alternative systems of reporting which may mean more to the unsophisticated user of financial reports ought to be explored.

Readability

Making something readable and comprehensible is no easy matter. Layout, legibility of type, an interesting approach, absence of difficult words and ease with which a passage can be read are obviously important factors. Readability formulae, such as the Flesch's readability formula, have met with a varied reception; they have been welcomed as guides to good writing and attacked vigorously as mechanistic devices used to stifle creativity and debase literature.[36] When the objective is to maximize the communication of simple messages — such as those found in advertisements, cookery books, instruction leaflets and training manuals — they are said to be appropriate. However, literary or scientific writings may lose in aesthetic value or in intellectual precision when oversimplified.[6]

The Flesch readability formula yields two measures — a "reading ease" score and a "human interest" score. The reading ease score is based on the average word length in syllables and the average sentence length in words. The human interest score is derived from the percentage of personal words, such as proper nouns and personal pronouns, and the percentage of personal sentences, such as spoken sentences, questions and other remarks directed to the reader, and exclamations. These measures are used on a continuous 100-word passage. When financial reports of companies were studied using the Flesch readability formula it was found that over a period of time these reports had become less and less readable and as a consequence less comprehensible.[37] When measures of readability, such as the Flesch readability formula, were applied to the P1 tax guide, the overall results suggested that the guide is easier to read than *The Times,* but significantly harder than *The Sun.*[16]

Interpretation of Marketing Information

In this section brand image, price and risk are discussed as important factors perceived by the consumer of products.

1. Brand Image.   It is conceivable that perceived differences between products rest more with the efforts of marketeers interested in building up a distinctive brand image than in the differences in the physical make-up of the products. Beer drinkers, who were credited with the ability to perceive differences between certain categories of beer on the basis of such characteristics as bitterness, strength, body, after-taste, foam, aroma and carbonation, were asked to drink from unlabelled bottles of beer and distinguish differences in taste on a brand basis. None of the drinkers placed their preferred brand ahead of the others, and carbonation was the only characteristic where there was a significant difference noted between the beers tasted. When the same drinkers drank from labelled bottles, there was a marked tendency to express preferences for their favourite brand.[38]

There are a number of complex and interrelated factors that influence brand perception — i.e., the appeal of the label and packaging; the quality of advertising associated with the product; the consumer's experience of the product and disposition towards it; the product's reliability and the personal satisfaction derived from its use; specification of attractive features of a product; and the desirable health or environmental factors associated with the product — such as health foods and lead-free petrol.[10] Another aspect of brand perception is quality. Overstatements by a manufacturer of the product's quality tended to produce more favourable evaluations of the product and higher expectations of its performance in the mind of the consumer. When the product, in this case a tape-recorder, did not perform well, the high expectations did not lead to disappointment and low evaluation of the product.[39]

2. Price.   Information on price produces different responses among consumers and perception of price can easily be distorted. Sometimes people think that the higher the price the greater the risk if things do not work out, but at other times it is felt that the higher price produces less risk because of the association of an expensive product with greater reliability and quality. When different types of product were presented at three different price levels — low, medium and high — it was found that 50% of the people tested chose the high-priced tennis rackets and portable stereo equipment, while 60% chose the low-priced toothpaste, coffee and suntan lotion. The high-priced products were perceived as possessing quality and greater financial risk, as well as being socially conspicuous. The consumers who chose the low-priced products perceived an insignificant relationship between price and quality and felt that the choice of brand had little social meaning and that the wrong purchase would not be disastrous.[40] The more conscious consumers are of prices the more likely they are to have a developed price perception. A price that is compatible with quality is important for some consumers. Traditionally Marks and Spencer's stores appeal to consumers who stress competitive prices in relation to quality, while Tesco's stores used to attract consumers who placed the primary emphasis on price. With the growth of competition on the High Street the situation depicted here may not be as clear-cut today.

A strong emphasis on price generally comes from the full-time housewife who has the time to shop around, whereas the consumer who goes out to work full-time may be less discriminating in this respect. However, the situation is likely to be more complex than that; perceptions of locational convenience, service, quality of the product, cleanliness of the shop, type of customer, and absence of queues at the check-out point are also important considerations. Apparently a number of studies point to the importance of price perception in relation to the quality of the product.[41] A high price is sometimes considered desirable for cosmetic products, such as perfumes, which puts them into the luxury class, though this is unlikely in the case of related products such as suntan lotion or hand cream.

3. Risk. The consumer tries to avoid psychological insecurity, does not like uncertainty, but has to live with the fact that all purchase decisions have unanticipated consequences. Certain purchases are high in psychological and social risks, such as purchases of clothing. Since clothing is so intricately tied up with our self-image, and the image others have of us, it is a risk purchase to some extent. Frequently there are risks attached to purchases, but in order to reduce risks we can engage in information-seeking. A particular man may pay £10 for a London theatre seat to see a stage musical. He was initially attracted to the musical by one particular song from the show which he had already heard and liked. However, he was disappointed to find that a number of other songs from the show did not live up to his expectations. In future he is more likely to establish the quality of the repertoire of songs rather than just one song in order to reduce the risk.

To remove uncertainty about the outcome of a purchase, the following avenues are open to the consumer: speak to somebody with experience of the product; read an analysis of the product if, for example, it is featured on the pages of the magazine *Which*; read a detailed description of the product in an advertising leaflet, brochure, newspaper or magazine; and finally, if possible, take advantage of a demonstration of the product. Another way to remove uncertainty is to develop loyalty to a brand known to be reliable. Sometimes the consumer is given an opportunity to try a new product without having to take risks. This could arise when the manufacturer distributes a free sample — e.g., a soap or detergent. Where a consumer has a strong brand loyalty, this might be the only way of getting him or her to sample an alternative brand. Risk perception varies from one individual to another, and whereas some consumers actively engage in information-seeking in order to reduce risks, others seem to enjoy the opportunity to sample new products and make purchase decisions with little or no attempt to reduce risk.

Interpretation by Computer

In the age of the computer the interpretation of stimuli is not confined only to the human being. A computerized surveillance system, consisting of a camera linked to a database, which contains the registration numbers of all recently stolen vehicles, has been developed by scientists at the British Home Office.[42] The camera scans a stream of traffic and the computer checks the car numbers. When the computer comes across the number of a car reported as stolen, it automatically alerts the nearest police station or patrol. The whole process takes little more than a second. The computer supplies the police with a full description of the vehicle, and even the traffic lane in which it is travelling. The thief who tries to beat the system by using false number plates will not succeed because the computer has access to every valid registration number ever issued. If the camera picks up a number that is not on file, the alarm will be raised automatically. Stealing a car at night is not a way to get round the system because the camera uses infra-red light. However, dirty number plates or bad weather can create a problem. The expected recognition rate is 70%.

PERSON PERCEPTION

As an extension of the previous section on *Perceptual Interpretation* we now turn to social interaction in the context of the interpretations we place on other people's behaviour. Person perception is concerned with the manner in which we perceive the personal characteristics of others, in particular their current mood and their total personality. Various dynamic cues — such as posture; gesture; body movement; facial expression; direction of gaze; tone of voice; rate, amount and fluency of speech; orientation; and distance — are picked up in the course of social interaction and they influence the interpretations placed on other people's behaviour. However, in a number of circumstances, such as those described below, misinterpretations are likely to arise.

Implicit Personality

Implicit personality theory is part of our cognitive set; which, in essence, means a set of concepts and assumptions used to describe, compare and understand people. Implicit personality theories vary with the individual and the differences are greatest between people of different cultures. In one study a number of children at a summer camp were asked to describe the others in their own words. There were wide variations in the descriptions used by different children to describe any specific child, but is was found that each child used the traits important to his or her central personality theory when describing all the other children.[43] In attributing characteristics to people we can arrive not only at static perceptual judgements (e.g., enduring characteristics such as age, beliefs, ability, manner, personality traits) but also at dynamic perceptual judgements of characteristics that change, such as specific rather than general actions, moods, emotions and intentions.[44]

Logical Error

Implicit personality theory could lead us to form hypotheses or assumptions about what traits go together in a person. Almost intuitively we use this interpretation to form an extensive and consistent view of other people when faced with incomplete information. This is often referred to as the logical error, the assumption being that certain traits are always found together. An experiment was conducted to test this principle in which students on a psychology course were given descriptions of a guest speaker before he addressed the class. He was described to one half of the class as "warm" and to the other half as "cold." The lecturer then entered the class and led a discussion for about 20 minutes. When he left the classroom the students were asked to describe him. The students who were told that he was going to be "cold" were more likely to attribute to him traits such as self-centredness, unsociability, humourlessness, and ruthlessness than were the students who were told he was "warm". The students who thought of the lecturer as "warm" were also more likely to interact with him during the discussion.[45]

What appears to be happening is that changes in person perception arise from varying even minor cues or stimuli, leading to a totally altered view of the person perceived.

Halo Effect
Another tendency similar to logical error is called the halo effect. This materializes when we perceive people in terms of the concepts of good and bad; all good qualities are possessed by the former and all bad qualities by the latter. Somebody given an adverse evaluation at a particular stage of his or her career may find that subsequently, when his or her profile has improved, an evaluation bears the scars of the earlier assessment. Likewise, in an interview situation, if an interviewer perceives in the interviewee a desirable attribute similar to one of his or her own, as a result he or she may make a favourable overall assessment. The reverse would be true when a deficiency is identified at the outset. There is evidence to suggest that our perceptions of people are markedly influenced by our initial good/bad evaluations of them. It has been suggested that our overall attitudes towards others can to a large extent be determined by our evaluations of them along three dimensions: (1) activity (active vs. passive); (2) strength (strong vs. weak); and (3) evaluative (good vs. bad).[46] The third dimension is considered the most influential.

Stereotyping
Another phenomenon similar to logical error is stereotyping. This is connected with our tendency to label people with traits or qualities which typically belong to a reference group. For example, we may consider a Scot to be mean or thrifty, or a Jew to be a shrewd businessperson. Therefore we attribute to a member of the race in question the characteristics of the stereotype. Biased perception arises when we rely on the stereotyped image and ignore critical information concerning the individual. Stereotyping does not necessarily result only in the creation of negative images; they can also be positive. Neither is it a wasteful activity, as one study has shown. Subjects

described a student in accordance with a stereotype, as they had no further information on which to work. At a later stage when the subjects became acquainted with the student, they described him for a second time and on average it was found that the initial descriptions were the more accurate.

In connection with stereotyping, a study was carried out in which students whose attitudes towards blacks were known to researchers rated a number of pictures according to 25 traits.[47] The pictures depicted ten Negroid faces and five Caucasian faces. The Negroid faces reflected a wide range of Negroid features. Ten of the traits described characteristics of the individual which could be determined from the features of the Negroid faces. The other 15 were personality traits widely accepted as part of the stereotype of the black.

Once a student selected a picture as that of a Negroid face there was a tendency to assign to it the personality traits associated with blacks as he or she construed them. The student paid no attention whatsoever to the individual differences depicted in the pictures. The results of the study were the same for students with either a less-pronounced prejudice or a well-developed prejudice. Stereotyping occurred because of a strong tendency to assign traits to an individual on the basis of group membership, despite the fact that individuals vary in the extent to which they exhibit the characteristics of their group. What we should try to do is to examine to what extent our impression of others is based on stereotype alone, so that we can make adjustments accordingly.

How do we react when we are presented with information about an individual which contradicts our stereotyped image? The answer can best be presented by reference to a study.[48] Two groups of college students were presented with different descriptions of a working man as follows.

Group I	*Group II*
He works in a factory, reads a newspaper, goes to movies, is of average height, cracks jokes, is intelligent, strong and active.	He works in a factory, reads a newspaper, goes to movies, is of average height, cracks jokes, is strong and active.

The only difference in the descriptions given to the groups was that for Group I the man was also described as intelligent. The actual description given by the students of Group II in response to the above stimulus typified the description of the average American working man, i.e., likeable and well-liked, mildly sociable, healthy, happy, uncomplicated and well-adjusted, down to earth, not very intelligent but tries to keep abreast of current trends, interested in sports and engages in simple pleasures. The introduction of the word "intelligent" in Group I had the effect of disturbing the group members' set of beliefs about factory workers, but most of them tried to protect their original systems of cognition by the following means.

1. Denial of the influential quality of intelligence: "He is intelligent but not so much, since he works in a factory."

2. Modification of the influential quality of intelligence: "He is intelligent, but doesn't possess initiative to rise above his group."

3. Denial of the fact that he is a shop-floor worker: some students maintained that the man was not a worker by promoting him to a foreman.

4. Recognizing the incongruity but adhering to the original cognition: "The traits seem to be conflicting but most factory workers I have heard about are not too intelligent."

The four responses reported above serve as a defence of the stereotype. In fact this finding suggests that stereotypes can prevent accurate perception in a number of different ways.

Assumed Similarity

This is the tendency to see others as having characteristics more like our own than is really the case.[49] We are inclined to project our own emotional or motivational state on to others. In an experiment where subjects were anticipating the receipt of a painful electric shock it was found that those subjects who reported feeling fear themselves were the subjects who predicted others would be afraid. In other experiments it was shown that those who were asked to predict the behaviour of others usually tended to make predictions more like their own behaviour than like the behaviour of the person about whom the prediction was made. This evidence may be explained as follows: we operate the *ego*-defence mechanism of projection (see chapter 1) by attributing to others the motives and emotions which we possess but feel uncomfortable about, and we act relying on our own experience with the disadvantage of not knowing the internal state of the other person.

Some of the pitfalls in person perception have been identified here, and there are a number of situations in business where employees make unrealistic generalizations about the personal characteristics of those with whom they come into contact.

Attribution Theory

A variation of the theories of person perception is attribution. Attribution theory has been proposed to develop explanations of how we judge people differently depending on the meaning we attribute to a given behaviour.[50] The theory suggests that as we observe a person's behaviour, we try to establish whether it was caused by internal or external forces. When something is internally caused, it is under the personal control of the individual; if it is externally caused, it is the result of the power of the situation which confronts the individual.

This can be illustrated by the use of a simple example. An employee is late for work. One might ask whether the cause is attributed to sleeping in because of being at a late-night party the previous night, or whether it is a matter of being caught up in a traffic queue due to a road accident. If the former were the case, that would be an internal interpretation. If the latter, it would amount to an external interpretation.

As a broad generalization we tend, as observers of social behaviour, to assume that other people's behaviour is internally controlled, but for ourselves we exaggerate the extent to which our own behaviour is externally determined.[51] The tendency to take more account of the situation in explaining our own behaviour and less account of the situation in explaining other people's behaviour is sometimes called the fundamental attribution error. In appraising the performance of an employee in an organization, effort or ability is often referred to when explaining performance with reference to internal factors. But when performance is explained with reference to external factors, often luck or the difficulty of the job is mentioned. Obviously the attitudes of the appraiser to the person being appraised will have an influence on the final outcome.[52] Prejudice could be a factor in determining whether an event is seen as either internally or externally caused. For example, in one study the successful performance of female managers was attributed to luck and being an easy task (an external interpretation) by prejudiced male managers, but in the eyes of unprejudiced male managers it was attributed to skill and hard work (an internal interpretation).[53]

The concept of attribution is said to be subjected to the following considerations.[54]

1. Distinctiveness.   This refers to how different the behaviour being observed is from other behaviour. Is it unusual or not? For example, if an employee's attendance record is exemplary, and this is reinforced by an overall satisfactory performance at work, a recent bout of absenteeism could be considered unusual. Therefore, in these circumstances the observer attaches an external attribution to this behaviour (i.e., the absenteeism is outside the control of the employee). If, however, the absenteeism fits into a general pattern, and is not unique, an internal attribution will be attached to the behaviour in question (i.e., the employee is personally responsible for his or her behaviour).

2. Consensus.   If everyone who is faced with a similar situation reacts in the same way, we can conclude that the behaviour shows consensus. For example, a particular employee's late arrival at work is observed. When the observer establishes that all those who took the same route to work as the particular employee were also late, possibly because of delays due to bad weather, the conditions necessary for consensus arise. If consensus is high, one is likely to attach an external attribution to the particular employee's lateness. However, if the other employees who travelled the same route arrived at work on time, the consensus factor would be absent and an internal interpretation could be attributed to the particular employee's lateness (i.e., it was his or her fault).

3. Consistency.   The observer of a person's behaviour takes consistency into account. For example, if an employee is responding in the same way over a period of time (e.g., he or she comes in late to work regularly over a six – month period), his or her behaviour is consistent. This could be contrasted with an example of an employee arriving late on the odd occasion. The more consistent the behaviour the more likely the observer is inclined to attribute the behaviour in question to internal causes.

4. Summary.   The above considerations focus on judging actions in a situational context. An attribution perspective is important because the way an observer perceives an action or behaviour will influence his or her response and provide a foundation for predicting future events. Therefore, it has significance in a motivational sense. Of course there is a danger in attributing causation to particular actions or behaviour, because we may end up basing our attribution on an over-simplification of reality. As a result, there may be bias in the way we judge others. People in organizations are continuously judging each other. Superiors judge the performance of subordinates, employees generally judge the amount of effort their colleagues put into their work, and new members of staff are judged by their peers.

The Selection Interview

One of the best known forums for judging the suitability of someone to join an organization or progress within it is the selection interview. The selection interview entails interaction between people, and has been referred to as a "conversation with a purpose." Achieving the purpose of the interview involves complex transactions of obtaining and giving information. Both the interviewer and interviewee bring hopes, fears, expectations, misconceptions, and many other cognitions to the interview process. By using appropriate behavioural strategies, the interviewer and interviewee hope to realize their objectives, and roles are adopted to further the aim of a successful outcome. If the parties to the interview process act skilfully, this should improve the quality of the interactive episode.[55]

However, a satisfactory outcome to the interview process also requires adequate preparation for the actual event. The interviewer should be well briefed, rehearse the interview, and anticipate the actions required. In a job interview it is important to put across information about the organization and an adequate description of the advertised job. The skilful performance of both parties, referred to above, is a function of skills connected with self-awareness, awareness of social interaction processes, and self-presentation based on an appropriate foundation of knowledge or information.

It is suggested that research on interviewing, as a device to select people for jobs, is fragmented and produces findings of little value to selectors.[56] However, on the basis of a recent comprehensive review of evidence about selection interviews, it was concluded that the following features were present:

1. The selection interview offers some insight into a person's sociability and verbal fluency from a sample of his or her total behaviour.

2. Though the selection interview may not be a valid process, it is easy to arrange and interviewers have faith and confidence in their judgement in interview situations.

3. Though the selection interview may not be a valid process, it presents an opportunity to sell the job to the candidates being interviewed. It is difficult to identify an equally efficient alternative.[57]

Apart from the modest claims to success stated above, the interview process has been subjected to some fundamental criticisms. Many of these criticisms are levelled at the interviewer. In panel interviews a proper role for each interviewer is sometimes not adequately specified. This is compounded by poor interviewing skills of individual panel members. Generally, there are too many occasions when interviewers spend time on irrelevant matters, missing the opportunity to explore a significant point in detail. Also, the public relations aspect of interviewing is ignored.[55] Other criticisms hinge on the following observations.[54]

1. Interviewers make perceptual judgements that are often inaccurate.

2. Interviewers are poor at reaching agreement when rating interviewees.

3. Different interviewers see different things in the same interviewee, and thus arrive at different conclusions.

4. Interviewers arrive at early impressions that quickly become entrenched in their perceptual judgement. Negative impressions arising from negative information received early in the interview can become more heavily weighted than the same information given later.

5. Many decisions are arrived at by interviewers early in the interview and change very little after the first five minutes of the interview. So the absence of unfavourable characteristics early on in the interview could act to the advantage of the interviewee.

COMMUNICATION PROCESSES

Perception is an important part of the communication process, and at work you will find different types of communication. That which is officially inspired is often referred to as formal communication, while communication that is unofficial, unplanned and spontaneous is classified as informal. A communication system can transmit information up, down and sideways within an organization on a one-way or two-way basis. When communication is one way there is no opportunity to receive a reaction from the receiver of the message. But in two-way communication the receiver of the message can provide a response and is encouraged to do so.

Ways of Communicating

There are many ways to communicate. When we use the spoken word, either face-to-face, in a small group or over the telephone, the sender of a message has the opportunity to observe feedback, answer questions and provide additional information by way of clarification. It is often faster than other forms of communication and has the advantage of being personal. For example, the safety practitioner may use the spoken word when he or she feels it necessary to impress upon a supervisor the absolute necessity of maintaining permanent machine guards in conditions where a certain laxity with regard to their use has developed. A disadvantage of the spoken word is the absence of a written record of the dialogue, though conversations can, of course, be taped.

A formal meeting usually consists of both the spoken and written word. The written component is the agenda, the minutes of the last meeting and papers previously distributed. The meeting itself relies substantially on the spoken word. A meeting of a safety committee is an example of a forum to exchange information on health and safety matters, and decide on appropriate action. In certain meetings visual aids could be used to emphasize technical issues. Apart from the use of the written word at meetings, a letter, memorandum or report allows the communicator to organize his or thoughts carefully, and provides a written record of happenings and transactions for future reference.

Although written communication is an impersonal process, it is generally possible to provide more information to the receiver by this means than through the spoken word. Written communication is somewhat more time-consuming than the spoken word, and it provides little opportunity for the sender to observe feedback and to provide clarification. Written communication amounts to a one-way communication system with a delayed response. Management information systems are an example of an elaborate interlocking system of written communication, aided by computerized and telecommunication systems.

Effective Communication

This amounts to putting a thought or feeling into a message, and transmitting the message so that the receiver interprets the message as intended.

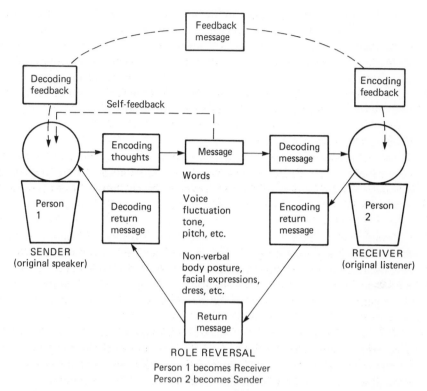

FIG. 3.18   The communication cycle. Source: Curtis, J. D. & Detert, R. A. (1981) *How to relax – a holistic approach to stress management*. Palo Alto, Cal. Mayfield Publishing. p.177.

The communication cycle appears in Fig. 3.18.

The message is transmitted to the receiver by word symbols, body postures, tone of voice, fluctuations in the voice, and various gestures. Other manifestations of non-verbal communication are: appearance; dress; facial expression; mannerisms; physical proximity; expression in the eyes; and attentiveness. Many of the senses are involved in sending and receiving messages. As can be seen in Fig. 3.18 a number of steps are involved in the communication process.

1. Have a clear idea of what you want to convey in your message.

2. Encode the communication by putting the ideas into a suitable form. Choose the proper words to convey the idea you have in mind, preferably using the language of the receiver.

3. Choose the most appropriate communication medium to transmit the message. You may ask yourself with regard to oral communication, "Shall I convey information by calling a meeting or, alternatively, use the telephone?" In the event of using the written word, the communication

could take the form of a memorandum, a letter, a report, a telex, or some form of electronic transmission. Sometimes we build redundancy into the transmission process by providing the same information in more than one form. In a specific safety sense, the word "danger" can be flashed on a screen and at the same time an audible signal denoting danger can be used.

4. Make sure the message gets to the receiver, though the receiver should take it upon him or herself to listen to or take note of the message.

5. The communication should be decoded in such a way that the intended meaning is actually conveyed.

6. If the receiver is to take a specific course of action after receiving the message, check that this is done. Of course, the receiver may not be required to take positive action, other than to store the information for future use.

7. Elicit feedback from the receiver.

Understanding is a critical factor in the communication process, and it is often said that people are only 25% efficient when they are engaged in listening and remembering. Vital information with respect to safety hazards should be repeated at intervals. The FIDO principle is worth noting. This states that learning through communication is enhanced by:

Frequency: the more often a message is repeated, the more likely it is to be remembered;

Intensity: the more vivid, enthusiastic, personalized and positive a communication is, the better it will be received and remembered;

Duration: short, pointed messages are more likely to get the attention, understanding and retention needed for good communication;

Over Again: learning is enhanced by spaced and frequent repetition; messages are imprinted in the mind bit by bit.

The process of projecting good safety practice could lend itself to many different types of communication and this could be reinforced by the good example set by executives in matters connected with safety regulations and practice. The safety and health aspects of company policy and safety standards should be well communicated, particularly to new and transferred employees. In job training the positive relationship between safety and efficiency or productivity should also be well communicated.

Communication Barriers
A number of pitfalls can hinder effective communication:

1. The communicator may be unable to think clearly about what he or she wants to say.

2. Though the communicator may have good ideas, he or she has dif-

ficulty in encoding the message properly, i.e., in putting ideas into a suitable form of words. Likewise, the communicator may be unable to put him or herself into the position of the receiver and fails to empathize, and as a result writes or talks as if he or she was communicating with him or herself and no one else.

3. Transmission of the message can be interrupted by "noise". There are two categories of noise, one physical and the other psychological. Physical noise could be interference on a telephone line or in a television receiver. It is comparatively easy to recognize and eliminate. Psychological noise is different and is more difficult to cope with. It consists of biases, attitudes, and beliefs held by people in the communication process and can block the transmission of ideas. Information overload could also lead to noise. With regard to the design of displays, one should endeavour not to undermine seriously the worker's reliability by providing too much information or providing information that cannot conveniently, easily and accurately be used; in such circumstances the excessive information has become noise. Overload arises because of the temptation to include certain items on the basis of convenience, or when we act in the belief that there is a remote chance that the worker may find use for the information sometime.

4. Selectivity in the reception, interpretation and retention of information is exercised. A manager receives a report on many facets of the company's operations. There is advice in the report about ways in which he or she should execute his or her managerial responsibilities for health and safety at work. This particular manager happens to be very interested in financial issues and ignores the safety considerations. Because of the manager's financial orientation, he or she may be adept at seeing the financial implications of various operational issues, but turns a blind eye to the critical safety matters. Likewise he or she tends to be better at remembering the financial rather than the safety implications.

5. The receiver of the message is too quick to jump to conclusions or becomes defensive. The speaker may be offended by an unjustified interruption or a premature assessment of what he or she has reputedly said. The quality of the delivery may be affected accordingly. If the *ego* of the receiver is bruised by what has been said, feelings of insecurity, inferiority or hurt can develop. The receiver adopts a defensive stance, and may strike back even though the speaker is offering a legitimate viewpoint or a constructive criticism. This can undermine the quality of the communication process. In the earlier section on interpersonal processes, the effects of stereotyping and the halo effect were found to distort interpersonal perception.

6. An unsuitable environment acts as an impediment to good communication. A noisy factory setting is not the best place for the safety practitioner to give serious advice on health and safety matters to a chargehand or supervisor with a lukewarm attachment to such advice.

7. A misinterpretation of feedback from the receiver of the message arises, or there is no perceptible reaction from the receiver. In either case, the sender of the message is denied insight into the position of the receiver with regard to a particular communication.

8. Rumour fills the gaps in the formal communication system, and is normally associated with the grapevine. The grapevine, however, which is part of the informal communication network, often feeds accurate information into the system. By definition rumour is false information, and it frequently arises because people are kept in the dark about important matters.

Communication Problems

Perceptual problems are frequently encountered in organizations; these are often referred to as communication problems. Communication within the finance department of business is likely to be better than between groups drawn from marketing and finance departments. Likewise communication between personnel within a geographical location is usually better than between groups in different locations. Sometimes we find the communication between the "staff specialist" in management accounting or product planning and the line manager — e.g., production manager — leaves much to be desired, and is likely to be aggravated by a difference of outlook or orientation. Another area which is often identified as a source of perceptual problems is the relationship between superiors and subordinates within the hierarchy of organizations.

In a study of 58 pairs of managers, who were asked various questions about the duties of subordinates, only about half were able to agree on their duties.[58] When it came to questions on the difficulties or obstacles that interfere with the performance of subordinates, only 8% of the pairs of managers were in agreement on more than half the topics discussed. Here we find that either the subordinates were not fully aware of what their superiors expected of them or the superiors did not know what work the subordinates were required to do. Whatever the cause, we would like to know more about the quality of communication that exists between the two with regard to specifying the requirements of the job of the subordinate. Obviously part of the problem arises from authority and status differences which inhibit individuals from communicating freely with their superiors about important job matters.

In a study of a large public utility top management and foremen were asked to express their ideas on how free the foremen felt when discussing important aspects of their jobs with top management. About 90% of top management felt that foremen were very free to discuss such issues with them, but only 67% of the foremen felt this to be so. The same question was asked of foremen and workers, and this time about 85% of foremen felt that the workers were very free to discuss important issues with them, but only

51% of the workers believed this to be so. Perhaps superiors are more likely than subordinates to believe in high quality communication processes. It was also found that there were marked differences in perception between superiors and subordinates when it came to assessing the nature of consultation. For example, 70% of the top managers believed they almost always got their subordinates' ideas and opinions in problem-solving sessions on the job, but only 52% of foremen believed this to be so. Like the top managers, 73% of the foremen believed that they almost always got their subordinates' ideas and opinions in problem-solving sessions on the job, but only 16% of the workers believed this to be so.[59]

In a survey of the opinions of full-time or part-time safety managers, together with a cross section of shopfloor workers in 26 factories in the London area, it was concluded that there were problems of communication with respect to safety.[60] There was profound ignorance among employees about the safety policy, but those who were aware of safety policy obtained it from a notice-board or from a personal copy of the document. Few employees knew about the Health and Safety at Work Act 1974, except that they were aware of the fact that an individual employee could incur criminal liability. There was surprising ignorance of the operation of safety committees, and there were problems with the reporting of hazards. In fact many employees were not very conversant with the business conducted in safety committees, though they were aware of the existence of them. Likewise, there were problems with reporting procedures for accidents, and there appeared to be little knowledge of first aid facilities. Apparently trade unions were a rather more important source of information on the Health and Safety at Work Act than management, though in one company management was a significantly more important source than trade unions.

One remedy for misperceptions encountered by managers and others in organizations, is a comparatively new technique developed at the Durham Business School.[61] The technique is known as the "Expectations Approach" and has been widely tested. It is claimed that it is operationally possible to audit the quality of communication among senior and middle management in any organization, and where poor communication is found this is the starting point to provide a basis for improving inter-personal communication. For a communication auditing system to be useful requires an effective audit of what Manager X says he or she wants from Manager Y, and what Manager Y thinks Manager X wants from him or her. The Expectations Approach to auditing communication systems obtains information in the simplest way possible. Each manager in the group whose communication is to be audited goes through the following motions:

1. Each manager writes down the expectations that he or she holds of each member of the group, identifying the various things others are expec-

ted to do (e.g., to operate equipment and machinery efficiently and effectively).

2. The manager then writes down the expectations that he or she perceives each member of the group has of the manager, identifying the various things others expect him or her to do (e.g., provide the accountant with budget targets for inclusion in the master budget).

After writing down the various expectations, they can be processed and filed on a computer. Each participating manager receives an Expectations Approach communication audit report which shows the expectations held of him or herself, in the audit data. This technique enables managers to identify rapidly where communication channels have broken down. The report gives no indication of whether or not the expressed expectations are organizationally appropriate, but it does highlight the need to analyse whether or not communication should exist between the two managers concerned. The Expectations Approach places the responsibility for auditing a manager's communication upon the individual manager as opposed to the manager's superior or some other person. This is said to be advantageous for a number of reasons. Managers are immersed in the detailed content of the job so their views about the job are crucial; they are well placed to judge how effective the other person's expectation of themselves are; they are obviously concerned about how desirable and reasonable the expectations are, and they have a vested interest in this accuracy.

SUMMARY

The basic processes in perception are reception of stimulus, attention, organization, interpretation and response. Stimuli are picked up by the senses which consist of vision, hearing, smell, taste, touch, warmth, cold, pain, kinesthesis, and vestibular. Safety practitioners, advertisers and producers of accounting information recognize the importance of attracting the attention of the perceiver, although this is not always easy. In this context absolute and differential thresholds are crucial. When they fluctuate this is known as sensory adaptation. The internal state of the individual is something else to consider when trying to attract the attention of the perceiver.

Before interpreting the information contained in a stimulus, it has to be organized. The Gestalt Laws of Organization govern the organization of perception. Marketeers and accountants are naturally concerned with the question of grouping stimuli into an organized whole, but sometimes problems arise. For example, a problem arises when a high level of technical language is used in financial reports. The individual adheres to constancy when organizing stimuli, though this can be undermined by illusions. Illusions can result from the use of different accounting bases.

Perceptual Interpretation follows organization and various cognitive aspects of our total personality are activated so that meaning can be ascribed to the information at our disposal. The interpretation of safety signals, published accounts and tax forms can present some difficulties. The perception of a brand, the price of a product and the risks attached to a purchase are important considerations for the consumer. The interpretation of stimuli by a computerized surveillance system is a feature of the era of new technology.

In person perception the following factors feature in a prominent way: implicit personality, logical error, halo effect, stereotyping and assumed similarity. An additional factor is the concept of attribution. The selection interview is a good example of person perception at work. Finally, perceptual issues in organizations were explored through the medium of communication processes. Techniques such as the Expectations Approach can assist with minimizing the negative aspects of organizational communication.

QUESTIONS

1. Identify the senses considered most crucial for registering stimuli of a safety, accounting or marketing nature.
2. What steps can the marketeer, accountant and safety practitioner take to attract the attention of the target audience?
3. Are there any circumstances in which a consumer can perceive below the absolute threshold?
4. Distinguish between absolute and differential thresholds.
5. The disposition or orientation of the perceiver of cost and revenue statements is crucial. Discuss.
6. Using accounting illustrations, explain what is meant by the organization of perception.
7. Identify circumstances when constancy is no longer valid. How do illusions manifest themselves in accounting?
8. In what way does the private shareholder experience difficulties in interpreting financial reports?
9. What significance does the consumer attach to the brand image and price of a product, and the risk associated with it, before making a purchase?
10. What insights derived from interpersonal perception should a sales representative, who is concerned with improving his or her social or communication skills, take into account?
11. What do you understand by attribution theory?
12. Assess the strengths and weaknesses of the selection interview.
13. Examine typical communication problems that arise in organizations and suggest ways and means of solving them.

REFERENCES

1. Thomas, A. (1978) Some perceptual illusions in accounting. *Accountancy*, June, 54–56.
2. Held, R. & Hein, A. (1963) Movement-produced stimulation in the development of visually guided behaviour. *Journal of Comparative and Physiological Psychology*, 5, 56, 872–876.
3. Gibson, E.J. (1969) *Principles of Perceptual Learning and Development.* New York: Appleton-Century-Crofts.
4. Voke, J. (1982) Colour vision problems at work. *Health and Safety at Work*, January, 27–28.
5. Feldman, M. (1971) *Psychology in the Industrial Environment.* London: Butterworth.
6. Anastasi, A. (1974) *Fields of Applied Psychology.* New York: McGraw-Hill.
7. Berg, D.H. (1967) An enquiry into the effect of exposure to advertisements on subsequent perception of similar advertisements. *Journal of Applied Psychology*, 51, 503–508.
8. Oliver, G. (1980) *Marketing Today*, London: Prentice-Hall.
9. Starch, D. (1961) Do inside positions differ in readership? Danial Starch and Staff. (Consultancy Report cited in Anastasi A, *Fields of Applied Psychology.* McGraw-Hill, 1979).
10. Berkman, H.W. & Gilson, C.C. (1978) *Consumer Behaviour: Concepts and Strategies.* California: Dickenson Publishing Co.
11. Hayne, C. (1981) Light and colour. *Occupational Health*, April, 198–204.
12. Christensen, J.M. (1981) The human element in safe man-machine systems. *Professional Safety*, March, 27–32.
13. Kanugo, R.N. & Pang, S. (1973) Effect of human models on perceived product quality. *Journal of Applied Psychology*, 57, 172–178.
14. Brown, P. (1970) The impact of the annual net profit report on the stock market. *The Australian Accountant*, July, 277–283.
15. Lothian, N. (1978) Bad language in financial reports. *Accountancy*, November, 42–46.
16. Lewis, A. & James, S. (1981) Understanding tax forms. *Certified Accountant, February* 48–52.
17. Day, R.H. (1969) *Human Perception.* Sydney: J. Wiley & Son.
18. Bobbitt, H.R., Breinholt, R.H., Doktor, R.H. & McNaul, J.P. (1978) *Organizational Behaviour, Understanding and Prediction.* Englewood Cliffs, NJ: Prentice-Hall.
19. McConnell, J.V., Cutler, R.L. & McNeil, E.B. (1958) Subliminal Stimulation: An overview. *American Psychologist*, 13, 229–242.
20. Latey, P. (1982) Computing can damage your health. *Practical Computing*, July, 126–127.
21. Robson, A.P. (1965) Eliminating weaknesses in management accounting. *Management Accounting*, June, 200–205.
22. Beresford Dew, R. & Gee, K.P. (1973) *Management Control and Information.* London: Macmillan.
23. Cyert, R.M. & Marsh, J.G. (1963) *A Behavioural Theory of the Firm.* Englewood Cliffs, NJ: Prentice-Hall.
24. Dearborn, D.C. & Simon, H.A. (1958) Selective perception: A note on the departmental identification of executives. *Sociometry*, 21, 2, 140–144.
25. Bruner, J.S. & Goodman, C.C. (1947) Value and need as organizing factors in perception. *Journal of Abnormal and Social Psychology*, 42, 33–44.
26. McGinnies, E. (1949) Emotionality and perceptual defence. *Psychological Review*, 56, 244–251.
27. Lee, T.A. & Tweedie, D.P. (1977) *The Private Shareholder and the Corporate Report*, London: Institute of Chartered Accountants in England and Wales.

28. Lothian, N. (1978) Bad language in financial reports. *Accountancy, November*, 42–46.
29. Stamp, E. (1978) Review of 'The Private Shareholder and the Corporate Report by T.A. Lee and D.P. Tweedie, ICAEW 1977' in *Accounting and Business Research, Autumn*, 285–288.
30. The Royal Society (1985) *The Public Understanding of Science*, (Report).
31. Warr P.B. & Knapper G. (1968) *The Perception of People and Events*. Chichester: J. Wiley and Son.
32. Gregory, R.L. (1966) *Eye and Brain*. London: Weidenfeld & Nicolson.
33. MacKay, K. (1973) *An Introduction to Psychology*. London: Macmillan.
34. Reason, J. & Mycielska, K. (1982) *Absent-minded? The Psychology of Mental Lapses and Everyday Errors*. Englewood Cliffs, NJ: Prentice–Hall.
35. Smith, J.E. & Smith, N.P. (1971) Readability: A measure of the performance of the communication function of financial reporting. *The Accounting Review, July*, 552–561.
36. Flesch, R. (1949) *The Art of Readable Writing*. New York: Harper.
37. Soper, F.J. & Dolphin, R. (1964) Readability and corporate annual reports. *The Accounting Review, April*, 358–362.
38. Allison, R.I. & Uhl, K.P. (1964) Influence of beer brand identification on taste perception. *Journal of Marketing Research, 1*, August, 80–85.
39. Olshavsky, R.W. & Miller, J.A. (1972) Consumer expectations, product performance and perceived product quality. *Journal of Marketing Research, 9*, 19–21.
40. Lambert, Z.V. (1972) Price and choice behaviour. *Journal of Marketing Research, 9*, 35–40.
41. Monroe, K.B. (1973) Buyers' subjective perceptions of price. *Journal of Marketing Research, 10*, 70–80.
42. Traini, R. (1983) Computer detection. The *Sunday Times*, 16 January.
43. Dornbusch, S.M., Hastorf, A.H., Richardson, S.A., Muzzy R.E. & Vreeland, R.S. (1965) The perceiver and the perceived: their relative influence on the categories of interpersonal cognition. *Journal of Personality and Social Psychology, 1*, 434–440.
44. Cook, M. (1971) *Interpersonal Perception*. Harmondsworth: Penguin.
45. Kelly, H.H. (1950) The warm–cold variable in the first impressions of person. *Journal of Personality, 18*, 431–439.
46. Osgood, C.E., Suci, G.J. & Tannenbaum, P.H. (1955) *The Measurement of Meaning*. Urbana, Ill: University of Illinois Press.
47. Secord, P.F., Bevan, N. & Katz, B. (1956) Perceptual accentuation and the Negro stereotype. *Journal of Abnormal and Social Psychology, 59*, 309–315.
48. Haire, M. & Grunes, W.G. (1950) Perceptual defences: processes protecting an original perception of another personality. *Human Relations, 3*, 403–412.
49. Feshback, S. & Singer, D. (1957) The effects of a vicarious aggressive activity. *Journal of Abnormal and Social Psychology, 63*, 381–385.
50. Kelly, H.H. (1971) *Attribution in Social Interaction*. Morristown, NJ: General Learning Press.
51. Nord, W.R. (1976) *Concepts and Controversy in Organizational Behaviour*, 2nd Edition. Pacific Pallisades, California: Goodyear, 27.
52. Fletcher, C. (1984) What's new in performance appraisal. *Personnel Management, February*, 20–22.
53. Garland, H. & Price, K.N. (1977) Attitudes towards women in management and attributions of their success and failure in managerial positions. *Journal of Applied Psychology, 62*.
54. Robbins, S. (1983) *Organizational Behaviour: Concepts, Controversies and Applications*. Englewood Cliffs, NJ: Prentice-Hall.
55. Wicks, R.P. (1984) Interviewing: practical aspects. In C.L. Cooper & P. Mackin (Eds.) *Psychology for Managers*. Basingstoke, Hants: BPS and Macmillan Publishers.

56. Lewis, C. (1984) What's new in selection. *Personnel Management, January*, 14–16.
57. Arvey, R.D. & Campion, J.E. (1982) The employment interviews: a summary and review of recent research. *Personnel Psychology, 35*, 281-322.
58. Maier, N.R.F., Hoffman, L.R., Hooven, J.J. & Read, W.H. (1961) *Superior-subordinate communication in management*. New York: American Management Association.
59. Likert, R. (1961) *New Patterns of Management*. New York: McGraw-Hill.
60. Barrett, B. & James, P. (1981) How real is employee participation in Health and Safety. *Employee Relations, 3*, 4, 4–7.
61. Machin, J.L.J. (1980) *The Expectations Approach: Improving Managerial Communication and Performance*. New York: McGraw-Hill.

4 LEARNING AND MEMORY

4 Learning and Memory

Learning and memory are interdependent concepts. Generally learning is concerned with the acquisition of knowledge and skills whereas memory is largely associated with retention and retrieval. The earlier part of this chapter is devoted to a study of learning, followed by a study of memory. The discussion of learning is sub-divided into classical conditioning, operant conditioning, and cognitive learning. Programmed learning and behaviour modification are discussed as techniques which derive their strength from operant conditioning. Memory is sub-divided into short-term and long-term, and various processes with respect to the functioning of memory are discussed. Finally, the transfer of learning (training) is examined.

LEARNING

Learning covers virtually all behaviour, and is concerned with the acquisition of knowledge, attitudes and values, emotional responses, such as happiness and fear, and motor skills such as operating a computer keyboard or riding a bicycle. We can learn incorrect facts or pick up bad habits in the same way that we learn correct facts and acquire good habits. Learning can take place surreptitiously through the process of socialization in a particular culture. A generally accepted definition is that learning involves a relatively permanent change in behaviour that occurs as a result of previous practice or experience.[1] This excludes the process of maturation, physical damage or disease and temporary changes in behaviour resulting from fatigue, drugs, or other causes. Learning cannot be observed directly; we can only observe a person's behaviour and draw the inference from it that learning has taken place. Sometimes a person may have the potential to perform and display what he or she has learned, but unfortunately anxiety intervenes to under-

163

mine actual performance. This could occur in an examination, when the anxious student does not perform in accordance with the tutor's expectations.

A distinction has to be made between learning and performance. Performance is evaluated by some quantitative and qualitative measure of output—e.g., the number of calls a sales representative makes to customers or the quality of an executive's chairmanship of a committee meeting—but learning acts as a constraint on the outcome. Normally we cannot perform any better than we have learned, though there are occasions when the right motivational disposition and a supportive environment helps to raise the level of performance. Increased motivation may improve our performance up to a point, but beyond this increased motivation may cause a lowering of the level of performance.[2] An approach to the investigation of learning which has been very influential, is the behaviourist approach. This draws on the insights derived from classical conditioning and operant conditioning, discussed in this chapter.

CLASSICAL CONDITIONING

Classical conditioning is an association of one event with another that results in a pattern of behaviour. The name of Pavlov is associated with classical conditioning.[3] He was a physiologist who originally experimented with digestive secretions in dogs, and noticed that the dogs not only produced secretions when they saw food, but also responded to any stimulus which had regularly been associated with the food, i.e., the sight of the food pan or the sound of the keeper's footsteps. These events prompted Pavlov to investigate the dogs' tendency to salivate in response to a stimulus (called a reflex action). Pavlov rang a bell each time he brought food to the dog, and gradually the dog began to associate the ringing of the bell with the presentation of food.

Unconditioned and Conditioned Stimulus

The unconditioned stimulus (US) is the presentation of the food; the conditioned stimulus (CS) is the ringing of a bell. The act of salivating by the dog is the response. This is often referred to as a conditioned response (CR) when associated with CS, and as an unconditioned response (UR) when associated with US. Before any learning can take place an association must exist between US and UR. Actual learning occurs from the pairing of the bell (CS) and the presentation of a pan of food (US). Classical conditioning also functions in a human context. If a puff of air is blown into the human eye, a blink automatically occurs. There is an association between the puff of air (US) and the blink (UR). If, however, a new stimulus—e.g., a light appears—is placed close in time with the US, the new stimulus (CS) brings about the blinking of the eye (CR).[4] Another example of human conditioning involves a physiological reaction. The small blood vessels close to the body surface constrict in order to try to keep the body warm when it is exposed to the cold; this is known as vasoconstriction. We are unaware of this response when our hands are placed in ice-cold water. After a number of joint presentations of a buzzer and putting a hand in ice-cold water it was established that vasoconstriction (CR) occurs in response to the buzzer (CS) alone.[5]

Extinction and Spontaneous Recovery

A conditioned stimulus will not last indefinitely unless it is accompanied by an unconditioned stimulus. If the conditioned stimulus is repeatedly introduced without being followed by the unconditioned stimulus, there will be a gradual weakening of the strength of the conditioned response. This is known as extinction, and amounts to a reversal of learning. Pavlov's dog ceased to salivate at the sound of a bell because food did not appear after a number of occasions when the bell was rung. A conditioned response that has been extinguished may spontaneously recover some of the strength lost in extinction after a period of rest. This is manifest when, after a night's rest, Pavlov's dog increases the number of drops of salivation to the first ringing of a bell the following morning. The degree of spontaneous recovery after extinction will depend on the strength of the association that exists between the conditioned and unconditioned stimuli, and the nature and frequency of the rest periods.

Illustrations of the Association between US and CS

The marketing executive is interested in creating public awareness of the company's product, and through the medium of advertising attempts to establish a strong association between the conditioned stimulus—the image of the product portrayed in the advertisement—and the unconditioned stimulus (the product itself). With a limited advertising budget a decision will have to be made whether the expenditure should be allocated to one or two major campaigns in a year, or whether it should be spread through smaller but more frequent advertising campaigns throughout the year. For a new product it may be worthwhile to use the budget on an intensive campaign in order to create a strong association for the product; for an established brand the nature of the product and the likely activities of competitors would dictate the desired course of action.[6] The aim of a marketing strategy could be to associate some feeling of euphoria or satisfaction with the product, so that when consumers enter a store and see the product the associative feeling is aroused.

This is reflected in a number of cinema and television advertisements. A scene showing a girl enjoying herself on a tropical beach is followed after a few seconds by a picture of a bottle of a particular brand of alcoholic drink. When the consumer is contemplating the purchase of an alcoholic drink at the off-licence or supermarket, the advertised brand on display can trigger off the image or emotional connotation of the beach and the girl. A Hovis bread advertisement depicted the bygone rural conditions of life, followed by people eating brown bread. When this product is seen on the supermarket shelf it is hoped that the consumer will experience a pleasant association between it and the ancient country setting. In order to entice a consumer to purchase a product, a discount in the price may be offered. The consumer purchases the product because of the price reduction and continues to do so after the discount has been withdrawn. In this example an association is established between the desirable reduction in price (unconditioned stimulus) and the product brand (conditioned stimulus). If the product in question compares well with the quality and performance of competing brands, the association initially established as a result of the price-reduction strategy could continue. In the short term at least the product may be chosen by the consumer despite the absence of a discount.

Once an action becomes repetitive, such as the continued purchase of the product initially with a price discount, a habit is formed. Many consumers rely on habit so as to alleviate the problem of choice. They tend to buy the same shampoo, coffee, and baked beans that they bought last time. A deliberate advertising strategy to foster brand loyalty is reflected in an overt association between the product and the brand. The slogan incorporating the misspelled name of the product and the name of the brand—Beanz meanz Heinz—is a good example of this strategy. A car manufacturer may adopt a different type of association in the form of a comparative claim, though the legal implications of such a strategy have to be considered. A comparative claim may take the following form: "The Ford Granada consistently rode as quietly as the Mercedes Benz."[7]

Associations between social groups and lifestyle are exploited by advertisers, so as to promote products to particular social groups. It is highly unlikely that an advertisement would show a prestige car against the background of a dilapidated small house in a run-down area. A more likely image would be for the car to appear in a context of affluence—near a large house driven by an attractive, well-dressed woman. However, if an advertiser wishes to enlarge the market for a particular product, then the product will be shown in a number of different settings, each designed to appeal to a particular social group.

Generalization

The phenomenon of generalization, related to classical conditioning, occurs when we attribute to a similar stimulus the characteristics of the conditioned stimulus. For example, Pavlov's dog salivated, though to a lesser extent, to the beat of a metronome as well as to the sound of a buzzer. The greater the similarity between the conditioned stimulus (the bell) and the new stimulus (the buzzer) the more pronounced is generalization. The concept of generalization can be viewed as the substitution of a new conditioned stimulus for the originally learned conditioned stimulus. It accounts for our ability to react to novel situations where we perceive similarities to familiar situations. The accountant when dealing with a new tax problem may see certain similarities between it and a past problem, and as a consequence is able to draw inferences from the past situation to illuminate the present. This is an act of generalization on the part of the accountant.

It is often assumed when a consumer has a satisfactory experience with a product—e.g., a Philips or Hitachi radio cassette recorder—that this will be generalized to other products, such as a video recorder, made by the companies concerned. Generalization may work to the firm's disadvantage, if an unfavourable experience with a product or service is transferred to a new product or service introduced by the firm. An example would be clients who are dissatisfied with the auditing service they receive from a firm of chartered accountants. Subsequently, the firm creates a first-rate management consultancy service, but the clients concerned feel unable to use the services of this firm although in need of consultancy advice.

Generalization is also evident in the following situation. A child, accompanied by a parent, pays a visit to the dentist. The child will probably respond with anxiety to the odd sensation as the tooth is drilled. But while in the dentist's chair the child registers a variety of stimuli: the dentist in a white coat, the "smells" of the surgery, the whine of the drill, and so on. The conditioned response of the child to pain is to be frightened, and this response becomes associated with the other stimuli registered by the child. On the way home the parent and child visit a chemist shop to buy some medicine, and it would not be surprising if the child were frightened when the chemist appeared in a white coat. Many people experience strong emotional reactions to certain situations because in the past these reactions have been paired with some painful or unpleasant experience.

Anxiety could be produced following a car accident on a particular road. Subsequently when driving down a similar road (cs) the driver experiences anxiety (cr). In fact, an anxiety or fear could spread or be generalizable to other stimuli which bear some relationship to the original stimuli—e.g., riding a bicycle or motorcycle, or using a taxi.

Emotional Reactions

An experiment conducted by Watson many years ago shows how emotional reactions may be classically conditioned in humans.[8]. At the beginning of the experiment a child named Albert was presented with a small white rat and played quite happily with it. However, when the small white rat (cs) was paired with a loud noise (us) and this was done several times, Albert developed a very strong aversive reaction to the rat and would whimper and recoil when it came into sight.

Discrimination

The opposite of generalization is called discrimination. This refers to the capacity to be able to distinguish between two stimuli so that the appropriate response to the correct stimulus is made. If Pavlov's dog salivates to the ringing of a bell but does not salivate when the telephone rings, we can conclude that he has discriminated between the appropriate and inappropriate conditioned stimuli. When product differences are easily recognizable—i.e.,the distinctiveness of a Mini Metro or Volkswagen—it is relatively easy for consumers to discriminate. In other cases terms such as "new" and "improved" are used in advertisements as discriminatory cues, though the continuing influx of new products to the market has deadened the impact of these frequently used words.

Stores, such as Harrods and Marks and Spencer, place overwhelming influence on the discriminatory cue of quality. Advertisers therefore have to give due care to the strategy of differentiating between the advertised product and competing products. Differentiation is evident when a car manufacturer highlights the positive design features of a particular car when compared with similarly priced competitive models. However, generalization which could result in a sales increase not only for the particular brand advertised but also for competing brands may be difficult to prevent in particular circumstances. Take for example an advertisement for Pepsi Cola which stresses that those who drink it are part of the in-crowd. There is a danger that this could be generalized to Coca Cola as well and result in increased sales of that product.

Thorndike, a learning theorist, also gave much thought to the relationship between stimulus and response. He came to the conclusion that problem solving, at least in lower animals, involves a slow, gradual, and at times, tortuous trial and error process.[9] He considered learning as a gradual stamping in of correct responses and a gradual stamping out of incorrect responses. Two basic principles govern trial and error processes: the law of repetition and the law of effect. The latter states that responses which satisfy the needs of the organism tend to be retained while those which fail to satisfy these needs tend to be eliminated. So if the person gets satisfaction from performing a particular act, that act will tend to be repeated. If you find that paracetamol is particularly effective in removing a headache over a period of time, this remedy is likely to be repeated.

Another theorist, Hull, recognized the importance of intervening variables in the stimulus-response equation, though Pavlov and Thorndike played down their significance.[10] These consist of drive, habit strength, and incentive. A response to a need—e.g., consumption of a particular product—could reduce the search (drive) for this product, and satisfaction with its consumption could lead to the formation of a habit, though the habit could vary over time. Hull's theory is sometimes described as a theory of conditioned learning, and it incorporates aspects of the work of both Pavlov and Thorndike. However, Hull's real contribution is acknowledging that the internal state of the organism, and particularly motivation, must be considered in explaining learning.

OPERANT CONDITIONING

The basic difference between operant conditioning and classical conditioning is that in operant conditioning the learner must make some response before his or her behaviour is reinforced or rewarded.

Reinforcement
The major proponent of the theory of operant conditioning is Skinner, and his work could be considered an elaboration of Thorndike's law of effect. In a basic experiment, Skinner placed a hungry rat in a box in which there was a lever. When the lever was depressed it activated a mechanism to deliver a food pellet. The rat tended to explore the box and by chance pressed the lever and a food pellet dropped. It began to press the lever more and more frequently to obtain the food. The food is the reinforcement for the behaviour.[11] This type of experiment was also conducted with pigeons, who pecked a disc in return for food pellets. The animals developed discriminatory behaviour in the sense that the lever was pressed, or the disc pecked, when a light was on but not when it was off. Food is a major form of reinforcement for animals, and this is evident in the training of circus animals who do interesting manoeuvres in return for rewards.

With humans factors such as attention, praise, approval, success and money are major reinforcers. The teacher who pays attention to the troublesome behaviour of a pupil is reinforcing that behaviour. Such behaviour ought to be ignored, while acceptable behaviour ought to be reinforced by praise or reward. A child may find that asking a parent a question in a civil manner produces hardly any response; however, screaming and shouting in order to attract attention does produce a response, and subsequently the child may adopt this ploy again.

The following are examples of operant conditioning processes in an organization. An executive is asked to speak at a board meeting. The stimulus is the request to speak, and the executive responds by giving certain views on matters within his or her area of responsibility. The executive's response may be reinforced by nods and smiles from a prominent director. The effect of the reinforcement increases the likelihood that the executive will respond with the same or similar views at future meetings. In another situation a safety practitioner on an inspection in a factory is impressed by the system of control relating to potential hazards. He or she provides reinforcement by praising those responsible and writing in favourable terms about this experience in the company newsletter. For a reinforcer to work it must be perceived by the recipient as being useful and relevant. For example, receiving public praise in the classroom may not be regarded as a reinforcement by the young schoolchild who does not want to be seen as the teacher's favourite. The child might work less hard in the future to avoid this embarrassing situation.

The principles of CONTIGUITY and CONTINGENT apply to reinforcement. The bigger the gap between behaviour and reinforcement generally the lesser the likelihood that the behaviour will be strengthened or diminished. For conditioning to occur there should be only a small delay between behaviour and reinforcement (contiguity). Therefore, when a consumer enters a store to buy a new product which has been intensively advertised it is important that it appears on the shelf. Likewise, the commuter on the underground railway who is peckish would prefer to use a vending machine while waiting for the train, rather than satisfy his or her hunger at the end of the journey. Reinforcement should be contingent on the appropriate response; that is, it should be provided only when the desired behaviour occurs, and it should not come too late otherwise it may be associated with more recent but inappropriate behaviour.

If reinforcement is expected but is not forthcoming, the responses associated with it could become extinguished. For example, if the rat in Skinner's box no longer receives food after pressing the lever, it would gradually stop pressing and go back to the previous random exploratory behaviour.

Though reinforcement and reward are associated, reward is not synonymous with reinforcement. For example, a reward could be given without any effect on behaviour. A reinforcer is only a reinforcer if it maintains or increases the probability of responding at a high level.[12] The learning involved in operant conditioning is sometimes referred to as instrumental conditioning, because the response of the organism is instrumental in obtaining the reinforcement.

Primary and Secondary Reinforcement

Reinforcers used in most animal-learning experiments are examples of primary reinforcers. Food, drink, and sex fit into this category. A secondary reinforcer is one which has derived and developed its reinforcement qualities from being associated with one or more primary reinforcers. Money would fall into this category. When monkeys performed certain actions to secure poker chips that could be exchanged for food, they responded to the secondary reinforcers (the poker chips).[13] These became reinforcers because the monkeys learned that the chips could secure the food. To be effective, secondary reinforcers must be paired with primary reinforcers.

Positive and Negative Reinforcement

A number of examples of positive reinforcement have already been given. Skinner's rats and pigeons received positive reinforcement in the form of food. When a person picks up a magazine from a news stand and derives satisfaction from reading it, then that person experiences positive reinforcement. The same would apply to other fast-moving consumer products; continuous satisfaction from the consumption of the product leading to a learned response and the development of brand loyalty.

With negative reinforcement and punishment the organism responds to avoid an unpleasant situation. The animal in a maze soon learns not to behave in a certain way in order to avoid receiving an electric shock (a negative reinforcement). An employee may work hard during a period in which the company is going though a difficult time to avoid being made redundant, rather than for the positive reinforcement of success. The motorist with little petrol left in the tank pulls in to a filling station with low standards of service, and unavoidably receives a negative reinforcer in the form of a surly, discourteous service.Next time he or she will avoid patronizing this filling station if possible. In this case negative reinforcement can lead to AVOIDANCE CONDITIONING because cues have been picked up indicating that the same standard of service is likely to prevail in the future.

Responses based on avoidance conditioning do not easily disappear, as most organisms are unlikely to try and establish whether or not the original negative reinforcement is still operating. Another illustration serves to highlight negative reinforcement and avoidance conditioning. A product is found to be faulty, or it does not live up to the customer's expectations in some way—i.e., it falls short of the manufacturer's claims. In this case the purchase of the product will be negatively reinforced, and the customer may consciously avoid purchasing it again. This could create problems for the manufacturer because it could be difficult to extinguish a negatively reinforced response. A car manufacturer may experience problems if a product had developed a reputation for rust or faulty parts leading to a more-than-average breakdown record. It could take a long time to overcome this reputation even though corrective action was instituted soon after the difficulties were reported.

Even though positive reinforcement is said to be more effective than punishment in regulating behaviour, punishment seems to be used as much as reward in society. The link between action or response and reward is visible in positive reinforcement, unlike punishment where it is evident that the action is wrong but the correct response is not specified. However, punishment can play a useful role in stamping out inappropriate behaviour and regulating behaviour in the short-term at least. If a lecturer shouts at a student guilty of disruptive tactics in the classroom, the misbehaviour is likely to cease immediately. The sudden cessation of the undesirable behaviour is very reinforcing for the lecturer. Though punishment has a role to play in changing behaviour, it should be used sparingly. If it is not severe, and there is a clear distinction between good and bad (playing on the road or with matches could be considered bad child behaviour, for example), then problems are unlikely to arise in terms of behavioural abnormalities. But if punishment is very severe in conditions where it is not easy to distinguish between right and wrong, it may negatively affect both the bad behaviour and other, similar, good behaviour. Administering hard punishment to a child, for instance, for answering back may not only extinguish this type of response but also it may eliminate intelligent discussions with parents and perhaps others as well. Therefore it produces unwanted side effects. Many chronically shy unassertive individuals report that extremely punitive measures were used against them in childhood, not only when they challenged parental commands but also occasionally when they only tried to voice their opinions on some issue or other.[12] Often people feel hostile towards punishment because it is viewed as a process that engendered anxiety in the first instance. Many children have failed to fulfil their scholastic potential because of negative feelings towards teachers and schools which have arisen through earlier traumatic experiences in an educational setting.

To produce the maximum effect, the punishment should come immediately after the undesirable behaviour.[12] Note the paradox of the heavy drinker, for example, who, despite warnings about cirrhosis, has another drink. If death from cirrhosis was the immediate consequence of having another drink, he or she would decline it. But in reality the immediate pleasure of the alcoholic drink outweighs the distant worry of possible liver failure. Generally, to stop the undesirable behaviour enough punishment must be meted out early in the process and the recipient must know which aspects of his or her behaviour are looked upon with disapproval. It is always wise to have a positive reinforcement in mind.

Schedules of Reinforcement

Examples were given earlier of the nature of reinforcement with respect to animals and humans. Here we examine different ways in which reinforcement is administered. When behaviour is reinforced each time it occurs it is referred to as continuous reinforcement. However, reinforcement is not necessary every time a response is made; in fact intermittent or partial reinforcement may suffice.

Intermittent or Partial Reinforcement. Intermittent or partial reinforcement, which amounts to reinforcing responses only some of the time, can be categorized as (1) Fixed Ratio, (2) Variable Ratio, (3) Fixed Interval, and (4) Variable Interval.

1. Fixed Ratio. A fixed ratio could be the reinforcement of, say, every fifth response. The fixed ratio schedule keeps the response fairly low after the moment of reinforcement, with a build up to a crescendo just before the next reinforcement when, for example, Skinner's pigeon would be extremely active pecking the disc in anticipation of obtaining more food pellets.

2. Variable Ratio. A variable ratio could be the reinforcement of, for example, the third, tenth, and then the fifth response. Under the variable ratio schedule the pigeon produces a very high and steady response rate as it has no idea when reinforcement will come. The variable ratio schedule is the one which is generally not resistant to extinction because the individual or animal never knows when reinforcement will appear again. While continuous reinforcement is essential in establishing behaviour initially, when behaviour is learned it is best maintained on a partial reinforcement schedule, such as the variable ratio basis.[12]

It is the irregularity of the reward schedule that makes gambling so difficult to eradicate since the gambler always feels he or she may be lucky next time. In an experiment people were allowed to gamble using slot machines. The machines were tampered with so that some paid out on every operation of the lever (continuous reinforcement) while other machines functioned like normal slot machines and paid out on a periodic basis (partial reinforcement). Then a significant modification took place in the experiment whereby everybody played on a machine that was adjusted in such a way that it would never pay out; in other words there would be no reinforcement whatsoever. The subjects who had experienced partial reinforcement were much more resistant to extinction of their responses and they continued to play long after the subjects on continuous reinforcement had finished.[14]

3. Fixed Interval. A fixed interval could be the reinforcement of response, say, every 10 minutes. With the fixed interval schedule there would be a reduction of activity just after the moment of reinforcement.

4. Variable Interval. A variable interval could be the reinforcement of responses at varying time intervals. The variable interval schedule produces a steady and high response rate.

Applications of Partial Reinforcement. The most appropriate partial reinforcement schedule has to be considered in relation to work and business practice. It would be impossible to use the variable ratio schedule as the only method for providing rewards to employees. People expect to obtain their salary on a regular basis (fixed interval), whatever the evidence in support of the variable ratio schedule. However, rewards such as bonuses and praise may materialize on a variable basis. A random partial reinforcement can be used as a basis for sales promotion schemes such as competitions. The consumer may be encouraged to purchase a certain product because it also provides an opportunity to enter a competition and a chance to win a holiday or car. But only a tiny minority of consumers are likely to receive the stated reinforcement—to win the competition. However, a large number of people may be persuaded to buy the product because of the competition, and then find that the product satisfies their needs. Its purchase has become a learned response.

Continuous Reinforcement. As stated earlier, continuous reinforcement amounts to the reinforcement of every response. The findings of certain studies indicate that continuous reinforcement can be as effective as partial reinforcement. In a study of workers planting pine seedlings it was found that a variable ratio schedule based on incentives was no better than a continuous reinforcement schedule; if anything it was less effective.[15]

Another study focused on trappers who were paid to catch rats who eat young trees planted for reforestation purposes. After an initial period on regular hourly pay, half the trappers operated on the basis of hourly pay plus a continuous reinforcement schedule (a specified bonus per rat trapped). The remaining trappers operated on the basis of hourly pay plus a variable ratio schedule (a bonus was paid for an average of every fourth rat trapped). Later these reinforcement schedules were reversed. Both reinforcement schedules contributed to an improvement in the performance of the trappers, but the continuous reinforcement schedule was at least as effective as the variable ratio schedule. However, when the trappers were split into experienced and inexperienced groups, the variable ratio schedule was superior among the more experienced trappers. But the less experienced group, who were presumably still learning, operated better under a continuous reinforcement schedule.[16] These findings would indicate that one should pay particular attention to differences between individuals when specifying the most appropriate reinforcement schedule. An alternative theoretical framework for examining the relationship between rewards and performance is the expectancy theory of motivation, which is discussed in Chapter 2.

PROGRAMMED LEARNING

Programmed learning can be discussed with reference to linear programming and branching.

Linear programming

Linear programming, which involves presenting very small pieces of information at an acceptable level of difficulty to the learner, sometimes using machines, is linked to Skinner's concept of operant conditioning. It is a deliberate attempt to utilize the experimental findings of the psychological laboratory in the classroom, and is a major component of programmed learning. The learner goes through a sequence of frames and makes a response. For learning to be effective under linear programming, reinforcement should follow immediately after the response; only acceptable behaviour, such as the right answer, is reinforced; and there must be sufficient reinforcements otherwise lack of interest will lead to an extinct response. When the desired response is emitted, the learner is positively reinforced by being told that the correct answer has been given. An incorrect response is negatively reinforced by repeating the question. Linear programming can be reduced to the following basic principles:

1. The subject matter, process or skill is defined, analyzed, and broken down into its elements.
2. Material is presented step by step in a prearranged sequence, the steps being so small that the error rate should be near enough to nil.
3. At each step the learner is given just enough information to ensure he or she makes an active correct response before going on to the next item.
4. Learners receive immediate confirmation of the results emanating from their responses, work at their own rate and check their own progress.

While individuals work at their own pace, some take longer than others to get through the programme. The major disadvantages seem to be that once written programmes become inflexible, they also become impersonal. They can become boring after the initial novelty wears off. The personal intervention of the teacher, particularly the development of personal relationships, which is absent in programmed learning, is often considered to be critical in helping the student's interest and motivation. Perhaps this would not apply to the teacher with poor teaching skills. Skinner developed his teaching machines because he believed that classroom learning was inefficient due to reinforcements being either delayed too long or being absent.[17] This might be an over-simplification, because although animals like to receive reinforcements without much delay, the evidence for humans is that they generally favour delayed reinforcement.[12] Humans have the capacity to retain information about reinforcements over a substantial period of time.

Branching

Another technique of programmed instruction is branching. Material presented in branching frames is usually more difficult and mistakes are more frequent. The questions at the end of the frame are designed to determine what, if anything, the learner has misunderstood. This can be achieved by directing the learner to remedial frames which deal with the specific misunderstandings, and then direct the learner back into the mainstream of the programme.

Programmed learning is not in widespread use; an enormous number of prepared programmes would be required for large-scale use and presently the demand for, and supply of, programmes appears to be at a modest level. However, with a substantial growth in the use of computer hardware and software this situation could change in the future.

BEHAVIOUR MODIFICATION

This is a technique which draws its strength from operant conditioning. It is used to control and change behaviour by reinforcing in a systematic way those actions which are considered important or desirable. A related approach to the control and change of behaviour, which preceded the use of behaviour modification techniques, is that of shaping.

Shaping

An appropriate reinforcer is selected to suit the occasion, and all positive reinforcements are contingent on the organism coming increasingly close to the desired behaviour. Gradually a chain of behaviour is built up and once the desired behaviour is achieved it will be reinforced continuously at first and subsequently on a variable basis.

For example, a pigeon may be taught to pick up a marble in its beak and deposit it in a box. The pigeon is accustomed to receiving food pellets in a small area, and when the pigeon happens to move near the marble the trainer uses the reinforcement. As a result the pigeon will now be more likely to spend time near the marble. The trainer waits until the bird looks in the direction of the marble. The looking increases and the trainer waits until the bird happens to bend towards the marble before it receives a reinforcement. So in progressive steps circumstances emerge whereby reinforcement is withheld until the bird performs the complicated movement that is required. In another experiment Skinner found that when a hungry pigeon engaged in a particular behaviour at the time it received a reinforcement (i.e., rotating in an anti-clockwise manner when the food came), this behavioural pattern developed into a conditioned response. Between the food giving sessions the pigeon would perform anti-clockwise dances two or three times until the food was presented again.

Skinner imputes to the pigeon a certain superstition, in the sense that the bird behaves as if its pattern of behaviour was the cause of the food. As mentioned earlier, shaping is used to control the behaviour of circus animals, and Skinner also trained pigeons to play tennis; they poked a table tennis ball across a table, trying to get it into a trough on their opponent's side.[11,17]

Shaping is also common in human learning. Tennis coaches, driving instructors, teachers and parents all guide their clients to the desired performance, be it manual, linguistic, social or emotional behaviour. In an encounter between a customer and a sales representative the customer emits an operant—e.g., a remark which need not be directly related to the topic that is of principal interest to the sales representative. The sales representative moves closer to the customer by a process of reinforcement. This could take the form of a nod, smile, saying "that's a good point," "how interesting," and so on. Part of the behavioural strategy is to have a large repertoire of reinforcers and to select those most appropriate to a particular situation. Reinforcement which the customer considers relevant can lead to the emission of another operant. Subsequently the sales representative should be selective in the use of reinforcers, that is, he or she should provide reinforcement when the conversation of the customer shifts a little nearer to the technical matter which interests the sales representative. The sales representative will tend to be effective if he or she is able to provide appropriate reinforcements to satisfy the psychological needs of the customer, on the assumption that the more the customer enjoys the encounter the more he or she will believe the technical case put forward by the sales representative.

Modelling

An applied learning procedure associated with shaping is modelling. The desired behaviour is firmly kept in mind before selecting the appropriate model capable of exemplifying the way to proceed. This could be an ideal style of supervision. Then a supportive learning situation is created, using role-playing. The desirable consequences of adopting the model's behaviour are emphasized, and reinforcement is provided when the model behaviour is achieved. Initially reinforcement can be continuous, and subsequently provided on a variable basis.

The modelling procedures can be illustrated with reference to a study which was conducted at the General Electric Company in the U.S.[18] The aim of this study was to assist in facilitating the retention of disadvantaged employees. Films were developed to use with both employees and their supervisors. The supervisor films showed and modelled rewards for tact, coolness, patience, thoroughness, and control. The employee films emphasized the courage needed to succeed, the value of working at a job, and success in a job. Other situations depicted were: not quitting; how to teach a task; developing trust; pride in work; reactions to ostracism; the new environment; absenteeism; and lateness. Each film was introduced and summarized by a member of the management team, such as a plant manager in the case of the supervisors, and a famous black athlete in the case of the employees.

During the training session role-playing was introduced in between breaks in the film show, and instructors and other members of the training group provided continuous social reinforcement when role-playing behaviour was similar or identical to the behaviour of the models portrayed. In all there were five two-hour sessions for both the supervisors and employees, and the outcome was very favourable from the point of view of the company.

A variant of the above study was a behavioural analysis exercise conducted in a small business. In a grocery store in a particular neighbourhood two employees were engaged in stock and sales activities. Their performance, covering a variety of duties, was initially monitored. Subsequently, the clerks were trained in desired work behaviour, through discussion, modelling and role-playing. Reinforcement took the form of time-off with pay, feedback in visual form and self-recording undertaken by the employees. Following behaviour modification interventions, performance increased significantly in terms of the employees' presence, assistance given to customers and the completeness of the stock position.[19]

Organizational Behaviour Modification

Two prominent contributers to behaviour modification in an organizational context are Hamner and Luthans. Both adopt a Skinnerian approach, though Luthans goes further than Hamner in his adherence to Skinner's ideas. There is obviously an overlap between the two, but it is useful to present their views separately.

Hamner's Approach.   Hamner has set out certain steps or stages that should be followed in introducing a positive reinforcement programme in a company[21,20]. The emphasis is on performance maximization, maximum positive reinforcement and minimum negative reinforcement; the attitudes of workers are generally ignored.

1. Performance should be defined in behavioural terms, and the company should be as objective as possible in devising measures of performance.

2. Specific and reasonable performance goals should be set for each worker in a form that can be measured; these goals are not meant to be personal goals, they are organizational goals.

3. The employee should maintain a continuous record of his or her work so that the relationship between the performance goal and actual audited performance is clearly visible. The objective is to highlight behaviour that is associated with positive reinforcements; therefore, the measurement of performance should be frequent rather than infrequent.

4. The supervisor glances through the employee's own feedback report, as well as examining other indicators of performance such as sales or production records. With reference to the previously set goals and audited performance, the supervisor praises the positive aspects of the employee's performance. This amounts to "extrinsic" reinforcement and it should strengthen the employee's resolve to achieve performance goals. The witholding of praise for sub-standard performance in relation to the goals set should give the employee an incentive to improve performance. Working on the assumption that the employee is already aware of his deficiencies, there is no reason for the supervisor to be critical. This is said to be the case because the use of positive reinforcement leads to a greater feeling of self-control, while the avoidance of negative reinforcements keeps the individual from feeling controlled or coerced.

Luthans' Approach. The approach of Luthans is called the BE-HAVIOURAL CONTINGENCY MANAGEMENT MODEL for organizational behaviour modification. It seeks to identify and manage the critical performance-related behaviour of employees in organizations, and consists of a five-step procedure.[22]

1. The critical behaviour necessary for satisfactory performance should be identified. The causes of good performance or bad performance should be noted, and techniques such as discussion and observation may be used to carry out this procedure.

2. A measure should be used to determine the strength or frequency of the relevant behaviour, using tally sheets, time sampling, and so on.

3. A functional analysis of the behaviour is carried out, and this exercise poses a number of questions. What factors caused the behaviour in the first place and what is sustaining it in terms of reward or avoidance of punishment? It is essential to have a view of the factors that may be maintaining the behaviour in question. This can be exemplified by an example of a sales manager who is concerned about the large number of visits by the sales representative to the home base; the visits are seen to be unproductive chats with colleagues.[23]

The sales manager is acutely aware of the time-wasting involved and is unhappy about the fact that the sales director keeps making comments that large numbers of the sales force are sitting at the home base doing nothing. It would be logical to establish the apparent rewards for returning to base. The chance to relax and avoid the pressures of being on the road may be one factor to consider. Another, and perhaps more important, may be that the sales representatives have the opportunity for social interaction with their colleagues. It is perhaps the reinforcing effect of the social interaction which is maintaining the undesirable behaviour from the company's point of view.

TABLE 4.1

Organizational Behaviour Modification Rewards

Contrived On-The-Job Rewards				Natural Rewards	
Consumables	Manipulatables	Visual and Auditory	Tokens	Social	Other
Coffee-break treats	Desk accessories	Office with a window	Money	Friendly greetings	Job with more responsibility
Free lunches	Wall plaques	Piped-in music	Stocks	Informal recognition	Job rotation
Food baskets	Company car	Redecoration of work environment	Stock options	Formal acknowledgment of achievement	Early time off with pay
Easter hams	Watches	Company literature	Passes for films	Invitations to coffee/lunch	Extended breaks
Christmas turkeys	Trophies	Private office	Trading stamps	Solicitations of suggestions	Extended lunch period
Dinners for the family on the company	Commendations	Popular speakers or lecturers	Paid-up insurance policies	Solicitations of advice	Personal time off with pay
Company picnics	Rings/tiepins	Book club discussions	Dinner and theatre tickets	Compliment on work progress	Work on personal project on company time
After-work wine and cheese parties	Appliances and furniture for the home	Feedback about performance	Holiday trips	Recognition in house organ	Use of company machinery or facilities for personal projects
Beer parties	Home shop tools		Coupons redeemable at local stores	Pat on the back	Use of company recreation facilities
	Garden tools		Profit sharing	Smile	
	Clothing			Verbal or non-verbal recognition or praise	
	Club privileges				
	Special assignments				

Source: Luthans, F. & Kreitner, R. (1975) *Organizational Behaviour Modification.* Glenview, Ill: Scott Foresman.

The above analysis could lead to the adoption of a behaviour modification programme as a means of encouraging sales representatives to make fewer visits to the home base. However, the strategy of discouraging them from making frequent visits to the home base as a means to make better use of their time could be defeated if opportunities for relaxation existed elsewhere, or if it was possible to stagger the visits so that only small numbers were at the home base at any time.

4. After conducting functional analysis, an intervention process gets underway to modify the appropriate behaviour. Care has to be exercised so that only desired behaviour is reinforced, and it is important to consider the context of the behaviour—e.g., tasks and organization structure. A wide variety and range of rewards are available, and some do not involve costs, such as friendly greetings and compliments. In Table 4.1 there is a list of possible rewards for use in organizational behaviour modification. This approach represents a major alternative to the expectancy theory of motivation discussed in Chapter 2.

5. The final step in the procedure is evaluation. The primary aim of evaluation is to establish to what extent the intervention has modified the behaviour. The intervention process could be removed or reversed and then the consequences are noted. Various combinations for manipulating the situation can be used in order to assess the impact of the behaviour modification programme.

Applications in Safety

Apparently getting workers to use personal protective equipment, such as earplugs or spectacles, is a significant problem in many manufacturing plants, and there is no doubt that a fair number of accidents at work could be avoided if personal protective equipment was appropriately used. The challenge then is to change the workers' behaviour as a means of avoiding work hazards.

This challenge was taken up in a study, using a behaviour modification programme to modify the habits of workers with regard to wearing ear protectors in two companies.[24] Some workers tend to be resistant to wearing ear protectors because they perceive certain costs associated with it, including a very unpleasant adaptation period, a continual concern for cleanliness when using earplugs, and increased sweating around the ear when using ear muffs. Since no penalties accrue for not wearing the ear protectors in a number of situations, and the prospect of hearing loss is too distant to be considered significant, the incentive to wear personal protective equipment of this nature is weak.

Attempts were made to change the behavioural balance in favour of wearing earplugs by introducing new reinforcers on a less-than-permanent basis. It was considered appropriate to enlist the support of supervisors in the design and execution of the programme. In this way it was felt that there could be mutual superior and subordinate reinforcement, and this could sustain the modified behaviour after the programme had terminated. In a metal fabrication plant of a company with 2000 employees the management style was production-orientated and authoritarian. Industrial relations were poor as evidenced by the company's history of frequent strikes and high staff turnover. But the company was known for its outstanding safety record primarily due to top management's involvement in all safety-related issues. Management had tried to increase the use of earplugs by workers before the study was conducted, using group lectures, poster campaigns and disciplinary action. These efforts seemed to have had limited success.

Control and experimental groups were drawn from two departments involved mainly in lathe-type operations characterized by high-frequency noise levels averaging 90 decibels. Both groups received a standard lecture on hearing conservation. But only the experimental group received immediate feedback as a reinforcer. In order to gauge hearing loss, short audiometric tests were administered at the beginning and end of a work shift, and the audiograms from these tests were shown to the workers immediately after the test. The differences between the beginning and end of the work shift tests were expressed in terms of temporary hearing loss.

One copy of the audiogram was given to the workers, and a second was placed on a special bulletin board in the production area. Besides the data on temporary hearing loss, other information such as the worker's name, age, and number of years in the department also appeared on the bulletin board. Workers were encouraged to try to use earplugs during one of their testing days so that they could observe the effect of noise on temporary hearing loss during that workshift. On the other testing day there would be no such condition. The testing procedure was terminated after all the workers were tested. For a period of five months thereafter (the follow-up period) the researchers sampled the behaviour of earplug use.

The results indicate that in the experimental department the use of earplugs rose appreciably (from 35% to a new 85%) at the end of the five-month period. But the control group, who did not participate in the experiment except for listening to the standard lecture on hearing conservation, did not experience any noticeable change. It took some time for the dramatic rise in earplug use in the experimental group to take place. The effects of the experimental conditions were complemented by a management prescription requiring the compulsory use of earplugs in the production area. This was an important adjunct to the experiment because in the changed environment deviant behaviour (not wearing earplugs) could result in corrective or punitive responses by supervisors. Therefore, this changed the balance in favour of earplug use.

In the weaving department of a textile factory with 1200 employees, another company tried to encourage workers to use earplugs in a noise environment averaging 106 decibels. Previous promotion campaigns and disciplinary action aimed at increasing ear protector use proved to be ineffective. This company then decided to introduce a programme whereby tokens were dispensed at random times by managers to workers wearing earplugs. A token consisted of a slip of paper carrying the factory's official letterhead and a serial number used for monitoring purposes. The tokens could be used to acquire a variety of inexpensive consumer products, and each product had a price expressed in terms of the number of tokens required for its purchase. Wall charts were also used to show earplug usage rates. The results of the experiment indicated that a substantial improvement in earplug use occurred.

The experiments conducted in the two companies relied on individual feedback and the token economy system, and the expenditure involved was no higher than the costs of a conventional promotion campaign to encourage the use of personal protective equipment. The experimental evidence strongly supports the effectiveness of the behaviourist approach for promoting the use of personal protective equipment.

Criticisms of Organizational Behaviour Modification

Despite its apparent success, organizational behaviour modification has been the subject of a number of criticisms. The most favourable results emanating from the use of behaviour modification techniques are associated with highly controllable situations such as a straightforward process in a small business or variables that are independent and easily isolated (e.g., absenteeism). As research studies move into more complex situations involving complex interactions between people, and where jobs are interdependent, the success of behaviour modification techniques is open to question. Furthermore, almost all the research studies have focused on employees at the bottom of the organization, paying less attention to the behaviour of managerial or professional staff. At the bottom of the organization employees experience greater supervisory control and encounter less complex jobs, and it is said that these conditions facilitate the obtaining of positive results from the use of behaviour modification techniques.[25]

The ethical problem of behaviour control and modification has to be considered and some argue that the systematic manipulation and control of people undermines freedom and is an affront to the dignity of the individual.[23] Others argue that operant conditioning principles lack the capacity to explain human action because they are not concerned with the internal functioning of the person.[26] This criticism may have had greater validity in the past, because more recent work on behaviour modification acknowledges that behaviour is better understood as a function of both the situation and the person, and the interaction between the two.[27] Acknowledging the interaction between situational and personal factors, encapsulated in social learning theory, is said to be more productive than the purely situational view contained in operant conditioning. Reference has already been made to a social learning approach in the discussion of personality in Chapter 1.

Relevance of Social Learning Theory

In social learning theory, the internal cognitive processes are said to have some effect on behaviour. This could be reflected in a person's expectations about the outcome of a particular piece of behaviour. The individual realizes from experience that certain actions will produce valuable benefits, and other actions will result in avoiding future trouble.[28] For example, business people do not have to wait until they experience the shock of a burning warehouse before they are prompted to take out fire insurance cover.

Social learning theorists maintain that though people respond to external reinforcement (e.g., money, praise), people often control and develop patterns of behaviour through the use of self-reinforcement. A positive self-reinforcement could arise when an athlete, having appraised his or her performance in finishing in fifth place in an important race, nevertheless feels extremely satisfied because of the strong competition. Another athlete, having appraised his or her performance, feels intensely dissatisfied with the outcome and amidst angry overtones rebukes him or herself. It is now apparent that internal processes, such as self-reinforcement and expectations as to the outcome of behaviour, should be placed alongside external reinforcement when considering the application of behaviour modification techniques.

COGNITIVE LEARNING

The main difference between a behaviourist approach to learning and a cognitive approach is that in cognitive learning there is a change in what the learner knows rather than what he or she does. The processing of knowledge is therefore important. Cognitive learning consists of two components—insight learning and latent learning.

Insight Learning

Much learning involves understanding what is being learned and thinking about it. Even animals behave sometimes as if they had insight into the situation to which they are responding. In a normal experiment in insight learning a problem is presented, followed by a period of time when no apparent progress is made and finally a solution *suddenly* emerges. A feature of insight learning is that it can be generalizable to other similar situations.

Kohler placed chimpanzees in an enclosed play area where food was kept out of their reach.[29] Potential tools such as poles and boxes were placed in the enclosure, and the chimpanzees rapidly learned how to use a box to stand on or a pole to move the food in their direction. At times the poles were used for pole-vaulting. In this experiment learning did not appear to develop as a result of trial and error and reinforcement, but came about in sudden flashes of insight. The chimpanzee would roam about the enclosure for some time, and then suddenly would stand on a box, grasp a pole and strike a banana suspended out of normal reach above the enclosure. When the chimpanzees were moved to new situations, the previous learning seemed to be transferred and the problems were solved quickly.

Latent Learning

Latent learning is not manifest at the time learning takes place. The learning goes on in the absence of reward, but when a suitable reward is available the information previously learned can be used. We tend to store knowledge about positive and negative reinforcements acquired through past experience. For example, a certain type of previous job was a source of satisfaction whereas another proved unsatisfactory. Likewise, the individual forms many kinds of cognitions about the way the career in which he or she is interested is structured from the trainee stage right up to the highest position of responsibility.

Cognitions from several different learning experiences may be integrated so that the individual can adapt to new situations and achieve personal goals. An early contribution to the concept of latent learning was made by Tolman.[30] He placed a rat in a maze, and the rat developed a cognitive map or mental picture of the maze. The rat learned something about the spatial arrangement of the maze; but this learning was not evident until a reinforcement motivated the animal to behave—i.e., to use an alternative escape route when the original was blocked.

Cognitive learning is closely related to other topics discussed elsewhere in this book. For example, selective perception (Chapter 3) and information processing (Chapter 5) are important ingredients in the cognitive process. But the heart of cognitive learning is memory.

MEMORY

Memory performs many functions and is involved in nearly every aspect of behaviour. In order to remember new information the individual needs to process or encode the information, store or retain it until it is called for, and then be able to retrieve it when required to do so. If any of these processes breaks down for any reason, the result is a failure to remember, or in other words, forgetting. Research on learning usually emphasizes the acquisition of knowledge and skills, whereas research on memory is largely concerned with retention and retrieval. However, learning and memory are inter-dependent. The human memory can be supplemented by an external memory. There are many situations where information is available without the need for it to be stored in the individual's memory. Packaging infor-mation, shopping lists, buyer's guides, or advertisements cut out by the con-sumer are part of the consumer's external memory. Memory is divided into two types: short-term and long-term.

Short-term Memory

Short term memory (STM) is said to have limited storage capacity and be capable of holding a small amount of information for a short time. Normally we can remember around seven names, or seven letters in the alphabet, although each of the names may contain many more than seven letters. A feature of STM is the rapid loss of information; therefore, we tend to repeat the information over and over again in order to retain it.

An employee is verbally given a customer's telephone number and asked to ring the customer immediately. Without writing the number on a piece of paper, the employee retains the number in his or her STM while dialling it. After making the telephone call he or she is likely to forget the number. Likewise, an accounts clerk holds a list of numbers in his or her STM for a brief period while engaged in mental arithmetic.

Long-term Memory

At some stage in the learning process information is transferred from the STM to the long-term memory (LTM). When material can be recalled reliably after a day or a week, it is safe to conclude that the information is recalled from LTM. Before the transfer takes place a fair amount of information can be lost, but unlike the STM, the capacity of the LTM is substantial and for-getting is slower.

Encode or Process

The storage capacity of STM is, as stated above, limited to around seven items or CHUNKS of information.[31] A chunk may be a single letter or digit or a combination of letters or digits, each combination being a chunk. We can remember a long telephone number because it can be chunked. A chunk is in essence an organized cognitive structure that can grow in size as informa-tion is integrated into it. A brand name could be considered the summary of more detailed information about a product in the eyes of a consumer familiar with that product. When chunking words the load on the memory is eased considerably. In order to facilitate memorization the following words may be chunked to form a sentence.

company	a
The	Acquisition
of	reorganization
necessitates	another

The sentence reads: *The acquisition of another company necessitates a reorganization.*

One important type of information in memory which is related to chunks is memory SCHEMATA. A schemata is an internal structure developed through experience which organizes incoming information in relation to previous experience.[32] The experienced stockbroker draws on a well-organized strategy (schemata) in buying or selling shares, and utilizes a wide repertoire of dealing strategies, as well as interpreting the mood of the stock market using his or her knowledge or experience. In addition, the broker may be able to rely on rapid recall from LTM about possible deals. The novice stockbroker would find each item of incoming information difficult to deal with. The information cannot be related quickly and easily to existing stored material because his or her schemata is underdeveloped. This could result in confusion and a lack of ability to process and respond to incoming information at the early stages of learning. A related notion to that of the schemata is the SCRIPT; this amounts to expectations about how various types of event will unfold themselves.

As a means of keeping information activated in STM, REHEARSAL is used. REHEARSAL is an activity which recycles the same items of information in STM. For example, a new word encountered in the study of a foreign language is repeated over and over again. Rehearsal is said to occur when items of information are repeated silently or overtly by the individual and is limited by the capacity of STM to around seven items or chunks circulating in the system. It must not be confused with mere repetition, and it implies an active, conscious interaction with incoming information. Material that is rehearsed is then transferred to LTM.

It is suggested that there are two basic ways of representing information in memory—two coding systems.[33] One is verbal, and the other is nonverbal and uses imagery. The latter could arise when you imagine a scene described by a sentence or caption. A brand name may be associated with some mental image of that brand. On an aerosol can of freshener a scene depicting a beautiful garden in springtime is obviously designed to create the appropriate imagery. However, it is important from a manufacturer's point of view for the consumer to process the verbal or semantic information in the advertisement. Otherwise a consumer who processes the imagery only (e.g., a waterfall or a beautiful scene) and fails to relate the claims made in the advertisement to his or her experience of the product, will be badly informed when confronted with product choice in a store. This is an example of the background of the advertisement diverting attention from the message. It is well to bear in mind that in processing material individual differences with respect to priorities, preferences, and prejudices play an important part.

Store or Retain

Various methods are employed to ensure the retention of the incoming information. Obviously there is a limit to what can be stored in STM. An eight-digit number (13456839) could be broken into manageable chunks (13–45–68–39) making four items, which will facilitate short-term retention. While LTM can be greatly improved by the individual becoming more proficient at encoding information, there is a distinct limit on the improvement of STM. A high priority is given to information that helps to achieve personal objectives and information that can be easily stored.[34]

For example, a consumer plans to compare specified foods on the basis of nutritional content in the supermarket using only the information printed on the package. All that is required in this particular situation is to commit to memory the brands that the consumer plans to compare in the supermarket. However, if the information on nutritional content appeared in an advertisement or in an article in a health food newsletter, and not on the package, the consumer would have to put more information into his or her memory. Events which are surprising, novel, inconsistent with our expectations, and so on will often be given priority when it comes to processing and storage—e.g., a new price or an interesting new feature in a well-established home computer.

Advertising can facilitate the retention of a message about a product. Frequently new products require the support of an intensive advertising campaign to capture the attention of the consumer. Special promotions such as free gifts or substantial discounts for a set period produce a similar effect. A different strategy is likely to apply to advertising the older familiar brands. The objective then is to foster long-term awareness and to mount a continuous but less saturated advertising campaign.[35]

Hierarchical Model.   A model for the structure of LTM to facilitate retention is the hierarchical model. This proposes that memory is structured with specific ideas categorized under more general ideas. Thus the concepts of a canary and an ostrich are categorized under birds, and birds are categorized under animals. At the highest level of the hierarchy presented overleaf in Fig.4.1, there are a small number of general concepts, and at the bottom many specific concepts.[36]

A similar model could be applied to the structure of information about accounting systems. Accounting could be sub-divided into financial and management accounting. Financial accounting would include items such as trial balance, profit and loss account and balance sheet, and management accounting has sub-divisions such as direct and indirect costs and various methods of allocating them. The CONCEPTUAL HIERARCHY, depicted in Fig.4.1, is a potent tool for facilitating learning. In one experiment the group who had a brief exposure to 112 words presented in the form of a conceptual hierarchy were far more effective in reporting orally the words they could remember than a random group who did not receive the words in an organized form.[37]

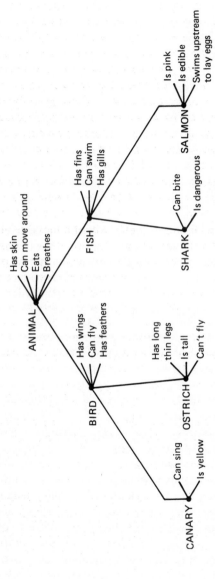

FIG. 4.1. A conceptual hierarchy. Source: Collins, A.M. & Quillian, M. (1969) Retrieval time from semantic memory. *Journal of Verbal Learning and Verbal Behavior, 8,* 240–247.

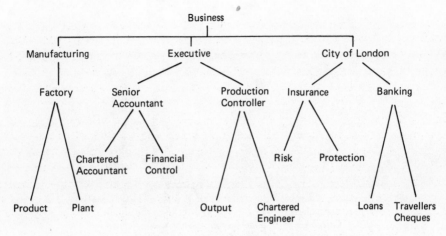

FIG. 4.2.   An associative hierarchy.

When a tree of items are associated, but not necessarily as a conceptual hierarchy, it is called an ASSOCIATIVE HIERARCHY. This is depicted in Fig.4.2.

The outcome of experiments on the associative hierarchy is similar to the results achieved with the conceptual hierarchy, but it would appear that the conceptual hierarchy is more organized and meaningful.[37]

Conceptual Similarity.   Another way of organizing material is the use of a conceptual category. In examining the association between words, one may be able to conclude that certain things are conceptually similar, while others are not.[38] Words of both low and high similarity appear in Table 4.2. These were used in a memory experiment. Lists of words high and low in conceptual similarity were spoken by the experimenter. The subjects were told nothing about the differences between the lists shown in Table 4.2. After each list was read, subjects were asked to reproduce as many words as they could, in any order.

You will notice that the words listed under high similarity can be grouped under the names of people, animals, clergy and dances; the scope to cluster words does not exist with the low-similarity items. Those who participated in an experiment, but were unaware of the differences specified in Table 4.2, experienced a high success rate when they unwittingly clustered the words in accordance with the type classification suggested above. Those who did not cluster the words on the basis of high similarity fared badly. When the experiment was changed in the way it was run and participants were asked to be on the look out for word similarities, the best results in remembering were achieved. The message from these studies is that if the individual learns a way of relating items to one another and is able to place them in a particular category, then this framework can be used as a retrieval

TABLE 4.2
Words that are High and Low in Conceptual Similarity

Low Similarity		High Similarity	
Apple	Cruiser	Bob	Foxtrot
Football	Trumpet	Rabbi	Joe
Emerald	Doctor	Cow	Bishop
Trout	Head	Rumba	Dog
Copper	Wide	Bill	Tango
Theft	Blue	Priest	John
Hat	Gasoline	Horse	Minister
Table	Cotton	Waltz	Cat

Source: Adapted from Underwood, B.J. (1964) The representativeness of rote verbal learning. In A. W. Melton (Ed.), *Categories of Human Learning.* New York: Academic Press, 48–78.

plan in reconstructing the items from memory. Performance in learning should improve as a consequence.

Personal System of Categorization.   There are many occasions when words or meaningful material are presented to us without the assistance of prior categorization. In such circumstances it can greatly assist the learner if he or she devises a personal system of categorization. Words arranged according to a classification system devised by the learner were more readily recalled than words arranged in a predetermined sequence that the learner had to comprehend and follow.[39] The very act of organizing the material is in itself an aid to learning, particularly when the learner is involved in developing the system of organization that is used. This evidence appears to be at variance with the evidence on prior categorization presented earlier. The principle of one's own system of categorization can be seen in action in a management training course when, for example, a large group of participants is divided into syndicates to discuss information and present a summary of the syndicate's position.

Retrieval

Retrieval from memory can range from almost immediate access for familiar items to involved problem search processes for other items. It is dependent upon the quality of the coding and organization of the information transferred to memory. Sometimes an item of information cannot be remembered, but then some event occurs which gives the "clue" needed to retrieve the item. For example, a consumer realizes that some item is needed which is not on the shopping list, but is unable to recall the item unaided. However, while shopping in the supermarket the consumer sees a related item, or the item itself, which suddenly triggers off recall.

People sometimes use real-life episodes to help them remember when certain events occurred. In a study of memory the date of the assassination of President Kennedy was tied to the date of some event in the life of the person being questioned.[40] A child of the respondent may have been born on that day, so the date of the assassination is then worked out by inference. A number of people can vividly recall what they were doing when they heard the news of the assassination. When recalling what happened at a party, or who was there, the person may engage in imagery retrieval by visualizing the room in which the event took place. This may facilitate the recall of the names of those present when the party-goers are known to the person engaged in recall. With regard to marketing, an advertiser may use location and imagery to facilitate recall of the identity of the product; for example, a picture depicts the user of a particular brand of air-freshener relaxing in the woods near a cool, idyllic stream.

Mnemonics. Mnemonics is a method of remembering items by imposing a structure of organization on the material to be memorized. The example of the advertisement for the brand of air-freshener, referred to above, could be used as a mnemonic device. This device is known as the METHOD OF LOCI, in which people or objects to be remembered are associated with familiar locations. It is a peg system which provides an organizational framework for learning material as well as offering good retrieval cues. Many of the popular mnemonic devices rely on visual imagery. People tend to learn verbal materials better when they are connected with some visual image.

For example, manufacturers incorporate imagery in the brand names of their products—Thick and Zesty tomato sauce, and Easy-Off oven cleaners.[7] If a learner wants to remember a particular item in a series (e.g., the third), then a peg system using numbering is useful. A popular system using numbers is as follows: one is a bun, two is a shoe, three is a tree, four is a door, five is a hive, six is sticks, seven is heaven, eight is a gate, nine is mine, and ten is a hen. This facilitates the development of a mental image of each item. Another mnemonic device is the key-word (e.g., cognition, bureaucracy) which publishers frequently use. In the March 1982 issue of *Protection* (a magazine about safety), a safety practitioner provided a mnemonic check list. Part of this list, which helped him to remember courses of action by heart, is reproduced in Table 4.3.

Mnemonic devices appear to be suitable when long lists of separate items need to be remembered. By relying on visual imagery, there could be problems when the learner tries to memorize abstract words. The mnemonic devices have been criticized because they do not foster the development of understanding and reasoning. But this criticism is unfair, because really these devices are only appropriate to rote-memory tasks.[41]

TABLE 4.3
Mnemonic Check-lists for Safety Practitioners

FIRST AID	ACCIDENTS AND INVESTIGATION
P – *preservation of life*	L – *looking after the injured*
M – *minimizing effects of illness and injury*	I – *isolate the hazard*
I – *immediate presence of trained personnel*	F – *feeling for other employees*
M – *minor injuries which do not need medical attention*	E – *enquiry afterwards*
	P – *persistence*
HEALTH	R – *respect for witnesses' statements*
I – *identification of hazard*	O – *open mind*
E – *eliminate*	B – *background*
S – *substitute*	E – *explanation*
I – *isolate*	
P – *protection*	I – *injury*
	A – *accident*
S – *first signs of over exposure*	U – *unsafe act or condition*
I – *illness(es) due to over exposure*	H – *human failing*
C – *conditions of over exposure*	B – *background*
C – *consequences of over exposure*	
	LPG
FIRE	C – *cutting off supply*
R – *rapid spread in the early stages*	E – *evacuation (erect barrier)*
L – *late discovery*	C – *containing spillage*
L – *late call of the fire brigade*	A – *avoid ignition sources*
H – *harrassment of fire fighting facilities*	A – *approach downwind*
	A – *avoid splashing on clothing*
O – *occupancy*	
C – *construction*	
T – *time to evacuate building*	
E – *number of exits*	
T – *travel distance to exit*	

Recall

The level of arousal—whether calm or active—can affect the ability of the person to recognize and recall. There is a difference between recognition and recall, and this is apparent when we recognize somebody but cannot recall the name of that person. There is reason to believe that recognition and recall improve as a consequence of exposure to repeated messages, though eventually the effects are less pronounced.[42] A number of difficulties arise with the recall of certain types of information. Material which is meaningful poses less of a problem. For example, the word *college* or *office* is associated with a number of events and experiences. But the same cannot be said of a nonsense syllable (e.g., *nac*).[43] Nonsense syllables, such as *dax, ruf,* or *koj,* are fairly unfamiliar to all learners, and we cannot rely on previous experiences to facilitate recall. However, there could be some familiarity with nonsense syllables—*dax* may be associated with a town in the south-west of France, *ruf* sounds phonetically like rough, and *koj* are the first three letters of the American TV policeman, Kojak. But not everybody would establish these associations.[12]

One can never know whether memory genuinely represents what was originally seen, or whether it represents a plausible reconstruction, with perhaps the addition of details that were never present in the first place. There is substantial evidence indicating that human beings have a tremendous capacity for describing what they believed happened, but these descriptions may have little relationship to what actually happened.[44] Often people are unaware that their account of a happening is either invented or inaccurate. It is therefore not surprising to find conflicts of evidence in courts of law when two witnesses provide entirely different accounts of what happened and each swears that his or her account is the correct one.

When experimental subjects recalled stories, distortion occurred, changes were found in the meaning of passages, and reproductions got shorter with the omission of details.[44] To achieve coherency, a story, though differing considerably from the original, would become a story in its own right, re-vamped with additional material in order to make sense out of it. People's names and numbers appeared to get lost. In an experiment two groups were presented with a short passage of prose describing some aspects of the life of a girl.[45] Group A was told that the girl's name was Carol Harris and group B was told that the girl's name was Helen Keller. A week later the groups were asked whether the passage of prose included the statement that the girl was deaf, dumb, and blind. Only 5% of group A said "yes," but 50% of group B said "yes." The information on the girl's disability was not included in the original passage of prose, but apparently Helen Keller was known to a number of people in group B as being actually deaf, dumb, and blind, and they convinced themselves that they were given this information originally. This study shows how substantial inaccuracies in recall arise when we amend material to fit our preconceptions.

Though our preconceptions tend to promote inaccurate recall, there are occasions when this can be helpful as far as memory is concerned. In another experiment two groups were presented with an account of a female patient, Nancy, who consults a medical practitioner.[46] The experimental group was told that Nancy might be pregnant; the control group was not given this information. This was the only distinguishing feature in the reports given to the two groups. The groups were tested subsequently for purposes of recall. The experimental group reported more items of information than the control group, and these items were not included in the original story; in fact, they were inferred or invented.

Forgetting

Forgetting arises when we cannot recall material at a particular time. It may not be due to a loss of information from our memory, but an inability to retrieve the information because the index system guiding the search is lost or inefficient, or because material has been classified in an inappropriate way so that the normal cues for retrieval are not effective.[47] A number of other explanations are put forward to account for why we forget. As time passes the "memory trace" of what was originally perceived decays. An alternative explanation is that certain processes interfere with the specific information committed to memory, and this undermines our ability to recall that information. There is experimental evidence to suggest that the INTER-FERENCE explanation is more important than the DECAY explanation.[48]

Interference can be expressed in a variety of forms. Some of the important ones are as follows:

1. Retroactive.   The placing of new information in the memory undermines the recall of previously recorded information. For example, a practising accountant has changed his or her telephone number. After committing the new number to his or her memory the client may find it difficult to retrieve the old number.

2. Proactive.   Information that was previously committed to memory undermines the recording of new information. For example, a sales representative who has regularly dealt with the previous manager of a store finds it difficult to remember the name of the new manager.

3. Repression.   The individual subconsciously avoids retrieving information associated with unpleasant events. A patient might forget an appointment arranged with a medical practitioner because of some traumatic experience associated with a previous visit to the doctor's surgery.

4. Emotion.   Anxiety can inhibit the retrieval of information. A student's anxiety about failing an examination may inhibit his or her attempts to retrieve information in the examination room.

When information enters the memory for the first time, it could be argued that it receives more attention than information entering when storage capacity has built up. However, it appears that the more recently acquired information can be retrieved more easily (recency effect). But imposing a delay of 30 seconds before recall, eliminates the recency effect completely, whereas it does not significantly affect the power of recall of information acquired earlier (primacy effect).[49]

There are some ways of counteracting the effects of forgetting. It has been found that when a period of sleep intervenes between learning and recall, recall is greatly improved.[50] Perhaps the absence of the distractions of wakefulness, and the relative inactivity of sleep, may account for this finding. However, if one dreams during sleep, a period when the brain is relatively active, there is some evidence to suggest that more forgetting occurs.[51]

Rehearsal is said to prevent forgetting because it keeps replenishing the memory trace. An involved story about an event or happening must of necessity be repeated frequently to facilitate retention and avoid forgetting. Finally, a number of the measures discussed earlier in connection with the systematic organization and arrangement of material prior to transfer to memory assist in combating forgetting.

TRANSFER OF LEARNING (TRAINING)

The basic psychological principle underlying the transfer of learning is that of generalization of stimuli, referred to earlier in connection with operant conditioning. When a stimulus is similar to the original conditioned stimulus it tends to elicit the same response.

Transfer

The transfer of learning (or training) is the process by which the effects of training in one form of an activity are transferred to another form. A claim often made is that the learning of mathematics, or at least the training involved, improves the learner's ability to solve problems requiring logic, whether these are of a mathematical nature or not. The classical curriculum of Latin, Greek, and rhetoric was considered important in the development of logical reasoning. Many educational programmes are built on the assumption that people have the ability to transfer what they have learned in one situation to another. If transfer was not possible, there would be little justification for formal education; every element of knowledge, skill and capacity would have to be taught separately.

1. Lateral Transfer. Lateral transfer involves performance at the same level of complexity as the initial learning, but in a different context. If a child has experience of arithmetic calculations with the aid of blocks or beads in the classroom, this understanding could be transferred laterally at home if the child, having removed two tennis balls from a box of six, realizes that four are left.

2. Sequential Transfer. Sequential transfer occurs when we build on a learning foundation. A fact learned today in a subject may have some relationship to a fact or idea learned tomorrow. For example, multiplication draws on an understanding of addition.

3. Vertical Transfer. Vertical transfer occurs when learning at one level, such as comprehending facts about addition and subtraction, facilitates the solution of problems utilizing these arithmetic operations. It amounts to a transfer from the simpler components of a task to the more complex.

4. Positive Transfer. When training or performance in one task can be transferred to another, positive transfer is said to occur. Positive transfer manifests itself in the following situations: learning Latin may aid the learning of Italian; having learned the skills of ice-skating could mean that learning to roller skate is that much easier; and mastering the skill of driving a car results in positive transfer to lorry driving.

5. Negative Transfer. Negative transfer is said to occur when previous learning in a particular task hinders learning in another task. This is obvious when a motorist from the U.K. switches from driving on the left-hand side of the road to the right-hand side while holidaying in France.

Errors may arise in a factory when an employee with experience of driving one particular model of fork-lift truck drives another model. The pedals for braking, reversing and accelerating can differ in sequence from one model to the next. This can be contrasted with the standardization universally applicable to cars, apart from the difference in the positioning of the steering wheel between British and foreign cars.

The typist of yesteryear may have experienced both positive and negative transfer when changing from a manual to an electric typewriter. Positive transfer occurs when the keys are tapped correctly, but negative transfer occurs when the typist takes action to return the carriage to the beginning of the line. On the manual machine this is done by hitting a lever on the left, and on the electric machine by depressing a key. When the typist changes from a manual to an electric machine performance is initially slowed down by the persistent habit of raising the left hand to hit the lever, which now does not exist, at the end of every line.

Skill Acquisition

A number of factors are said to influence the acquisition of skilled performance. Most of these factors were proposed following simulated training sessions, rather than real-life training situations. However, they command a certain degree of acceptance.

1. Knowledge of Results or Feedback. Feedback comes from two sources, one from the external environment and one from the internal environment. The external environment could be the display section of a machine in front of an operator. The internal environment could be the operator's own muscles and nervous system. Both these sources provide continuous feedback, so that in effect the operator is always receiving knowledge of results. In driving a car the learner has a feel for the car while operating the clutch and accelerator pedals simultaneously (feedback from the internal environment), and receives feedback from the external environment when reading the dials on the dashboard. The driving instructor will provide augmented feedback in the form of verbal knowledge of results by telling the learner that he or she is engaged in movements which are either right or wrong. The instructor could also offer explanations to assist the learner.

Knowledge of results, preferably with appropriate comments, is important to the student on a course where continuous assessment is used, and to the business executive who wants to know how well operations are progressing, so that remedial action can be taken if necessary, and objectives modified accordingly. Feedback should be precise and the trainee should be given adequate time to assimilate it.[52] Feedback should be appropriate to the stage of learning which the learner is at, and it should concentrate on those aspects of the task that are critical for good performance. A trainee can become very dependent on feedback, and removing it could cause a deterioration in performance; this would be particularly so if its removal took place early on in learning.

2. Part or Whole. Using the part method the task is broken down into sections, and this method is suitable where learning does not suffer from compartmentalizing a body of knowledge. So if the task lends itself to chunking, and where some elements of the task are more difficult than others and require more time to be devoted to practising them, then this can be a useful method. Typing is an example of an activity best learned by this method, where each letter is practised on the keyboard before attempting whole words. Likewise with swimming, where the components of breathing, arm stroke and kicking are practised separately at first. Though the part method may appear appropriate for the actor learning the lines of a long play, and it may have beneficial motivational effects in the sense that the learner can reach the learning objective more quickly, it has disadvantages. For example, in linking the parts to form the whole the learner might get the sequence mixed up.

The total task is practised until mastered when the whole method is used. The tasks that are best learned by this method include those where integration and rhythm are the critical features of the skill. For example, the task would lose its meaning if broken into chunks—i.e., learning to drive a car. In addition, the whole method is preferable when the total task is small enough to avoid resorting to numerous rests and the learner is quick to learn and is intelligent.

A compromise between the two methods described is the PROGRESSIVE (CUMULATIVE) PART method which has been used for training older workers.[53] The task is broken into its constituent elements; the first element is practised until mastered, when the trainee proceeds to the second element and practises it in combination with the first. When this combination is mastered the third element is added, and so on until the whole task has been learned.

The older trainee suffers from an impairment of short-term memory and if the task is learned by the part method the first element is forgotten by the time the last element is learned. However, the whole method is also unsuitable because it tends to overload the older trainee. The progressive part method attempts to prevent overload and minimizes the likelihood of forgetting the earlier elements of a task by a constant process of rehearsal.

3. Massed or Distributed Practice.   Should the elements of learning a task be massed together or should they be spaced or distributed over a period of time? When the student is cramming in preparation for an examination, he or she is engaged in massed practice. In such circumstances some students could be highly motivated, with less time to forget the study material. For some people massed practice can result in boredom and fatigue and impair performance. However, this condition could be alleviated by the introduction of suitable rest pauses. Massed practice would appear to be particularly suited to a problem-solving exercise where it is important to persevere with the task until a solution is found.

Distributed or paced practice seems to be more beneficial for motor-skill learning (e.g., typing) than for verbal or more complex learning. But as the material to be learned increases in quantity and difficulty, then paced practice has a useful function.[54] In a verbal-learning experiment paced practice was found to be superior to massed practice.[55] Two groups of subjects learned a list of twelve nonsense syllables. One group, who adopted massed practice, had a six-second rest between each run through the list. The other group, who adopted paced practice, had a two-minute rest. The two groups were then given scores for the number of syllables that were reported correctly. The spaced practice group was superior to the massed practice group. It would be unwise, however, to generalize this result to all instances of verbal learning.

Learning Curves

The trainer must realize that learning takes place in a piecemeal fashion along increasingly difficult paths, and this can be depicted in the form of a learning curve which is shown in Fig.4.3. During the course of training the learning curve sometimes shows a levelling off after which it rises again. The point on the curve where little or no learning seems to be occurring was termed a plateau in a classic study of trainee telegraphists.[56] One suggestion to account for the shape of the curve is that the first plateau denotes the point at which the trainees mastered the motion of tapping individual letters but had not yet progressed to tapping whole words. The second plateau denotes the point at which the trainees mastered whole words but not

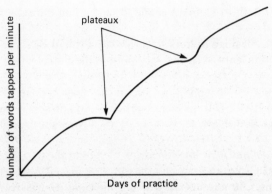

FIG. 4.3.   A learning curve. Source: adapted from Bryan, W.L. & Harter, N. (1899) Studies on the telegraphic language: The acquisition of a hierarchy of habits. *Psychological Review, 6,* 345–375.

phrases. These plateaux were supposed to represent a period in the learning process when the skill concerned was in the process of reorganization. This has been challenged in the light of subsequent studies in this field.[57] It should be noted that the plateaux do not appear during the learning of all skills, but where they can be identified the trainer should take particular care in explaining to the trainees the reasons for their lack of progress, otherwise the trainees may become demotivated. In a study of taxi drivers it was noted that driving performance improved by a factor of 50% in seven weeks, but then it remained constant (a plateau) for twelve weeks. Over the following ten weeks additional training brought about another 50% improvement in performance.[58] When learning to drive, much effort goes into the development of hand-foot co-ordination. As driving proficiency increases the driver pays more attention to monitoring road conditions, predicting the reactions of other drivers, and so on.

Alternative Approaches

The above approaches to training when applied in an organizational context place a lot of control in the hands of trainers. They set training objectives, specify the contents of the training programme in terms of realistic tasks and skills, and finally ensure that the achievement of the targets embodied in the programme is of the required standard. This overall approach has been referred to as the traditional approach to learning.[59] It is considered valid in the realms of operative, supervisory and management training when knowledge and experience of a technical process are required. For example, the technical aspects of procedures governing machine operation and maintenance, budgetary control, and production planning and control would lend themselves to the traditional approach.

The alternative approach incorporates the belief that learning is an active process best done when individuals participate in and take responsibility for their own learning. This offers the trainee the opportunity to have a say in what the training programme should accomplish, to exercise greater self-direction and control, and to remove barriers to the attainment of the learning objectives. This bears some similarity to the ideas associated with participative leadership in Chapter 8. The eventual outcome is said to increase sensitivity and lead to a continuing growth in self-awareness.[59]

Out of this training perspective came management development programmes with a firm humanistic flavour. The emphasis was on improving the sensitivity and self-awareness of the individual as a person and as somebody who interacts with others to bring about changes for the better in organizations. One example of this approach, which has been severely criticized, grew out of the study of group dynamics by Kurt Lewin (see Chapter 7). It is referred to as sensitivity training ("T" groups).

The aim is to bring about change in the individual through group membership. The desired change is the development of self-insight, sensitivity to other people's behaviour, awareness of factors that facilitate or impede the smooth functioning of the group, and the acquisition of skills in understanding and influencing inter-personal processes.

Approaches to management training and development in the 1980s are much broader than sensitivity training and related techniques. Although the human relations aspects of management are still important, there is less attachment to the idea that focusing on inter-personal processes alone will solve the significant problems confronting organizations in a period of change.

SUMMARY

Learning, which cannot be observed directly, embraces most of our behaviour and can be distinguished from performance. Three major approaches to the study of learning are: classical conditioning; operant conditioning; and cognitive conditioning. Classical conditioning was discussed, with the aid of a number of illustrations derived from business practice, under the following headings: unconditioned and conditioned stimulus; extinction and spontaneous recovery; generalization; discrimination; and emotional response.

Operant conditioning consists primarily of reinforcement. The principles of "contiguity" and "contingent" apply to reinforcement. This concept was discussed with reference to primary and secondary reinforcement, positive and negative reinforcement (including avoidance conditioning) and schedules of reinforcement. Schedules of reinforcement, appropriately illustrated, were sub-divided into intermittent or partial reinforcement and continuous reinforcement. The former were listed as (1) fixed ratio, (2) variable ratio, (3) fixed interval, and (4) variable interval.

Programmed learning, which is linked to the concept of operant conditioning, consists of linear programming and branching. Linear programming and branching are techniques of programmed instruction. Behaviour modification, also related to operant conditioning, was discussed in terms of shaping and modelling, and specifically in an organizational context. Certain applications of behaviour modification in safety were introduced. Criticisms of the concept and the relevance of social learning theory were also discussed in the section on behaviour modification.

Cognitive learning can be categorized as insight learning and latent learning. This concept is closely related to selective perception and information processing, and draws heavily on memory.

Memory was classified as either short-term or long-term, and critical functions of memory were identified as encoding, storing and retrieving information. Chunking, the use of schemata and rehearsal facilitate the encoding process prior to the transfer of information to the long-term memory. Verbal and non-verbal coding systems are used to represent information in our memory. As a means to facilitate the storage of information in the long-term memory, devices such as the conceptual hierarchy, the associative hierarchy, conceptual similarity, and a personal system of categorization can be used.

Retrieval depends on the quality of the coding system and the organization of information transferred to memory. In this context mnemonics and recall were explained. For a variety of reasons distortions in the retrieval of information occur, and forgetting occurs when we fail to retrieve information. A number of explanations were put forward to explain why we forget, and there was a brief reference to ways of counteracting the effects of forgetting.

Transfer of learning (training) was referred to as a process by which the effects of training in one activity are transferred to another. Different types of transfer were described—(1) lateral, (2) sequential, (3) vertical, (4) positive, (5) negative. Factors likely to influence skill development in a training context were identified as (1) knowledge of results or feedback, (2) part or whole, and (3) massed or distributed practice. The relevance of learning curves was emphasized. Finally, learner-centred approaches, as opposed to the traditional trainer controlled approaches to learning, were acknowledged.

QUESTIONS

1. Distinguish between learning and performance.
2. Define the following processes in classical conditioning:
   a. generalization;
   b. extinction;
   c. conditioned stimulus;
   d. discrimination.
3. What is the significance of the association between an unconditioned stimulus and a conditioned stimulus in the field of marketing?
4. Explain the following terms:
   a. primary and secondary reinforcement;
   b. positive and negative reinforcement;
   c. avoidance conditioning;
   d. contiguity and contingent.
5. Assess the relative strengths of different schedules of reinforcement in a business context.
6. Comment on the differences between programmed learning and behaviour modification.
7. Discuss behaviour modification as a technique used to promote good safety practice at work.
8. Compare and contrast operant conditioning and cognitive learning.
9. Identify the difference between short-term and long-term memory.
10. Using examples from business practice to illustrate your answer, what do you understand by:
    a. an associative hierarchy;
    b. mnemonics?
11. Explain the following terms:
    a. chunk;
    b. schemata;
    c. rehearsal;
    d. interference and decay;
    e. primacy and recency effects.
12. Describe the traditional and alternative approaches to the transfer of learning in an organizational context.

REFERENCES

1. Hilgard, E.R., Atkinson, R.C.S. Atkinson, R.L. (1975) *Introduction to Psychology*. *6th Edition*. New York: Harcourt Brace.
2. Spence, K.W., Farber, I.E. & McFann, H.H. (1956) The relation of anxiety (drive) level to performance in competitional and non competitional paired – associated learning. *Journal of Experimental Psychology*, 52, 296–305.
3. Pavlov, I.P. (1927) *Conditioned Reflexes*. New York: Oxford University Press.
4. Hall, J.F. (1976) *Classical Conditioning and Instrumental Learning*. Philadelphia: Lippincott.
5. Menzies, R. (1937) Conditioned vasomotor response in human subjects. *Journal of Psychology*, 4, 75–120.
6. Williams, K.C. (1981) *Behavioural Aspects of Marketing*. London: Heinemann.
7. Cohen, D. (1981) *Consumer Behaviour*. New York: Random House.
8. Watson, J.B. & Rayner, R. (1920) Conditioned emotional reactions. *Journal of Experimental Psychology*, 3, 1–14.
9. Thorndike, E.L. (1911) *Animal Intelligence*. New York: Macmillan.
10. Hull, C.L. (1943) *Principles of Behaviour*. New York: Appleton-Century-Crofts.
11. Skinner, B.F. (1951) How to teach animals. *Scientific American*, 185, 26–29.
12. Burns, R.B. & Dobson, C.B. (1984) *Introductory Psychology*. Lancaster: M.T.P. Press.
13. Wolfe, J.B. (1936) Effectiveness of token rewards for chimpanzees. *Comparative Psychology Monographs 12*, Whole No. 60.
14. Lewis, D.J. & Duncan, C.P. (1956) Effect of different percentages of money reward on extinction of a lever pulling response. *Journal of Experimental Psychology*, 52, 23–27.
15. Yukl, G.A., Latham, G.P. & Elliott, D.P. (1976) The effectiveness of performance incentives under continuous and variable ratio schedules of reinforcement. *Personnel Psychology*, 29, 221–231.
16. Latham, G.P. & Dossett, D.L. (1978) Designing incentive plans for unionized employees: a comparison of continuous and variable ratio reinforcement schedules. *Personnel Psychology*, 31, 47–61.
17. Skinner, B.F. (1961) *Analysis of Behaviour*. New York: McGraw-Hill.
18. Goldstein, A.P. & Sorcher, M. (1974) *Changing Supervisor Behaviour*. New York: Pergamon.
19. Komaki, J., Waddell, W.M. & Pearce, M.G. (1977) The applied behavioural analysis approach and individual employees: improving performance in two small businesses. *Organizational Behaviour and Human Performance*, 19, 337–352.
20. Hamner, W.C. & Hamner, E.P. (1976) Behaviour modification on the bottom line. *Organizational Dynamics*, 4, 3–21.
21. Hamner, W.C. (1977) Worker motivation programmes: the importance of climate, structure and performance consequences. In W.C. Hamner & F.L. Schmidt (Eds.), *Contemporary Problems in Personnel*. Chicago: St. Clair, 256–284.
22. Luthans, F. & Kreitner, R. (1975) *Organizational Behaviour Modification*. Glenview, Ill: Scott, Foresman.
23. Robertson, I.T. & Cooper, C.L. (1983) *Human Behaviour in Organisations*. Plymouth: Macdonald & Evans.
24. Zohar, D. (1980) Promoting the use of personal protective equipment by behaviour modification techniques. *Journal of Safety Research*, 12, 78–85.
25. Miner, J.B. (1980) *Theories of Organizational Behaviour*. Hinsdale, Ill: The Dryden Press.
26. Locke, E. A. (1977) The myths of behaviour modelling in organizations. *Academy of Management Review*, 4, 543–553.

27. Davis, T.R.V. & Luthans, F. (1980) A social learning approach to organizational behaviour. *Academy of Management Review*, 5, 281–290.
28. Bandura, A. (1977) *Social Learning Theory*. Englewood Cliffs, NJ: Prentice-Hall.
29. Kohler, W. (1927) *The Mentality of Apes*. London: Routledge.
30. Tolman, E.C. (1948) Cognitive maps in rats and men. *Psychological Review*, 55, 189.
31. Miller, G.A. (1956) The magical number seven, plus or minus two: some limits in our capacity for processing information. *Psychological Review*, 63, 81–97.
32. Mander, J.M. & Parker, R.E. (1976) Memory for descriptive and spatial information in complex pictures. *Journal of Experimental Psychology: Human Learning and Memory*, 2, 38–48.
33. Paivio, A. (1969) Mental imagery in associative learning and memory. *Psychological Review*, 76, 241–263.
34. Shiffrin, R.M. & Atkinson, R.C. (1969) Storage and retrieval processes in long-term memory. *Psychological Review*, 76, 179–193.
35. Myers, J.H. & Reynolds, W. (1967) *Consumer Behaviour and Marketing Management*. Boston: Houghton Mifflin.
36. Collins, A.M. & Quillian, M. (1969) Retrieval time from semantic memory. *Journal of Verbal Learning and Verbal Behavior*, 8, 240–247.
37. Bower, G.H., Clark, M., Lesgold, A. & Winzenz, D. (1969) Hierarchical retrieval schemes in recall of categorized word lists. *Journal of Verbal Learning and Verbal Behavior*, 8, 323–343.
38. Underwood, B.J. (1964) The representatives of rote verbal learning. In A.W. Melton (Ed.), *Categories of Human Learning*. New York: Academic Press, 48–78.
39. Mandler, G. & Pearlstone, Z. (1966) Free and constrained concept learning and subsequent recall. *Journal of Verbal Learning and Verbal Behavior*, 5, 126–131.
40. Warrington, E.K. & Sanders, H. (1972) The fate of old memories. *Quarterly Journal of Experimental Psychology*, 23, 432–442.
41. Eysenck, M.W. (1984) *A Handbook of Cognitive Psychology*. London: Lawrence Erlbaum Associates Ltd.
42. Bettman, J.R. (1984) Memory factors in consumer choice—a review. In I. Fenwick & J.A. Quelch (Eds.), *Consumer Behaviour for Marketing Managers*. Newton, Mass: Allyn and Bacon, 55–74.
43. Ebbinghaus, H. (1885) *Memory: A Contribution to Experimental Psychology*. New York: Columbia University, Teachers College.
44. Bartlett, F.C. (1932) *Remembering: An Experimental and Social Study*. London: Cambridge University Press.
45. Sulin, R.A. & Dooling, D.J. (1974) Intrusion of a thematic idea in retention of prose. *Journal of Experimental Psychology*, 103, 244–262.
46. Owens, J., Bower, G.H. & Black, J.B. (1979) The soap opera effect in story recall. *Memory and Cognition*, 7, 185–191.
47. Tulving, E. (1968) Theoretical issues in free recall. In T. Dixon & D. Horton (Eds.), *Verbal Behavior and General Behavior Theory*. New Jersey: Prentice-Hall.
48. Waugh, N.C. & Norman, D.A. (1965) Primary Memory. *Psychological Review*, 72, 89–104.
49. Glanzer, M. & Cunitz, A.R. (1966) Two storage mechanisms in free recall. *Journal of Verbal Learning and Verbal Behavior*, 5, 351–360.
50. Jenkins, J.G. & Dallenbach, K.M. (1924) Oblivescence during sleep and waking. *American Journal of Psychology*, 35, 605–612.
51. Ekstrand, B.R. (1972) To sleep perchance to dream (about why we forget). In C.P. Duncan, L. Sechrest & A.W. Melton (Eds.), *Human Memory*. New York: Appleton-Century-Croft.

52. Rogers, C.A. (1974) Feedback precision and post-feedback interval duration. *Journal of Experimental Psychology*, *102*, 604–608.

53. Belbin, E. (1964) *Training the Adult Worker*. (Problems of Progress in Industry, No. 15) London: HMSO.

54. Bass, B.M. & Vaughan, J.A. (1966) *Training in Industry: The Management of Learning*. Belmont, California: Wadsworth.

55. Hovland, C.I. (1938) Experimental studies in rote learning theory, 111. Distribution of practice with varying speeds of syllable presentation. *Journal of Experimental Psychology*, *23*, 172–190.

56. Bryan, W.L. & Harter, N. (1899) Studies on the telegraphic language: the acquisition of a hierarchy of habits. *Psychological Review*, *6*, 345–375.

57. Keller, F.S. (1959) The phantom plateaux. *Journal of the Experimental Analysis of Behaviour*, *1*, 1–13.

58. Chisseli, E. E. & Brown, C.W. (1955) *Personnel and Industrial Psychology, 2nd edition*. New York: McGraw-Hill.

59. Blackler, F. & Shimmin, S. (1984) *Applying Psychology in Organizations*. London: Methuen.

5 HUMAN INFORMATION PROCESSING AND DECISION-MAKING

5 Human Information Processing and Decision Making

Information processing and decision making are overlapping and related concepts, but there is a tendency among scholars to discuss them separately. In fact the individual acts as a processor of information right through to the final decision stage. This chapter starts with a definition and illustrations of information processing. There follows an examination of three major approaches to the study of human information processing. Next is a description of a decision cycle, followed by a discussion of three descriptive decisionmaking models. A distinction is made between structured and unstructured decision processes. This distinction is important when analyzing decision making under conditions of uncertainty. The development of decision support systems in the age of the computer is acknowledged before closing the discussion with an examination of individual and organizational influences on human information processing and decision making.

HUMAN INFORMATION PROCESSING

A human information processing perspective is essentially a cognitive view of Man. Human beings approach only a few situations in a unique way as information processors. Instead information from a person's environment is processed through pre-existing systems of knowledge abstracted from various memory schemata and experiences. These would include beliefs, theories, propositions and schemes. Effectively they are structures of knowledge that provide people with an important interpretative function capable of attaching meaning to incoming information as well as augmenting it. These structures also help to resolve certain ambiguities and to draw inferences, sometimes unconsciously, from the incoming information; and they create a much broader scene than could be justified by a literal interpretation of the material just received.

Production managers, like most people, have personal goals and aspirations and are motivated to achieve them. They are fortunate if their personal goals coincide with the goals of the organization for which they work. In the pursuit of achieving the organizational goals, expressed as a specified quantity and quality of output, they have to place reliance on information, not always accurate, about the availability of raw material and manpower, stock levels, product quality and the needs of customers. This and other information is used as a basis for making predictions about the business environment that influences the production function and to which it has to adapt.

The processor of information is essentially concerned with identifying and registering cues or stimuli which are perceived to be useful. The intelligent investor will not only pick up cues or information from the published accounts of a company, but will also rely on information from non-accounting sources, such as stock brokers, financial analysts and the financial press, though some of this information may have its origin in the accounting system of a company. The auditor establishes the appropriate starting point for an audit, and the extent of the assignment, after registering cues from early exploratory work. If the internal control system is perceived to be strong, less extensive tests of a substantive nature are likely to be performed. But if the internal control system is perceived at the outset to be on the weak side, more testing of entries in the accounting records is likely to be undertaken. The next step is to translate and transform the cues or information into a meaningful pattern in order to facilitate the choice of an appropriate response. Before doing so, however, the information will be evaluated and that which is considered inappropriate will be rejected.

Having conducted the audit of the accounting information systems, and having evaluated the data at his or her disposal, an auditor is faced with the task of formulating opinions about the "true and fair" state of the client's financial statements. Before expressing an opinion, professional judgement will be exercised to determine the amount of information to collect, when to collect it, the manner in which it is to be collected, and the implications of the information collected. The information is rarely, if ever, perfectly reliable or perfectly predictive of the "true and fair" state of the client's financial affairs. Nevertheless, the auditor may be held liable in law should the audited financial statements prove to be unrepresentative of the "true and fair" state when the latter is certified as being the case.

Approaches

There exist at least three major approaches to the study of human information processing. These are the Lens model, the Cognitive and the Process Tracing approaches.

1. Lens Model. The basic principles of this model are that the nature of the task environment exerts a powerful influence on behaviour, that the numerous cues from the environment within the grasp of the individual are usually imperfect, and that these cues are not very effective at predicting the environment with which the individual has to cope. As a result of the low level of predictability, the individual has to develop a range of processes that act as a response capability in order to achieve the objectives associated with the task.[1] The Lens model uses linear statistical procedures or Bayesian decision theory. A primary objective of certain researchers using this approach in the accounting field is to build mathematical models designed to show the relative importance of different sets of information and to measure the accuracy and consistency of judgement; the measurement of consensus and predictability is also attempted.

The Lens model is a normative model. A normative model in this context is concerned with how people solve problems, how they predict events, how they make decisions, and so on. To test the model, actual behaviour can be compared with what the model predicts, and if there is a perfect match the model is said to be robust. If there is a mismatch, it is hoped that the discrepancies are reflected in a systematic way. In the making of a major capital investment decision in a company, techniques based on normative principles could be used. Subjective probabilities will also be considered, since certain benefits or costs are expected to accrue following the making of the decision. Subjective probabilities are really different degrees of belief in the truth of a particular proposition. People revise their subjective probabilities as new information is received, so in these circumstances we can expect the company to revise the predictions based on its investment decision. Research on the Lens model identifies the prevalence of conservatism.[2] This means that when people receive new information they revise their subjective probabilities in the direction indicated by the normative model, even though the revision may be very small. Misperception and bias in the handling of data emanating from the person's task environment explains to some extent the onset of conservatism. When significant revisions are built into a normative model, it would appear that one is gravitating towards a descriptive model; such a model would describe rather than prescribe the way the individual processes information.

A valid question to ask is whether individuals terminate the search for information at a point before the best or optimal stopping point as specified by the normative model. Sometimes it would appear that individuals have accumulated enough evidence to satisfy their own standards and stop short of the ideal position for the cessation of the search for information. Somebody wishing to buy a video recorder may be advised to consult the *Which* report on video recorders. A thorough analysis of the strengths and weaknesses of the various brands specified in the report could be considered a prerequisite to a purchase decision. However, consumers may leaf quickly through the report without studying it closely or completely, and terminate the search for information before the optimal stopping point, feeling that they have enough information to make an acceptable decision. In recent times the usefulness of Bayesian decision theory, which is used in the Lens model, has been questioned; criticism is levelled at the static nature of algebraic models for evaluating and combining information, and it is suggested that time would be better spent observing the decision-making process (descriptive theory).[3]

2. Cognitive Approach. The focal point of attention with this approach is information-seeking behaviour in a complex environment. The assumption is that it is both possible and useful to classify individuals according to how they use information—i.e., their customary style of processing information. Accounting studies based on this approach attempt to classify users of information by their personal characteristics, using personality measures and decision style, the objective being to design information systems best suited to the individual style of the decision-maker.[4] However, it is likely to be very difficult to accommodate a tailor-made information system compatible with the personality needs of various individuals in an organization; though it is recognized that certain information-processing tasks are more capably performed by people with particular cognitive approaches. For example, in examining the problem-solving ability of schoolboys, it was found that those who were studying sciences and proposing to continue with their studies to degree level were showing tendencies to be convergers; in other words, they tended to be analytical and symbolic in their thinking rather than being imaginative, fluent and flexible. Those in the arts stream, however, showed a tendency to be divergers—i.e., imaginative, fluent and flexible rather than analytical and symbolic.[5]

A rather crude extension of the different problem-solving orientations to work organizations might suggest that the converger may feel more at ease with tasks that are highly structured, whereas the diverger may find the less structured tasks more suited to his or her mode of operation. The highly structured tasks, exemplified by tight procedures and management techniques, are more prevalent further down the organizational hierarchy than at the top where the number of relatively unstructured tasks is probably greater. Therefore a convergent outlook would seem to be particularly appropriate at the lower echelons of the organization. But would a divergent outlook be suited to life at the top of the organization? Apparently successful chief executives tend to rely more on "feel" and intuition (divergency-type characteristics) than systematic reasoning, they synthesize rather than analyze, they intuitively know more than they can communicate, and they revel in ambiguity and dislike regularity.[6]

The cognitive approach is associated with the theories of Schroder et al.[7] This work focuses on the reaction of a person's information processing system to changes in the complexity of the decision environment, particularly changes in the information load. Cognitive complexity has been referred to by Schroder and others as having three main features: (1) differentiation (numbers of parts); (2) integration (the degree to which the parts are related); and (3) order (the clarity with which the layers are arranged in a hierarchy).

Cognitive complexity is a function of past experience, and this can be expressed as the amount of information received and the degree of success in negotiating problems in the past.

People facing increasing inputs of information to their processing systems are expected to develop relatively complex cognitive structures. These people tend to rely on more complex sources of information and spend more time searching for and processing information, as if to suggest that they can handle larger amounts of information and are motivated to seek an optimum level of information. A person with an ability to utilize complex conceptual processes, that are integrated in nature, is likely to understand and react favourably to complexity in his or her decision environment. A difficult tax problem is more likely to be resolved by a competent tax specialist than by an accountant with a peripheral interest in taxation. Speed and an ability to cope with a substantial amount of complex data would be a feature of the performance of the former. Apart from information load, the format for the display of information and the order in which the information is presented are also important considerations.

3. Process Tracing Approach.   Unlike the other two approaches to human information processing, this approach goes beyond input-output analysis and attempts to obtain measures of events or processes between the input and output stages.[8] In both the Lens model and the cognitive approach, one draws inferences about how the information processing system works by looking at the relationship between the information received from the task environment and the end result (i.e., the judgement or decision). With process tracing one seeks evidence relating to the actual information processing activities. The evidence is most commonly sought by asking individuals to describe their thought processes. In a study comparing the decision-making processes of experts and novices in the context of a financial analysis task, differences in the style and depth of analysis between the two groups were detected. The research method used in the study was process tracing or PROTOCOL ANALYSIS.[9] Decision-makers were asked to verbalize while engaged in financial analysis, and these verbalizations were recorded on tape. The resulting transcripts, called concurrent or thinking-aloud protocols, provide the data for the protocol analysis.

Each subject was given a number of financial cases to process during the financial analysis task. A case contained a general description of the firm and a three-year set of financial statements, consisting of a balance sheet, income statement and pages with financial ratios, sales figures and production data. Each subject was asked to evaluate quickly the financial position of the firm, and to identify the underlying problems, if any.

Protocol analysis starts with splitting up the evidence provided by individuals into phrases, and coding or classifying these phrases with respect to the decision-making activity that they exhibit. (An example of a decision-making activity would be computing a financial trend or comparing costs and revenue.) Next the decision-makers' goals are identified. (An example of a goal would be the objective of the individual to explore indicators of the economic health of the firm, or to discover unusual features of the financial statements.) The next step in protocol analysis is the identification of the decision-making processes in terms of the individual's analysis in relation to the goals he or she has set.

The final step in protocol analysis is to present a visual representation of the sequence of events leading from the initial examination of the information through to the making of the final decision. A methodological weakness of protocol analysis stems from the difficulties in eliciting verbal descriptions from subjects. It is the degree of complexity of the task to be performed that exerts an influence on the way the information system functions in the process tracing approach. The task environment determines the extent of the problem, or "problem space" as it is called. The problem space will then determine the processes used to come up with a solution.

In an accounting exercise a student is confronted with a statement indicating that "land was purchased for £45,000 cash." The student is asked to make the required book-keeping entry, and begins by constructing a problem space, which means identifying the type of problem to be solved.[3] In this case it is an accounting problem. The student will then proceed to identify key words in the statement. The word "land" is compared with accounting words stored in long-term memory. When it is identified, it is categorized by type. For example, a definition of an asset is recalled and is then checked to see if land possesses the characteristics of an asset. If it does, it would be classified as an asset. Next, the entry in the asset account will be determined by an evaluation of the word "purchased." The information with respect to acquiring an asset would be combined with the student's understanding of the principles of debit and credit. In this case, it would be a debit entry of £45,000 to the land account. The same process would apply to cash, but here it is a credit entry of £45,000 in the cash book. Obviously the manner in which the total process is activitated will depend on the skill of the student. What is critical in this example is the interaction of the task environment and the expertise of the information processor in doing the exercise.

The example given is a simple problem, but the basic processes involved in solving it apply to more complex problems. For instance, if land was leased rather than purchased, the problem would be more complicated. The student would have to establish whether it was a rental lease or a capital lease. He or she would go ahead with the construction of the problem space, combining his or her internal knowledge with the external information provided, using a process more involved than that described in the previous example.

DECISION MAKING

Decision-making models are of two types: prescriptive and descriptive. Earlier in the discussion of the Lens model, a normative approach was considered prescriptive, in the sense that the model tells us what ought to be

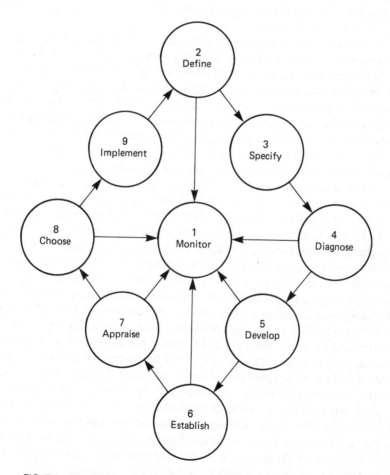

FIG. 5.1   The decision process. Source: Archer, E. (1980) How to make a business decision: An analysis of theory and practice. *Management Review, February.*

done. The normative or prescriptive model attempts to impose on the decision-maker the framework reflected in the assumptions of the model. A descriptive model, on the other hand, describes the steps involved in making a choice from among various courses of action open to the decision-maker. As we shall see later this is not always a rational process.

Decision Cycle

A study of over 2000 managers, supervisors and executives was undertaken in order to determine what steps in the decision cycle they used and found helpful. Out of this study came a simple nine-step framework, though the outcome of other studies had a part to play as well.[10] This is depicted in Fig.5.1 as a decision process, and it is discussed with reference to a description of a relatively simple decision.[11]

1. Monitor. The environment should be constantly monitored to obtain feedback. The decision-maker monitors the environment to detect deviations from plans or pick up signals on the need to take a decision. For example, a company makes specialized quality testing equipment for the food processing industry. The general manager of the company, having monitored the environment, has become aware of the fact that the number of late deliveries of testing equipment to customers is on the increase. Subsequently this information is reinforced by a complaint from an important customer who has just received a second late delivery.

2. Define. The problem or situation has to be precisely defined. The information picked up at the monitoring stage could relate to the symptoms of the problem, but not the causes. From initial inquiries it appears plausible that communication difficulties between the production and marketing functions is a contributory factor in the problem of late deliveries. The general manager writes a letter to the marketing and production managers asking for information on the delivery service to customers and the present utilization of manufacturing capacity.

3. Specify. The decision objectives have to be specified, and the likely risks and the constraints should be considered. What the decision-makers expected to be achieved is clarified.

4. Diagnosis. The problem or situation is more thoroughly analyzed and the causes of the problem are scrutinized. The general manager discusses the problem with the production manager, who states that the reasons for the late deliveries are the unrealistic delivery promises made by sales staff, who are also at fault in not giving manufacturing staff enough notice to plan production when large new orders are received. Faced with this evidence the marketing manager in conversation with the general manager defends the sales staff. He or she maintains that prompt delivery is crucial in highly competitive market conditions, and that the company must react quickly to get new business. Inevitably the manufacturing staff cannot expect much notice of new orders. The marketing manager also maintains that the problem is inadequate capacity in the production area due to under-investment in plant over a period of time. Therefore the production function does not have sufficient flexibility to meet delivery times. The general manager at this stage feels that due to communication difficulties neither the production manager nor the marketing manager has critical information at their disposal when making decisions.

5. Develop. Alternative courses of action or solutions are developed. The options open to the company have been discussed at length and the critical options are listed as: (a) introduce a computerized information system; (b) all sales staff are required to check with production control before making promises related to delivery; (c) put aside an afternoon each week for a meeting when operating managers can discuss matters of prime importance; and (d) all sales staff are required to complete weekly reports on the likelihood of receiving orders from customers in the near future. It is felt that any combination of the above options is feasible.

6. Establish. At this stage the methods or criteria to be used in the appraisal of the options or alternatives are established. This could be any process that ensures the provision of an adequate amount of information to facilitate realistic promises with respect to deliveries of testing systems to customers, and to improve performance of the delivery service at acceptable cost levels.

7. Appraise. Alternative solutions or courses of action should be appraised. Each alternative or option is evaluated in terms of the quantity and quality of information it would provide for the production and marketing functions. The costs of implementation of the alternatives would also be appraised. Both costs and benefits would be expressed in quantitative and qualitative terms.

8. Choose. The best alternative solution or course of action is chosen. In this case a management committee made the decision, and chose two (rather than one) options for implementation. The options 5.a and 5.d above were either too expensive or were unlikely to produce much useful information. The eventual decision was that 5.b and 5.c should be implemented.

9. Implement. The best alternative solution or course of action is implemented. The detailed operational plan is discussed at the regular afternoon management meeting. In addition the marketing manager issues instructions to sales staff to check with a certain person in production control before stating delivery times.

This decision process could revert back to stage 1, when monitoring activity resumes. In this case it was felt that the system had improved, but the general manager was not totally satisfied with the outcome. At a meeting of the management group the problem was redefined to include some fundamental issues which affected the way the production function was organized, and the decision process started again. In practice the process of decision making is unlikely to be as smooth as the model depicted above would suggest. "Real decision behaviours can exhibit frequent backtracks and jumps forward before an option is finally selected. Thus the decision process may not be smooth but a jerky and hesitant progression involving at times, one step forwards and two steps backwards."[11]

The descriptive decision process described above would be classified by Behling and Schriesheim as the "econological model of decision making."[12] Other descriptive models of decision making, which they acknowledge, and which will be analyzed later, are the "bounded rationality" and "implicit favourite" models.

Econological Model

This model describes a logical and orderly way of processing information and arriving at a decision. The resultant decision is considered to be based on rationality. However, there is some evidence to suggest that consumers do not make decisions in the way outlined in the econological model. For example, in the literature on consumer behaviour a decision model similar to the econological model is adopted,[13] but in a critical analysis of research studies on pre-purchase decision behaviour, it was concluded that for many purchases a decision process never occurs, or if purchase behaviour is preceded by a decision process, this process of choice is likely to be very limited. It typically involves the evaluation of only a few alternatives, it entails little external search for information, few evaluative criteria are used, and the evaluation process is a simple one. It may be more realistic to consider the potency of a personal recommendation from a friend or relative, coupled with limited search for and evaluation of information prior to a purchase decision. Other influences on purchase behaviour may be conformity to group norms, imitation and so on.[14]

Two main factors may account for the limitations of the econological model. One is concerned with the information available to decision-makers, and the other with the processing capability of the individual.

1. With regard to availability of information, only a small number of alternative courses of action in the decision situation come to mind, knowledge of a given alternative is incomplete, and when outcomes of the decision process are considered the values attached to these outcomes are imperfectly anticipated.[15] A real difficulty is the problem experienced by the decision-maker in selecting even a limited number of alternative courses of action, because of knowledge deficiencies.[16]

2. With regard to the information-processing capability of the individual, there are constraints in the way we seek solutions to problems. Even if the decision-maker has full knowledge of all alternatives and outcomes, complete rationality could not be achieved because of the restrictions imposed upon the decision process by the capabilities of the human mind as an information-processing system. The system accommodates only one process at a time, it cannot work in a parallel fashion; and as was stated in Chapter 4, on learning and memory, the inputs and outputs stemming from problem-solving activity are initially stored in a small short-term memory with very limited capacity. Of course the human information-processing system has access to a substantial long-term memory with fast retrieval but slow storage. All these factors impose restrictions on the way in which the individual's information processing system seeks solutions to problems.[17]

Given the limiting factors identified above, it would appear that decision processes which are amenable to a consideration of a number of alternatives and outcomes cannot be made in the form postulated by the econological model. Basically, we suffer deficiencies when comparing alternatives in a simultaneous fashion, rather than a sequential arrangement, and our memory storage system can be a handicap. Likewise, the exercise of placing values on various outcomes of the decision process, and ranking alternatives in order of preference, is constrained by the limitations of our memory. Again we find that being able to select the alternative that will generate the greatest benefit is extraordinarily difficult.[18]

Bounded Rationality Model

This model is more reality-orientated, and it recognizes the constraints acting on the ability of the individual to process information. Individuals and organizations seek the best solutions when faced with a choice among alternatives, but they usually settle for considerably less than they would like to have. The ideal decision would make too great a demand on their data-processing capabilities. Bounded rationality explains decision making in terms of three main processes: (1) consideration of alternative solutions in a sequential fashion; (2) use of heuristics to identify the most promising alternatives; and (3) satisficing.

1. Consideration of Alternative Solutions in a Sequential Fashion.
When things are going well there is a tendency not to scan the environment
in a serious way. But if the external environment poses a threat to the organization, then a search for solutions to the problems encountered takes
place; this is akin to the notion of strategic planning. The search process is
said to have three main characteristics.[19] The search is motivated in the sense
that it is activated in response to a current problem. It is simple minded in
that it begins with the obvious solutions, and only considers other solutions
if the simple-minded solutions prove inadequate. Finally, it is biased because the search for solutions is influenced by the individual's *ego*, training,
experience, hopes and aspirations, and other factors which serve to distort
his or her view of the world. Unlike the treatment of alternatives in the
econological model, which requires that all alternatives under consideration
be identified before any evaluation takes place, here in the bounded rationality model the various alternatives are identified and considered one at a
time. Those that prove inadequate in the light of the evaluative criteria are
discarded before other alternatives are considered.

2. Use of Heuristics.   Heuristics are rules which guide the search for
alternatives into areas where there is a good chance of finding satisfactory
solutions. They reduce to manageable proportions the number of possible
solutions through which the decision-maker must sift.[17] Heuristic models do
not attempt to optimize, though they can do so by chance, but they aim to
achieve satisfactory sub-optimal solutions. The heuristic approach adopts
short cuts in the reasoning process, and it uses rules of thumb, such as the
following, in the search for a satisfactory solution.[20] "Buy when prices on
the stock exchange move rapidly in a particular direction with a heavy
volume of trading." "When the stock of goods gets down to four, that is the
time to buy more." "For accounting purposes value assets at cost or market
value, whichever is the lower." In production scheduling the motto is "first
come, first served or schedule urgent jobs first."[21] Heuristic models are generally more complex than these rules of thumb, but equally they can be
relatively simple.

3. Satisficing.   In the econological model the best or optimal course
of action is chosen after considering all possible alternatives. On the other
hand, satisficing as a bounded rationality process operates on the assumption that decision-makers judge alternatives one at a time against certain
standards of acceptability and accept the first alternative which meets the
minimal acceptable criteria or the minimum conditions for success. So the
decision-maker need not evaluate all possible alternatives, but only search
until an adequate one is found. Therefore, satisficing means the acceptance
of a satisfactory outcome. As a result, the decision-maker engages in a

lesser amount of information processing activity than would be the case if an optimal alternative was sought. An insight from an expectancy theory of motivation, which is discussed in Chapter 2, could be applied to the behaviour of the decision-maker intent on satisficing. As decision-makers explore the various alternative solutions, their aspiration level rises and next time round they may be a little more adventurous in their search. But as they find it difficult to discover satisfactory solutions, their aspiration level falls and that makes it easier on the next occasion to obtain satisfactory solutions.[22]

The bounded rationality model appears to be a more accurate description of the individual's decision-making process than is found in the econological model, but the evidence to support this assertion is not totally conclusive.[12] Much of the supporting evidence comes from computer simulations of the decision-making process, and the decisions studied seem to have a number of characteristics found in programmed or structured decisions.

Structured or Programmed Decisions.   A structured or programmed decision is well defined; the decision-maker is aware of the extent of the decision, and there exists a clear set of options from which a choice can be made. The method of evaluating the options has been established and is straightforward. Therefore the decision-maker has a well specified and agreed decision procedure at his or her disposal.[23] The following is an example of a structured decision.[11] A manager has to choose a new packaging machine from a selection of two models, both of which are similar to an existing machine and are known to be reliable. The manager chooses the machine which offers the most attractive post-tax discounted return calculated over a five-year period. This involves collecting details, such as price and operating costs, of each machine using a formula approved by the organization for capital expenditure proposals. An order is then placed for the selected machine and the goods received section and accounts department are duly notified. An example of non-programmed or unstructured decision making is given in the commentary on the implicit favourite model.

Implicit Favourite Model.   In an analysis of the job-search behaviour of graduate business students it was concluded that decisions were made in a way that could not be adequately explained by either the econological model or the bounded rationality model.[24] However, in accordance with the predictions of the econological model, the students searched for alternatives in a parallel fashion and evaluated several alternatives at a time. But a departure from the econological model was evident with respect to the lack of weighting attached to the evaluation criteria; neither was the evaluation criteria used in making the final choice. (The criteria used in evaluating alternative jobs may, for example, relate to a number of characteristics such as salary level, job interest and challenge, and location.) It was also established in this study that the alternatives were not ranked in some order of preference.

An important finding of the study was that the search for information continued after a satisfactory alternative (the implicit favourite) was identified, e.g., the choice of a particular type of job that offers interest and challenge with a modest initial salary. What happened next was a lengthy process of investigation soon after the search for alternatives ceased. This took the form of justifying the choice of the implicit favourite by offsetting against it the most attractive of the rejected alternatives, e.g., a job with an attractive initial salary, but rather limited challenge and prospects. Then a rationale was created to show that the implicit favourite was superior to the best of the rejected alternatives. Once the implicit favourite was chosen, information on the outcome of alternatives was biased in its favour. Also, evaluation elements (e.g., minimum salary, challenging jobs) used in the choice of the most appropriate alternative were adjusted to fit the desired outcome. From an outside objective assessment of the decision process it was clear that the implicit favourite was based only on a limited number of dimensions of the decision criteria. A decision was not announced at the time of the choice of implicit favourite; it was not until the most attractive of the rejected alternatives was ruled out in a rather biased analytical exercise that a decision was declared.

In a criticism of the implicit favourite model it is alleged that the model is more a model of decision rationalization than of decision making. It concentrates on the justification for the choice of the implicit favourite but it says very little about how the implicit favourite is selected.[12] The model was created as a result of individual decision making in pursuit of a job, and may not be applicable to organizational decision making where bargaining and political processes could act as significant constraints.

Decision Making under Uncertainty

The evidence discussed in the previous section relates to a non-programmed or unstructured decision, which is described further here.

Non-programmed or Unstructured Decisions. Non-programmed or unstructured decisions are not clearly defined either in terms of what the objectives are or who is involved in the decision. In fact the decision situation is blurred, not well understood and difficult to tackle. The alternative solutions to be considered are not immediately apparent, simply because the situation facing the decision-maker has not been seen in its present form before, or under the prevailing circumstances. Because of the novelty of the decision, the decision-maker has an unclear view of how to tackle it; in fact different executives are likely to have different views on both the decision itself and how to tackle it. The following is another example of a non-programmed or unstructured decision.[11] A manager is keen to make a decision about the nature of the company's product portfolio in the medium term. Reports from sales representatives indicate that the existing product range appears somewhat obsolete in relation to that offered by competitors. The manager has to face a decision either to update the existing range of products or alternatively to offer a new range. This presents a dilemma, more so because the eventual decision will affect a number of areas within the company. The manager proceeds to consult and seek advice from colleagues in other functional areas of the business on the feasibility of his or her own initial ideas about the best way to go ahead. He or she recognizes that a new product range will provide a firm foundation for the long-term security of the company, but also realizes that any significant expenditure incurred at this stage could threaten the delicate cash-flow position of the company in the short term. It is no easy task to take the right decision in these circumstances.

Apparently the uncertainty associated with the making of a non-programmed or unstructured decision also makes its presence felt at the implementation stage. This was highlighted in a study of the implementation stage of a non-programmed decision.[25] A decision was made to transfer staff from one location of a company to another. The chief executive decided that a specified number of staff were involved in the move, and a senior personnel executive had responsibility to implement the decision. The personnel executive was given wide discretionary powers to use standard operating programmes and to develop new programmes or modify old ones through discussion and analysis. His first line of action was to initiate problem-solving activity by calling a meeting of individuals qualified to contribute to the process of implementing the decision. Out of this meeting came an action programme.

However, as the implementation process neared completion it was evident that matters were not progressing at the level originally anticipated. Because of a reluctance of some staff to move, quality considerations had to be relaxed and lower-calibre staff were transferred in particular circumstances. In addition, the reluctance of certain staff to move created organizational slack in the donor site and this was condoned by the workers and union officials alike. The unanticipated consequences flowing from the implementation process, which acted to the disadvantage of the company, were the creation of organizational slack at the old site and the introduction of lower-calibre staff at the new site.

As a final comment on unstructured decisions, it is worth noting that a certain type of unstructured decision, i.e., a strategic decision in an organization, may be underpinned by a basic structure. From a field study of 25 strategic decision processes, together with a review of the related empirical literature, it was concluded that strategic decision processes, as opposed to tactical decision processes of a routine problem-solving nature, are immensely complex and dynamic; but yet they are amenable to conceptual structuring.[26] To finalize this section we shall examine an important decision process which exemplifies uncertainty; the process of negotiation.

Negotiation. Negotiation is an example of decision making under conditions of uncertainty. It pervades many aspects of organizational life; for example, negotiations are conducted between union representatives and management, between sales executives and clients, and between managers within an organization on matters connected with the allocation of scarce resources. Before decisions are made, delicate behavioural processes can be detected during the course of negotiations. Morley has analyzed these processes, and the more important ones will now be discussed.[27]

Negotiators take certain courses of action on the basis of their perception of the likely response of the other party in the negotiation process. Negotiators will strive to attain the maximum benefits from the encounter, but equally they are aware of the need to reach an agreement acceptable to all parties. Obviously this necessitates compromise and modification of positions when circumstances dictate such a course.

Negotiators have to come to terms with two major forces which impinge on the situation. First, there are the social processes and relationships built up with the opponents at the bargaining table. Second, the negotiators are conscious of the fact that they are acting as representatives of a group who are outside the bargaining process. For example, union representatives are acting on behalf of their trade union, which may have specified the desired result. The relative strength of the two forces can change as negotiations proceed.

At the bargaining table it is possible for friendly relationships to develop between the protagonists. This in turn facilitates the free flow of information, and eventually contributes to a co-operative rather than a competitive spirit and the development of mutual trust and respect. Of course there is also the potential for conflict, and this could be injected into the proceedings from the outside environment. Another source of conflict stems from inconsistencies in the judgements of negotiators. Deviousness may be attributed to a negotiator because his or her judgement is considered inaccurate or incomplete.

The bargaining process can be complex and clouded with uncertainty. Critical information may not be readily available, or if it is, it may be ambiguous. Alternatively, there may be a lot of information available in numerous documents and the negotiators may find it difficult to grasp their brief. As arguments are presented and manoeuvres worked out, the interests and power base of participants become critical. Uncertainty is often created when a negotiator tries to answer questions on the validity of information presented by the other party. Likewise, negotiators may doubt their ability to defend their position, and are concerned about giving too much away too quickly. ("Shall we continue in the hope of negotiating a better deal?") Negotiators are continuously trying to make sense out of the dialogue and to put it into an ordered perspective.

Eventually, the outcome of the negotiations will depend upon the accuracy of the negotiators' diagnosis of the delicate inter-personal processes, and the skill with which they make the appropriate moves. Those endowed with a perceptive outlook, who possess a good facility in presenting a case and are shrewd, operate at an advantage. In complex negotiations, particularly of a multilateral nature, a breakthrough in the negotiations may be difficult to achieve. The desired outcome of most negotiation processes is likely to embrace a favourable agreement, the avoidance of a disaster, and improved relationships between the parties concerned.

Decision Support Systems

A decision support system is a system which provides information to supplement rather than replace managerial decision making.[11] It generally consists of a database which accommodates internally generated data (e.g., costs), but can also include external data (e.g., economic forecasts). The data could be analyzed or rearranged using, for example, a computer model. The computer models vary in levels of sophistication. There are those used in financial analysis where data on cash flow analysis, financial forecasting, and balance sheet projections are available. By contrast, databases in a marketing information system could include sales figures, pricing data and the costs of marketing a product. This data could be merged with an external marketing database to provide a forecast of sales and the effects of different marketing decisions.

The examples given above are related to systems providing decision-oriented data with the aid of a small computer model. A more sophisticated model would be a system that proposes a decision or a specific recommendation for action. In this situation the decision support system has the capacity to give solutions based on the appropriate software and data input. An example is a system for calculating the premium attached to an insurance policy. The premium is calculated by the system using standard statistical and actuarial data and details of the proposed policy.[28] At the other end of the scale is a simple decision support system which is effectively a file drawer system. This is a computer-based version of a manual filing system. All it does is provide access to a particular item of data (e.g., the cost of a spare part in the offices of a dealer in the car trade).

How do policy makers respond to systems based on computer models? In one study the extent to which computer-based modelling systems were used by public agencies was investigated. It was found that the eventual choices of alternatives in decision processes were rarely influenced directly by the analyses from these systems. An interesting finding was that in relevant cases the computer analyses (results) were used to support policies already decided in advance. If the results were considered by the policy makers to be influential, they would call in the expert (computer modeller) who would play a prominent part in the making of a decision.[29]

In another study the constraints surrounding the operation of computer models in a changed context were emphasized.[30] The following computer systems, using small to medium-sized computers, carried out functions normally done by middle managers:

1. Inventory and marketing analyses in a plant in the U.K.
2. Patient scheduling in a hospital in the U.K.
3. Scheduling production in a radio factory.

The results emanating from these systems were unsatisfactory. All three systems were too inflexible to meet changing demands. With regard to (1), bad weather accompanied by unexpectedly heavy snowfalls led to problems with transportation, and this disrupted inventory planning. With regard to (2), the system was disbanded because it failed to respond to the basic needs of doctors and patients. Finally, in the case of (3), changes in the taxation system resulting from new regulations in the European Economic Community made the marketing of the radios extremely difficult.

Are certain types of decisions more amenable to decision-support systems than others? It appears that decisions on the borderline between structured and unstructured decisions are compatible with the computer models of the decision support systems.[31] Well structured decisions can be accommodated by the conventional management information systems. But when top management face novel and unpredictable conditions, which require the taking of unstructured decisions, programmed packages may be too restrictive to deal with these circumstances.[32] In decision situations which are highly unstructured the decision-maker will rely heavily on experience, judgement and even intuition.

INDIVIDUAL AND ORGANIZATIONAL INFLUENCES

Individual and organizational factors influence the way in which information is acquired, processed and used in the making of decisions. The influence exerted by the group on decision making is specifically referred to in Chapter 7. Some individual considerations in connection with cognitive complexity were discussed earlier, in the section of this chapter on the cognitive approach to information processing.

Personality

With respect to specific personality factors related to information processing, it has been suggested that dogmatic and authoritarian personality types display a marked lack of tolerance for ambiguity and uncertainty and consequently are less likely to search for information. They are less capable of dealing with inconsistent information and are unlikely to be flexible in the positions they adopt.[33] A fuller discussion of personality types appears in Chapter 1.

Decision-makers with Machiavellian tendencies could view information as a tool for achieving their personal objectives, possibly resulting in the withholding of information so as to maintain control or to win favours from influential people. The withholding, ignoring and distorting of information for whatever reason can be detrimental to decision-making that rests on the combined or co-operative efforts of a number of employees. Social motives play an important part in interactive episodes or contacts between employees, and as a consequence can affect the quality of decisions where an exchange of information is critical in the decision process.

Brainstorming

Brainstorming is a technique used in an organization to facilitate the search for alternative solutions to a problem.[34] The important thing is to be tolerant of all suggested solutions to a problem, however unconventional or unworkable they appear to be. The technique is used in group situations, and its main purpose is to generate ideas with little censorship or criticism.

Trained Incapacity

A situation sometimes develops where the training provided by the organization actually interferes with the individual's approach to decision making and problem solving. This arises particularly when the decision rules or procedures do not fit the problem or decision under review. But the individual has been trained to operate the rules and procedures, and is not prepared to modify or adjust them to suit the decision or problem in hand. This is referred to as "trained incapacity," and it acts as a process to compartmentalize incoming information and problems into a limited number of categories in a procedure or decision process.[35] This may have an advantage from the employee's point of view because less time is spent on analyzing the problem and searching for alternatives, and it provides consistency and predictability in the processing of information.

However, it tends to produce rigidity and impairs the capacity of the organization to react effectively to changed circumstances, when problems cannot be categorized neatly by a pre-determined procedure. Trained incapacity is said to portray an approach to decision making whereby the decision-makers become so accustomed to making programmed decisions that they even attempt to solve non-programmable problems in a programmed way.[36]

Division of Labour

Division of labour within organizations provides a number of operating advantages. It permits specialization with the potential for greater efficiency, but the introduction of functional specialists breeds the growth of specialized language and terminology. Production managers have their own unique vocabulary just as accountants have their technical language. These and other factors, such as conventions and outlook on commercial life, make the transmission of information for purposes of decision making across functional or unit boundaries rather difficult and may result in distortions and omissions.[37]

Organizational Hierarchy

Apart from the division of tasks into specialist functions, an organization is invariably characterized by an arrangement of tasks in a hierarchical form. For example, senior managers perform different tasks from those performed by first-line supervisors. The organizational hierarchy may pose problems for the processing and transfer of information. Sometimes information is modified by a subordinate so that it complies with the preferences and prejudices of the superior. This may be done in order to obtain the approval of the superior. There are many occasions when employees of the same status in the organization frequently provide information and feedback on performance to one another as a normal part of social interaction, but the incidence of feedback is much less between different layers of the organization. There appears to be a tendency for subordinates to feel uncomfortable when they are engaged in exchanging information with superiors rather than with their peers.[38] They tend to overinterpret and overreact to messages sent by superiors.

In addition to the problem of communication of information between layers of the organization, there is the problem which results from the tendency of the organizational system itself "to filter information by providing less and less detailed information to the top of the organization."[39] As the information makes its way up the organization, summaries with expressions of opinion, conclusions and recommendations for action are very prevalent. So it is the inferences drawn from the primary data collected at the lower levels of the organization, not the detailed data itself, that is transmitted upwards. Therefore the people further down the organization who prepare the summaries and draw inferences from the detailed information can exert considerable influence on the decision-makers at the higher level. Since the top decision-maker is unlikely to inspect the raw primary data, he or she should be aware, to an acceptable extent, of the credibility of the major sources of information within the organization.[40] However, advances in information technology make it possible for senior managers in certain circumstances to gain direct access to information generated further down the hierarchy. A full discussion of new technology and management appears in Chapter 8.

The Grapevine

Not all communications take place within the formal hierarchy of organization. Nearly all organizations make extensive use of informal communication processes, partly to compensate for the deficiences generated by the formal processes. Informal communication can arise spontaneously within an organization, and can be seen to make a contribution in terms of lightening the burden of the overloaded formal communication channels. The grapevine consists of a network of informal relationships and it transmits information unofficially. Sometimes this information is accurate, and sometimes it is inaccurate. It is now patently obvious that communication processes within organizations can have a material effect on the quality of information processing and decision making, particularly when the information flows through the layers of the hierarchy. A fuller discussion of communication takes place in Chapter 3.

This concludes a brief examination of some important individual and organizational influences on human information processing and decision making.

SUMMARY

Human information processing and decision making are related concepts. A human information processing perspective, which amounts to a cognitive view of man, was discussed with reference to the production manager, the investor and the auditor. Three approaches to the study of human information processing were identified. These are the Lens Model, and the Cognitive and Process Tracing approaches.

Two types of decision models were referred to, but most of the discussion was devoted to an analysis of descriptive rather than prescriptive models. This reflects the interests of behavioural researchers who study applied decision making. The steps in a decision cycle were illustrated with respect to a description of a relatively simple decision. Three models of decision making were introduced; the econological model, the bounded rationality model and the implicit favourite model. Heuristics and satisficing are two of the features of the bounded rationality model.

Decision making was examined with respect to conditions of uncertainty. Two types of decision were defined as structured and unstructured. The unstructured decision lends itself to conditions of uncertainty, whereas stable or more predictable situations are compatible with a structured decision. Negotiation and bargaining were discussed as examples of decision making under conditions of uncertainty. Decision support systems, using computer models, were acknowledged as a process that supplements managerial decision making, though one must recognize the constraints that affects the operation of computer decision models in changed circumstances.

The chapter was brought to a conclusion with an examination of some individual and organizational influences on decision making. These are personality, brainstorming, trained incapacity, division of labour, organizational hierarchy, and the grapevine.

QUESTIONS

1. Define Human Information Processing with examples drawn from business life.
2. Describe three approaches to the study of Human Information Processing. Select one approach and show how it can be applied to an accountancy problem.
3. Distinguish between a converger and a diverger in an organizational context.
4. Identify the steps in the decision cycle. To what extent do decisions in real life follow this process?
5. Comment on the conditions appropriate to (1) unstructured decisions, and (2) structured decisions.
6. List the models of decision making reported by Behling and Schriesheim.
7. Collective bargaining is a complex negotiation process. Discuss.
8. What do you understand by the notion of decision support systems?
9. List the influence exerted by individual and organizational variables on Human Information Processing and Decision Making.

REFERENCES

1. Brunswik, E. (1955) Representative design and probabilistic theory in a functional psychology. *Psychological Review, May,* 193–217.
2. Snowball, D. (1980) On the integration of accounting research on human information processing. *Accounting and Business Research, 10,* 307–318.
3. Dillard, J.F. (1984) Cognitive science and decision-making research in accounting. *Accounting, Organizations and Society, 9,* 343–354.
4. Libby, R. & Lewis, B.L. (1982) Human information processing research in accounting: the state of the art in 1982. *Accounting, Organizations and Society, 7,* 231–285.
5. Hudson, L. (1966) *Contrary Imaginations.* London: Methuen.
6. Bobbitt, H.R., Breinholt, R.H., Doktor, R.H. & McNaul, J.P. (1978) *Organizational Behaviour: Understanding and Prediction.* Englewood Cliffs, NJ: Prentice-Hall.
7. Schroder, H.M., Driver, M.J. & Streufert, S. (1967) *Human Information Processing.* New York: Holt, Rinehart & Winston.
8. Hayes, J.R. (1968) Strategies in judgemental research. In B. Kleinmuntz (Ed.), *Formal Representation of Human Judgement.* New York: John Wiley and Sons.
9. Bouwman, M.J. (1984) Expert vs novice decision making in accounting: a summary. *Accounting, Organizations and Society, 9,* 325–327.
10. Archer, E. (1980) How to make a business decision: an analysis of theory and practice. *Management Review, February.*
11. Cooke, S. & Slack, N. (1984) *Making Management Decisions.* Hemel Hempstead, England: Prentice-Hall.
12. Behling, O. & Schriesheim C. (1976) *Organizational Behaviour: Theory, Research and Application.* Boston: Allyn & Bacon.
13. Engel, J.F., Blackwell, R.D. & Kollat, D.T. (1978) *Consumer Behaviour.* Hinsdale, Ill: The Dryden Press.
14. Olshavsky, R.W. & Granbois, D.H. (1979) Consumer decision making—fact or fiction. *Journal of Consumer Research, 6,* 93–100.
15. Simon, H.A. (1957) *Administrative Behaviour.* New York: The Free Press.
16. Terry, G.R. (1968) *Principles of Management.* Homewood, Ill: Richard D. Irwin.
17. Simon, H.A. & Newell, A. (1971) Human problem solving: the state of the theory in 1970. *American Psychologist, 26,* 145–159.
18. Von Neumann, J. & Morgenstern, O. (1953) *Theory of Games and Economic Behaviour.* Princeton, NJ: Princeton University Press.
19. Cyert, R.M. & March, J.G. (1963) *A Behavioural Theory of the Firm.* Englewood Cliffs, NJ: Prentice-Hall.
20. Hinkle, C.L. & Kuehn, A.A. (1967) Heuristic models: mapping to maze for management. *California Management Review, 10,* 59–68.
21. Weist, J.D. (1966) Heuristic programs for decision making. *Harvard Business Review, September/October,* 129–143.
22. Simon, H.A. (1957) *Models of Man.* New York: John Wiley & Sons.
23. Simon, H.A. (1960) *The Science of Management Decisions.* New York: Harper & Row.
24. Soelberg, P.O. (1967) Unprogrammed decision making. *Industrial Management Review, 8,* 19–29.
25. Dufty, N.F. & Taylor, P.M. (1970) The implementation of a decision. In L.A. Welsch & R.M. Cyert (Eds.), *Management Decision Making.* Harmondsworth: Penguin.
26. Mintzberg, H., Raisinghani, D. & Theoret, A. (1976) The structure of unstructured decision processes. *Administrative Science Quarterly, 21,* 246–275.
27. Morley, I. (1984) Bargaining and negotiation. In C.L. Cooper & P. Makin (Eds.), *Psychology for Managers (2nd Edition).* Basingstoke, Hants: British Psychological Society/ Macmillan Publishers.

28. Alter, S. (1977) A taxonomy of decision support systems. *Sloan Management Review, Fall.*

29. Greenberger, M., Crenson, M.A. & Crissey, B.L. (1976) *Models of the Policy Process: Public Decision Making in the Computer Era.* New York: Russell Sage Foundation.

30. Bjorn-Anderson, N. (1979) Myths and realities of information systems contributing to organizational rationality. *Proceedings of the IFIP 2nd HCC Conference, June.* Amsterdam: North Holland Publishing.

31. McCosh, A.M. & Scott-Morton, M. (1978) *Management Decision Support Systems.* London: Macmillan.

32. Oborne, D.J. (1985) *Computers at Work: A Behavioural Approach.* Chichester, England: John Wiley & Sons.

33. Dermer, J.D. (1973) Cognitive characteristics and the perceived importance of information. *Accounting Review, July,* 511-519.

34. Osborn, A. (1957) *Applied Imagination.* New York: Scribners.

35. Merton, R.K. (1957) *Social Theory and Social Structure.* Glencoe, Ill: Free Press.

36. Kerr, S., Klimoski, R.J., Tolliver, J. & Van Glinow, M.A. (1975) Human information processing. In J. Leslie Livingstone (Ed.), *Managerial Accounting: The Behavioral Foundations.* Columbus, Ohio: Grid Publishing.

37. Litterer, J.A. (1973) *The Analysis of Organizations (2nd Ed.).* New York: John Wiley & Sons.

38. Blau, P.M. & Scott, W.R. (1962) *Formal Organizations.* San Francisco: Chandler.

39. Richards, M.D. & Greenlaw, P.S. (1972) *Management: Decisions and Behavior.* Glenview, Ill: Richard D. Irwin.

40. March, J.G. & Simon, H.A. (1958) *Organizations.* New York: John Wiley & Sons.

6 ATTITUDES

6

Attitudes

After a definition of attitudes, this chapter continues with a brief commentary on attitude formation. This is followed by a section on the functions of attitudes. Next, the notion of prejudice is introduced, and this leads to an analysis of attitude change. The discussion moves on to focus on attitude measurement, and finally there is comment on the relationship between attitudes and behaviour.

DEFINITION

Attitudes are enduring systems of positive or negative evaluations, emotional feelings, and action tendencies, with respect to the individual's social world.[1] Attitudes can also be defined as mental states developed through experience, which are always ready to exert an active influence on an individual's response to any conditions and circumstances that the attitudes are directed towards.[2] (For example, an attitude to safety could predispose the individual to react in a certain way to hazardous conditions at work.)

Three components of an attitude can be identified (see Table 6.1). They are classified as *belief* (cognitive), *feeling* (affective), and *action* (conative) and each component can be either positive or negative. The *feeling* or *affective* component of an attitude is of prime importance and it can have a significant impact on the other two components. There are occasions when the cognitive, affective, and conative components of an individual's attitudes will be consistent with one another; this is called *intra-attitude consistency*. The person who visits a pub frequently (action-tendency), probably believes that the publican gives a good service (cognitive), and feels that the service and atmosphere is good (affective). However, intra-attitude consistency may not always be achieved, as will be seen later.

239

TABLE 6.1
Components of An Attitude

Component	Positive	Negative
Belief (cognitive)	Kerry is safety conscious.	Kerry is careless in the way he operates machinery.
Feeling (affective)	Kerry can be trusted.	Kerry cannot be trusted.
Action (conative)	It is easy to relate to Kerry.	It is difficult to relate to Kerry.

Attitudes and Values

There is a difference between attitudes and values. Having an attitude implies the existence of an object towards which an attitude is directed. A value is an ideal to which the individual subscribes; it offers a standard that will guide our conduct and acts as a process to evaluate and judge our own behaviour and that of others. The motivational impact of a value is apparent when we strive to attain a particular ideal.[3]

Attitudes and behaviour are the consequence of adhering to a particular value. For example, if an individual places a high value on equality for different races in society, one could expect him or her to have a positive attitude to ethnic minorities and behave accordingly. However, the relationship between attitudes and behaviour is not always predictable. An attitude can spring from a value; a person who places a high value on honesty, may develop a negative attitude towards another person who consistently tells lies. In another context a person who values justice may develop a positive attitude towards a public figure who is seen to be fostering this cause.

Attitudes as Filters

A person tends to select information that is consistent with his or her attitudes and ignores information that is opposed to them. The expression of an opinion amounts to an interpretation of what has been observed after filtering it through the medium of attitudes.

In the processing and use of accounting information, for example, the attitudes of those involved assume a primary importance.[4] The attitude of the accountant to the processing of accounting information will be influenced by the emphasis put on formal information processing systems by management in organizations, by the extent of the value placed by senior management on both accounting information and the contribution of accountants, and by the emphasis put on the notion of communicating data of a financial nature both inside and outside the organization. The extent to which accounting information is used is likely to be influenced by the attitudes of the user or decision-maker to accounting information.

Positive and Negative Attitudes

A positive attitude is likely to exist if decision-makers consider the information to be useful, where they welcome it, have confidence in it, and place value on it when compared to other types of information about the business. The quality of accounting information and accounting systems is likely to be associated with the quality of the accountant as perceived by the users of accounting information. The decision-maker or user of accounting information may have negative attitudes towards certain types of information because these are considered irrelevant, even though in practice the information may be of utmost importance to the decision-making process. On other occasions accounting information is wrongly or inefficiently used, or alternatively it is discounted because in specified circumstances decision-makers are attached to preconceived notions about the right decision.

An example of a negative attitude to safety at work could be the acceptance of a situation where machinery guards in a factory are frequently removed by workers, where workers are sometimes forced by supervisors to work in unsafe conditions, where supervisors do not listen when workers report unsafe conditions, where supervisors do not act to put right unsafe conditions when reported, and when they are not very receptive to requests for personal protective equipment.[5] The importance of adhering to positive attitudes when faced with machine hazards at work hardly needs stating.

A large number of accidents result from inadequately guarded machine tools and machinery. Though certain machines are difficult to guard, for example, milling and grinding machines, the manager with a positive attitude towards safety will give serious consideration to the provision of sturdy and all-round guarding and ensure that switches for emergency stops are placed in a prominent position. Automatic guards, using a trip device, are now manufactured to prevent access to dangerous parts of machines; when the trip device is activated, the dangerous parts stop. A similar principle is the photo-electric system, whereby the machine cuts itself off if a light curtain is interrupted.

Management can also adopt positive attitudes towards personal protective equipment. This type of equipment includes items such as safety glasses, ear plugs, hard hats, face shields, gloves, knee pads, safety shoes, respirators, and the like. In a survey of worker attitudes to safety, it was found that 75% of male respondents stated that they always or almost always wear the personal equipment available on the job. However, only 40% of female respondents reacted to the same extent in the use of the equipment.[5]

The latter group may be concerned with their appearance; if so, safety practitioners should work on the motto that the "safe look" is the "smart look."

ATTITUDE FORMATION

Personality in terms of introversion or extraversion is said to create a disposition favourable or unfavourable to the acceptance of attitudes. Introverts are more susceptible to socializing influences and are more prone to accept the values of society than extraverts who tend to be under-socialized.[6] The authoritarian personality is likely to display attitudes such as deference to superiors, hostility towards inferiors, disinclination to be introspective, and inclination to project unacceptable impulses on to others. It is suggested that highly authoritarian individuals are those who have been exposed to harsh and threatening discipline in the home early in life, and they retain an attitude of latent hostility towards their parents.[7] A more comprehensive discussion of personality types can be found in Chapter 1.

Membership of a group can be influential in determining the attitudes of individuals. This is illustrated in the Bennington College study on groups reported in Chapter 7. Socializing influences at work also influence the formation of attitudes. It is widely acknowledged that during the training period professional people develop attitudes towards the practice of their chosen vocation that colour their vision and affect their approach to the reality of the work situation. This process of socialization, by which members of a profession subscribe to the values and beliefs nurtured by the professional group, is termed *professionalization*. It involves modification of attitudes during the training phase and conformity to group standards, and it embraces acceptance of specific obligations to colleagues, clients, and the public. Thus entrants to the profession come into contact with various segments of the profession during the training period. Apart from the necessary skills, they become acquainted with the typical responses, postures, thought processes and expectations of the qualified professional.

In a survey of chartered accountants the attitudes shown in Table 6.2 were said to be nurtured during the chartered accountants' training.[8]

Using the framework in Table 6.2 an exploratory study of the attitudes of chartered accountants working both in industry and the profession was conducted in the early 1970s.[9,10] The results indicated that the accountants showed a preference for *caution* in their approach to business problems, and this was more marked in the case of accountants employed in a professional practice. Similarly with respect to *exactitude,* the accountants working in a professional practice displayed a firm attachment to this attitude, whereas their counterparts in industry were less concerned with exactitude. With regard to *anti-theoretical pragmatism,* accountants in professional practice exhibited a strong tendency towards acceptance of this

TABLE 6.2
Attitudes Developed by Chartered Accountants in Training

Caution	– a preference for certainty, predictability, and avoidance of risk.
Exactitude	– a preference for the maximum attainable precision in ouput independent of the cost and value of achieving it.
Anti-theoretical pragmatism	– a preference for convention-based rather than analytical approaches to problems, and for experience rather than theory.
Professional exclusiveness	– a preference for the qualities of chartered accountants when compared with those of other accountants.
Quantification	– a preference for numerical methods of working and items which can be quantified.
Rationality	– a preference for systematic logical approaches to problem solving as opposed to other methods such as intuition.

attitude. They tended to rely on experience rather than theory, and they showed a preference for the status quo as opposed to innovation in accounting and auditing. By contrast, the accountant in industry seemed distinctly less attached to antitheoretical pragmatism.

Both groups of chartered accountants seemed to regard their qualification as being better in most respects than that of other qualified accountants, although industry-based accountants considered themselves slightly less *exclusive*. Chartered accountants in professional practice frequently perceived their fellow members as possessing better education—both general and professional—higher professional integrity, more social presence, greater independence of mind and a wider breadth of business vision than their certified and cost and management counterparts. Finally, as one would expect, all the sampled accountants showed a very clear preference for *quantification* in dealing with problems; as one respondent observed, numerical ways of thinking and working are developed during the period of training.

FUNCTIONS OF ATTITUDES

Attitudes help individuals to adopt a stable view of the world in which they live. We can only cope with our environment if that environment is reasonably orderly and predictable so that the individual, the group or society may know where they stand and what to do.[11] Attitudes facilitate the organization of diverse thoughts into a coherent pattern. This contributes to the reduction of uncertainty and allows the individual to operate without the discomfort of having to evaluate all stimuli impinging on his or her senses in order to make the correct response. The mere fact that we impose some order on our social universe makes it easier for others to communicate and relate to us, particularly when they have some insight into our attitudes. Likewise, an insight into the attitudes of others helps us to understand and interact with them. However, as we saw in Chapter 3 on perception, we still experience difficulties in perceiving and evaluating people and events in everyday life. It is generally recognized that humans have a need to experience themselves as free agents, and are not just entities reacting to an ordered environment; there are occasions when we exert influence on our environment. The major functions of attitudes, which have not been experimentally tested to any great extent, have been identified by Katz as instrumental or adjustive, *ego* defensive, expressive, and acquisition of knowledge.[12]

Instrumental or Adjustive

Individuals strive to maximize rewards and minimize sanctions or penalties in their external environment. They develop favourable attitudes towards objects which satisfy their needs and unfavourable attitudes towards objects which thwart their needs. In the latter case a consumer may develop a particular attitude towards a product category and avoid items which it contains. For example, a consumer chooses not to use electric hairbrushes because of a previous bad experience with electric hair rollers. On the other hand, a successful stay in a hotel may give rise to a favourable attitude that manifests itself in return visits to that or a similar hotel.

Ego Defensive

Individuals develop attitudes designed to protect themselves from exposure to undesirable basic truths or certain realities in their environment. A consumer may attempt to ward off threats to self-esteem by developing positive attitudes towards products, such as grooming aids or an impressive car, that may enhance the self-image. Another consumer develops favourable attitudes towards mechanisms of defence, such as mouthwashes or deodorants, in order to defend the *ego*. There are other occasions when the individual projects his or her weaknesses on to others as a means of self-protection, and in the process develops unfavourable attitudes towards the target group; this could arise in the case of prejudice directed at minority groups.

Ego-defensive attitudes may be aroused by internal and external threats, by frustrating experiences, by the build-up of pressures previously repressed, and by suggestions or directives from an authoritarian source. *Ego*-defensive attitudes are difficult to change because of the misdirected nature of the impulses associated with them. For example, an employee encounters a frustrating experience at work and feels aggressive as a consequence because of the hurt to his or her *ego*. However, the employee displaces this aggression by directing it at a completely different target such as a member of the family or a pet. Though *ego*-defensive attitudes are difficult to change, it is possible to remove the threats to the attitudes through therapeutic means in a supportive environment by giving individuals insight into the dysfunctional parts of their defence mechanism.

Expressive
This attitudinal function contains three main aspects. It helps to express the individual's central values and self-identity. Consumers express their values in the products they buy, the shops they patronize and the lifestyle they exhibit. The expressive function also helps individuals to define their self-concept, and facilitates the adoption of sub-culture values considered important. The teenager may dress and behave in a certain way in order to foster his or her status in an in-group. Finally, the expressive function helps the individual to adopt and internalize the values of a group he or she recently joined and as a consequence he or she is better able to relate to the group. An individual who has joined an ecology group may now express values manifest in the purchase and use of a bicycle and the recycling of bottles.

Knowledge
Individuals need to maintain a stable, organized and meaningful structure of their world in order to prevent chaos. Attitudes provide the standards or frames of reference by which the individual judges objects or events, and attitudes that provide consistency in our thinking are particularly relevant. The efficiency of the knowledge function of attitudes is readily observable in consumer behaviour. Attitudes predispose the purchaser to prefer a particular make of car, and he or she do not have to re-examine their values, habits and lifestyle prior to the decision to buy. However, if existing attitudes are inadequate in resolving a particular issue, then the acquisition of new knowledge could bring about a changed attitude. Consumers are generally information-seekers; they have a need to know and this drives them to gain information that gives meaning to their social world. But sometimes individuals take the easy option and rely on stereotypes to simplify reality. Of the four major functions of attitudes, the knowledge function is perhaps the weakest in theoretical significance.[13]

Demands of the Work Environment
Earlier there was reference to specific attitudes developed during the chartered accountant's training. Whether these attitudes are functional depends on the type of work environment in which the chartered accountant works. With reference to the industrial, as opposed to the professional, accountancy environment, it has been suggested that adherence to *quantification* is

generally functional, but adherence to *caution, exactitude* and *anti-theoretical pragmatism* is on balance dysfunctional.[8] Caution may manifest itself in the industrial or commercial world in an undue amount of checking of figures and records. The accountant who is very attached to caution may be ill-prepared to cope with decisions in the work situation as he or she moves up the organizational pyramid. An example of dysfunctional exactitude in business is the calculation of figures to the nth decimal place where approximations to the nearest thousand may suffice. Anti-theoretical pragmatism in the business situation can be evidenced, among many other instances, in the failure to approach decision problems on an incremental cash-flow basis. The accountant's preference for caution, coupled with anti-theoretical pragmatism, may explain the emphasis on and attachment to conservatism in the preparation and presentation of accounting information.

At the level of professional practice attachment to anti-theoretical pragmatism may help to explain much about stagnation in the development of a framework of financial accounting. Preference for experience rather than theory may lie at the heart of the profession's failure to get to grips with financial reporting relevant to the needs of existing and potential shareholders rather than merely detailing stewardship in the traditional manner.

PREJUDICE

Although it is possible to encounter a continuum of prejudice, ranging from extremely favourable to extremely unfavourable in terms of attitudes, in practice, however, the word "prejudice" is mainly used with a negative connotation. The prejudiced person tends to hold a negative view of, for example, racial groups or certain practices. In rural India it is not uncommon to find prejudice against the introduction of new farm machinery or the general acceptance of contraception. Prejudice may find expression in a negative view of certain safety procedures used by a company.

The prejudiced person with, for example, a stereotyped view of people of a particular race or creed may have that view dispelled on meeting somebody who does not fit the stereotype. But equally the prejudiced person is capable of rationalizing the situation in such a way as to conclude that the person he or she met is unique in some respects and is unlike the stereotype. Therefore the prejudiced view prevails. For example, an anti-Semite will not be swayed in his or her view of Jews by evidence of their charitable behaviour, nor will those who have a deep prejudice against black people by coming in contact with intelligent and industrious people in this racial group. A successful encounter with an estate agent, whereby a person's house was sold in record time to a reliable purchaser, may not dispel a prejudice against estate agents harboured by that person—the experience may be viewed as atypical. The prejudiced person can easily slide into behaviour known as *discrimination*.

Influence of Personality and Culture

Factors such as personality, home background, culture and conformity can influence prejudice. Earlier the authoritarian personality was considered important in the context of attitude formation. In a study conducted by Adorno and his colleagues it was concluded that the most highly prejudiced people displayed an authoritarian personality.[7] These people put a high premium on status both inside and outside the home, and had a clear view of dominance and submission. They were basically insecure and tended to repress or deny their own personal conflicts, they were conventional in approach to life with explicit values and rules to guide behaviour, they adhered to socially acceptable behaviour that promoted their interests and tended to be aggressive to groups who do not share their views.

A study of anti-Semitism among female university students concluded that those girls who harboured deep prejudice against Jews displayed repressed hatred, jealousy and suspicion of parental figures.[14] In effect they projected on to Jews feelings that would normally be directed towards parents and other authority figures in their life.

Culture can determine the nature and level of prejudice. In Japan the culture is supportive of flexible working practices, whereas Britain has a reputation for rigid demarcation lines between jobs and skills. Demarcation-line disputes have been a feature of industrial life in Britain, particularly in the past.

From the results of a survey of South African whites three main reasons were inferred to explain prejudice against black people.[15] One reason was the manner in which the historic strife between black and white has been presented in schools, in textbooks and at home. The whites were the goodies and the blacks were the baddies, and invariably the blacks were presented as perpetrating atrocities on the whites. Another reason was associated with the way of life. Blacks were poorer, had no political rights and had the least attractive jobs. Finally, the way blacks were treated was considered important. Blacks had to carry identity cards and if they were imprisoned they were forced to work, a requirement not imposed on the whites.

Influence of Group Norms

Conformity to the dominant norm of a prejudiced group is a critical factor in prejudice. When the individual conforms to a prejudice held by the group, he or she can be seen as favouring the maintenance of this prejudice. Conformity can legitimize extreme behaviour which is based on prejudice. At work this could lead to active discrimination and ill-treatment of minorities.

The victims of prejudice are generally held in low esteem by the prejudiced person and this is considered an ample justification for prejudice and discrimination. Sometimes the social status of the prejudiced person is low or declining, and using a scapegoat to compensate for feelings of internal unease is one way of trying to cope with the frustration experienced.

Ways of Reducing Prejudice

A number of suggestions have been made about ways of reducing prejudice. As was mentioned earlier, contact with the victim of prejudice *may* help to change the attitude of the prejudiced person, but this does not always happen. There are circumstances where the prejudiced person, having worked with the victim of prejudice, concludes that, contrary to expectations, his or her work mate is not lazy after all. However, the prejudice may remain firm when generalized to situations outside work.[16]

Discussion is said to reduce prejudice when the prejudice is of a lower order, but to intensify it when it is of a higher order.[17] When people with opposing prejudices work in an interdependent fashion to achieve a common objective, this can have the effect of reducing prejudices on both sides. As described in the next chapter on groups, hostility between two groups was reduced by creating situations which made it necessary for both groups to co-operate in removing obstacles.

ATTITUDE CHANGE

A variety of factors are responsible for bringing about a change in attitudes. For instance, the marketing executive could try to modify those attitudes that strongly influence the purchase of a particular type of product. He or she tries to bring attitudes into line with what the company is going to offer. Take the British Rail advertisement with the simple message of "Let the train take the strain." It draws attention to the convenience and relaxation of a train journey compared with a similar journey by car. Other examples of marketing strategies designed to change attitudes towards a product, by attracting attention to the characteristics of the product which have an edge over competing products, are as follows: A manufacturer may add a characteristic to the existing characteristics of a product—a mouthwash ingredient may be added to a toothpaste, and a fabric softener to a washing powder. In other situations the emphasis could be placed on an important product attribute. For example, Volvo may stress the special anti-rust proofing its cars receive, and a washing machine manufacturer may attract the consumer's attention to a "no-tangle" washing action.

Sources of Attitude Change

Kelman recognizes three sources of attitude change as compliance, identification and internalization.[18]

1. Compliance.   Compliance arises when an attitude is adopted for ulterior motives, such as the desire to make a favourable impression on the individual's boss or client.

2. Identification.   Identification arises when the individual adopts an attitude in order to establish or maintain a satisfying relationship with others. A student wishing to establish a good working relationship with a lecturer may adopt an attitude reflected in listening attentively at lectures and contributing intelligently at seminars.

3. Internalization.   Internalization arises when the new attitude is embraced as part of a cluster of attitudes because the individual feels comfortable subscribing to that attitude.

Factors Contributing to Attitude Change

A number of specific factors giving rise to a change in attitudes can be identified. These are group membership, exposure to the mass media, forced contact, rewards, communication, and persuasion.

1. Group Membership.   In a study conducted at Bennington College there was evidence of a noticeable shift in attitudes as a result of group membership, though there were marked individual differences.[19] It was concluded that the main factor influencing the student's decision to change or not to change her attitudes was the relationship to the family or college. Where the student decided to be independent of her family, and affiliated with and derived prestige from the college group, she tended to adopt a radical position on the left of politics. But where she maintained strong family ties, coming from a home where conservative attitudes were more prevalent, there was a tendency to ignore the influence of the college; this was expressed as withdrawal or active resistance. Membership of a group at work, whereby the individual is influenced by some prevailing ideology or practice, can likewise contribute to a change in attitudes. There must be many examples of workers changing their attitude to safety after joining companies with sound and progressive safety practices.

2. Exposure to the Mass Media.   The mass media (press, radio, and television) are often held responsible for a change in attitudes. For instance, periodically campaigns are mounted in the mass media with a strong safety connotation—"clunk click every trip" in connection with the wearing of car seat belts, or highlighting the risks of driving with excess alcohol in the bloodstream—so as to influence attitudes to safety. On examining the influence of the mass media on attitudes to certain issues, an unexpected conclusion emerged in one study.[20] Messages presented via newspaper, radio, and television produced insignificant attitude changes initially. However, having re-measured these attitudes some weeks later, the researchers found significant changes. They put forward the following explanation for the delayed shifts in opinion. Most people are to begin with affected in a very small way by what they see and hear in the press, on radio and on television. But then people are likely to discuss these issues with others whom they know and whose opinions they value and trust. It is only then that attitude change will occur to any marked degree.

3. *Forced Contact.* Closely related to the influence exerted by the group in changing attitudes is the notion of forced contact. For example, placing a worker with negative safety attitudes in a vibrant safety group, whose terms of reference are to promote good safety practice in a company, could result in a change in safety attitudes. But the success of such a venture is likely to depend upon the degree of involvement of the recalcitrant worker in the work of the group. When black and white people were forced to live in integrated housing schemes—i.e., where families were allocated flats and houses irrespective of their race—the three aspects of attitudes (beliefs, feelings and actions) towards black people by white people improved. A control group observed in segregated housing schemes did not produce a similar effect.[21] A related finding was reported during the Second World War when black troops were integrated into previously all-white U.S. combat divisions. Where black and white soldiers experienced field service together, only 7% of the white soldiers in the mixed units said they disliked this form of integration. In units which were all-white 62% of the troops opposed the integration.[22] It is now clear that forced contact in the housing and military situations described above led to a decrease in racial prejudice.

4. *Rewards.* Some form of reward may have to be forthcoming in some cases before a person changes an attitude. Take, for example, a prejudiced politician with strong views on immigration. Having had a number of refusals from selection committees in constituencies where he would like to stand, paradoxically he is eventually adopted by a constituency with a strong immigrant community. In nursing the constituency his behaviour is at variance with his private beliefs. Where he receives social approval for the way he conducts himself politically, it is conceivable that he will adopt the attitude implicit in his political role. In this case social approval is the reward that leads to attitude change. As a means to encourage workers to use personal protective equipment, changes could be made to both the design and the material to improve the comfort of the wearer.[23] In effect this is offering the prospect of reward to those prepared to adopt a more positive attitude to safety practice. Also campaigns could be initiated consisting of awards for success in safety competitions.

5. *Communication.* Communication of a message designed to change attitudes may be ONE-SIDED or TWO-SIDED. The following findings emerged

when propaganda was used to change the attitudes of soldiers.[24] A soldier who had received a high school education was more influenced by a two-sided communication, whereas the soldier with a poorer education was more influenced by a one-sided communication. Arguments contained in one-sided communication are effective if the receiver's attitude is in sympathy with the attitude based in the message. But an argument contained in a two-sided communication would be more effective if the initial attitude of the receiver was at variance with the attitude based in the message. These findings may not be valid in the long term and in conditions where counter-propaganda exists. This principle is illustrated by the following examples.

A productive social encounter in an organization might arise when A, a credible communicator with a deep-seated positive attitude to safety, tries to influence B who has a lukewarm attitude to safety. If A and B held diametrically opposed views on safety, the encounter could be quite different. A manufacturer of electrical appliances provides information in a one-sided communication when a user's manual goes with the product, though there is scope for two-sided communication when the consumer asks questions of a sales assistant in the store where the appliance was bought. This offers an opportunity to clear up any confusion or difficulties with respect to the operation or use of the product.

The order in which two opposing arguments are presented is likely to have a bearing on the effectiveness of the communication. Where the first argument put across has the greatest effect, this is referred to as the PRIMACY EFFECT. But where the second argument put across has the greatest effect, this is referred to as the RECENCY EFFECT. Attachment to the notion of the primacy effect may be implied from the behaviour of a lawyer acting for the prosecution in a court of law. He or she presents the prosecution's case before the lawyer acting for the defence. On the other hand a politician may feel that the best moment to make a final address before an election is the day after his or her major rival does so; this politician obviously believes in the recency effect. There is support for the superiority of the primacy effect in certain circumstances.[25] A first communication is likely to be more effective if both sides of an argument are presented by the same person, and provided the listeners are unaware that conflicting views are to be presented. If at the end of the presentation the listeners make a public commitment, this is an important factor in endorsing the primacy effect.

PUBLIC COMMITMENT is a powerful strengthener of attitudes. In an experiment conducted by Hovland and his associates a group of students were asked to write an essay on their attitudes to reducing the legal voting age to 18 years. This came after a session where they were exposed to an argument which was favourable to the idea of reducing the legal voting age to 18 years. Half the group—the public commitment group—were asked to sign their essays and were told that their work would be published in full in the school newspaper the following week. The other half—the private commitment group—were not asked to sign their essays, and in addition were assured that their views would remain anonymous. Both groups were then presented with an argument which was strongly in favour of retaining the minimum voting age at 21 years, and they were invited to write a short paragraph stating their frank opinions on this matter. The results of this experiment suggest that only 25% of the public commitment group shifted or changed their attitudes, whereas 50% of the private commitment group (whose views remained anonymous) were able to change their attitudes.

Here we see that the effect of making a public commitment is to make the person relatively resistant to change in the face of counter-propaganda. But situations like this are rather complex, because people differ in their interest in a particular issue. Likewise, if the issues are difficult to grasp, the intelligence of the person is an important factor. Other factors to consider are the nature of the propaganda to which the individual is exposed, and the nature of the group in which a public commitment is made.

Is the manner in which the message is put across critical in terms of changing attitudes? To answer this question a group of researchers conducted two experiments based on the court system in the U.K.[26] A written legal case was presented to subjects and they were asked to reach a decision on whether they considered the accused guilty or innocent. However, before they reached a decision they were asked to study the defence argument put forward by the accused. The defence argument was submitted to two groups, and though the content was identical the presentation was different in each case. In the first group the experimenters put forward the arguments in a confident tone of voice—e.g., a statement would be prefaced with, "Obviously . . .," "I believe . . .," "I am sure . . . ." In the second group the experimenters presented the arguments with more tentative expressions in the text, such as, "I don't know . . .," "I am not positive . . .," "I am unsure . . . ." It was found that when the case for the defence was put forward in a confident verbal manner in the first group the number of subjects agreeing with the submission for the defence was significantly higher than was so in the second group.

In a second experiment an actor used a tape to submit a plea of "not guilty," and this submission was presented in alternative forms, that is, in either a confident or neutral or doubtful manner. So the subjects were exposed to different modes of presentation. The number of subjects who were sure that the plea was correct was highest when the actor behaved confidently. This was followed by neutral and doubtful modes of presentation in that order. It hardly needs stating that confidence is an important factor in influencing people in business, and one feels that the able communicator is likely to rely on non-verbal expressions as a means of supplementing the verbal delivery when transmitting confidence to an audience.

When dealing with THREATS and FEAR, how gruesome should a message be? An advertisement on road safety showing a really gruesome illustration of road accident victims may not produce the desired effect, whereas a more temperate reference to road accident victims might be more productive. The effects of different levels of threats to get high school students to adopt recommended practices of dental care was experimentally studied.[27] An illustrated lecture on dental care was given to three similar groups, but a different level of fear-arousing message was used in each group. In the mild-level threat group the students were shown decayed teeth cavities, mouth infections and visits to the dentist. In the moderate-level threat group there were similar illustrations to those presented in the mild-level threat group, but in addition warnings of pain from toothache and dental work were given. In the strong-level threat group the threats already stated in the other two groups were reiterated and these were reinforced by warnings of possible intense suffering from secondary diseases, such as blindness and cancer, and major dental surgery.

Apart from the three experimental groups, a control group, which received a talk on a different topic, was used. In order to measure the response to the message, the experimenters noted the students' reported changes in teeth-brushing practices and the extent to which they attended a dentist during the following week. It was found that the mild-level threat produced the greatest change in responsive behaviour (37%) followed by the moderate-level threat (22%), with the strong-level threat producing a small change (8%). The mild-level threat group responded significantly more than the control group. But the strong-level threat group was no different from the control group who did not get a pep talk. These findings indicate that the greater the threat, or the greater the intensity of a fear-arousing message, the lesser the intensity of dental protective action.

The three experimental groups were exposed to counter-propaganda (a different message) a week later. The mild-level threat group was more resistant to this message than the other two groups and the least resistance was felt by the strong-level threat group. This is understandable since the former group had already significantly changed their attitudes, whereas the latter group experienced an insignificant change of attitudes following the initial fear-arousing message. An explanation put forward to account for the initial reaction of the strong-level threat group suggests that stimuli that appeal to intense fear arouse anxiety in the listeners. To try and reduce this anxiety people become hostile to the speaker and as a result are likely to reject the message.[27] The conclusion from the above study is that threats should be used with great care, and although a little fear may be a good thing, a lot of fear may be a bad thing.

The common-sense view, unlike the view emanating from the study reported above, would suggest that a high-level threat is likely to produce a better response in terms of attitude change. Support for this view came from the findings of a study assessing the effect of a talk on the seriousness of tetanus and the need for anti-tetanus injections.[28] This created strong fear arousal leading to a behavioural change in the form of obtaining an innoculation if this was easily available, though such a course of action could be considered medically desirable behaviour requiring little prompting. It is also suggested that a strong fear appeal in a message is superior to mild fear in changing attitudes when a threat is posed to an individual's loved ones, when the subject matter of the message is presented by a highly credible source, and when the recipient, though vulnerable, has a high degree of self-esteem.[29] In a particular situation a speaker with high credibility can arouse high fear in the recipients of the message, but the logical consequences of total acceptance of the message may not materialize. For example, when subjects were subjected to high fear arousal with respect to the hazards of smoking, they were willing to cut down on smoking but less willing to have a chest X-Ray.[30]

The DISSIMILARITY or SIMILARITY of the attitudes of both the communicator and listener also has to be considered. If the communicator advocates a position which is close to that held by the listener, the listener will perceive a greater similarity between the two positions than exists in reality; this is referred to as ASSIMILATION. On the other hand, if the communicator advocates a position which is rather distant from that held by the listener, the latter perceives it as more distant than it really is; this is referred to as CONTRAST.[13] Maximum attitude change can be expected when the listener does not hold an extreme attitude on the matter, the issue is not one that appeals to his or her *ego* but is likely to be neutral, and the communicator has high credibility. This might very well describe the conditions in a psychology laboratory, because the typical laboratory setting creates a high credibility source (academic or scientific staff), the issues dealt with are unimportant when compared to real life events, and therefore it is no wonder that experimenters usually obtain attitude change.[31] However, this criticism may be unfair if levelled at all studies of attitude change, since attitude change as an outcome of field studies has been observed.

6. *Persuasion.*   Persuasion is an important process in attitude change. An extreme form of persuasion was employed by the Chinese with respect to the re-education (brainwashing) of prisoners of war. Soldiers were coerced into reading aloud pro-communist propaganda over the camp's loud-speaker system. The reason for this was that other prisoners were more likely to accept such ideas from their own colleagues than from the enemy. In one camp a soldier reared in Brooklyn, New York, on the east coast of the U.S., delivered the message with a deadpan expression in an exaggerated southern Dixieland drawl as an act of defiance.[17]

Persuasion exemplified in promotional efforts in the field of marketing would appear to be more subtle. A company wishes to change one or more of the attributes of its product or service in order to enhance the corporate image. For example, an airline, primarily a domestic carrier, now wishes to be considered an international carrier. In another situation the consumer is asked to reassess the value of a particular attribute of the product or service. A building society, moving to a banking type of service, in addition to its normal service, stresses the convenience of being open on Saturday mornings. (Partly in response to increased competition from the building societies, some commercial banks now offer a limited banking service on Saturday mornings.) A pharmaceutical company may stress the absence of an undesirable attribute in its product—e.g., paracetamol, unlike aspirin, is not very harmful to the stomach. In order to increase the overall attractiveness of a brand, a new attribute of the product is given particular attention in advertisements. Here are a few examples: a birth control element in dog food; the addition of a deodorizing feature to socks; the inclusion of a "light to show the way to escape" in smoke detectors; the incorporation of protein in a dishwashing product for "softer hands;" a revolutionary roll-on antiperspirant that goes on dry; and the wonderloaf that is nutritionally superior. Also a manufacturer of roll-on deodorants may wish to capitalize on a social trend and stress the advantages of the roll-on product over spray products.

The advertiser may wish to influence the OPINION LEADERS either individually or in groups. Opinion leaders are people of roughly the same social standing as those who will be subjected to their influence. They tend to be better informed, often more intelligent and pay more attention to the channels of communication than those subjected to their influence. There could be an opinion leader for different pursuits, e.g., fashion, sport, and politics. Those who succumb too readily to persuasion are said to be anxious.[13] Their lack of self-confidence as a result may make them vulnerable and their preoccupation with their own thoughts and fears may create a disposition whereby they do not pay enough attention to the persuasive message.

The CREDIBILITY of the source of a message has already been acknowledged above; it is equally applicable to persuasion. The perceived STATUS (the position or role occupied by the persuader) is also important. Credibility depends on the general trustworthiness, qualifications, dynamism, or energy of the person.[17] What effect has the credibility of the persuader on whether or not one yields to his or her message? The impact of the credibility of the persuader in a classroom situation is demonstrated in the following study.[29]

A lecturer, introduced as Dr. Hans Schmidt, an internationally renowned research chemist, was presented to a group of students. Dr. Schmidt wore a white laboratory coat and spoke with a German accent. The students were asked to report, by putting up their hands, when they smelt a new chemical vapour he was about to release. The lecturer pulled the stopper of a small glass beaker giving the impression that he was releasing the vapour. Then the students sitting in the front of the lecture hall raised their hands, and their reaction spread throughout the hall. Later the students were told that the beaker had not contained any vapour, merely distilled water, and that Dr. Schmidt was a lecturer from the Department of German. This experiment illustrates the power of suggestion emanating from an apparent expert or credible source. One wonders whether the same effect would be produced if a student dressed in jeans went through the same motions as Dr. Schmidt.

In another experiment the opinions of students on certain important issues were obtained.[32] One week later the students were presented with four newspaper articles dealing with the issues on which the students had earlier expressed an opinion. Each article dealt with one of the important issues, and the articles contained a mixture of arguments for and against the topics discussed. The students were unaware of the title of the publication from which the articles were extracted. Subsequently, one group of students was told that an article came from a credible source; for example, from a medical journal in the case of the use of drugs. Another group was told that the article came from a low credibility source; for example, from a mass-circulation newspaper, again in the case of drugs. Once again the attitudes of the students to the issues raised earlier were assessed, and they were compared with the attitudes which prevailed prior to the experiment. A 22% change in attitudes was observed for the group exposed to the high-credibility source, as opposed to 8% for the low-credibility source.

What is the relevance of the notion of credibility to a commercial organization? The credibility of a trading company can be enhanced by creating a corporate reputation. This could be achieved by reliable products, good after-sales service, sound warranties and guarantees, using friendly and helpful staff, and acting in a socially responsible manner. Likewise, a supplier could use well-respected stores or speciality shops for an unknown brand, and this could contribute to improved sales. The high credibility of the source is evident in a magazine such as *Which*, because of its established reputation for expertise in providing information on different products. A source with low credibility could be effective if it argued against its own interest.[33] For example, a tobacco company would have low credibility if it argued that there was no relationship between smoking and lung cancer, but the company could be very persuasive in changing people's attitudes if it publicly argued that smoking definitely leads to lung cancer.

When considering "source credibility" it is well to acknowledge the SLEEPER EFFECT. This develops when, after a lapse of time, a person will be more persuaded by the content of the message and less influenced by the credibility or non-credibility of the source. It is said that credibility is of importance only to attitudes relating to issues in which subjects have a mild interest. But if the latter's *ego* involvement in an issue is high, the importance of credibility is minimal.[34] Perhaps where there is greater involvement of the self in an issue, this leads the subject to a position whereby he or she pays more attention to the content of the message and less to the source.

The subject's firm attitudinal attachment to a particular issue is the crucial factor in this situation and the credibility of a source which may challenge this state of affairs is likely to be considered unacceptable.

Sometimes it is suggested that *overhearing* and taking notice of a message on an issue in which one has a high personal involvement—instead of being the direct recipient of the message—can produce the intended effect. At least the communicator cannot be accused of attempting to influence directly the eventual recipient who overheard the message. But where the communication is presented directly, the communicator may be suspected of giving desirable information to further his or her own ends.[35,36]

It is probably better to think of credibility as applicable to a particular situation, rather than it having general applicability, because the credible source may have only a specific expertise to offer. Finally, is it important for the persuader to draw an explicit conclusion at the end of the message? The persuader, on the grounds of effectiveness, does not have to be explicit if the listener is motivated or intelligent enough to draw his or her own conclusion. However, the explicit conclusion is more likely to be effective with the less-intelligent listener.[37]

Balance and Consistency

A key concept in attitude change is balance and consistency. It is suggested by Festinger that people try to establish internal harmony, consistency or congruity among their opinions, attitudes, knowledge and values.[38] Consistency theory developed in a climate of conformity in the U.S. when it was believed that people do not like to behave in a manner inconsistent with their attitudes. Consistency could equally be applied to the structure of a given attitude, whereby the cognitive, affective and conative components of an attitude are consistent with one another. In a sense consistency could be internally rewarding and this is tantamount to internal reinforcement. The concept of consistency can be applied to a cluster of attitudes within the attitudinal frame of the individual, though it is possible to condone minor inconsistencies.[39]

Consistency Theories

Consistency theories have been divided into three categories—balance theory, congruity theory and cognitive dissonance theory.

1. Balance Theory. Balance theory is concerned with both balance and imbalance in attitudes.[40] There are times when our intuition tells us that a particular situation is unbalanced or uncomfortable in a cognitive sense. For example, the Finance Director of a company welcomes the appointment of a new Director of Marketing because he or she believes they share an outlook in common about efficiency and the future direction of the company. However, the Finance Director suddenly senses that the Marketing Director has serious reservations about proposed cost-cutting plans. As a result the Finance Director expects friction to arise at the next board meeting. This gives rise to imbalance and produces tension, which the Finance Director attempts to alleviate. In these circumstances the Finance Director, in order to restore balance, could change his or her attitude to the Marketing Director from positive to negative, or revise his or her opinion about the matter on which there is likely to be fundamental disagreement, or alter his or her perception of the Marketing Director's attitude towards the proposed cost-cutting plans. It should be recognized that people have different thresholds or levels of tolerance for imbalance, and some people may function well in certain states of imbalance and not feel it necessary to reduce the accompanying tension.

2. Congruity Theory. Congruity theory is also concerned with positive and negative attitudes but in addition attempts to measure the strength of these attitudes.[41] For example, if someone such as a first class actor for whom we have great respect, and who we evaluate as +3 (highly favourable) on an Osgood semantic differential scale (see Table 6.5, page 266), praises a product in a television advertisement—again which we evaluate at +3—then there is no discrepancy. However, if somebody whom we admire greatly (say, +3) makes many complimentary remarks about a product or service for which we have a low regard (say, −2), then there is a discrepancy of 5. To reduce the discrepancy, the individual could think less well of the admired figure and view the product or service in a less negative way; this might help to bring the attitudes in question more into line. Factors to consider when adjustments to attitudes are contemplated are the strength of the attitudes (because generally speaking the stronger the attitude the more difficult it is to change), and the extent to which the person believes in the information disseminated by the admired figure. A consumer could arrive at a conclusion that the admired figure is putting forward favourable views about the product, not because he or she thinks highly of it, but merely because there is a handsome fee for promulgating the message.

There are occasions when people actively seek information consistent or consonant with their attitudes. In one study recent purchasers of new cars were asked to read advertisements for various makes of car including their own.[42] The results showed that they were much more likely to read advertisements for their own car, which they presumably had favourable attitudes towards, than advertisements for cars which they had either ser-iously considered buying at one stage or cars that had been given little or no consideration. There are other occasions when people strive for consistency by bringing their attitudes into line with newly adopted behaviour. When workers were promoted to the job of foreman they tended to acquire mana-gerial attitudes consistent with their new organizational role. However, when some of them returned to their previous positions as workers they experienced a significant dilution of their recently acquired managerial attitudes.[43]

The consistency between attitudes and behaviour may not prevail in every situation. In a study of hotel owners' attitudes towards certain racial groups it was concluded that there were discrepancies between attitudes and behaviour. In their response to items on a questionnaire some hotel owners resident in the southern part of the U.S. expressed an intention to dis-criminate against a Chinese couple, accompanied by a white American, in the provision of accommodation.[44] But when they came face to face with a well-dressed Chinese couple, travelling with a white American, accommo-dation was not refused to the travellers. Perhaps it is more difficult to dis-criminate in a face-to-face situation than in private on paper. But equally it is often easier to be liberal on paper than in face-to-face encounters. In this situation the hotel owner may have had to come to terms with conflicting attitudes, and maybe the business attitude to making a profit took preced-ence over the racial attitude or prejudice.

3. Cognitive Dissonance Theory.   Cognitive dissonance theory is pro-bably the most important cognitive consistency theory. Cognitive disson-ance arises when individuals act in a manner inconsistent with what they feel. If an attitude is not terribly important to the individual, then the be-haviour which is inconsistent with it creates relatively little dissonance. Dif-ferent situations create different levels of dissonance. For example, a child may experience greater dissonance when having to choose between buying a book and going fishing, than between going to the cinema or going to the theatre. Choice in the face of alternatives then becomes a critical issue. The positive aspects of a rejected alternative and the negative aspects of the chosen alternative are inconsistent or dissonant with the action taken.[38] The easiest way to get rid of this psychological discomfort—i.e., to reduce the dissonance—is to change the attitude to the decision so that it corresponds more closely with the outward behaviour.

One may hypothesize that this may be achieved by deliberately playing down the attractiveness of the rejected alternative and reinforcing the chosen alternative by providing supportive information after the decision was made.[45] This hypothesis was subjected to empirical testing in the follow-ing study.

A group of women was asked to rate the desirability of a number of household products. They were told that the manufacturer wanted consumer reactions for which they would receive a reward of one product from a set of two that was available for this purpose. Half the group could choose from two products where there was only a slight difference in the attractiveness of the products (High Dissonance group)—this makes the act of choice more difficult. The other half could choose from two products where the difference in the attractiveness of the products was great (Low Dissonance group)—this makes the act of choice easier. When both groups made their choice of product they were asked to read four research reports which contained commentaries on the products used in the study. The high dissonance and low dissonance groups were divided into sub-groups, whereby half the members in each sub-group were given a report on the products which constituted the first choice; the other half were given reports dealing with products not the subject of choice. Therefore, those provided with reports on products chosen had the opportunity to peruse relevant technical data after they had made their decisions.

The experimental test was repeated when the subjects were asked to rate the desirability of the household products once again. The results showed that the attractiveness of the previously chosen product increased and the attractiveness of the previously rejected product decreased in the high dissonance group irrespective of whether or not relevant information about the product was received. In other words, the provision of relevant or irrelevant post-decision information did not have a material effect on individual efforts to reduce the state of dissonance. In the low dissonance group it was the irrelevant information that increased the attractiveness of the previously chosen product and decreased the attractiveness of the previously rejected product. Since the results show that dissonance was reduced by the provision of information unrelated to the product choice after a decision was made, the hypothesis cited above (i.e., the use of supportive information reinforces the chosen alternative and plays down the attractiveness of the rejected alternative) must be rejected. However, the manner in which the research was conducted in this study has been subjected to criticism.

The threat of PUNISHMENT or the promise of REWARD is relevant in the context of cognitive dissonance.[46] If the individual is forced to comply, following the use of sanctions or rewards, there will be a tendency for the individual to change his or her attitude so that it is brought into line with his or her behaviour. However, this statement needs qualification in the light of whether or not the force to bring about compliance is strong or weak. If the pressure used to force compliance is strong, the individual is much less likely to change his or her attitude so as to bring it into line with enforced behaviour. Why should this be so? Because it could be argued that if you were made to change your actions or behaviour by a strong force, you can always say that if you had the freedom to express yourself you would do so and would not take the enforced action. In this case dissonance would be minimal because the individual has little choice in the matter. On the other hand, if the pressure to force compliance is weak, i.e., the force exerted to make you act or behave in opposition to your inner attitude is weak, then dissonance is strong. This might arise, for example, when under the threat of a minor social sanction you behave in a manner contrary to your privately held attitude. To reduce the dissonance would necessitate bringing the attitude into line with the behaviour.

The above hypotheses were subjected to experimental laboratory tests.[46] Students were asked to carry out boring, repetitive tasks. One group was paid one dollar to participate in the test and the other group was paid 20 dollars. The first batch of students who performed this task was told to tell the next batch that the tasks were interesting and enjoyable; in fact the students were asked to tell a lie. The students complied with the experimenter's request, and later the two groups were tested privately on their attitudes towards the original laboratory tasks. The first group, who received the smaller payment, said the tasks were enjoyable, but the second group, who received 20 dollars, said the tasks were boring and uninteresting. Therefore, in accordance with the prediction specified in the previous paragraph, the first group of students had little pressure applied to them and they changed their attitude by acknowledging that the tasks were interesting and enjoyable. This group could hardly justify telling a lie for the money, so dissonance was high. To reduce the dissonance the students had to change an inner attitude by an unconscious means to arrive at the view that tasks were quite interesting and enjoyable. But the second group of students were subjected to greater pressure to tell a lie, in the form of an incentive of 20 dollars, and felt it unnecessary to change their inner attitude to the task; the students were prepared to tolerate dissonance because the rewards for doing so were worthwhile. In experimental studies like the one described, we cannot always be sure of the exact nature and seriousness of the subject's response and when it is the best time to introduce the rewards.

The following are examples of observations on cognitive dissonance in the literature on consumer behaviour. In advertisements one should be careful not to exaggerate the positive features of a product, because if the product does not live up to the expectations of consumers, dissonance is likely to occur. The disappointed consumers may feel more at ease later when, having received unfavourable word-of-mouth communication about the product from members of their consumer peer group, they negatively evaluate the product. This could produce the effect of reducing dissonance. Incentives, such as free samples or coupon offers, can be used to entice consumers to experiment with a product they might not normally buy. Dissonance could occur if the act of acquiring and using the product is inconsistent with the specific attitude towards the product. Of course the consumer could avoid dissonance by not responding to the incentives because of a firm view of the unacceptable nature of the product.[47] In practice one might encounter a number of situations in which free samples may result in the product not being given a fair trial, in the sense that consumption ceases when the supply of free samples is depleted; in such circumstances dissonance may be of a small magnitude. This might account for the mixed success of incentive offers in contributing to a larger market share for a product.

A consumer chooses a product which has created dissonance. Subsequently, the consumer reads an advertisement that emphasizes the desirable features of this product. The effect of this could be that dissonance is reduced to such an extent that at a future date the consumer develops a favourable attitude towards the brand in question. For example, a car manufacturer by emphasizing the desirable features of the vehicle—i.e., its high trade-in value, the length of time the car will remain fashionable—is trying to reassure the consumer that the right purchase decision was made, and in the process is contributing to the reduction of post-purchase dissonance. In a study of consumer behaviour with respect to cars, it was found that, though the consumer considered a large number of alternative models, more advertisements connected with the make of car finally chosen were read.[42] The notion of post-decision dissonance is likely to be more important for consumer durables than for convenience goods.

Do individuals critically appraise the information they seek in order to reduce dissonance? It is suggested that people tend to prefer information supporting consonance or cognitive consistency rather than avoiding information likely to promote dissonance.[42] Festinger identifies some of the possible reactions to a state of dissonance as follows: individuals seek new information that is supportive of their outlook, and will avoid sources of new information that are likely to increase the existing state of dissonance. New information likely to increase the existing state of dissonance could be misperceived or misinterpreted. The company of others who agree with a particular attitude that one wants to establish or maintain is sought, and efforts are made to solicit greater social support for one's desired position. Finally, the individual plays down the importance of the factors contributing to the state of dissonance, and loss of memory intervenes and helps remove key dissonant elements.[38]

Cognitive dissonance theory has been subjected to much criticism on the grounds that attitudes have often been found not to predict behaviour, and that results supporting the theory often turn out to be based on vulnerable experimental evidence. In addition, most people seem able to tolerate great logical inconsistencies and do not necessarily avoid information favourable to alternatives not chosen. Neither do most people over-expose themselves to favourable information and, finally, dissonance seems to explain the past rather than predict the future.[48] A particular criticism of the measures used to gauge cognitive dissonance is the rarity of circumstances in which subjects engage in self-reporting. With regard to our tolerance of inconsistencies, it is argued that people grow used to and expect a certain amount of imbalance in their cognitive make-up and over time have managed to adapt to a certain level of incongruity.[49] Therefore, up to a point, they are not too concerned with means of coping with dissonance reduction.

ATTITUDE MEASUREMENT

How do we measure attitudes? Attitude measurement usually implies measurement of the cognitive component (i.e., the thinking aspect) of an attitude. The most basic way of doing this is to ask a single question, but this is rarely a satisfactory method because it does not take into account the many parts of attitudes. Many general attitudes possess a number of facets; therefore, it is preferable to use an attitude scale composed of many questions. Attitudes cannot be directly observed as such, but can be measured indirectly. We need measures to help us compare the attitudes of individuals or groups, and to be able to register changes in an individual's attitudes over time. The aim is to record numerically what a person thinks about a particular issue—e.g., nuclear disarmament or the political party most suited to governing the country—and it is important that the questions asked have the same meaning for all those who participate in the attitude survey. Among the widely used techniques are the following methods.

Thurstone Scale

This was one of the first systematic approaches to attitude measurement and was developed by Thurstone and Chave in 1929.[50] The first step is to write out a large number of statements, perhaps 100 or more, each of which expresses a particular view. These statements should express all possible viewpoints from extremely favourable to extremely unfavourable. An ex-

TABLE 6.3
An Example of a Thurstone Scale Measuring Employee Attitudes

Statements	Scale Value[a]
The company values my contribution.	9.50
My job is safe as long as I turn out good work.	8.25
My boss lets me know what he or she thinks of me.	7.20
The company offers rewards commensurate with efforts.	6.50
The company needs to improve its training programme.	4.80
The company's policy of dealing with people is rather vague.	3.00
My job offers little opportunity for the exercise of discretion.	2.65
My boss never lets me know what he or she thinks of me.	1.50
Many employees stay with the company because they cannot find another job.	0.70

[a]These values would not appear on the scale.

ample of statements used for the measurement of employees' attitudes using this method is illustrated in Table 6.3.

Each statement is typed on a separate piece of paper, and a judge is asked to place each statement in anything up to 11 piles. There are 9 statements in the example in Table 6.3, therefore, the piles range from statements judged to express the least favourable viewpoint (pile 9) to statements judged to express the most favourable viewpoint (pile 1). Statements judged to express varying degrees of favourableness in between these extremes on a continuum are put into the appropriate pile. In the construction of the attitude scale the services of as many as 100 judges or assessors are used. The judges are asked not to express their own attitudes, but to be as objective as possible in indicating the extent to which the statement is favourable or unfavourable towards the topic in question. The purpose of allocating statements to piles is to determine the scale value of the various statements. For example, if all judges place a statement in piles toward the favourable end of the continuum of attitudes, we could conclude that the statement expresses a favourable attitude toward the company.

The number of times each statement is placed in each pile is calculated, and a further calculation is made to determine the average location of the statement in order to arrive at a scale value. An imaginary scale value is shown in the above example. The consistency of the judges' assessments for each statement is analyzed. Statements placed by all judges in one or a limited number of categories have the greatest degree of reliability. Statements that are placed by the judges over several categories are eliminated. It is sensible to begin with many more statements than are required for the final scale, and to settle for 10 or more statements that are spread over the entire range of the continuum; these statements would have been consistently evaluated by the judges. The final material for the attitude scale comprises the selected statements and their scale values. In the administration of an attitude scale, statements appear on printed paper in random order without the scale values that appear in Table 6.3. All employees participating in the attitude survey are requested to tick all statements they agree with and their identity remains anonymous. The attitude of each employee is usually calculated as the average or median scale value of the statements ticked. An average of 6.52 would be the outcome of an attitude survey where the second, fourth, and fifth statements shown in Table 6.3 were ticked by an employee. The calculation is as follows:

$$\frac{8.25 + 6.50 + 4.80}{3} = 6.52$$

This employee's average score is at the favourable end of the scale, and therefore it indicates a favourable attitude toward the company. On the other hand, an average of 1.73 would emerge if the sixth, eighth, and ninth statements reflected the preferences of the employee. This score would be arrived at as follows:

$$\frac{3.00 + 1.50 + .70}{3} = 1.73$$

The average of 1.73 would indicate an unfavourable attitude toward the company.

Likert Scale

This method of measuring attitudes is somewhat simpler than the Thurstone method, and is probably the most commonly used attitude scale.[51] The individual is asked not only to indicate agreement or disagreement but also to signify how strongly he or she agrees or disagrees with a number of statements relevant to the attitude being measured. This is normally done on a five-point scale, though it is possible to use a seven-point scale. The normal practice is to incorporate the various statements in a questionnaire. The following selection of items is extracted from a questionnaire used in a study of union and management attitudes to safety:[52]

1. Many accidents happen because a worker tries to make things easier or faster at the expense of safety.
2. Industrial accidents are part of life and must be accepted as such by management and workers.
3. Many of the present-day occupational illnesses from which people suffer cannot be anticipated or avoided.
4. The benefits of safety outweigh its costs.
5. Safety is the most important element of the working environment.

The subject is asked to respond to the above items or statements indicating the extent of his or her agreement or disagreement using the scoring method illustrated in Table 6.4.

TABLE 6.4
An Example of a Likert Scale

Scoring	Attitude Intensity
1	Strongly Disagree
2	Disagree
3	Tend to Disagree
4	Neither Agree nor Disagree
5	Tend to Agree
6	Agree
7	Strongly Agree

In the example a value is given to each response category in order to produce a numerical score. The different scores in each category are added together to arrive at a total score. A high overall score can be viewed as a positive attitude to the issues raised in the questionnaire; a low overall score denotes a negative attitude.

The statements chosen for inclusion in the Likert Scale are usually found from experience to be connected with the attitude concerned and would be provided by knowledgeable people. In order to analyze statistically the data on the scale, it is important that a zero point is absent. However, this entails forcing a subject to express an attitude when in fact he or she does not hold one, and this reduces to some extent the validity of the exercise. Because of the way the Likert Scale is constructed, most of the scores will fall at the two ends of the scale, and there is less power of discrimination as we move nearer the neutral point.

Osgood's Semantic Differential

This technique was devised by Osgood and his colleagues as part of a study of the meaning of words; it consists of pairs of adjectives opposite in meaning.[53] An abbreviated example of pairs of words used by Fiedler to create a profile of the least preferred co-worker in the contingency model of leadership, referred to in Chapter 8, is given in Table 6.5.[54]

In Table 6.5, a seven-point rating scale is used with O standing for neutral or "don't know." Numerical values cover a scale from +3 to –3; alternatively a scale ranging from 7 to 1 can be used with 4 as a mid-point. The respondent is asked to give an immediate reaction to each pair of words listed in the table and describe the person he or she prefers the least by placing an X in one of the seven spaces between each pair of words. The

TABLE 6.5
An Example of a Semantic Differential Rating Scale

	+3	+2	+1	0	−1	−2	−3	
Pleasant	–	–	–	–	–	–	–	Unpleasant
Friendly	–	–	–	–	–	–	–	Unfriendly
Accepting	–	–	–	–	–	–	–	Rejecting
Helpful	–	–	–	–	–	–	–	Frustrating
Enthusiastic	–	–	–	–	–	–	–	Unenthusiastic
Relaxed	–	–	–	–	–	–	–	Tense
Close	–	–	–	–	–	–	–	Distant
Warm	–	–	–	–	–	–	–	Cold
Co-operative	–	–	–	–	–	–	–	Unco-operative
Supportive	–	–	–	–	–	–	–	Hostile
Interesting	–	–	–	–	–	–	–	Boring
Self-assured	–	–	–	–	–	–	–	Hesitant
Cheerful	–	–	–	–	–	–	–	Gloomy

individual's score is his or her total score on all scales of the measure used; the higher the score the more favourable is the respondent's impression of the person assessed.

The semantic differential deals with factors concerned with evaluation (Good←→Bad), with potency (Strong←→Weak), and with activity (Active←→Passive). It could be used in the study of interpersonal perception, and also could be applied to measuring attitudes to work where the emphasis is on the emotional reaction of the subject. The semantic differential technique measures attitudes in a rather global way and can be used to advantage among the less literate subjects.

Other measures of attitudes are now briefly acknowledged.

Social Distance Scale

This scale was designed by Bogardus and comes closest to measuring the conative or the "tendency to act" component of an attitude.[55] The concern of Bogardus was to design a measure that would give an indication of the extent to which a native would accept or reject foreigners. For example, a native would be asked, with respect to a foreigner, which of the following statements were acceptable:

1. I have no objection to intermarriage.
2. I would invite this person to my club as a personal friend.
3. I feel this person should have only visitor status in my country.
4. I would exclude this person from my country.

It is a very useful and relatively simple method, though its main limitation is its preoccupation with issues that are often perceived in a negative way (e.g., foreigners).

Sociometry

Using a natural group, every member of the group is asked to name their preferred partner for a specified activity.[56] They then rank the remainder of the group in order of preference, with reference to questions such as, "Who would you most like to sit next to?" Some knowledge of the "thinking" and "emotional" aspects of an individual's attitude can be obtained by asking, "Why do you want to sit next to the most popular person?" The least popular person can also be identified by this method. This technique has not been extensively used in the measurement of attitudes.

Reliability and Validity

Qualities that are essential to any kind of measure are reliability and validity. A reliable measure is one that will provide the same reading if that which is measured remains constant. If the same jar of marbles is weighed twice within a day, one expects it to weigh the same on both occasions. This procedure can then be used to test the scales, because the jar's weight can be relied on to remain the same. However, with attitudes one cannot get away with the assumption that they remain the same over time; in fact attitudes may change as a result of being measured. Therefore, the reliability of an attitude measure is more difficult to establish. A valid measure is one which measures what it claims to measure, though this is sometimes difficult in psychology because we normally try to measure something that cannot be observed from the outside (i.e., how somebody thinks and feels about an issue). So the appropriate criterion for establishing validity is often difficult to determine. For a measure to be valid it must first be reliable, though a measure may be reliable but lacking in validity.

ATTITUDES AND BEHAVIOUR

The relationship between attitudes and behaviour is more complicated than one might expect. A positive attitude towards road safety is just one factor among many that influence safe driving (behaviour on the road). Other factors, such as driving habits, social conventions, temperament when provoked by another driver, the attitude of the police to speeding or reckless driving, have to be considered. The relationship between an intention to behave and actual behaviour has been the subject of rigorous investigation by Fishbein and Ayzen.[57] Intentions with regard to behaviour, such as intentions to devise safety procedures for a paint shop in a factory, are influenced by the safety practitioner's attitude towards implementing safety policy and by various organizational and social influences about the acceptability of this line of activity. The safety practitioner may ask him or herself the following questions. What will the group of workers in the paint shop think of my ideas for their safety, and what is likely to be the most acceptable formula for devising a workable procedure? If the workers object to some or all of my ideas, how should I proceed?

Influenced by the ideas of Fishbein, a study was conducted whereby an attempt was made to identify attitudes and social influences that would predict a motorcyclist's behavioural intention to wear a helmet in a U.S. State without a helmet-use law.[58] Attitudes in the form of beliefs about the advantages and disadvantages of helmet use were far more important than social influences in determining the intention to wear a helmet. This was particularly so for users of helmets rather than non-users. It is interesting to note the beliefs held by the motorcyclists with respect to the use of helmets. On short trips and riding in city and suburban streets there appeared to be a low frequency of helmet use, even though the risk of accidents is high; the miles recorded for these journeys were relatively high over a set period of time. Apparently 65% of motorcyclists, who reported that they use helmets on and off depending on conditions, indicated that they always use a helmet when riding on long highway trips. Is the risk of an accident or threat of hazardous conditions on the road perceived to be greater in the eyes of the long-distance traveller? If it is, hence the need for precautionary measures, though the helmet's effect in providing protection from injury at high speed appears to diminish! This is reminiscent of the attitude to wearing seat belts in motor vehicles in the U.K. on long journeys prior to the statutory requirement to wear seat belts by the driver and front seat passenger.

The frequency of helmet use was also influenced by weather conditions. It is a comfortable prospect to wear a helmet in cold or wet conditions; and the perceived possibility of having an accident in wet road conditions could prompt the motorcyclist to take protective action. The helmet users appeared to be generally better informed about the benefits, in terms of safety and prevention of injury from wearing a helmet, than were the non-users. Those who did not use a helmet appeared to be misinformed about the effects of wearing helmets, and were possibly unaware of the likely serious consequences that could befall the non-user. The type of belief held by the motorcyclist who did not wear a helmet was as follows: "Using a helmet would adversely affect the motorcyclist's ability either to hear or see, or both, when riding and therefore would interfere with the safe operation of the motorcycle; and there is a likelihood that a helmet might actually result in the wearer receiving a neck injury if he or she was involved in an accident when riding the motorcycle."

Consumers tend to give different weightings to different attributes of a particular product. With regard to paper towels, one consumer wants extra absorbency, another wants colourful paper, and somebody else stresses price and the cheapest brand available. The evaluation placed on a product amounts to an aggregation of the individual attitudes attached to each attribute (e.g., price, design, packaging, durability) that the consumer perceives as important. A distinction has to be made between an attitude towards an object (e.g., a product) and an attitude towards behaviour (e.g., buying the product). For example, a consumer may have a positive attitude towards a particular brand, but may not have a positive attitude towards buying that brand for perfectly understandable reasons. This is exemplified in the following example. A consumer believes that high pile carpeting is warm, comfortable, luxurious, and prestigious. Having positively evaluated these attributes, the consumer is likely to have a positive attitude towards high pile carpeting. But is it practicable to buy this type of carpeting if there are pets and young children in the consumer's house?[59] Therefore, a consumer's intention to purchase a product is dependent upon an assessment of how favourable the outcome is likely to be in terms of utility or satisfaction.

Sometimes the attributes of a product gain in importance as a result of external factors, quite independent of any marketing strategy used by a company. For example, dietitians promulgate the view that products high in fibre content are good for people's health. This in turn is likely to influence substantially the sale of selected high-fibre foodstuffs. An interest in jogging has led some bra manufacturers to develop "sweat" and "support" bras for female joggers. The widespread use of tea bags in the U.K. has fundamentally changed some people's attitudes to the purchase of tea bags, though initial promotion campaigns may have been influential in changing consumer attitudes.

SUMMARY

In defining attitudes the three components (cognitive, affective, and conative) of an attitude were identified. A distinction was made between attitudes and values, and it was stated that attitudes, which can be either positive or negative, act as filters in the selection of information. Personality and socialization are important influences in the formation of attitudes. The influence of socialization at work, in the context of attitude formation, was mentioned with reference to the training of chartered accountants.

Attitudes perform an important function in helping the individuals adopt a stable view of the world in which they live. The functions of attitudes were discussed with reference to Katz's system of classification, i.e., instrumental or adjustive, *ego*-defensive, expressive, and knowledge. In this context, a brief reference was made to the demands of the work environment.

With respect to prejudice, which mainly has a negative connotation when discussing attitudes, the influence exerted by personality, group, and culture was noted. Suggestions were made about ways of reducing prejudice.

Attitude change was examined from three angles: sources of attitude change, factors contributing to attitude change, and balance and consistency. Using Kelman's system of classification, the sources of attitude change are compliance, identification and internalization. Factors contributing to attitude change were identified as group membership, exposure to the mass media, forced contact, rewards, communication, and persuasion. These factors were illustrated with reference to appropriate examples. A key concept in attitude change is balance and consistency. Basically this means that people strive for consistency between the components of an attitude as well as between attitudes and behaviour. Consistency theories were discussed with reference to balance theory, congruity theory, and cognitive dissonance theory. The relevance of the latter to consumer behaviour was noted.

The notion of attitude measurement was acknowledged, and the following techniques were described: Thurstone Scale, Likert Scale, Osgood's Semantic Differential, the Social Distance Scale, and Sociometry. Qualities essential to any kind of measure—reliability and validity—were briefly explained. Finally, the relationship between attitudes and behaviour, drawing on the work of Fishbein, was introduced and illustrated with examples drawn from safety and marketing.

QUESTIONS

1. Explain what is meant by the components of an attitude.
2. Distinguish between attitudes and values.
3. Comment on attitudes as filters in the context of accounting information in business.
4. Identify certain attitudes developed by accountants in the course of training.
5. What functions do attitudes perform?
6. Explain what is meant by prejudice and discuss the factors which give rise to it.
7. In what way does compliance differ from internalization when focusing on sources of attitude change?
8. Communication and persuasion were identified as two of the six processes contributing to a change in attitudes. In this context explain the following terms:
   a. Two-sided communication.
   b. Primacy effect.
   c. Public commitment.
   d. Threats and fear.
   e. Assimilation.
   f. Opinion leaders.
   g. Credibility.
   h. Sleeper effect.
9. Discuss any one of the consistency theories and explore its application to business practice.
10. How do we measure attitudes to work?
11. Is there a direct relationship between attitudes and behaviour?

REFERENCES

1. Krech, D., Crutchfield, R.S. & Ballachey, E. (1962) *Individual in Society*. New York: McGraw-Hill.
2. Allport, G.W. (1935) Attitudes. In C. Murchison (Ed.), *Handbook of Social Psychology*. Worcester, Mass: Clark University Press.
3. Rokeach, M. (1973) *The Nature of Human Values*. New York: Free Press.
4. Lee, T.A. (1972) Psychological aspects of accounting. *Accounting and Business Research, Summer,* 223–233.
5. Re Velle, J.B. & Boulton, L. (1981) Worker attitudes and perceptions of safety, Part. 1. *Professional Safety, December,* 28–34.
6. Eysenck, H.J. (1970) *Psychology Is About People*. London: Allen Lane Press.
7. Adorno, J.W., Frenkel-Brunswick, E., Levinson, D.J. & Sandford, R.N. (1953) *The Authoritarian Personality*. New York: Harper & Row.
8. Hastings, A. (1968) *The Chartered Accountant in Industry: A Study of Values*. (Unpublished Ph.D. thesis) University of Birmingham.
9. Buckley A. & McKenna E.F. (1973) The practising chartered accountant—job attitudes and professional values. *Accounting and Business Research, Summer,* 197–204.
10. McKenna, E.F. (1972) *Leadership Styles in Industry* (Unpublished M.Sc. thesis), University of Lancaster.
11. Kelman, H.C. (1969) Patterns of personal involvement in the national system. A social psychological analysis of political legitimacy. In J.N. Rosenau (Ed.), *International Politics and Foreign Policy*. New York: Free Press.
12. Katz, D. (1960) The functional approach to the study of attitudes. *Public Opinion Quarterly, 24,* 163–204.
13. Reich, B. & Adcock, C. (1976) *Values, Attitudes and Behaviour Change*. London: Methuen.
14. Frenkel-Brunswick, E. & Sanford, R.N. (1945) Some personality factors in anti-Semitism. *Journal of Psychology, 20,* 271–291.
15. MacCrone, I.D. (1957) *Race Attitudes in South Africa*. London: Oxford University Press.
16. Secord, P.F. & Backman, C.W. (1974) *Social Psychology*. New York: McGraw-Hill.
17. Mackay, K. (1973) *An Introduction to Psychology*. London: Macmillan.
18. Kelman, H.C. (1961) Processes of opinion change. *Public Opinion Quarterly, 25,* 57–78.
19. Newcombe, T. (1943) *Personality and Social Change: Attitude Formation in a Student Community*. New York: Holt, Reinhart & Winston.
20. Katz, E. & Lazarsfield, P.F. (1955) *Personal Influence*. New York: Free Press.
21. Deutsch, M. & Collins, M.E. (1951) *Inter-Racial Housing*. Minnesota: University of Minnesota Press.
22. Stouffer, S.A., Suchman, E.A., Devinney, L.C., Star, S.A. & Williams, R.N. (1949) *The American Soldier: Vol.1, Adjustment During Army Life,* Princeton, NJ: Princeton University Press.
23. Zohar, D. (1980) Promoting the use of personal protective equipment by Behaviour Modification Techniques. *Journal of Safety Research, Summer, 12,* 78–85.
24. Hovland, C.I., Lumsdaine, A.A. & Sheffield, F.D. (1949) *Experiments in Mass Communication*. Princeton, NJ: Princeton University Press.
25. Hovland, C.I., Harvey, O.J. & Sherif, M. (1957) Assimilation and contrast effects in reactions to communication and attitude change. *Journal of Abnormal and Social Psychology, 55,* 244–252.

26. Maslow, C., Yoselson, K. & London, M. (1971) Persuasiveness of confidence expressed *via* language and body language. *British Journal of Social and Clinical Psychology, 10,* 234–240.

27. Janis, I.L. & Feshbach, S. (1963) Effects of fear arousing communication. *Journal of Abnormal and Social Psychology, 48,* 78–92.

28. Leventhal, H.R., Singer, P. & Jones, S. (1965) Effects of fear and specificity of recommendation upon attitudes and behaviour. *Journal of Personality and Social Psychology, 2,* 20–29.

29. Karlins, M. & Abelson, H. (1970) *Persuasion.* London: Crosby Lockwood.

30. Leventhal, H., Watts, J.C. & Pagano, F. (1967) Effects of fear and instructions on how to cope with danger. *Journal of Personality and Social Psychology, 6,* 313–321.

31. Himmelfarb, S. (1974) Resistance to persuasion induced by information integration. In S. Himmelfarb & A. Eagley (Eds.), *Readings in Attitude Change.* New York: John Wiley and Sons.

32. Hovland, C.I. & Weiss, W. (1951) The influence of source credibility on communication effectiveness. *Public Opinion Quarterly, 15,* 635–650.

33. Koeske, G. & Crano, W. (1968) The effect of congruous and incongruous source statement combinations upon the judged credibility of a communication. *Journal of Experimental Social Psychology, 4,* 384–399.

34. Johnson, H.H. & Scileppi, I.D. (1969) Effects of *ego* involvement conditions on attitude change to high and low credibility communications. *Journal of Personality and Social Psychology, 13,* 31–36.

35. Walster, E. & Festinger, L. (1962) The effectiveness of overheard persuasive communications. *Journal of Abnormal and Social Psychology, 65,* 395–402.

36. Brock, T.C. & Becker, L.A. (1965) Ineffectiveness of overheard counter-propaganda. *Journal of Personality and Social Psychology, 2,* 654–660.

37. McGuire, W.J. (1968) Personality and susceptibility to social influence. In E. Borgatta & W.W. Lambert (Eds.), *Handbook of Personality Theory and Research, Vol. 3,* Chicago: Rand McNally.

38. Festinger, L.A. (1957) *Theory of Cognitive Dissonance.* Evanston, Ill: Row, Peterson.

39. Sherif, M. & Sherif, C.W. (1967) Attitude as the individual's own categories: the social judgment–involvement approach to attitudes and attitude change. In C.W. Sherif & M. Sherif (Eds.), *Attitude, Ego–involvement and Change.* New York: John Wiley and Sons.

40. Heider, F. (1946) Attitudes and cognitive organizations. *Journal of Psychology, 21,* 107–112.

41. Osgood, C.E. & Tannenbaum, P.H. (1955) The principle of congruity in the prediction of attitude change. *Psychological Review, 62,* 42–55.

42. Ehrlich, D., Guttman, I., Schonbach, P. & Mills, J. (1957) Post-decision exposure to relevant information. *Journal of Abnormal and Social Psychology, 54,* 98–102.

43. Liberman, S. (1956) The effects of changes in roles on the attitudes of role occupants *Human Relations, 9,* 385–402.

44. La Piere, R.T. (1934) Attitudes vs actions. *Social Forces, 13,* 230–237.

45. Brehm, W.J. (1966) A Theory of Psychological Reactance. New York: Academic Press.

46. Festinger, L. & Carlsmith, J. (1959) Cognitive consequences of forced compliances *Journal of Abnormal and Social Psychology, 58,* 203–210.

47. Engel, J.F., Blackwell, R.D. & Kollat, D.T. (1978) *Consumer Behaviour.* Hinsdale Ill: Dryden Press.

48. Tedeschi, J., Schlenker, B. & Bonoma, T. (1973) Cognitive dissonance—private rationalization or public spectacle. In W. Scott & L. Cummings (Eds.), *Readings in Organizational Behaviour and Human Performance.* Homewood, Ill: Richard Irwin.

49. Driver, M.J. & Streuffert, S. (1966) *The General Incongruity Adaptation Level (GIAL) Hypothesis: An Analysis and Integration of Cognitive Approaches to Motivation.* Paper No. 114, Krannert School of Industrial Administration, Purdue University.

50. Thurstone, L.L. & Chave, E.J. (1929) *The Measurement of Attitudes.* Chicago: University of Chicago Press.

51. Likert, R. (1932) A technique for the measurement of attitudes. *Archives of Psychology, 22,* 1–55.

52. Price, D.L. & Lueder, R.K. (1980) Virginia union and industry management attitudes toward safety and the Occupational Safety and Health Act. *Journal of Safety Research, 12, Fall,* 99–106.

53. Osgood, C.E., Suci, G.J. & Tannenbaum, P.H. (1957) *The Measurement of Meaning.* Urbane, Ill: University of Illinois Press.

54. Fiedler, F.A. (1967) *Theory of Leadership Effectiveness.* New York: McGraw-Hill.

55. Bogardus, E.S. (1925) Measuring social distance. *Journal of Applied Sociology, 9,* 216–226.

56. Moreno, J.L. (1953) *Who Shall Survive?* New York: Beacon.

57. Fishbein, M. & Ayzen, I. (1975) *Beliefs, Attitudes, Intention and Behaviour: An Introduction to Theory and Research.* Reading, Mass: Addison-Wesley.

58. Allegrante, J.P., Mortimer, R.C. & O'Rourke, T.W. (1980) Social-psychological factors in motorcycle helmet use: implications for public policy. *Journal of Safety Research, 12,* 115–126.

59. Cohen D. (1981) *Consumer Behaviour.* New York: Random House.

7 GROUPS

7 GROUPS

The opening section of this chapter is devoted to a definition of a group. There follows an analysis of important characteristics of groups, and some reasons are given why people join groups. Next, the main focus is on key processes within groups. These consist of reference groups, social comparison, co-action and affiliation, social control, decision making (including risky shift and groupthink), and inter-group conflict. A listing of the characteristics of the effective and ineffective group concludes the chapter.

DEFINITION

How do we go about defining what we mean by a group? In the first instance we can observe interpersonal relationships in a group and note that people communicate verbally and non-verbally. The behaviour of members of the group is influenced by shared norms (e.g., standards of behaviour or expectations), and members strive to achieve a common objective normally under the influence of a leader or chairman. This definition of a group might not include a silent order of nuns who do not interrelate in a dynamic way; also, there are occasions when members of a committee (a group) may not share group norms, and although they work together one member could achieve his or her goals at the expense of the others. So it is difficult to arrive at an all-embracing definition of a group. Groups can be referred to as belonging to certain types, and a classification of groups by type follows.

Formal or Informal

Groups can be classified as either formal or informal. In a formal group important objectives and roles performed by members are pre-determined. For example, the quantity and quality of output, and the requirement to adhere to safety standards and desired behaviour in dealing with charge-hands and colleagues are either implicit or made explicit. In formally constituted groups it is also possible to find informal norms and behaviour. By contrast, the informal group develops in a spontaneous fashion and the objectives and roles found in this type of group arise from the current interactions of members. Once these objectives and roles are established a member normally subscribes to them because he or she considers him or herself a group member or wishes to be considered as such.

Primary or Secondary

Groups can also be classified as either primary or secondary. A primary group is small in size, face-to-face contact is generally frequent and relationships tend to be close and often intimate. A family, a play-group, a sports team, or a tightly knit group of accountants or safety practitioners in an organization could constitute a primary group. A secondary group assumes more of an impersonal nature and may be geographically distant. A company, a hospital or school could fall into this category. This type of group is not necessarily a psychological group, but membership of it could influence a member's outlook.

Classification by Skill and Level of Interaction

Sayles maintains that the technology of a plant has the effect of creating different types of work groups, which he distinguishes primarily on the basis of skill and level of interaction.[1]

1. *Apathetic*. A relatively unskilled group, the members of which tend to work as individuals. There is little sense of group solidarity, morale is low and the group is regarded as unsatisfactory by management.

2. *Erratic*. The group is unskilled with a relatively large amount of interaction among members. On occasions the group develops solidarity; it is not usually shrewd about choosing the right situation in which to express grievances. The group consists of unpredictable members led by authoritarian leaders.

3. *Strategic*. The group consists of skilled members, who interact to a great extent. The group is highly calculating in its strategy and is accepted by management.

4. *Conservative*. This is the most highly skilled group. It maintains a strong sense of group identity, even when its members are dispersed. It is primarily concerned with the stability of traditional wage differentials.

Because the workers categorized above were drawn from mass production industries only, one could question the validity of this exercise if generalized to other groups. However, it shows that groups in industry display different orientations. For example, as a result of introducing new technology in the coalmining industry, Trist et al. showed how group loyalty and cohesion were adversely affected by the change and the miners reacted strongly against having to forego their traditional independence.[2]

CHARACTERISTICS OF GROUPS

Some key characteristics of groups such as norms, communication, and group dynamics are discussed in this section. Related topics, such as reference groups and decision making, will be dealt with later in the section on *Group Processes*.

Norms
Social norms regulate the relationships between individuals in groups; in fact they are guides to behaviour. Norms are collective because they are shared by many members of a group; they are only guides or expectations about what behaviour should be and as such allow us to anticipate other people's behaviour in specified circumstances. They are not necessarily followed in all circumstances. However, they can be enforced and people are either positively rewarded for complying with them or punished for not complying. Norms usually reflect the values of the group.[3]

Though norms regulate behaviour in groups, some norms can be viewed more seriously than others simply because of the sanctions associated with contravening them. To depart from a group norm in a street gang could produce significant sanctions, and so members of the gang may break society's laws in order to escape the sanctions. Yablonsky has shown how an ordinary youth, a member of a violent gang, gets involved in brutal behaviour as a response to group pressure.[4] This illustrates a powerful compulsion to adhere to group norms considered by many people to be crude and unacceptable. But for the individual member of the gang the fear of sanctions far surpasses general moral inhibitions. There are other circumstances depicted in experiments where deviation from a group norm would not activate any significant sanctions apart from the anxiety that would arise as a result of departing from the consensus established by a group.

The above are examples of INTERNALLY IMPOSED norms. EXTERNALLY IMPOSED norms in, for example, an active military group, are various forms of discipline to which military personnel are required to adhere. Sanctions for the infringement of these norms can be heavy. By contrast, a sports team may typify a situation where norms are externally imposed, but sanctions applicable to deviations from the norms are modest; for instance, a footballer may receive only a caution for indulging in illegal play. Somebody who chooses to ignore a group norm by, for example, persistently ignoring safety regulations at work, can be referred to as a DEVIANT.

Pressure can be put on deviants to conform to group norms and this can take the form of verbal abuse, physical assault, silence, blacklisting and physical exclusion from the group. Sometimes one or more of these sanctions are levelled at a worker who fails to respond to officially approved strike action; he or she is considered to be a deviant by contravening the norm to withdraw labour in specified circumstances. Norms are associated with the internal working of the group, but to the outsider it is generally the group's external image that is visible. The outsider recognizes private language, technical slang and in-jokes as alien but may attribute them to a particular group. Likewise, the distinctive way in which members of the group dress conveys the group's identity (e.g., a nun or priest).

When members of a group share a similar outlook and face a common problem it appears to be in their interest to conform to group norms. COHESIVENESS—the extent to which norms are upheld by members—depends on the reasons for joining the group, the meaning the group has for members, and the opportunities for joining other groups.

The individual has also to balance the costs of changing his or her behaviour or opinions—so as to conform to the group—with the rewards of being liked, supported, and respected by other people in the group. The greater the benefit members derive from the group, the greater the likelihood of developing a cohesive group. But a cohesive group can have antisocial aims, as we discovered above with the example of the street gang, as well as aims which are laudable (e.g., the aims of a well-knit safety group in an organization). The danger of too much cohesion is that it could lead to an insufficient exploration of issues considered by the group. This is a topic which will be elaborated on later when discussing "groupthink". In a marketing study the cohesiveness of the group as a determinant of the degree of brand loyalty of members was subject to analysis. Apparently the power of group cohesiveness is greater in predicting choice of products high in social involvement (e.g., cigarettes, beer) than of products low in social involvement (e.g., deodorants).[5]

Members can improve their self concept with the help of the reflected impression they make on others in certain groups. The THERAPEUTIC nature of face-to-face contact is generally recognized. In a group such as Alcoholics Anonymous a member who is dependent on drink can unburden him or herself and expect to receive sympathy and support from the group. Likewise, a member may derive moral strength to control his or her weight from membership of a group such as Weight Watchers. But groups can also produce negative effects. According to Laing, mental illness has its origins in faulty interactions in the patient's primary group (i.e., the family).[6] Deviance can spring from group membership when young people are integrated in groups with norms at variance with those of wider society, as was described earlier with reference to a street gang.

Communication

In studies of communication networks groups of four or five people were engaged in problem-solving tasks in different forms of groupings.[7] Each person in a group receives a list of symbols (e.g., star, circle, wavy line). Though each list is different, all lists contain one symbol in common. The task is to find out as quickly as possible which is the common symbol. Subjects are only permitted to communicate with one another by written notes. The situations depicted in these studies are not like the small group in which communication is face-to-face and everyone can hear everyone else. They are rather more like situations found in large organizations where a number of people in different parts of the organization are in touch with one another only indirectly or, if directly, then frequently through relatively impersonal media such as a telephone or memorandum.

The communication networks studied by Leavitt are shown in Fig. 7.1. The problem was solved more quickly, there were fewer mistakes, and fewer messages were required in the more centralized network—i.e., the wheel. The person at the centre enjoyed himself much more than the other members of the group, and he was perceived as leader. In the decentralized network—the circle—performance was slower, more erratic, but enjoyable. It is suggested that centralized networks, such as the wheel, lend themselves to the efficient execution of simple tasks, but more complex tasks were found to be more effectively performed by less highly centralized networks, such as the circle or a network in which everybody communicates with everybody else.[8] The complex tasks required more than the mere collation of information in exercises connected with the construction of sentences and solving arithmetic problems. The central person in the wheel could be overwhelmed and overloaded when dealing with incoming messages and manipulating data in the complex tasks; so a centralized network would be inappropriate in these circumstances.

Spatial factors such as GEOGRAPHIC PROXIMITY can also affect group relationships, and the greater the opportunity to interact with other people the greater the likelihood that such meetings will give rise to the development of group norms and consensus.[9] It would appear that homogeneity, in

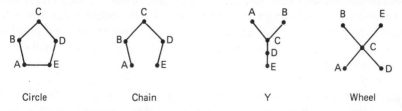

Circle   Chain   Y   Wheel

FIG. 7.1   Communication networks. Source: Leavitt, J. J. H. (1951) Some effects of certain communication patterns on group performance. *Journal of Abnormal and Social Psychology, 46*, 38–50.

terms of age, intelligence and social class, among subjects is important in this context. Different seating arrangements in groups were associated with different types of group task. Where children were given a competitive task, they chose to sit at right angles at a table, but when they were given a cooperative task they sat side by side.

Students participated more in discussions when the seating arrangement was a circular layout of chairs.[10] It is clear that decisions customarily taken by architects and interior designers have a marked effect on group structures and relationships. It is sometimes suggested that the ideal arrangement is the loose oval seating plan adopted by five or so people meeting for informal discussion. A rule of thumb is to increase the distance of people from the hub or centre until they are almost out of the bounds of communication. Then the desks and apparatus required for work can be positioned. Ancillary facilities, such as communal files, rest areas, and soft drink dispensers should be widely placed so that people are encouraged to stand up and walk around for at least two in every twenty minutes. It should be borne in mind that our bodies do not like immobility and our span of attention is limited.[11]

Group Dynamics

A psycho-analytical view of the dynamics of a group recognizes the group's emotional impact on the individual's behaviour because of considerations of conformity, loyalty, and identification with and reaction to the group. According to Freud, libidinal or sexual impulses are inhibited and identification with the leaders takes place, though this could lead to envy and competition between members for the chance to replace the leaders.[12] A full discussion of the psycho-analytical view appears in Chapter 1 on personality. It is conceivable that when the individual is acting alone he or she is more reality orientated and more efficient intellectually than when exposed to the stultifying effect of interaction in a group. From his observational experiments with groups of soldiers undergoing therapy, Bion refers to the unconscious contributions by members to the group mentality.[13] For example, an atmosphere of hostility in a group does not come out of nowhere; members unconsciously contribute to it even though individually they may deny it. Bion recognizes the existence of a mechanism, made up of three functions, which exists below the surface of the group with the express purpose of resolving group tensions. The three functions are flight/fight, dependency and pairing.

1. Flight/Fight. Although designed to protect the group and ensure its survival, this could be destructive. The group appears to want to fight somebody in the group, including the leader, or ignore issues by replacing them with anything other than the appropriate issues.

2. Dependency. The group is concerned with procedural matters (e.g., good committee practice) so that it can feel secure. The concern is to ensure that the group continues to exist and function in a predictable way.

3. Pairing. Two members of the group, one of whom could be the leader, enter into discussion while the remaining members listen and are attentive. The matters under discussion could hinge on a change of leadership or a change in the direction of the group in order to improve its effectiveness.

Anxiety and discomfort can arise as a result of the fight or flight function, complacency and security can stem from dependency, and guilt from pairing because the group is not making headway in the task to change the situation. Pressures are internally generated, arising from the dynamics of the group, as well as externally imposed, for example, nursing mentally handicapped patients in understaffed conditions. The psycho-analytical view emphasizes the dysfunctional aspects of group dynamics, but it should be noted that the working life of the group is not always dominated by these pressures.

REASONS FOR JOINING GROUPS

People have a need to develop relationships with others, and therefore companionship is one reason why people join groups. Sometimes a job may not be very interesting, but belonging to a work group could provide the interest and diversity that is lacking in the job. When a person enters a new situation or encounters unfamiliar surroundings he or she may feel lost or lonely; it is in circumstances like these that a friendly group can be of immense benefit. Another reason for joining a group is the need to identify with the group. Belonging to a group where one can share the experiences of one's immediate colleagues can be an important source of job satisfaction; as a result loyalty to the group can override loyalty to the organization. The group may also provide a sympathetic ear when we experience tension or frustration. Likewise, we rely on the group to provide guidance on the correct behaviour to adopt in particular circumstances or to provide answers to difficult questions. This could apply to an inexperienced recruit in a technical safety or marketing group within an organization.

People sometimes join groups in order to obtain power, because they wish to control others or want the status that accompanies a leadership role. Some, however, have a desire to be dependent or submissive. Associating with others may not be prompted by a need for dependence; instead it may be a self-protection strategy employed by the individual when, for example, he or she joins a trade union. Finally, groups provide a refuge for those who seek a certain degree of anonymity in a social setting.

GROUP PROCESSES

Group processes are discussed by focusing on reference groups, social comparison, co-action and affiliation, social control, decision making and intergroup conflict. Groups can exert a powerful influence on the attitudes and behaviour of members. People are not only influenced by groups to which they currently belong, but also by reference groups which they consult in arriving at an opinion or judgement.

Reference Groups

These groups may provide a normative or comparative reference point or both. They may not always be real groups; it may be a single individual who symbolizes a group perspective on life, or it may be a group which never meets, e.g., "well-rounded people." A NORMATIVE reference group is one from which the individual obtains certain standards. The individual is influenced by the norms, values, and attitudes of the group as well as its total outlook on life. The aspiring entrant to a profession such as chartered accountancy may be profoundly influenced by the persona of chartered accountants before being admitted to professional membership. This is referred to as ANTICIPATORY SOCIALIZATION. A COMPARATIVE reference group is used as a focus when the individual compares the predicament and characteristics of members of the reference group with his or her own situation or that of his or her group. The reference groups chosen may be those seen as very similar to the individual's own group or one with which he or she can identify. These groups are important in determining whether the individual feels relatively satisfied or dissatisfied after engaging in the comparative exercise. Both normative and comparative reference groups may be used as positive frames of reference, when the groups are admired or envied or, alternatively, as a negative frame of reference from which the individual disassociates him or herself or which he or she rejects.

Newcombe uses the "reference" concept in his study of women students at an expensive American residential college (Bennington College).[14] In the 1930s most of the girls came from wealthy conservative families and on arrival at college held conservative political views. During the four-year stay at the college they were exposed to the more liberal or radical attitudes of the teaching staff and senior students. A feature of the educational approach at the college at that time was discussion of a wide range of social problems; this was partly prompted by the experience of the Great Depression and President Roosevelt's New Deal. There was also a belief that the girls should be exposed to issues affecting the contemporary world. Over the four years a number of the girls experienced a marked shift in their attitudes from relatively conservative to relatively liberal.

How can this phenomenon be explained? Bennington College was the girls' MEMBERSHIP group, but this in itself would not explain the shift towards attitudes held in high regard in the college. The crucial factor appears to be that the college community was taken as either a positive or negative reference group for the political attitudes of the students. The college community was taken as a negative reference group for the girls who remained conservative in outlook; they used the home or family group as a positive reference group. For some girls the college remained a negative reference group for political attitudes, but a positive reference group for social attitudes. But the vast majority of the students did alter their political outlook, taking the college as a positive reference group and possibly the parents as a negative reference point.

The girls who remained unaffected by the college's political attitudes may have had well-thought-out conservative opinions, rather than mere compliance with parental views, prior to joining the college. Alternatively, in the estimation of Newcombe, they were overdependent on their home and parents, or they had other interests and did not take either the college or home as a reference point for their political attitudes. Newcombe concluded that a change in attitude is affected by the way in which an individual relates him or herself to the total membership group and one or more reference groups within it.

A change in attitude could also depend on the strength of the initial attitude prior to exposure to group influences, the perceived discrepancy between the person's attitudes and the attitudes of members of the membership group, and the personality of the individual in the light of perceived pressures from the group. Therefore an operative in a factory with regressive safety attitudes who works in a progressive safety environment may not necessarily be influenced by the enlightened attitudes of his or her membership or reference group. Likewise, a stubborn and obstinate character may resist group pressures even though acceptance of such pressures could be beneficial to all concerned.

Reverting to the Bennington College study, Newcombe and his colleagues carried out a follow-up study 25 years later.[15] They found that very few of the women had reverted to the conservative attitudes which they had on entering the college. The women and their husbands, where appropriate, expressed more liberal attitudes than a comparable sample of American women of the same socio-economic grouping. One interpretation of this finding might indicate that the college remained a vital reference group and focus in the lives of the women, and the persistence of the liberal views was assisted by their choice of spouse and friends.

Reference Groups and Marketing.   Reference groups influence consumer behaviour in at least two ways. They set levels of aspiration for individuals by offering cues as to what lifestyle and related purchasing patterns they should strive to achieve; they also define the actual items considered acceptable for displaying this level of aspiration—i.e., the kind of housing, clothing, car, etc., appropriate for a member to retain his or her status in a group. Manufacturers place importance on getting their brand identified with a particular reference group, and advertisers have made effective use of reference groups in marketing a wide range of products. The conspicuousness of a product is said to be the attribute that has the greatest general bearing on consumers as far as their susceptibility to reference group influence is concerned.[16]

To be conspicuous the product must be seen and identified by others, and it must stand out and be noticed. To satisfy the second condition wide ownership of the product must not prevail. A high-performance car is open to more reference group influence than fresh vegetables. The advertiser has to be careful in the identification of the reference group. A toothpaste company launched a new product a decade ago in the U.K. aimed specifically at girls in their teens. The television advertisement alluded to a likely friendship between a member of a band and a girl at a dance hall. Unfortunately the band chosen had an image and musical style ten years out of date. The next advertising campaign dropped this particular approach and reverted to a yachting scene featuring a much older girl.[17]

In addition to the conspicuous nature of the product, three other factors affect reference group influence:

1. The amount of information and experience which the individual can draw upon is important. Where the consumer has limited information and personal experience of the product, he or she may seek the advice of informed people or observe the behaviour of influential consumers or role models.

2. The perceived risk in purchasing the product may be significant. A group discussion can influence the amount of risk to accept in a purchase decision, and the amount of risk the individual is prepared to accept can be increased or reduced as a result of any discussions he or she may have with others whom he or she respects.

3. The greater the credibility of the reference group, as perceived by the individual, the greater the likelihood that its standards will be accepted.[18]

Social Comparison

A reasonable degree of conformity, and hence predictability, is necessary for successful living in a social environment. When we find ourselves in a particular group situation, it is of immense value to have previously given some thought to what others consider the correct response to make in a particular situation—i.e., the best way to behave at an interview. Also, we may consider other people's views before considering the most suitable views to express on religious, social and political issues as well as the use of a particular vocabulary in conversation or the most suitable clothes to wear at a party. An able safety practitioner is continually comparing his or her views on safety with those of other experts in the field, as well as line managers who have something useful to say about the implementation of safety policy. It is natural for people to compare their own judgements on a particular issue with the judgement of others who are in close proximity to them so that they can check out the validity of these judgements.

Kelman identifies three processes of social influence which have an impact on the individual: compliance, identification and internalization (referred to in the previous chapter as the sources of attitude change).[19] Compliance arises when individuals conform to the expectations of the group because the group has the power to reward them if they conform to the group's norms or values, and to punish them if they fail to do so. Identification refers to the process of adopting the characteristics of the group in order to sustain a valued relationship. Internalization develops when individuals accept the group's influence because it appeals to their own values and can be instrumental in attaining personal goals.

These processes of social influence were examined in relation to their influence on the evaluation of a brand of instant coffee.[20] People perceived the product more favourably after seeing others evaluate the product favourably. The researchers, however, concluded that although people frequently buy products that others in their group buy, this purchase behaviour may not establish a role relationship with others (identification), or lead to a reward or punishment mediated by others (compliance). But the evaluation of products by other people provides information about the products, and the idea of a "good" product may be derived from the group. This influence could be invaluable in comparing and contrasting different brands or products (internalization).

Group Norms. As a social comparative influence, norms in work groups can assume a position of significant importance. A deviation from significant norms may initially invite disapproval that amounts to no more than reminding the culprit that a deviation has taken place. Subsequently disapproval may assume a stricter and harsher form. Norms can relate to work targets, sharing of resources, and mutual help and can be affected by events such as changes in work practices, rewards, and employment and economic circumstances.

The productivity level of the men engaged in wiring up telephone banks in the celebrated "Hawthorne" studies was well below what the men could have achieved. A variety of social influences were at work in this group; for example, those who wired up around 6,600 connections per day had approval and favours bestowed on them by the others. Those who exceeded this target attempted to conceal it, and those who worked below the productivity norm were shown various forms of disapproval by the group.[21] One of the findings in a study conducted by Lupton confirmed the bank wiring room finding, referred to above, but another finding did not.[22] There was a restrictive productivity standard in one factory, Jays, engaged in light engineering, and all employees referred to it as the "fiddle."

In the other factory, Wye, which was engaged in the manufacture of water-proof garments, each employee sought to maximize his or her earnings. Various explanations were put forward to account for the differences in group standards or norms. Jays operated in a stable market, had a history of union organization, a predominantly male labour force with interdependent work and relatively low labour costs. Wye operated in a small unstable market, had a weak union, a predominantly female labour force with independent tasks and high labour costs. What appears to be fairly clear is that attempting to maximize earnings in one organization was tantamount to deviant behaviour, but such behaviour in the other organization amounted to conformist behaviour.

Standard costs, as part of the accounting system in an organization, are typically used to evaluate individual performance. However, individuals may be faced with a conflict between the standards imposed by the formal organization and the informal peer group. It is suggested that formal control systems, of which standard costing is part, should be consistent with group norms. Otherwise individuals will face conflicting requirements and some will certainly bow to small-group pressure rather than conform to the organization's formal requirements.[23] Therefore, the task for the accountant is to design systems which do not pit the individual against the group, and this necessitates basing the system on group performance standards rather than individual standards. In examining congruency or fit between the requirements of the standard costing system and the small group, the accountant should be aware of variables such as group norms, cohesiveness and member control.

A classic study was conducted by Sherif, which deals with the emergence of group norms in ambiguous or uncertain conditions.[24] Individuals who participated in the experiment were given the job of judging the apparent movements of a stationary pinpoint of light. When the light is viewed in a completely dark room, without any reference points, it appears to move. This is a phenomenon known as the "autokinetic effect." Perception of the magnitude of this movement varies from individual to individual and is influenced by psychological factors residing in the person. When individuals work alone on different occasions, each develops a stable perception of the light. One individual may perceive relatively little movement (e.g., a few inches) in a particular direction, while another individual may perceive a large movement in a different direction. An individual norm or standard develops and this is repeated consistently from one episode of the experiment to another.

When individuals work in groups of two or three, announcing their judgements aloud without any collusion between them, each individual is affecting the other's judgement. Gradually group norms—shared expectations—rather than individual norms or standards are established. The group norm tends to reflect a compromise between the individual norms, whereby extreme estimates of the movement of the light are moderated. Individuals who had previous experience of the autokinetic phenomenon, and had established their own individual norms, gradually gave them up in response to the behaviour of the group. In fact, the group norms persisted even after the individuals were allowed subsequently to work on their own. A more rapid acceptance of group norms occurred among individuals who had no experience of the experiment before becoming a member of the group. As before, these group norms persisted in the period when individuals later worked alone.

The experiments conducted by Sherif illustrate dramatically the powerful effects of group membership on the individual and have some fascinating features. The individual has negligible past experience that can be applied in judging the position of the pinpoint of light. There is the absence of a yardstick, ambiguity is present, and as a consequence the individual is highly dependent upon others in arriving at judgements. In everyday life this happens with different degrees of ambiguity, but in many situations each of us usually has some past experience (knowledge, facts, beliefs, values, attitudes) which forms a basis for our judgement.

In a laboratory study, where subjects were asked to evaluate and choose the best suit from three identical men's suits, it was concluded that individuals who are exposed to a group norm will tend to conform to that norm in a decision-making situation that confronts them when no objective standards are available. However, if the individual's freedom is threatened by being induced to comply with a group norm, then there will be a lesser tendency to conform.[25] The marketing implications of this study would indicate that when objective evaluation is difficult consumers accept information on product quality or style provided by their peer, or reference, groups. Thus peer groups, friends, and acquaintances may be a major source of influence and information which deserves our attention at the stage of buying major products or services. But any attempt to restrict the independent choice of the consumer may be resisted under certain conditions. For example, a neighbour or relative may sell you an idea about a product, but not necessarily the brand to buy or the store to patronize because this advice could very well be ignored.[26]

Even when a situation is clear-cut, where conditions of uncertainty are absent, a group can exert a significant influence on the judgements of the individual. This would be particularly noticeable in situations where one individual is in the minority, and the majority hold a view which is contrary to the view of reality held by the individual. In a well-known study, conducted by Asch, groups of eight individuals each had the job of comparing a series of standard lines with several alternatives.[27] They were then required to announce, in the presence of the investigator, which of the alternative lines was the same length as the standard line in each case. Unknown to the one genuine subject in each group, seven individuals colluded with the investigator; each of them were secretly instructed on exactly how to respond. They offered the same incorrect answer before it was the turn of the genuine subject to pass comment. From this experiment emerged the sobering thought that for one-third of the time the genuine subjects were prepared to deny the information being conveyed by their senses and shifted his or her judgement, thereby making an error, so as to conform with the group norm or standard.

It is interesting to note that before the group task, each individual performed on a solo basis with virtually no errors. This suggests that perceiving the similarity or otherwise of the paired lines was not a particularly difficult task and errors can hardly be attributed to an ambiguous stimulus.

After the experiments, Asch confronted each individual who had succumbed to group pressure or influence with the fact that they had yielded to the group in the specified instances. When faced with their mistaken judgements, some individuals admitted that they had realized the seven other members of the group were wrong, but the unanimity in outlook of these members led them to experience severe distress about being deviant, which culminated in yielding to the perceived pressure. Others reported experiencing equal distress but, sensing the considerable weight of evidence against them, concluded they must have misunderstood the instructions and were wrong. A small proportion of those who succumbed to group influence were amazed at discovering their errors and reported not being aware of any conflict and could not recall being influenced by other group members.

Here we observe three quite different processes of social influence. First, the threat of disapproval or rejection because one is a deviant; it is up to the person to cope with the stress brought about by ignoring the group pressure, or to succumb to group pressure and avoid the stress. Second, the threat arising from the doubts about whether the requirements of the task have been correctly interpreted; this could give rise to a search for confirmation or disconfirmation of the accuracy of one's judgement, and dependent on the outcome of this search, yielding or not yielding to the group. Third, neutralizing the threat by denial or repression without being aware of this, and as a consequence accommodating oneself to the wishes of the group.

Apparently the subjects who did not yield to group pressure, and who remained independent, were those who experienced the greatest stress and discomfort. However, this condition was substantially alleviated when the genuine subject was supported by an ally (another genuine subject). Also, a growth in the minority representation—i.e., another genuine subject joining the group—gave rise to a lesser degree of compliance with the group judgement. Whether the individual yields to the group or resists it is likely to depend on the clarity of the stimulus (i.e., the degree of similarity of the paired lines), whether or not the genuine subject is the only deviant from the group norm, and the personality disposition of the genuine subject. A genuine subject, acting on his or her own, who perceives only a small difference between the standard and alternative lines, and acts invariably in a conformist way, may side with the group judgement.

Group influence may be particularly important in budgeting discretionary costs. These costs would be associated with non-programmable and non-routine tasks and would cover areas such as advertising, research and development, training and so on. There is no optimal solution as to the amount to spend and there is considerable latitude for the use of judgement in the determination of discretionary costs. The group may exert pressure to achieve uniformity of opinion or consensus even though this may not be the most appropriate way to act in given circumstances. In accordance with Asch's conclusions, a solitary voice of dissent within the budgeting group may yield to the majority view in circumstances when such a course of action is unwise. But a growth in the minority view may add strength to a position of justifiable resistance. Therefore this may suggest a vote in favour of heterogeneity in group composition so as to increase the likelihood that minority viewpoints will have at least some peer group support and not face unanimous opposition in the budgeting process. It may also suggest the need for group leaders to develop a group norm embracing the encouragement of responsible disagreement.

Co-action and Affiliation

Being in the company of others has a material bearing on the behaviour of the individual. In emergency situations it is said that we are more likely to respond quickly if we are on our own than if we are in a co-active situation in the presence of another person.[28] When we are in the presence of others in a group situation, we are inclined to leave it to other members and if they do not react perhaps the situation is perceived as not being serious enough. Until we see others acting in a decisive way, there may be a reluctance to act because of the lack of clarity surrounding the situation. This may occur in an emergency situation when life or property is at risk. If an individual experiences smoke in a room, he or she is likely to respond fairly quickly. However, if a group is confronted with the same stimulus, rapid response may be less likely because of the inclination to discuss the nature of the threat and how to tackle it.[29]

In the company of others, be they colleagues or observers, we tend to get aroused and this creates a state of drive which manifests itself in a behavioural response.[28] If the observer of the behaviour is an expert, who evaluates the subject's performance, the behavioural response of the subject is likely to be greater; in these circumstances the subject is likely to be apprehensive. A lesser behavioural response is likely when the audience consists of peers who are watching out of interest and the least behavioural response was noted when subjects acted on their own.[30] Imagine a situation when your own performance as a student or worker is being evaluated by an expert in your field!

Do people prefer the company of others to remaining in isolation? A classic experiment conducted by Schachter, who was concerned with the concept of affiliation, may throw some light on this question.[31] Groups of college girls in an American university were selected to participate in an experiment in a mythical Department of Neurology. They were greeted on arrival by Dr Gregor Zilstein, the psychologist performing the experiment, who wore a white coat and used a stethoscope. This image was intentional in order to influence the students' behaviour.

The psychologist told the girls that they were about to receive electric shocks that would be either painful but do no permanent harm or not painful, and in either case the electric shock would resemble more of a tickle or a tingle than anything unpleasant. The key question was what the girls would do in this frightening situation. They were told to choose whether to wait with other girls or alone, and to state their preference on a questionnaire. It should be noted that the instructions the girls received, and the presence of the doctor with his apparatus was merely a deception, in order to make the subjects feel afraid.

When the girls experienced strong fear, they generally preferred to wait with others, and they preferred to wait alone in conditions of low fear. Why do people affiliate with others when suffering from fear? Perhaps they want to compare their situation with others to see if their fears are justified. Apparently people are likely to reduce their anxieties while waiting for a painful experience, but more so when waiting in the company of others, irrespective of whether the people in the group communicate.[32]

Social Control
In social control the influence is exercised from above on a vertical basis, rather than on a horizontal basis as in social comparison. Experiments on obedience to authority, such as the famous study by Milgram, have shown that a significant number of people are prepared to inflict pain on others

because an authority figure instructs them to do so.[33] Subjects representing a cross-section of the population in an American university town were induced to inflict pain and danger on other people by increasingly large doses of electric shock as a punishment for making mistakes in a learning experiment. Those at the receiving end of the electric shocks—the victims—protested in a dramatic fashion and pleaded for the experiments to cease.

This put the subjects into an awkward and difficult position. They had to cope with the demands of the experimenter to continue with the experiment, the pleas of the victim for the experiment to cease and the demands of their own conscience. A number of people refused to take part in the experiments, and some withdrew after administering a small dose of electric shock. However, others continued to participate and, though troubled by their participation, they accepted the experimenter's logic that it is legitimate to administer electric shock to a learner who makes mistakes.

When colleagues of the experimenter were present, and they refused to continue with the experiments, this gave the subject encouragement to do likewise in most situations. The effects of group pressure are evident in this situation. The behaviour of the colleagues of the experimenter conveyed to the subjects that first of all disobedience is possible, that no adverse consequences stem from disobedience, and anyway the act of giving a victim an electric shock is improper. The good news is that the electric shocks were not real, though the subjects were not aware of this during the experiment. The cries of the victim's distress came from a tape recorder which was activated by pressing the "shock" lever. When victims were visible to the subject, through a glass partition, the role of the victim was played by an actor.

What was surprising in this series of experiments was the number of people who were prepared to administer electric shocks to somebody who made a mistake in a learning experiment. One of the striking aspects of the experiment is that the subjects are in a situation where demands are made on them while they cannot compare themselves with somebody in a similar situation. As such the conditions of the experiment do not correspond with those found in formal organizations. It is worth noting the operation of social comparison in one phase of the experiments. This occurred when colleagues of the experimenter decided to challenge his authority. From this incident we may conclude that social comparison may play an exceedingly important part in limiting the potency of demands from authority figures.

Milgram's aim was to establish conditions under which a person would blindly carry out the orders of another, even when the task was objectionable and the orders could not be supported by any kind of reasoning. He saw his research as contributing to a reduction of the threat of totalitarian authority systems. His critics felt that he should not have subjected his subjects to the stress they experienced from participating in the experiments, and that studies of such destructive forms of obedience are open to misuse by totalitarian authority figures.

Other forms of social control are institutional control and brainwashing. In institutional control the inmate in a prison is frequently stripped of personal props to his or her identity. For example, personal clothing and furniture are not permitted, the mail can be controlled and frequent association with relatives and friends is not allowed.[34] In brainwashing there is an attempt to undermine people's stability of mind and self-image by not permitting them to relate to friends or identify with their normal group. This is achieved by measures such as segregating members of the group, prohibiting group formation, fomenting mutual distrust, manipulating the news so that only the bad news gets through, and finally exposing the individual to the desired message in a state of social isolation.[35]

Individual differences have to be taken into account when considering the degree of difficulty in altering a person's values. It would be more difficult to induce Catholic missionaries to renounce their faith than to persuade army conscripts who are peace-loving civilians at heart to renounce their country's involvement in an unpopular war. Some manipulative measures manage to secure compliance only, but not identification and internalization. The value of this type of social control is lost when the individual returns to his or her old environment, but in severe situations the effect of coercive persuasion cannot be reversed.

Decision Making

Models of decision making and constraining influences were discussed in Chapter 5. Using groups to make decisions has been both strongly endorsed and seriously questioned by behavioural scientists and managers. From early studies of group dynamics the implication appears to be that people are more likely to accept new ideas from their colleagues and leader in the course of discussion than from a leader telling them what to do. It is believed that the individual sees a clearer picture of the situation and as a consequence feels involved in the decisions, and finds it easy to bow to the will of the group. This involvement is considered effective when the focus is on overcoming resistance to change. It is claimed that group discussion makes better use of the available talent or abilities of members. It promotes acceptability of decisions because people have had the opportunity to raise their anxieties or concerns in connection with the problems under discussion; and it is considered a democratic way of going about things, although this could be somewhat invalidated if the information put before the group is selectively chosen.

The early studies referred to above were conducted by Kurt Lewin.[3] Groups of housewives were persuaded to buy cheaper, unattractive cuts of meat, which were nutritional, to help economize as part of the war effort

Interesting and attractive lectures were given with supporting leaflets, emphasizing the vitamin and mineral value of offal as well as stressing the health and economic aspects of this type of food, with hints about the preparation of dishes. In the method devoted to group discussion a different approach was adopted. The group leader discussed the link between diet and the war effort and the discussion focused on the reasons why housewives were not keen to experiment with cheap foods (hearts, kidneys, etc.). It was found that 32% of those who discussed the issues in a group said a week later that they served at least one of the dishes recommended by their group. But only 3% of the housewives who attended the lectures took the minimum advice of the lecturer. Is the lecture an unsuitable medium in these circumstances? The listener is generally in a passive role, using personal experience to accept or reject the proposals advocated by the lecturer; the listener is generally ignorant of what others are going to decide and there is no "new social norm" to offer guidance.

By contrast, in the discussion group, people are encouraged to exchange views and consider the merits and demerits of buying different cuts of meat. There is an acknowledgement that other people have a valid point of view, and this could lessen a resistance to change. The advisability of buying offal is openly discussed, and recipes are introduced when the housewives are mentally prepared for a change. The decision which emerges from the discussion becomes a norm, and when members publicly support the group's decision this can consolidate the individual's intention to buy and in effect change her purchasing behaviour.

Lewin accepts the power of group decisions in influencing individual behaviour. To him the exercise of freedom of choice rather than high pressure salesmanship is critical. In the discussion group a minority position (to buy the cheap meat) developed into a majority position. In fact the previous majority position (not to buy the cheap meat) could now be considered deviant. One particular facet of this experiment should be noted, which is that the advocated new behaviour—save money and assist the war effort—was obviously an attractive proposition.

In the fields of marketing and safety, to name but two, efforts are made to change the individual's outlook, and group decision making may be used as a vehicle to achieve this objective. In a study adopting similar methods to those used by Lewin, housewives were encouraged to consume greater quantities of fresh and evaporated milk.[37] It was found that the group discussion was more effective in changing behaviour than the lecture; the influence of the personality of the leader of the discussion group was considered not to be an influential factor. The group was drawn from the same neighbourhood, and unlike the Red Cross Group in Lewin's experiment members of the neighbourhood group were not members of a club meeting regularly. This might suggest that group decision making can be effective in ad hoc groups. Lewin is of the view that group discussion could be used as an important method of bringing about social change which is potentially adaptive. However, group discussion as a method could be undermined (as is shown later in the analysis of "groupthink") if the discussion is limited and the group leader manipulates proceedings in a manner which is contrary to the interests of the group.

Risky Shift. Is there a danger that a group is more conservative and cautious than an individual in arriving at decisions, and as a result may produce poorer decisions? Or alternatively, are groups prepared to take greater risks? Apparently, some groups are prepared to take greater risks than are individuals; this is known as the risky shift phenomenon.[38] The following is an item from a questionnaire on Choice Dilemma used for measuring risk-taking.[39]

A corporation, dealing in light metals, is prosperous and has considered seriously the possibilities of expanding its business by building an additional plant in a new location. It is faced with a dilemma of choice. It can build a new plant in the home country which is politically stable, and where a moderate return on the initial investment could be achieved; or, it could build a plant in a foreign country where there are lower labour costs and easy access to raw materials. The latter action would mean a much higher return on the initial investment, but there is a history of political instability and revolution in the foreign country; in addition, the leader of a small minority party in the foreign country is committed to nationalizing all foreign investments.

As Finance Director, imagine you are advising the Chief Executive of the corporation. Several probabilities or odds of continued political stability in the foreign country under consideration are listed in Table 7.1, and you are asked to tick the lowest probability that you would consider acceptable

TABLE 7.1
Choice Dilemma Questionnaire - Probabilities
of Political Stability

Tick the lowest probability that you, as Finance Director, would consider acceptable for the Chief Executive to decide to build a new plant in the foreign country.

The chances that the foreign country will
remain politically stable are: 1 in 10   ____
                                   3 in 10   ____
                                   5 in 10   ____
                                   7 in 10   ____
                                   9 in 10   ____

Or: tick here if you feel that the Chief
Executive should not build, no matter
what the probabilities.   ____

for the Chief Executive to go ahead and build the new plant in that country.

The dilemma is a two-choice situation where the Finance Director is faced with a choice between a risky but highly desirable course of action, and a cautious but less desirable one. Failure in terms of the risky alternative can be assumed to lead to very unfavourable consequences. For the risky choice there are two possible consequences: (1) the probability of political stability and no nationalization; or (2) the probability of political instability and nationalization. In Table 7.1 a 1 in 10 chance represents a risky choice whereas a 9 in 10 chance represents a cautious one. When business executives decided on the ranking of investment projects, in a study outside the normal risky shift research studies, they agreed as a group to take more risky decisions than they had chosen as individuals. An appropriate question to ask at this stage is whether people would generally be more risk-taking in their behaviour when decisions are for real in the world of work?

What aspects of the group's experience account for the risky shift phenomenon? Before a consensus is reached certain aspects of the group discussion are important:

1. An upward influence on the level of risk an individual proposes to take emanates from information about the risks other members in the group are prepared to take.

2. The emotional interaction arising from the discussion may create a disposition for a shift towards risk to take place.

3. The act of committing oneself to a group decision is tantamount to lifting the burden off one's shoulders and transferring it to the group, and in the process the commitment becomes more risky. Because each member feels less personal responsibility for a potential loss, consensus is likely to move towards acceptance of more risk.[40]

It is also suggested that there may be a possibility of a CAUTIOUS SHIFT in group decision making, and this would co-exist with a risky shift. For example, certain items under review might be interpreted in a cautious direction after the discussion, whereas other items are biased towards risk. In other circumstances risk-taking may be ingrained in the culture of the members of the group. In such a case cultural values could act as a filtering process, whereby information generated by the group discussion is interpreted in a particular way. For example, risk-taking business executives from the U.S. engaged in committee deliberations to justify a decision, may select observations arising from the discussion which support their cultural disposition. On the other hand, cautious business executives from the U.K. may place a different interpretation on the group discussion. In the former case it is likely that persuasive arguments favoured risk, and in the latter case they favoured a conservative view.

Cohesion and Loyalty.   Sometimes the advantages of group decision making are undermined by powerful psychological pressures resulting from members working closely together and sharing the same set of values. At a time of crisis this puts people under considerable stress. Where a group is cohesive—that is, the group is very important to its members, or they have a strong need to stay in it—a high level of conformity can be demanded of its members. The conformity is likely to express itself in loyalty to the group, even in circumstances when the policies of the group are malfunctioning.

There are occasions when group loyalty makes a mockery of accident prevention. In one particular case the function of factory units was to modify rod-shaped machine tools by cutting or banding them.[41] Before modifying them, one end of each pen-sized tool was dipped in a protective molten plastic substance. After modification some of the tools were sandblasted to make them look better. Almost every one of these actions was undertaken in a grossly unsafe manner. One Monday the manager told six of his subordinates to make the place presentable because the Factory Inspector was coming round. Three of them were asked to tidy up around the machine and the other three to pick up the boxes of machine tools from the gangway and place them on a long bench.

The manager told the group that they could replace the boxes as soon as the visit was over, and gave them a wink, because the bench was required for other things. The Inspector seemed to be viewed as an enemy. The men grumbled about the visit, but the manager said, "Surely we don't want people like inspectors finding fault with our unit, lads!" This prompted jokes about setting booby traps for the Inspector. When the Inspector left there was evidence of a lot of anti-safety behaviour. This behaviour would suggest that there appeared to be mindless devotion to the group, particularly in the face of an outside authority figure with powers of sanction.

Groupthink   It has been suggested by Janis—a perceptive observer of the functioning of in-groups—that as a group becomes excessively close-knit and develops a strong feeling of "we-ness", it becomes vulnerable to a pattern of behaviour known as groupthink.[42] When consensus seeking becomes a dominant force, groupthink develops; this is a thinking process which tends to push aside a realistic appraisal of alternative courses of action. It is the outcome of group pressure and impedes the efficient execution of one's mental faculties and interferes with members' ability to test reality and preserve their judgement. Groupthink amounts to an unintentional erosion of one's critical faculties as a result of adopting group norms; this is to be distinguished from a similar occurrence as a result of external threats of social punishment. Though groupthink is more likely to affect cohesive in-groups, this is not always the case, and is particularly unlikely to be so where an atmosphere of critical inquiry is a normal feature of the decision-making approach.

The outward signs of groupthink are likely to manifest themselves in a number of ways. Members of groups formed to make decisions show a tendency to be lenient in their judgement of the ideas of their leader or fellow members for fear of being ostracized or disciplined. They go so far as being unnecessarily strict with themselves, placing controls on their own freedom of thought. There is an amiable atmosphere with an absence of aggravation so as to retain the comfortable "we-feeling." As cohesiveness in the group continues to develop there is a strong urge on the part of each member to avoid "rocking the boat" and this can be instrumental in persuading the individual to accept whatever proposals are promoted by the leader or a majority of the group's members.

On the face of it, the scope for deviant thought is considerable in a highly cohesive group, nevertheless the desire for consensus on all important issues is so prevalent as to discourage the individual from utilizing this advantage. When groupthink is forcefully present, deviant thoughts are relegated to insignificance by individuals establishing that their own reservations are not so overwhelming after all and should be set aside, and that the benefit of the doubt with regard to the remaining uncertainties should be given to the group so as to promote consensus.

Also, perhaps agreeing is considered more beneficial than the insecurity that is likely to be created should the individual suffer rejection because of persistent deviant thoughts. Groupthink places greatest emphasis on team-work with an inherent striving for unanimity within the collective membership. This presents a number of difficulties ranging from over-optimism and lack of vigilance to ineffectiveness and lack of realism in the formulation and implementation of policy. The following are key characteristics of groupthink.[42]

1. Illusion of Invulnerability. Many, if not all, members of the in-group share an illusion of invulnerability. This has some reassuring effect as regards obvious dangers and is responsible for members becoming over-optimistic and keen to take unjustifiable risks. It also causes them to fail to respond to clear warning signals. Here the group displays an unshaken belief in its endorsed course of action, and in the face of information or views to the contrary its belief remains intact. The group goes as far as discounting warnings or negative feedback by indulging in rationalizations of its action on a collective basis.

Inevitably this leads to a reconsideration and renewed commitment to both the underlying assumptions of policy pursued and the policy itself. A further line of action might be reflected in an approach whereby evidence to support the status quo is selectively chosen from any available source or, if necessary, by inventing specious forecasts. Some members of the group or committee may be aware of the misgivings of an outsider about the wisdom of pursuing the policy in question but display a reluctance to voice concern. Where the group believes it is invulnerable this can reduce anxiety about taking risks. An accountant acting in an advisory capacity may find that members of a management committee fail to respond to clear warning signals with regard to the financial advisability of pursuing a particular course of action. Because of the illusion of invulnerability, the group discount the warnings and engage in collective rationalization in order to maintain their view or belief.

2. *Belief in the Rectitude of the Group.* There develops an unquestionable belief in the morality or self-righteousness of the in-group. In this way one can choose to ignore the ethical or moral consequences of the decisions taken. A war cabinet, having placed the minimization of civilian casualties high on its priority list, may find it easier to prosecute or escalate the war without feelings of guilt. In much the same way a working party or committee within an organization, having reached a decision to introduce a scheme of job enrichment or industrial democracy, may appeal to the justness and ethical nature of the scheme when fully operational—i.e., it provides employees with the potential for self-fulfilment and self-determination.

A member whose doubts, following consideration of the scheme, are committed to writing is likely to suppress them when attending meetings. When an outsider is invited to express his or her observations on the feasibility or otherwise of the scheme, the chairman is likely to be quick off the mark when the speaker finishes, and to move on to the next item on the agenda if the speaker's observations express misgivings or doubts. At crucial meetings the obvious tactic would be for the chairman or leader not to call on the doubters to speak. Instead, an attempt would be made to tame the doubters, and in any case not to permit them to go so far as questioning the fundamental assumptions of strategy. This would be particularly so if the doubters are members of the in-group.

3. *Negative Views of Competitors.* There is a tendency to subscribe to negative stereotyped views of the leaders of enemy or competitor groups. Here we find the prevailing attitude of mind supporting the view that these leaders are either too weak or too stupid to meet the challenge of the in-group. In a military campaign this disposition could create an underestimation of the numerical strength of the enemy, or a totally inaccurate assessment of their true intentions. For example, it is reported that because of the rigid attachment of President Johnson's advisers to the domino theory, they ignored the nationalistic yearnings of the North Vietnamese

and their wish to ward off the Chinese. It was suggested by a social scientist in Britain, who has made a special study of decision making, that the U.K. government did not pick up certain critical signals prior to the Falklands war.[43] Similarities to the military analogy can be found within organizations among groups competing for scarce resources, and in an external context when policy-making groups make certain assumptions about the quality of the company's competitors.

4. Sanctity of Group Consensus.   There appears to be a natural tendency to steer clear of a deviation from what is perceived as group consensus. A member sharing this disposition remains reticent about personal misgivings or doubts and, in addition, is quite capable of convincing him or herself of the lack of substance in these doubts. Outside the group situation, in the corridor or dining room, this person may, however, feel strongly about the issues in question and convey the antithesis of his or her true feelings on the matter at the meeting. This individual may subsequently feel guilty for having kept silent, but it is probable that the circumstances surrounding the group discussion were such as to permit only the raising of matters of minor importance.

5. Illusion of Unanimity.   The illusion of unanimity creates the belief that all members' judgements are unanimous when they subscribe to the majority view. No doubt unanimity is fostered when members are insulated from outside views between meetings and where the emerging majority view reflects the declared choice of an influential figure (e.g., the chief executive) in the organization. The presumption of unanimity is upheld when members remain silent. There is an almost unstated assumption that members who respect each other will arrive at a unanimous view. The result of this proneness to validate group consensus is, in the absence of disagreements among members, the sweeping away of critical thinking and testing of reality. This can lead to serious errors of judgement, though it could be argued that the mutual bolstering of self-esteem and morale, which emanates from the process of seeking agreement, enhances the group's capacity to take action.

A range of divergent views about the riskiness of the preferred course of action could be mildly traumatic. The existence of disagreement could give rise to anxieties about the likelihood of making a serious error, and once unanimity is severely dented it is difficult to remain confident about the correctness of the group decision. The onus then falls on members to confront the uncertainties and assess the seriousness of the risks. Therefore, to eradicate this painful state, members are inclined, without realizing it, to prevent latent disagreements from coming to the surface, particularly when they are proposing to initiate a risky adventure.

However, a nagging doubt may persist if information about difficulties surfaces and is provided by a previous supporter of the group who is of high calibre. There now develops a movement towards emphasizing areas of convergence in thinking at the cost of fully exploring divergencies that might expose unresolved issues. The illusion of unanimity is maintained simply because, generally speaking, the major participants in the group discussion fail to reveal their own reasoning or discuss their assumptions or reservations.

An overview of the processes involved in the making of an investment decision by a policy group in a public corporation, screened on British television some years ago, provides ample evidence of unnatural striving for unanimity that might be engineered by the chairman of the corporation. The rationale for his preference was not always clearly stated, but alternative solutions which challenged the preferred solution seemed to be all too easily discredited and discarded in circumstances which justified more serious consideration of them.

6. Erecting a Protective Shield.   Finally, groupthink has the effect of erecting a shield to protect the leader and fellow members from adverse information that might shatter their shared complacency about the morality and effectiveness of past decisions. This situation arises when an influential group member calls a doubter or dissenter to one side and advises him or her on the desirability of backing the leader and the group. Where outside expert opinion is sought, invariably the chairman will retort by questioning the legitimacy of the assumption underlying it, or ensuring that insufficient time is devoted to discussing it, finally stating why the original decision seems to be a wise one. This type of behaviour manifested itself in the investment decision process referred to above. The accountant may be asked to submit a financial appraisal of a project to which the chief executive has a total commitment. Having presented the report, the accountant is horrified to find that the chief executive, instead of assessing the report on its merits, questions the legitimacy of the assumptions underpinning it, and puts aside insufficient time to discuss it. In effect, a shield is erected to protect the group members from what they consider to be adverse information likely to dislodge commitment to the chosen course of action.

The accountant then faces a dilemma: having presented an opinion, should he or she accept a committee decision which is quite contrary to it?; would it be better to insist that the report goes on record?; by being too persistent or regularly opposing the group, is there a possibility of increasing isolation and eventual rejection by the group or its leader?

The consequences that flow from groupthink symptoms, discussed above, are synonymous with the consequences of poor decision-making practices, and it follows that inadequate solutions to the problems under review are found. Discussion tends to be limited to but a few alternatives and there is a conspicuous absence of evaluation of many alternatives that should be considered in the decision process. No systematic consideration is given to the question of whether gains, which do not appear obvious in the normal course of events, have been overlooked; neither is any cost assessment placed on the alternatives which have been rejected by the group. Similarly, no serious attempt is made to get the views of experts on potential losses or gains.

A noticeable trend is for group members to display a positive interest in facts and options that support their preferred policy, while ignoring facts and opinions that challenge it. There tends to be a failure to establish contingency plans to deal with foreseeable setbacks such as bureaucratic inertia, mishaps or subtle political manoeuvring by opponents, which could pose a threat to the successful outcome of the course of action chosen. Given the dysfunctional effects created by groupthink, what steps can we take to prevent it?

Steps to Counteract Groupthink. There are a number of steps suitable to counteract groupthink.

1. Encourage individual members to evaluate what has been said in a critical fashion; place a high priority on an open discussion of doubts and objections where it is perfectly legitimate to disagree or be sceptical. The leader must be prepared to accept criticisms of his or her own judgement, which could have a healthy effect in arresting the rapid slide towards consensus with its adverse effect on critical thinking.

2. At the beginning of the discussion, as a means of encouraging open inquiry and an objective investigation of a wide range of policy alternatives, the leader should exercise impartiality and avoid stating preferences and expectations with regard to outcomes. Avoid arriving at conclusions on the basis of a consideration of an inadequate number of alternative courses of action. Encourage members to offer suggestions, and be aware at all times that early evaluation of a limited choice of alternatives could have a detrimental effect on ideas that are different, novel or lacking support.

3. At the stage of the meeting when an evaluation of policy alternatives is required, one member of the group should play the role of devil's advocate, challenging the evidence put forward by those promulgating the majority point of view.

4. Do not rush into a quick solution of the problem. When you arrive at a first solution or preliminary choice, let it rest for a while and come back to it later and analyze the problem afresh. Where feasible, allow each group member to report back to his or her section or department to establish what people feel about the proposals before a final decision is reached. However, security considerations may rule out such an approach in every case. Expose

the problem to outsiders with different special interests from those of the group members and ask them to challenge its assumptions and content. The outcome of this exercise would be reported back to the group.

5. Where appropriate, break up the group into sub-groups, with each sub-group having a chairman, to examine the feasibility and effectiveness of the proposed policy alternatives. Then the main group should reconvene to settle the differences. Ideally, create more than one group to examine the same question, each group working under a different leader.

6. Where the group is in competition with another group, it may be advisable to put aside a session to monitor information reaching the group from this source and write alternative models of the rival group's intentions.

This strategy, though desirable, could be costly in execution and might be considered inappropriate at a time of crisis.

Intergroup Conflict

Membership of a particular group could predispose members to view other groups with suspicion and sometimes hostility. A vivid illustration of inter-group conflict is provided by Sherif.[44] Boys attending summer camps were allocated to two different groups. Competitive games were used to develop a competitive relationship between the two groups, and when a hostile inter-group relationship emerged various procedures to resolve the conflict were used. Bringing members of the hostile groups together socially as a means of reducing conflict did not seem to work. Neither did it help when accurate and favourable information about one group was communicated to the other group. Even bringing the leaders of the two groups together to enlist their influence was not productive. In fact social contacts of the type described above can act as a means of intensifying conflict because favourable information about a disliked group may be ignored or reinterpreted to fit negative stereotyped notions about opponents.

Apparently the best strategy for achieving harmony between the groups in conflict is to bring the groups together to work towards the achievement of a common or superordinate goal. This requires a collaborative effort for the achievement of the superordinate goal, and in these circumstances favourable information about a disliked group is seen in a new light; in addition leaders are in a better position to take bolder steps towards co-operation. Examples of superordinate goals set by Sherif are the breakdown of the camp water supply which required inter-group co-operation to find the fault, and the breakdown of a lorry used for excursions which required all members of the groups to pull together on the same rope to get it started. After a series of activities based on different superordinate goals, inter-group conflict was progressively reduced and the two groups began to integrate. These principles can also manifest themselves in an organizational setting.

An organization consists of different groups (e.g., production and marketing functions) and one effect of group membership, in whatever function, is the development of group loyalties. This can result in a parochial view of overall organizational events, and there is a likelihood that each group actively pursues its own ends to the disadvantage of the organization as a whole. Conflict can arise when there is competition for scarce resources among the different groups. Budgeting can be used as a process for resolving inter-group conflict, but it may not always be successful in doing so. A significant threat to the survival of the organization may be instrumental in bringing about more constructive inter-group co-operation and the resolution of conflict.

Although the principle of setting superordinate or common goals as a means to reduce inter-group conflict is appealing, Sherif felt it may not be applicable in all industrial settings. The reason he gave was that some groups in industry possess notably more power than others. There is now greater interest in the significance of power as a dimension of inter-group relations.[45] The question of power is discussed in the next chapter.

EFFECTIVE AND INEFFECTIVE GROUPS

To conclude this chapter it seems appropriate to introduce the views of two prominent organizational psychologists on what constitutes the features of the effective group. One of them also had something to say about the characteristics of the ineffective group. McGregor has compared the features of both the effective and ineffective group.[46] Members experience the social climate indicated in Table 7.2 within both the effective and ineffective group.

Likert identified the profile and performance characteristics of the highly effective work group.[47] These are shown in Table 7.3 and could supplement the features of the effective group listed in Table 7.2.

Many of the characteristics of the effective group listed in Tables 7.2 and 7.3 are ideal types, and though people may strive to operationalize them there are formidable behavioural and organizational constraints likely to undermine the process. Nevertheless, they are indicative of good practice with respect to the functioning of groups.

TABLE 7.2

McGregor's Characteristics of Effective & Ineffective Groups

Effective	Ineffective
a) Informality; relaxed atmosphere; involvement; interest	Formality; tense atmosphere; indifference; boredom
b) Much discussion; high contributions	Domination by few; contributions often lack relevance
c) Understanding/acceptance of common aims	Aims ill-defined and misunderstood; conflict between private aims and common aims exists
d) Listen; consider; forward ideas	Unfair hearing; irrelevant speeches; members fear ridicule/condemnation
e) Examine disagreements; dissenters are not over-powered	Disagreements are suppressed or conflict develops; large minority are dissatisfied; disruptive minority imposes its views
f) Consensus decision making; member feels free to disagree	Lack of consensus; premature decision making; formal voting (simple majority).
g) Constructive criticism	Personalized destructive criticism
h) Feelings and attitudes are aired	Feelings remain under the surface
i) Awareness of decisions/actions; clear assignments	Lack of awareness of decisions; unclear assignments
j) Leadership role undertaken by most suitable member	Leadership role is jealously guarded
k) Frequent review of group operations	Not too concerned with deficiencies of the group

TABLE 7.3
Likert's Characteristics of the Effective Group

1. Social interaction skills (e.g., ability to relate to others) required by both the leader and members are well developed.

2. Relaxed working relationship among members of the group.

3. Identification with the group and loyalty to all members, including the leader.

4. High degree of confidence and trust among members, including the leader.

5. Individual values and needs find expression in the group's values and goals. Because the individual members have helped to shape the group outlook, they feel satisfied with the way in which the group is going.

6. Acceptance of important group values (e.g., loyalty or safety) by members.

7. Since individuals wish to achieve something and enhance their personal worth, they channel this motivation to achieve the important goals of the group and at the same time they abide by the major values of the group (e.g., achieve a high level of production without compromising safety standards).

8. Commitment to the group springs from sharing the group's values and deriving satisfaction from membership. The individual is keen to do his or her best and not let his or her colleagues down.

9. Supportive atmosphere governs all interactions, problem-solving and decision-making activities of the group. Suggestions, comments, ideas, information, criticisms, are forth-coming.

10. Linking functions with other groups: the group endeavours to adopt the values and goals of the groups with which it has a link.

11. The leader of the group who is carefully chosen adopts a participative management style.

12. The group is capable of setting attainable goals for members.

13. Mutual help is forthcoming in order to accomplish the group's goals.

14. The supportive atmosphere of the group stimulates creativity.

15. The group has a healthy respect for necessary bureaucratic practices.

16. A premium is placed on efficient communication processes, and there is little reason to doubt the credibility of the information communicated.

17. Members tend to exert influence on each other for the common good; this would apply to exerting influence on the leader. The ability of members of the group to influence each other contributes to the flexibility and adaptability of the group.

18. The attachment to common goals and shared values contributes to the stability of group activities. Members feel secure in using their initiative to make decisions in these circumstances.

SUMMARY

Having briefly introduced the notion of what is meant by a group, it was suggested that groups can be classified by type. Groups can be classified as formal or informal, primary or secondary, and by skill and level of interaction. The characteristics of groups were identified as norms, communication networks and group dynamics. Before examining group processes, some reasons for joining groups were briefly stated.

Group processes were identified as: reference groups; social comparison; co-action and affiliation; social control; decision making; and inter-group conflict. Reference groups were classified as normative or comparative, and as positive or negative. The relevance of the concept of the reference group to marketing was noted.

The significance of social comparison was explained. Group norms, as a social comparative influence, were illustrated with reference to production targets and standard costs. The influence exerted by the group in different experimental conditions (e.g., the studies conducted by Sherif and Asch) was acknowledged. Group influence was briefly discussed with respect to budgeting and discretionary costs.

With regard to co-action and affiliation, relating to others in different conditions (e.g., being evaluated by an expert or in a state of fear) can have a material bearing on the behaviour of an individual in a group setting. Social control is the influence exercised by an authority figure on a vertical basis, rather than on a horizontal basis as in social comparison. Social control was illustrated with particular reference to Milgram's experiments (i.e., obedience to authority). Other forms of social control are institutional control and brainwashing.

The nature and likely benefits of group decision making were discussed, initially with reference to the experiments conducted by Lewin. The risky shift phenomenon was explained and illustrated using an investment decision as an example. The focus on decision making was concluded with a discussion of groupthink. The key characteristics of groupthink were explained along with possible steps to counteract it.

The nature of inter-group conflict was briefly explained with reference to experimental evidence and its likely sources within a business organization. The chapter was brought to a close with a perspective on the social climate within both the effective and ineffective group.

QUESTIONS

1. Define what is meant by a group, and give examples of different types of group.
2. What is the difference between an internally imposed norm and an externally imposed norm? Into which category would you place a production target?
3. Explain the following terms which are used to describe the characteristics of a group:
   a. cohesiveness;
   b. communication networks;
   c. group dynamics;
   d. geographic proximity.
4. Give the reasons why you joined your favourite group other than your family.
5. What is the difference between:
   a. a membership group and a reference group;
   b. a normative reference group and a comparative reference group?
6. Discuss the suggestion that reference groups influence consumer behaviour.
7. What is the significance of the Hawthorne studies in the context of group norms as a social comparative influence?
8. "Formal control systems, of which standard costing is part, should be consistent with group norms." Discuss.
9. Comment on the relevance of the findings of Asch's experiment to a group involved in the budgeting process.
10. Describe Milgram's work on obedience to authority, and suggest the most appropriate type of organization where social control is legitimate.
11. With reference to decision making in groups, explain the following with examples from business practice:
    a. group discussion;
    b. risky shift and cautious shift;
    c. groupthink.
12. What strategy would you recommend for achieving harmony between groups in conflict?
13. Distinguish between effective and ineffective groups.

REFERENCES

1. Sayles, L.R. (1958) *The Behaviour of Industrial Work Groups*. New York: John Wiley & Sons.
2. Trist, E.L., Higgin G., Pollock, H.E. & Murray, H.A. (1963) *Organisational Choice*. London: Tavistock.
3. Zaltman, G. & Wallandorf, M. (1979) *Consumer Behaviour: Basic Findings and Managerial Implications*. New York: John Wiley & Sons.
4. Yablonsky, L. (1967) *The Violent Gang*. Harmondsworth: Penguin.
5. Witt, R.E. & Bruce, G. (1970) Purchase decisions and group influence. *Journal of Marketing Research, 7,* November, 533–535.
6. Laing, R.D. (1970) *The Divided Self*. Harmondsworth: Penguin.
7. Leavitt, H.J. (1951) Some effects of certain communication patterns on group performance. *Journal of Abnormal and Social Psychology, 46,* 38–50.
8. Shaw, M.E. (1964) Communication networks. In L. Berkowitz (Ed.), *Advances in Experimental Social Psychology*, Vol.1, New York: Academic Press, 11–47.
9. Festinger, L., Schachter, S. & Back, K. (1950) *Social Pressure in Informal Groups: A Study of Human Factors in Housing*. New York: Harper & Row.
10. Sommer, R. (1967) Small group ecology. *Psychological Bulletin, 67,* 145–152.
11. Latey, P. (1982) Computing can damage your health. *Practical Computing, July,* 126–127.
12. Freud, S. (1955) Group psychology and the analysis of the *ego*. Vol. XVIII. In J. Strachey, (Ed.), *The Complete Psychological Works of Sigmund Freud, Vols. I-XXIV*. London: Hogarth Press.
13. Bion, W.R. (1961) *Experience in Groups*. London: Tavistock.
14. Newcombe, T.M. (1970) Attitude development as a function of reference groups: the Bennington study. In *Understanding Society*. London: Macmillan (for the Open University), 585–594.
15. Newcombe, T.M. (1967) *Persistence and Change, Bennington College and its Students after 25 Years*. New York: John Wiley & Sons.
16. Bourne, F.S. (1957) Group influences in marketing and public relations. In R. Likert & S.P. Hayes (Eds.), *Some Applications of Behavioural Research*. Paris: UNESCO.
17. Oliver, G. (1980) *Marketing Today*. London: Prentice-Hall.
18. Schiffman, L.G. & Kanuk, L.L. (1978) *Consumer Behaviour*. Englewood Cliffs, NJ: Prentice-Hall.
19. Kelman, H.C. (1961) Three processes of social influence. *Public Opinion Quarterly, 25,* 57–78.
20. Burnkrant R.E. & Cousineau, A. (1975) Informational and normative social influences in buyer behaviour. *Journal of Consumer Research, 2,* December, 206–215.
21. Roethlisberger, F.J. & Dickson, W.J. (1939) *Management and the Worker*. Cambridge, Mass: Harvard University Press.
22. Lupton, T. (1963) *On the Shop Floor*. Oxford: Pergamon.
23. Flamholtz, E. (1975) Small group interaction and task performance: its implications for managerial accounting. In J. Leslie Livingstone (Ed.), *Managerial Accounting*. Columbus, Ohio: Grid Inc.
24. Sherif, M. (1936) *The Psychology of Social Norms*. New York: Harper & Row.
25. Venkatesan, M. (1966) Experimental study of consumer behaviour: conformity and Independence. *Journal of Marketing Research, 3,* November, 384–387.
26. Cohen, D. (1981) *Consumer Behaviour*. New York: Random House.
27. Asch, S.E. (1952) Effects of group pressure upon the modification and distortion of judgements. In C.E. Swanson, T.M. Newcombe & E.L.Hartley, (Eds.), *Readings in*

Social Psychology. New York: Holt, Rinehart & Winston.

28. Latané, B. & Darley, J. (1968) Group inhibition of bystander intervention in emergencies. *Journal of Personality and Social Psychology, 10,* 215–221.

29. Zajonc, R.B. & Sales, S.M. (1966) Social facilitation of dominant and subordinate responses. *Journal of Experimental Social Psychology, 2,* 160–168.

30. Henchy, T. & Glass, D.C. (1968) Evaluation of apprehension and the social facilitation of dominant and subordinate responses. *Journal of Personality and Social Psychology, 10,* 445–454.

31. Schachter, S. (1959) *The Psychology of Affiliation.* Palo Alto: Stanford University Press.

32. Wrightsman, L. (1960) Effects of waiting for others on changes in level of felt anxiety. *Journal of Abnormal and Social Psychology, 61,* 216–222.

33. Milgram, S. (1965) Some conditions of obedience and disobedience to authority. *Human Relations, 18,* 57–76.

34. Goffman, E. (1961) *Asylums: Essays on the Social Situation of Mental Patients and Other Inmates.* New York: Doubleday.

35. Schein, E.H. (1956) The Chinese indoctrination program for prisoners of war. *Psychiatry, 19,* 149–172.

36. Lewin, K. (1958) Group decision and social change. In E.E. Maccoby, T.M. Newcombe & R.L. Hartley (Eds.), *Readings in Social Psychology, 3rd Edition.* New York: Holt, 197–211.

37. Radke, M. & Klisurich, D. (1958) Experiments in changing food habits, cited by Lewin, K. in *Group Decision and Social Change.* In E.E. Maccoby, T.M. Newcombe & R.L. Hartley (Eds.), *Readings in Social Psychology, 3rd Edition,* New York: Holt, 197–211.

38. Stoner, J.A.F. (1961) A comparison of individual and group decisions involving risk. Unpublished Master's thesis, School of Industrial Management, M.I.T. quoted in Brown, R. (1965) *Social Psychology.* New York: Free Press.

39. Kogan, N. & Wallach, M.A. (1967) Risk taking as a function of the situation, person and the group. In T.M. Newcombe (Ed.), *New Directions in Psychology,* Vol III, New York: Holt, Rinehart & Winston, 111–278.

40. Wallach, M.A. & Kogan, N. (1965) The roles of information, discussion and consensus in group risk taking. *Journal of Experimental Social Psychology, 1,* 1–19.

41. Chapman, J. (1982) After the inspector's visit—when group loyalty made a mockery of accident prevention. *The Safety Representative, March,* 5.

42. Janis, I.L. (1972) *Victims of Groupthink: A Psychological Study of Foreign Policy Decisions and Fiascos.* Boston: Houghton Mifflin.

43. Heller, F. (1983) The danger of groupthink. The *Guardian, 31 January,* 9.

44. Sherif, M. (1967) *Group Conflict and Cooperation: Their Social Psychology.* London: Routledge & Kegan Paul.

45. Hartley, J. (1984). Industrial relations psychology. In M. Gruneberg and T. Wall (Eds.), *Social Psychology and Organizational Behaviour.* Chichester: John Wiley & Sons.

46. McGregor, D. (1960) *The Human Side of Enterprise.* New York: McGraw-Hill.

47. Likert, R. (1961) *New Patterns of Management.* New York: McGraw-Hill.

8 LEADERSHIP AND MANAGEMENT STYLE

8 Leadership and Management Style

This chapter examines the leadership process from a number of perspectives. It starts with a commentary on the trait approach, followed by the impact of personality on leadership and the different forms in which leadership finds expression. One of these forms is the participative leadership style, and this is examined from many angles because of its importance as a management style. Nowadays situational leadership is a fertile area of study, and therefore, it is appropriate to acknowledge a number of situational theories. Finally, there is reference to certain factors likely to have a bearing on the leadership process; these are culture, power, politics, and new technology.

TRAIT APPROACH

Early attempts to define leadership concentrated on defining the desirable qualities found in a leader. It was generally concluded that a leader has special powers and perceptive abilities unlikely to be found in a person not born to be a leader. The types of trait often mentioned are: quickness of decision; the courage to take risks; coolness under stress; intuition; and even luck.[1] One researcher extensively reviewed the literature a number of years ago and came to the conclusion that the personal qualities of the leader could be classified as follows.

1. *Capacity:* intelligence; alertness; verbal facility; originality; judgement.
2. *Achievement:* scholarship; knowledge; athletic accomplishments.
3. *Responsibility:* dependability; initiative; persistence; aggressiveness; self-confidence; desire to excel.
4. *Participation:* activity; sociability; co-operation; adaptability; humour.
5. *Status:* socio-economic position; popularity.[2]

317

Another researcher identifies particular personality characteristics. He feels that leaders tend to be better adjusted, are more dominant, more extraverted, more conservative, and have greater interpersonal sensitivity than non-leaders.[3] A drawback of these approaches to the identification of personality and personal qualities is that the traits in question may not be part of the innate abilities the leader had at birth. In fact they may have been developed as a result of training or performing the leadership role.

In popular journalism occasionally there is reference to the personal qualities of a leader, perhaps prompted by concern during an economic crisis or the prospect of an accelerating crisis. We are told that leaders who possess honesty, candour, vision, sheer physical stamina, and courage are in short supply. Other qualities are said to be: integrity; team spirit; loyalty; will power; persuasiveness; the ability to develop good will; and the power to inspire.

It is now generally accepted that the study of leadership is something more than the analysis of some combination of traits. The job to be done, the atmosphere within a group of subordinates, and the interaction between the two also contribute to patterns of leadership. This is a view that is expanded by Adair in his functional approach to leadership. He acknowledges that the trait approach has some relevance, but in organizations it is imperative to consider the need to achieve the common task, the need for group cohesiveness or team maintenance, and the needs of individuals.[4]

LEADERSHIP STYLE AND PERSONALITY

Leadership Style

In order to investigate some aspects of how a group functions under different types of group atmosphere and different types of leadership, experiments were conducted with groups of children.[5] The groups were engaged in mask-making and similar activities. Different styles of leadership—autocratic, democratic and *laissez-faire*—were deliberately introduced by the experimenters who were adults. For example, the formulation of policy, the techniques and methods to be used, the division of work activities and the allocation of individuals to work were determined by the autocratic leader without reference to the group, while the democratic leader actively involved the children in policy-making and generally in the job of dividing and allocating the work. The autocratic leader was very subjective in his criticism and praise and remained aloof from the group except when demonstrating how to do the work.

On the other hand, the democratic leader was objective in his criticism and praise and tried to be a regular group member in spirit without doing much of the actual work. The groups appeared to react very favourably to the imposition of democratic leadership practice. There appeared to be greater group purpose, the individual group members related well to each other and displayed less aggression and hostility and more group unity in the democratic groups than in the autocratic groups. The reaction of group members to the *laissez-faire* style was marked with a lower degree of efficiency, organization and satisfaction.

A criticism levelled at these studies is that the findings suffer severe limitations if they are applied to the field of industrial leadership.

Both the ideal autocratic and democratic leadership style have been considered in an organizational setting.[6] In the autocratic model there is a noticeable absence of credit for suggestions emanating from subordinates and a lack of formal recognition of the efforts of subordinates. The subordinate does not have the opportunity to participate in the decision-making process, and is therefore deprived of feedback which could contribute to a useful learning experience. He or she is prevented from developing an insight into the factors which must be considered in choosing among alternatives in a decision situation. Should the subordinate make a contribution he or she probably gets no credit for it. The subordinate, as a result, has little motivation to contribute beyond what is minimally expected.

Under an ideal democratic system, participation by subordinates is more frequent and more constructive. Managers are more prepared to discuss relevant issues with subordinates and to respect their suggestions. When suggestions are received and evaluated, the reaction is transmitted to the subordinate in the form of feedback. This is believed to contribute to a desirable level of motivation and to promote the quality of future suggestions. It is also said to lead to greater involvement and contributes to high performance standards.

Personality

A comprehensive treatment of Personality appears in Chapter 1. Here the way in which personality impinges on leadership is acknowledged.

A number of writers and researchers subscribe to the view that personality interacts with style of leadership. This would apply to the personality of both the superior and the subordinate. The subordinate is said to react adversely to the imposition of autocracy. When the subordinate is denied pertinent information because the superior monopolizes official communication, this creates certain problems. The subordinate is unable to perceive the significance of a number of dimensions in the work situation, and this results in emotionalism, lack of direction and alienation. Because the superior can interfere with the subordinate's freedom of action and the realization of personal objectives, the subordinate may feel frustrated.[7] An autocratic style of leadership is also said to interfere adversely with spontaneity and creativity on the part of the subordinate, and is likely to undermine processes of co-operation.[8] It can also promote much hostility and aggression, leading to the harbouring of latent discontent.[5]

However, there may be conditions where the subordinate's personality is compatible with an autocratic style of leadership. According to Argyris, autocracy appeals to the "infant" in the subordinate's personality and promotes a state of dependency and submissiveness. So if the subordinate has not sufficiently matured and not moved to the "adult" end of the personality continuum, then perhaps autocracy can be agreeable.[9] It is suggested that those with poor productivity records are prone to suffer some anxiety and as a consequence they prefer a more autocratic style.[10] By not disclosing at the outset the sequence of steps in the work cycle, having decided instead to reveal them in a piecemeal fashion, an autocratic leader may unintentionally manage to reduce anxiety and promote dependence.[5] This is understandable because it is easier to cope with a partial rather than a global view of the work cycle.

What conditions are required to ensure that the subordinate's personality is compatible with a democratic style of leadership? The subordinate with a high need for independence is likely to prefer a democratic style.[11] In a study of insurance salesmen it was concluded that the more successful salesmen, who felt the least threatened, preferred a democratic leadership style.[10]

Sometimes a person who acts as a subordinate in one capacity acts the role of superior in another. The exercise of authority by a superior has a number of psychological meanings. It relates to superiority, dominance, submission, guidance, help, criticism, and reprimand. It also conjures up images of manliness and virility.[12] A superior whose feelings of insecurity in an uncertain situation do not allow him or her to release control over the decision-making process may be unable to involve subordinates to the extent required by democratic leadership.[11] If such superiors have a strong need for predictability and stability, they may consider the act of releasing control as something that reduces the predictability of the outcome.

An executive in a new job may feel uncertain about the situations he or she is to confront, and is likely to seek elaborate counsel, but the self-contained manager prefers to deliberate alone and acts in an autocratic manner with hardly any subordinate involvement in the decision-making process.[13] Though this evidence may have credibility in some circumstances, there must be other occasions when the self-contained manager, who may well display self-confidence, invites a high level of subordinate involvement in the decision-making process. There are complicated reasons why superiors adopt autocratic leadership. Some superiors may identify with their own superiors who also use autocratic leadership.[7]

A superior may use an autocratic style as an outlet for repressed agression brought about because of being subjected to autocracy as a subordinate.[14] Others may resort to discipline of a harsh nature bearing the hallmark of autocracy, in order to express a deep-seated hostility need.[15] All these interpretations border on the realm of unconscious motivations in leadership behaviour, and though important it is difficult to identify and measure these processes.

LIKERT'S FOUR STYLES

An expansion of the notion of leadership style consisting of two extreme positions—autocratic and democratic—is provided by Likert.[16] He puts forward four styles of leadership to capture the management culture of the organization.

1. Exploitative Authoritative.   The leader uses fear and threats, communication is downwards, superior and subordinates are psychologically distant, and almost all decisions are taken at the apex of the organization.

2. Benevolent Authoritative.   The leader uses rewards to encourage performance, upward flow of communication is limited to what the boss wants to hear, subservience to superiors is widespread, and although most decisions are taken at the top of the organization some delegation of decision-making exists.

3. Consultative.   The leader uses appropriate rewards, communication may be two-way although upward communication is cautious and limited, by and large, to what the boss wants to hear; some involvement is sought from employees, and subordinates have a moderate amount of influence in some decisions, but again broad policy decisions are the preserve of top management only.

4. Participative.   The leader dispenses economic rewards and makes full use of group participation and involvement in fixing high performance goals and improving work methods and procedures. The emphasis is on a network of accurate information; subordinates and superiors are psychologically close, and group decision making is widely spread throughout the organization. There is a tendency for a number of individuals to belong to more than one work group in order to promote inter-group links and understanding.

PARTICIPATIVE LEADERSHIP

The participative style of leadership has been favourably endorsed in a number of studies. In a study of the role of first-line supervisors, it was concluded that the supervisor who frequently checked up on subordinates, gave them detailed and frequent instructions and generally limited the em-

ployees' freedom to do their work in their own way had a low productivity
record. This result was contrasted with the record of high productivity units
where there was a high frequency of contact between superior and subordinates, where decision making tended to be pushed down the hierarchy,
where superiors were helpful in a constructive way, and generally where
relationships between superiors and subordinates were evident. In low productivity units, on the other hand, contact between superior and subordinates was low and there existed a high degree of pressure to finish jobs
and meet production targets.[17]

The participative style is often conceived largely in terms of a "system of
values" governing behaviour with a commitment to full and free communication, a reliance on consensus rather than on the more customary forms of
coercion or compromise to tackle and manage conflict, and an atmosphere
that permits and encourages emotional expression as well as a healthy attitude to work.[18] It is argued that as the individual moves from the infant end
of a personality continuum (basically dependent and submissive, with few
and shallow abilities and a short-time perspective) to the adult end (endowed with relative independence, autonomy, self-control, many abilities
and a few in depth, and a long-time perspective) then we have to create
conditions to permit increased self-regulation, self-evaluation, self-
adjustment and participation in the setting of goals. By doing so, it is alleged, we bring about an improvement in productivity and attitudes.[9]

Contrary to general misconceptions, humans have within themselves
the capacity to exercise self-direction and self-control in the achievement of
objectives to which they are committed. Individuals are likely to assume
responsibility rather than to shed it, and if they are lazy, indolent, or passive,
it is not due to inherent human weaknesses but attributable to previous organizational experience.[19] There is a recognition that the full potential of
human resources is not realized in organizations.

This is the theme very much in evidence in a "Human Resources"
model of organization. This model maintains that there exists in organizations reservoirs of untapped resources and that these resources include not only physical skills and energy but also creative ability and the
capacity for responsible, self-directed, self-controlled behaviour. The
model also has something to say about the improvement of the quality of
decisions and company performance through effective delegation, and that
involvement in decisions applies to non-routine as well as to routine matters.
Also, providing the opportunity for the exercise of self-direction and self-
control should be a progressive step in line with the growth in the ability and
experience of the individual.[20]

Participation in Production
In one factory a group of female employees were given the opportunity to

determine their work rate by controlling their own conveyor belt. As a result, quality was maintained and production rose appreciably. It was not until the earnings of the female workers outstripped the earnings of many of the male workers in the plant, chiefly due to the size of productivity bonuses, that various pressures were brought to bear on management to remove the alleged pay inequity. In these circumstances the plant superintendent arbitrarily revoked, without consultation, the productivity bonuses the women had come to expect and he returned the plant's operations to the previous state. The end result was that things moved again at their "time study" speed, production dropped and within a month all but two of the eight women had left the company.[21]

In another factory an investigation was undertaken because the company experienced an acute resistance by employees to changes in both jobs and methods of work. The consequences of this resistance to change were high rates of staff turnover, many complaints, low efficiency and restriction of output. It was decided to create both an experimental and a control group, the experimental group participating in the evaluation and redesign of their jobs. The experimental group, unlike the control group, surpassed their previous performance, but only after experiencing an unsatisfactory contribution for a transitional period. During the transitional period 62% of employees whose jobs were modified suffered a chronic substandard performance or left the job during the retraining stage. An encouraging note to these experiments was the impressive performance of control groups when they worked in the same conditions experienced by the experimental groups.[8]

Management at ICI saw three main benefits accruing to participation at the shopfloor level.[22] First, the employees' unique knowledge of their job enabled them to identify waste which only they could know about. Second, proposed changes were discussed in a positive co-operative spirit with both management and employees making suggestions and evaluating them together, as opposed to management making proposals which would subsequently be rejected by the workers' representatives. Third, after formal acceptance of changes, the changes took place with speed and without disruption to the life of the enterprise. However, though management were encouraged to discuss matters with shopfloor workers, a disadvantage appeared to be the apparent erosion of the middle manager's role.

Participation in Budgeting
The concept of participation has been applied to planning and control processes (e.g., budgetary control) within organizations. There is a long stream of studies indicating the desirability of participation in the budgetary process, though one should take note of the qualifying statements. It is maintained that higher levels of participation in the budgetary process lead to a

higher level of motivation to meet budget standards, though this does not extend to the setting of financial standards.[23]

In one particular study it was found that those who participated in the setting of standards performed better than those who did not, but the outcome from another study suggests that the favourable consequences of participation are limited to the creation of favourable attitudes rather than improving performance.[24,25] In a participative process there is an opportunity to obtain feedback on the acceptability of the individual's proposals, and this is said to be a prerequisite to a commitment to the budget.[26] Likewise, the budget process is likely to be improved by the contribution of the individual's unique and localized knowledge of his or her area of work.[27].

In more recent studies the clarity of the budget goal or standard goes hand in hand with participation as factors giving rise to higher levels of motivation to meet: (1) budget standards; (2) actual budget achievement; and (3) job satisfaction.[28,29] It appears that the personality of the manager involved in the budgetary process is an important variable in the relationship between participation and positive outcomes in terms of satisfaction and performance. The relationship is said to be good for those individuals who feel they have a large degree of control over their destiny (internal locus of control), but bad for those who feel their destinies are controlled by luck, chance or fate (external locus of control).[30]

Sometimes participation in budgeting falls short of ideal practice. In budgetary control the illustration of pseudo-participation is embodied in a classic study which commented on the tactics of the controller who at one and the same time encourages an exchange of opinions and, believing that the line supervisors have little to contribute anyway, is very keen to get their signatures on the new budget signifying their approval.[31] The signatures are then evidence of their approval. One should note however that if supervisors accept half-heartedly a budget target or budget changes, and are bound by their signatures, it will almost inevitably follow that the initiators of the targets or changes will have to be constantly vigilant, and will have to pressurize the acceptors of the suggested course of action in order to ensure compliance. This is not a favourable situation to be in for somebody who subscribes to the notion of participation as a motivational tool.

There is also the danger of budget biasing taking root in a participatory budget system; this amounts to managers inflating costs or reducing revenue at the budget stage.[32] In the context of meeting the requirements of the corporate master budget, there is a view that the ability of large groups of lower-level personnel to participate in budget planning must be the subject of some doubt for the following reasons. They may lack the interest and expertise required for comprehending the range of factors to be balanced in the planning of sales, production, materials, and administration. Likewise, they may be limited in their ability to understand the need for identifying limiting factors and may be unable to co-ordinate their estimates with those of other draft sub-budgets. There may also be difficulties in comprehending the more sophisticated forecasting and simulation techniques as well as a lack of full understanding of the broader economic and other environmental factors affecting operations. Lastly, to finalize a budget with so many people contributing would present many problems for the accountant, and if planning were to start much earlier in order to accommodate this constraint, estimates may be out of date.[27]

Participation in Systems Design

With the growth in the computerization of administrative systems, the question arises as to the extent to which employees will be involved in the rearrangement of work and the redesign of jobs. It is suggested that the atmosphere implicit in the "Human Resources" model of organization referred to earlier, together with a supportive top management, is a necessary requirement.[33] On occasions the specialists (systems analysts) have too much responsibility for design and modification of information systems, and operating managers and their staff have too little. Therefore it is a prime requirement for systems analysts to communicate with the users of information. This view would find favour with Mumford, who puts forward participation as an effective process to bring about desired change to administrative systems.[34]

Consensus participation is the preferred strategy of Mumford, which she construes as an advanced democratic approach. It aims to involve representatives of all staff in the user department continuously throughout the systems design process. Representatives would be elected, and the services of analysts would be at the disposal of the group. The object is to exchange extensively ideas about new forms of work organization among colleagues, and allow the final decision to be taken by the department as a whole. The first task of the design group is to gather information about the impediments to efficiency and job satisfaction. This would be followed by proposals for alternative systems of work designed to overcome the problems identified, leading to the adoption of the most preferred alternative. The likely outcome is the advocacy of autonomous or self-managing groups for the most skilled employees and job rotation for those who do not mind doing routine jobs.

Participation in Safety

The pursuit of high standards of health and safety practice at work is a desirable objective, and the use of participative processes to attain that objective has been recommended. The Robens Committee in the U.K., who deliberated on safety and health at work, recognized the prime importance of worker co-operation with management if places of work were to be made safer; the committee believed that worker involvement would assist in overcoming the apathy which it felt was the primary cause of accidents at work.[35] The report went on to say that health and safety problems, unlike most other matters, have a greater effect in promoting common ground between management and workers. "There is no legitimate scope for bargaining on safety and health issues but much scope for constructive discussion, joint inspection and participation in working out solutions." The report sought to encourage employees to accept health and safety both as a personal responsibility and an important organizational objective, and to work co-operatively towards improving health and safety practices and standards.

The views of the Robens Committee were subsequently incorporated in the Health and Safety at Work Act 1974, and this created a legal framework for individual and collective involvement in health and safety issues at the workplace. The Act provides recognized trade unions with the right to appoint safety representatives from among their members. These representatives have the right to investigate potential hazards and dangerous occurrences, investigate the complaints of employees concerning health and safety and carry out routine inspections of the workplace. They are entitled to make representations to their employers on health and safety matters. The code of practice accompanying the statutory regulations stresses the need for open dialogue between management and representatives in order for participation to be effective. Recent evidence on health and safety practice at work indicates that the consultative process was in some respects deficient. One of the most common problems was simply the lack of responsiveness by line managers to the requests of safety representatives for information or action, though sometimes the managers did not have the information to give.[36]

Criticism of Participative Leadership

A challenge to the alleged benefits accruing to a participative style comes from a study conducted in four divisions within a company.[37] In two divisions a participative style was used, decision making was deliberately pushed down the hierarchy, supervisors were trained to use supervisory methods of a democratic nature and there was an appreciable increase in their freedom of action. In the other two divisions greater hierarchical control was introduced by an increase in the closeness of supervision and there was a noticeable shift upwards in the level at which decisions were made. These conditions prevailed for a year and approximately 500 employees were involved. It was found that both programmes contributed to a significant increase in productivity, surprisingly with a slight advantage accruing to the autocratic system.

Critics of the participative leadership school harbour a number of reservations. They see a tendency to place overwhelming emphasis on personal co-ordination and control to the detriment of bureaucratic or impersonal control techniques. The important role played by bargaining and the use of power in interpersonal relationships is overlooked; the democratic or participative style is conceived largely in terms of group harmony and compatibility between personal goals and organizational goals, but the importance of organization structure is neglected.[38] Although generally people would like to exercise some degree of control over their own environment, they may fear the participation process because it threatens their integrity and independence, or they believe they will be controlled to some extent by other participants. Should the rewards or benefits which result from co-operating with others prove inadequate, then withdrawal from the participative process is a likely outcome.[39] It is also suggested that participation might lack appeal for those who do not trust each other, who feel intellectually superior to their peers, and who do not have the patience to bother with it and feel it consumes too much valuable time.

Macro Participation

The foregoing discussion dealt with participation at the micro level (primarily at the operational level). Participation at the policy or macro level is discussed briefly here. In Britain participation at the macro level has never been a significant practical proposition, though the worker-director scheme at the British Steel Corporation is a notable exception. The Bullock Committee report in 1976 was followed by a white paper on industrial democracy in 1978. The white paper proposed a structure of joint representation committees composed of all unions at each place of work with a statutory right to discuss company strategy and have access to information. These measures were never enacted.

The European Commission's revised 1983 Draft Directive on "Procedures for Informing and Consulting Employees" (the Vredeling Directive) would, if implemented, give employee representatives, in organizations employing 1000 or more workers within the E.E.C., substantial general information on the group as a whole and specific information on their own company within the group. Certain business secrets would be withheld.

The British Employment Secretary said in a press release in November 1983, that:

> . . . the government welcomes moves to promote involvement of employees in the enterprises for which they work, but it believes that the main initiative is best left to employers and employees, who are in the best position to judge what best suits their particular circumstances. . . . I am very dubious of the value in the European Community issuing directives which conflict with well-established and perfectly legitimate differences in industrial relations policy and practice

between member states. There is evidence of significant growth in recent years of employee involvement under the voluntary approach preferred in the U.K., and the Commission has not even attempted to show why this approach should now be discarded.

In Sweden employee directors on the boards of companies have proved a successful venture, and in Germany, the Mitbestimmung provides an opportunity for employee representatives to influence policy formulation on supervisory boards.

A significant extension to industrial democracy practices in Sweden came about with the 1976 Act on "Employee Participation in Decision Making." In this legislation there is provision for collective agreements between employers and unions to embrace questions relating to concluding and cancelling employment contracts, to supervision and distribution of work or other aspects of management. The 1976 Act, though welcomed by trade unionists and certain politicians, has been received with hesitancy and anxiety by many employers and managers. They are afraid of increased union influence, and "cannot believe that it will be possible to run their companies in an efficient and profitable way under the new conditions."[40]

The reality surrounding the operation of Works Councils in Yugoslavia highlights some of the difficulties with participation at the macro level. For example, 90% of the talkers in the council were experts who had received higher education, the workers were inadequately motivated and the influence of a power élite and a small circle of competent and responsible people was conspicuous.[41] However, the rank and file workers participated more actively when the discussion moved from technical problems to human relations problems such as standard of living and social welfare, and to the hiring and placement of workers.[42]

A British social scientist, on reviewing some critical evidence of self-management in Yugoslavia feels the problems of alienation in the workplace cannot be magically solved by simply installing worker's councils but is himself inclined to the view that much less might be achieved in terms of industrial democracy if an even weaker system of worker participation had been arrived at, or is set up in future.[43]

On the basis of a personal impression of the drawbacks of participation in a sympathetic culture, the following observation was made by Child in studying Israeli industrial practices.

> The role of socialist principles in the establishment of Israeli institutions and indeed in the political life of the country even today cannot be overlooked. Bearing these factors in mind, one might conclude that if in that type of society schemes of participation and industrial democracy have on the whole become transmuted into techniques of management and have not substantially modified the industrial management hierarchy,

then in societies where social stratification is more strongly entrenched there is even less prospect that the establishment of formal systems of industrial democracy will lead to any fundamental change of social relationships within industry.[44]

Quality Circles

An extension to the basic philosophy of the participative process is the quality circle. This advocates participation in the setting of objectives, together with participation in processes leading to a removal of obstacles frustrating the achievement of agreed objectives. The consequences of the implementation of quality circles are said to be enhanced commitment to necessary changes in work practices. The quality circle has become an integral part of the management system in Japan, and the key factor appears to be the involvement of employees at all levels. It is used to improve productivity, product quality and safety at work, and the benefits claimed following its use are reduced waste, improved communication between management and workers, the creation of a problem-solving environment, increased job involvement and improved morale.

A quality circle is a small group of employees (four to fifteen) who do similar work and report to the same supervisor. The group meets regularly on a voluntary basis to identify and analyze work problems and provide solutions. A large plant could have many quality circles. Employees are encouraged to join a circle, not told to, and they can expect to experience a greater sense of control over their job environment. Members of a circle receive training in the basics of the technical aspects of the job, and in the skills of problem solving and making presentations to management. Interpersonal skills training is an important means of removing the barriers to interactions between people.

In the field of health and safety at work it is suggested that the quality circle training should make reference to safety hazard detection and problem-solving techniques such as: hazard recognition; accident investigation; elements of fire protection; industrial hygiene; incidence recall; damage control; loss run analysis; data collection; safety location diagrams; decision analysis; cause and effect analysis; and brainstorming. This type of training provides circle members with the tools needed to detect, analyze and solve health and safety problems and to assist them in making presentations to management.[45]

The usefulness of the concept of the quality circle must be properly understood, and to this end a publicity campaign could be launched within the company to explain the concept to the employees and request volunteers. The objectives of the circle must be endorsed by management. A quality circle consists of circle members, a circle leader, a facilitator, a steering committee and circle management. Circle volunteers are those who do the work and are interested in improving the quality of the work environment. The circle leader is a specially trained supervisor or somebody chosen from among the voluntary group. A facilitator, who has to be carefully selected and trained, provides training to circle members, provides a communication channel between different circles and acts as a liaison person between circles and between the steering committee and management. He or she provides feedback on various activities, exerts influence where appropriate and deals with conflicting groups. A steering committee is normally comprised of first-line supervisors, who have a brief to provide quick responses to requests for funds, and to make sure that the circles get support from technical specialists in the organization. Circle management provides support, funds, and facilities, and it reviews the solutions recommended by the circle in its management presentations. The presentations are the vehicle through which the group obtains recognition for the work done.

A meeting of a quality circle could last for no more than one hour per week in a quiet room. Members of the circle would identify problems which could affect the overall company plan; for example, how to improve productivity by 10% in 1988. The circle would prioritize the order in which problems are to be tackled, and having selected a problem (e.g., how to reduce product defects from 5% to 2%), circle members set realistic goals. Using appropriate analytical methods, a general plan and schedule for the solution of the identified problems is established. Drawing on internal expertise, and invited external specialists who act in an advisory capacity, and using external sources of data, the circle discusses several solutions to a problem.

The preferred solution would be tested and implemented after presenting management with a full analysis using appropriate statistical techniques. Where management decide to implement the solution, this should be widely publicized so as to provide circle members with the necessary recognition. Any rejection of a circle recommendation should have the reasons for non-acceptance well stated. The results emanating from circle initiatives should be monitored, and presentations of successful outcomes could go beyond the organizational level in which the circle functions. As an incentive for circle members it is not uncommon for directors of a company in Japan to be present and participate directly by asking questions at the presentation.

Some of the conditions necessary for the quality circle to work have been referred to above. The following conditions should also be given serious consideration.[46] The management should be modest in its expectations initially, and perhaps start with a low-profile pilot scheme. The support and commitment of management, and particularly senior management, is crucial. They should demonstrate their support for the programme, in both words and actions, by explaining what is involved, by providing training resources and other assistance, by attending regular presentations made by the circle, and by using the circle for its own purposes. The terms of reference of the quality circle should be clearly stated and communicated; the safeguard and assurances with respect to the impact it may have on bonuses, overtime earnings and job security have to be considered. The union is likely to be sensitive to the question of productivity gains and the way they are to be distributed. The importance of anticipating problems, rather than merely reacting to them, has to be stressed as well as the need to engage in innovative activities, such as new systems and products. Naturally, circle members would like to see their successes recognized at all levels of the organization.

In an empirical study of how quality circles work in practice in four U.S. companies, it was concluded that quality circles lend themselves to the solution of basic localized problems of an immediate and solvable nature. They also provide employees with an opportunity to learn how to influence their work situation.[47] The Work Research Unit of the Department of Employment in Britain has done much to publicize the concept of the quality circle, and is now concerned with the practical application of the concept. In a comparatively recent publication of the unit it was stated that it is too soon to draw conclusions about the applicability of the concept in the U.K., and acknowledged that the response to it has not been dramatic.[48] In the recent past the Work Research Unit organized a national conference on quality circles, which was sponsored by the National Economic Development Office in Britain. This was considered to be useful in stimulating and creating a renewed interest in quality circles, and had as its objectives the dissemination of knowledge based on practical experience, the sharing of useful ideas and suggestions, and the consideration of options and strategies for the future.[49]

In Japan the enthusiasm for the quality circle is evident, and the concept is adapted to meet particular organizational circumstances. As a result, there are variations in the manner in which the quality circle is implemented.[46] One practice common to all quality circles is that discussions go beyond quality; they include cost, use of equipment, efficiency, errors, and safety. In some cases there is a formal training programme for members; in other cases only leaders receive formal training, and there are also instances where no formal training is provided. In the latter case the skills of supervisors and experts in the group would be used. The circle leader can be the immediate supervisor of the group; in other cases the leadership role rotates, though it is likely that the majority of leaders come from the ranks of supervisors. Sometimes the norm is to hold meetings in the employees' time without payment, but there are also precedents for meetings to take place in the company's time, with overtime payments for meetings held in the employees' time.

Consideration and Initiating Structure

The manager using participative leadership has an employee-centred approach and would appear to rank high on *consideration* and *initiating structure*. These dimensions of leadership behaviour were isolated and identified by researchers at the Ohio State University. Both factors can be evaluated in an individual by using a questionnaire. *Consideration* indicates friendship, mutual trust, respect, and warmth. A high score on this dimension reflects a climate of good rapport and two-way communication.

Initiating structure indicates a concern with defining and organizing roles or relationships in an organization, and establishing well-defined forms of organization, channels of communication and ways of getting jobs done. A high score on this dimension characterizes individuals who play an active role in directing group activities through planning, communicating information, scheduling, trying out new ideas and practices, and so on.

The job-centred manager would appear to rank high on initiating structure and low on consideration. The Ohio studies found that the two factors were independent of each other—that is, how a leader scores on one factor has no influence on what he or she scores on the other, though other studies show that the two dimensions are related. This means that a leader can be directive in managing subordinates and at the same time can establish highly supportive relations with them.[50]

Features of both consideration and initiating structure are acknowledged by implication in a report on "Managing Safety" prepared by the Accident Prevention Advisory Unit of the Health and Safety Executive.[51] The report states that high standards of safety should be a management objective pursued in the same way as other management objectives, and wishes to stimulate managers to recognize the contribution that they can make to the assessment of safety and health problems for which they are responsible in the workplace.

The development and application of effective solutions to these problems would require effective information systems that will assist in the identification and assessment of hazards so that resources can be earmarked and priorities allocated to control or eliminate the hazards. A successful manager is described in the report as somebody who sets understandable and practical goals for safety; motivates and obtains commitment from the workforce; provides realistic resources for the implementation of safety policy; instils a need in the workforce to accept personal responsibility for safety; and evaluates standards of safety achievement in ways that clearly mark approval or disapproval of individual and group performances.

Hersey and Blanchard extended consideration (relationship behaviour) and initiating structure (task behaviour) to form four leadership styles ranging from direction to delegation.[52] They introduce the maturity of the subordinate as a major factor determining the effectiveness of leadership style. The maturity factor is defined as the ability and willingness of subordinates to take responsibility for their own behaviour and can only be considered in relation to the performance of a specific task. A subordinate could be mature in relation to one task but not another.

For example, a trainer may be an accomplished instructor but a poor administrator. In this case the superior of the trainer adopts relationship behaviour (e.g., delegation) when the trainer performs as an instructor; he or she is mature in the eyes of the superior. However, when the trainer is acting in an administrative capacity, the superior resorts to a task-centred or directive style because the subordinate is considered immature. This model has potential as a situational theory of leadership.

The Managerial Grid

Another approach to depicting different leadership styles, including an employee-centred or participative style, is The Managerial Grid developed by Blake and Mouton.[53] In this concept of leadership style concern for people

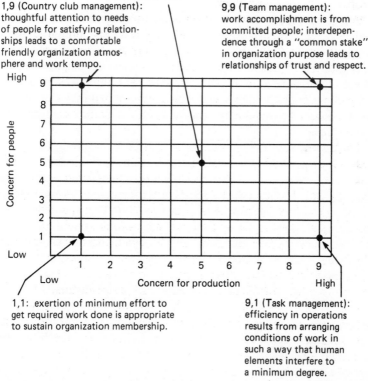

5,5: adequate organization performance is possible through balancing the necessity to get out work with maintaining morale of people at a satisfactory level.

1,9 (Country club management): thoughtful attention to needs of people for satisfying relationships leads to a comfortable friendly organization atmosphere and work tempo.

9,9 (Team management): work accomplishment is from committed people; interdependence through a "common stake" in organization purpose leads to relationships of trust and respect.

1,1: exertion of minimum effort to get required work done is appropriate to sustain organization membership.

9,1 (Task management): efficiency in operations results from arranging conditions of work in such a way that human elements interfere to a minimum degree.

FIG. 8.1   The Managerial Grid®. Source: Blake, R. R. & Mouton, J. S. (1985). *The Managerial Grid III* (Revised edition). Houston: Gulf Publishing Co. P.12. © 1985, reprinted by permission.

and production are treated as separate dimensions. Leadership style is not shown as a point on a leadership continuum but rather as a point on a two-dimensional grid. In Fig.8.1 the horizontal dimension of the grid represents the individual's concern for production and the vertical dimension represents his or her concern for people.

This concept is similar to the concept of employee-centred and job-centred leadership discussed earlier. In The Managerial Grid the individual can score anything between the maximum number (9,9) or the minimum number (1,1) on either dimension. The ideal of The Managerial Grid is to move towards the 9,9 style (team management) where there is an integrative maximum concern for both production and people; this appears to be in the same mould as participative leadership.

Blake and Mouton advocate a phased organizational development programme with the adoption of the 9,9 style in mind. The 9,1 style (task management) focuses wholly upon production and the manager in this category can generally be said to have acute problems in dealing with people, but is exceptionally competent in a technical sense. This style is entirely geared to a high level of productivity, at least in the short term. The superior makes the decision and the subordinate carries it out without question. Traditionally shopfloor conditions in the motor industry were considered to be a good example of the 9,1 leadership style, and the fact that its past record of industrial relations is punctuated with disputes might be indicative of the shortcomings of task management. It is conceivable that this style of leadership is a major contributor to the polarization of the superior and subordinate, resulting in the "them" and "us" thinking which is at the root of many industrial disputes.

By contrast, the 1,9 style (country club management) emphasizes people to the exclusion of their performance. People are encouraged and supported, but their mistakes are actually overlooked because they are doing their best—the maxim of "togetherness" applies. Direct disagreement or criticism of one another must be avoided, and as a consequence production problems are not followed up. This style of leadership can easily evolve when competition is limited.

SITUATIONAL THEORIES OF LEADERSHIP

There is a general belief that the particular circumstances in which the leader finds him or herself are influential in determining the most appropriate leadership style. In this section important situational perspectives on leadership are considered.

Leadership Continuum

The first theory to be examined is the revised continuum of leadership be-

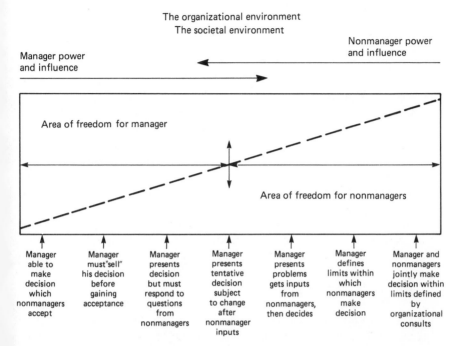

FIG. 8.2 Continuum of leadership behaviour. Source: Tannenbaum, R. & Schmidt, W. H. (1973) How to choose a leadership pattern. *Harvard Business Review, May–June,* p.167. Reprinted by permission of the *Harvard Business Review.* Copyright © 1973 by the President and Fellows of Harvard College; all rights reserved.

haviour proposed by Tannenbaum and Schmidt.[54] They conceive a continuum with an autocratic style on the left-hand side and a democratic style on the opposite side, with varying degrees of influence in between. This is depicted in Fig.8.2.

The term "non-manager" is used as a substitute for "subordinate"; this is said to reflect the newer organizational processes such as industrial democracy and participative management, where subordinates have a greater say in matters that affect them as well as frequently sharing managerial functions. The arrows indicate the continual flow of interdependent influence. The authors of the leadership continuum are inclined to associate a subordinate-centred style with the achievement of the following common objectives shared by many managers: (1) to raise the level of employee motivation; (2) to increase the capacity of subordinates to accept change; (3) to improve the quality of decisions; (4) to develop teamwork and morale; and (5) to foster the development of employees.

The theory also considers the situation in which leadership style operates. Situational factors that determine the manager's choice of leadership style are: (1) forces in the manager; (2) forces in the subordinate; and (3) forces in the situation.

1. Forces in the Manager.   A useful starting point is an understanding of the manager's attitudes and predispositions towards an appropriate leadership style. A manager may not subscribe to a participative style because he or she prefers to act alone. Likewise, managers may not wish to involve their subordinates because they lack confidence in them; or if the situation is uncertain, they may feel insecure and prefer to act independently.

2. Forces in the Subordinate.   Ideally a manager would expect the following conditions to exist before being prepared to allow the subordinate to participate in decision making. The subordinate has a relatively high need for independence; shows a readiness to assume responsibility for decision making; possesses a relatively high tolerance for ambiguity; is interested in the problem which is considered important; has the necessary knowledge and experience to deal with the problem; understands the goals of the organization with which he or she can identify; and has developed expectations to share in decision making.

3. Forces in the Situation.   The prevailing organizational culture may determine to some extent the type of leadership style that is best suited to a given organization. For example, behavioural characteristics of an autocratic nature may be considered functional in some organizations and are therefore reinforced.

Other forces in the situation which may somehow restrain the manager's manoeuvrability with respect to leadership style are the size of the working group, the geographical dispersion of subordinates, the secrecy of the issues in question, the level of relevant expertise of the subordinate, and the pressure of time. Where, for example, the size of the group is large, subordinates are scattered over many company sites, the issues are highly confidential and secretive, the subordinate does not have the kind of knowledge that is needed, and the organization is in a state of crisis, then an autocratic style may be appropriate. The opposite may be true when these situations are reversed. In the Tannenbaum and Schmidt model there is an interdependent relationship among and between the situational factors and leadership style, because what happens to one variable may have a bearing on another. The model is of some value as a conceptual scheme for identifying different leadership styles and the circumstances that influence them, but it lacks precision in suggesting the appropriate point on the continuum to choose in a given set of circumstances.

The Influence-Power Continuum

Another leadership continuum has been formulated by Heller.[55] He calls it

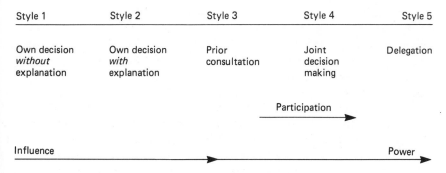

FIG. 8.3 The influence-power continuum.

the influence-power continuum (IPC) and it is used to evaluate the various degrees of sharing influence and power between the superior and subordinate. The main feature of IPC—depicted in Fig.8.3—is that it extends the normal concept of participation to incorporate the sharing of power through delegation. A detailed description of the IPC is as follows:

Style 1. *Own decision without detailed explanation.* These are decisions made by the manager, without previous discussion or consultation with subordinates, and no special meeting or memorandum is used to explain the decisions.

Style 2. *Own decision with detailed explanation.* The same as in Style 1, but afterwards the manager explains the problem and the reasons for the decision in a memorandum or special meeting.

Style 3. *Prior consultation with subordinate.* Before the decision is taken the manager explains the problem to his or her subordinates and asks for their advice and help. The manager then makes the decision. The manager's final choice may, or may not, reflect the subordinates' influence.

Style 4. *Joint decision making with subordinate.* The manager and his or her subordinates together analyze the problem and come to a decision. The subordinates usually have as much influence over the final choice as the manager. Where there are more than two individuals in the discussion, the decision of the majority is accepted more often than not.

Style 5. *Delegation of decision to subordinate.* The manager asks the subordinate to make the decisions regarding a particular subject. The manager may or may not request the subordinate to report back to him or her and seldom vetoes the subordinate's decisions.

Heller related the various leadership styles to specific situational circumstances and established certain relationships. The following sample of the findings of a study conducted in the U.S. are illustrative of a situational perspective. A large span of control on the part of a senior manager, which indicates a large number of immediate subordinates, is associated with time-saving decision styles at the extremes of the continuum, either highly centralized (Style 1) or decentralized (Style 5). When senior managers see big differences in skill between themselves and their subordinates, they use centralized or autocratic styles (Styles 1 and 2). When they see little difference in skill, they are more willing to share power with their subordinates and use democratic styles (Styles 3 and 4). This finding appeals to common sense, in that there is little point in sharing influence with a subordinate who is perceived as not possessing the necessary skill.

Closely related to the last finding is the finding that where senior managers have experienced subordinates (measured by age and length of time in the company), they are noticeably more inclined to use delegation (Style 5) and to avoid centralized or autocratic styles (Styles 1 and 2). General managers and personnel managers used the greatest amount of power sharing, while production and finance managers used the least. In recent years Heller's research programme has been extended to a number of European countries. This research provides tests of the original U.S. research and introduces some new variables, for example, skills and educational levels, and environmental turbulence and complexity. Taking the U.S. and European studies together it appears that managers in the U.K., Germany, and the U.S. are inclined to be more autocratic whereas Swedish and French managers are more democratic.[56]

The author adopted Heller's leadership continuum to measure the leadership style of chief accountants in the U.K. Among the situational factors that influenced their style were the nature of the decisions they faced, the extent of job specialization in the finance function, the calibre of section heads, the qualities or skills of their subordinates, the number of subordinates reporting to them and the psychological distance or closeness between them and their subordinates. Contrary to a general impression which suggests that accountants are autocratic in orientation, chief accountants placed almost equal emphasis on both autocratic and democratic leadership styles. What was particularly interesting was that they modified their style to suit prevailing situational circumstances.[57]

Fiedler's Model

One of the most influential and widely discussed theories of leadership in recent years is the contingency model of leadership effectiveness, postulated by Fiedler.[58] This theory attempts to predict how style of leadership, leader-member relations, the power vested in the position of leader and the structure of the job or task harmonize to determine the leader's ability to achieve productive output. The measure of the style of leadership is the esteem of the leader for his or her least preferred co-worker (LPC). The LPC is the person with whom the leader has found it most difficult to co-operate. To arrive at an LPC score, leaders were asked to rate both their most preferred co-worker (MPC) and their least preferred co-worker (LPC). Leaders who describe their MPCs and LPCs similarly are classified as "high LPC" leaders, whereas those who describe their LPCs much more negatively than their MPCs are classified as "low LPC" leaders. The co-worker evaluated in this way need not be someone the leader is actually working with at the time. According to Fiedler, the LPC score is best interpreted as a dynamic trait which results in different behaviour as the situation changes.

Leaders with high LPC ratings would be psychologically close to their group members; with low LPC ratings they would be psychologically distant. Leaders who describe their least preferred co-workers in a relatively favourable manner (high LPC) tend to be employee-centred in their relationships with group members. They gain satisfaction and self-esteem from successful interpersonal relations. Leaders who describe their least preferred co-workers in a relatively unfavourable manner (low LPC) tend to be autocratic, task-centred and less concerned with the human relations aspects of the job. They gain satisfaction and self-esteem from successful task performance. Therefore, the high and low LPC leaders seek to satisfy different needs in the group situation.

The three major variables in the work situation which can impede or facilitate a leader's attempt to influence group members are, as stated above, leader-member relations, the structure of jobs or tasks, and the power in the position of the leader. In the normal course of events the organization provides support for the leader by structuring jobs with the help of procedures, rules, and regulations.

The degree of structure in the job or task can be measured by establishing the extent to which work decisions can be verified, the degree of clarity surrounding the stating of the work goal, the number of methods available for achieving the goal and the extent to which one can be specific about the solution to the work problem. The leader finds it easier to force compliance in a structured job situation than in an unstructured job situation. In the latter situation leaders may find it difficult to exercise influence because neither they nor the group members can be dogmatic about what should be done; in fact, the leaders will have to pay attention to inspiring and motivating their followers.

Power in the position is the authority vested in the leader's position as distinct from any power arising from his or her skill and ability in handling matters arising within the group. It would include the rewards and punishment at the leader's disposal; the leader's authority to define the group's rules; and his or her appointment being immune from termination by the group.

The most important of these three dimensions is leader-member relations. A liked and respected leader, or one working in a smoothly func-

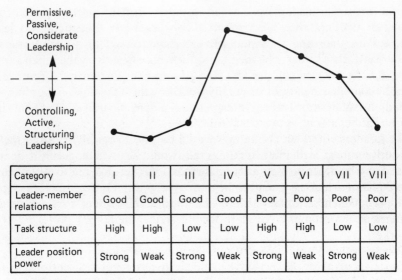

FIG. 8.4 Contingency model of leadership effectiveness. Adapted from: Fiedler, F.E. (1972) The effects of leadership training and experience: A contingency model interpretation. *Administrative Science Quarterly, December,* p.455.

tioning group, can do what would be difficult for a leader in different circumstances. Power in the position is the least important of the three dimensions because a well-liked leader can get results without institutional power, and likewise, will not need the power if the task is clearly structured.

Fiedler arrives at a continuum depicting the favourableness of the situation for the leader. This is shown in Fig.8.4. For example, the leader with a low LPC, who is autocratic and task-centred (controlling, etc.), was found to be effective in both favourable and unfavourable situations for the exercise of influence. This was found to be so when executive functions in complex organizations were examined. A favourable situation has a high job structure, good leader-member relations and strong power in the position. An unfavourable situation has low task structure, moderately poor leader-member relations and weak power in the position. But in between these two extreme positions, where the situation is intermediate in favourableness, the employee-centred leader (permissive, etc.), who has a high LPC, was found to be effective. This type of leadership orientation was associated with policy decision-making. The implications of Fiedler's model for improving organizational effectiveness are either to change the manager's leadership orientation, as reflected in the LPC score, so it is compatible with the above situational conditions, or alternatively to modify the situational conditions in order to bring them into line with the leadership orientation.

Fiedler's contingency theory of leadership has been the subject of a considerable amount of criticism.[59] Fiedler has consistently defended his approach, theory, research and interpretations of the research evidence. There are numerous rejoinders and counter rejoinders in the literature on the contingency theory of leadership. Criticisms hinge on the difficulty of measuring task structure, the problem of using the LPC score to differentiate task and human-relations-oriented leadership, and in particular the absence in many studies of a leader with an LPC score somewhere between high and low. Fiedler's view, with regard to the latter point, is that middle LPC leaders are not concerned with either task or human-relations issues and perform poorly in most leadership situations. But others would dispute this view. Fiedler's model focuses heavily on performance to the neglect of employee satisfaction and as a consequence provides an incomplete picture of leadership effectiveness. Finally, despite the criticisms of Fiedler's work, it remains an important landmark in the study of leadership.[60]

A Normative Model (Vroom and Yetton)

A "normative" or "prescriptive" model of leadership style, has been put forward by Vroom and Yetton.[61] Certain assumptions are made about the consequences of exercising different leadership styles. A significant feature of this model is that it provides a list of considerations a manager may dwell on before selecting a leadership style in different circumstances. Vroom and Yetton believe descriptions of leadership behaviour, such as employee-orientation and task-orientation, are not strictly operational because they are too imprecise. They maintain that a normative theory of leadership must be sufficiently precise in specifying the behaviour of a leader so that a person may be confident that he or she is acting in accordance with the prescription offered by the theory. To achieve this they put forward different forms of leadership or decision making behaviour to cope with both individual and group problems. These are depicted in Table 8.1, and they bear a similarity to the autocratic-democratic continuum shown in Fig. 8.2.

In Table 8.1, the approaches or styles classified as A are autocratic, C are consultative, G are group-dominated, and D are delegative; there are variations within each letter classification. The right-hand column of Table 8.1 refers to problems where only one subordinate is involved, the left-hand column refers to situations in which a group of subordinates is involved. The leader should only use an approach after seriously considering the type of problem faced and the context in which it is placed. Before selecting the most appropriate approach or style in a given situation, leaders must pay particular attention to what they would like the outcome of their deliberations and actions to be. Vroom and Yetton maintain that the leaders' approach to making a decision, or their leadership style, will be determined by the following attributes of the various problems and situations they face.

TABLE 8.1
Decision Methods for Group and Individual Problems

Group Problems	Individual Problems
A1. You solve the problems or make the decision yourself, using information available to you at the time.	**A1.** You solve the problem or make the decision by yourself, using information available to you at the time.
A2. You obtain the necessary information from your subordinates, then decide the solution to the problem yourself. You may or may not tell your subordinates what the problem is in getting the information from them. The role played by your subordinates in making the decision is clearly one of providing the necessary information to you, rather than generating or evaluating alternative solutions.	**A2.** You obtain the necessary information from your subordinate, then decide on the solution to the problem yourself. You may or may not tell the subordinate what the problem is in getting the information from him. His/her role in making the decision is clearly one of providing the necessary information to you, rather than generating or evaluating alternative solutions.
C1. You share the problem with the relevant subordinates individually, getting their ideas and suggestions without bringing them together as a group. Then you make the decision which may or may not reflect your subordinates' influence.	**C1.** You share the problem with your subordinate, getting ideas and suggestions. Then you make a decision, which may or may not reflect his/her influence.
C2. You share the problem with your subordinates as a group, obtaining their collective ideas and suggestions. Then you make the decision, which may or may not reflect your subordinates' influence.	**G1.** You share the problem with your subordinate, and together you analyze the problem and arrive at a mutually agreeable solution.
G2. You share the problem with your subordinates as a group. Together you generate and evaluate alternatives and attempt to reach agreement (consensus) on a solution. Your role is much like that of chairman. You do not try to influence the group to adopt "your" solution, and you are willing to accept and implement any solution which has the support of the entire group.	**D1.** You delegate the problem to your subordinate, providing any relevant information that you possess, but giving him/her responsibility for solving the problem. You may or may not request the subordinate to tell you what solution he/she has reached.

Source: Vroom, V. H., & Yetton, P. W. (1973) *Leadership and Decision-making.* Pittsburgh: University of Pittsburgh Press. p.13. © 1973 by University of Pittsburgh Press, reprinted by permission of the publisher.

I. *The importance of the quality of the decision.*

II. *The extent to which the leader possesses sufficient information or expertise to make a high-quality decision alone.* It is obvious that a leader who makes a decision alone only utilizes the knowledge and skills he or she possesses. But there are a number of occasions when the leader draws on the resources of the group.

Subordinates, as a group, may have the necessary information to generate a high-quality decision. For example, a decision to rationalize the administrative structure of an organization may require more knowledge and expertise than the leader possesses. In such circumstances one may ask if subordinates can make a valid contribution to the decision process. If not, it will be necessary for the leader to go outside the group for information.

III. *The extent to which the problem is structured or unstructured.* Structured problems are those for which the alternative solutions or methods for generating and evaluating solutions are known. An example of a structured problem is deciding when to take legal action on arrears in a customer's account where the amount is large and long overdue. Unstructured problems cannot be dealt with in a clear-cut manner and they appear to be elusive or complex. An example of an unstructured problem is defining the expected life of a new fixed asset for depreciation purposes.

IV. *The extent to which acceptance or commitment on the part of subordinates is critical to the effective implementation of the decision.* Acceptance of the decision by subordinates is critical when the effective implementation of the decision requires the display of initiative, judgement or creativity by all concerned. It is recognized that subordinates' participation in the making of a decision is likely to increase the probability of them accepting it.

V. *The likelihood that the leader's autocratic decision will be accepted by subordinates.* There might be circumstances when subordinates accept an autocratically-imposed decision. This may occur when the proposed course of action enshrined in the decision appeals to reason and is intrinsically attractive, (e.g., the leader awards his or her subordinates extra holiday entitlement because of their exceptional performance at work).

VI. *The extent to which subordinates are motivated to achieve the organizational goals as reflected in the problem under review.* It is possible to find situations where the personal goals of an employee are in line with those of the organization. But in other cases the employee's self-interest as reflected in his or her personal goals is out of line with organizational goals, expressed as targets and objectives, which he or she is expected to achieve. In such circumstances a leadership style, such as G2 in Table 8.1, could pose a potential risk to the quality of the decision because significant control resides in the group.

VII. *The extent to which subordinates are likely to be in disagreement or conflict over preferred solutions.* If there is disagreement, it may be possible to bring about agreement by allowing the group to interact. This could be achieved by using a group-dominated approach to decision making (e.g., c_2 or G_2 in Table 8.1) where subordinates interact in the process of solving the problem.

Having discussed the attributes of the problems and situations the leader faces, with reference to leadership behaviour, we now proceed to state the rules for choosing a particular approach to decision making or leadership. This is done by eliminating the approaches or styles, listed in Table 8.1., which seem to be inappropriate, leaving us with a feasible set of decision-making approaches.

I. Where the quality of the decision is important, and the leader does not possess enough information or expertise to solve the problem alone, eliminate the A_1 decision-making approach in order to avoid the risk of a low-quality decision.

II. Where the quality of the decision is important and the subordinates cannot be trusted to contribute to the solution of the problem with the goals of the organization firmly in mind, eliminate the G_2 approach.

III. Where the quality of the decision is important, the leader lacks the necessary information or expertise to solve the problem alone, and the problem is unstructured—i.e., the leader does not know what information is needed or where it is located because access to it is difficult—then eliminate the approaches A_1, A_2, and C_1. The approach A_1 militates against collecting the necessary information and the approaches A_2 and C_1 are cumbersome and less effective when a problem-solving orientation is required. In this situation it is the approaches c_2 and G_1, which require interaction among subordinates who are knowledgeable with respect to a particular problem, that are likely to generate solutions of a high quality.

In the case of I, II, and III above, the major preoccupation is to make sure that a decision of high quality is made in circumstances where quality is relevant. In the case of IV, V, VI, and VII below, the major preoccupation is to ensure that the decision is acceptable to subordinates when their acceptance of it is of importance.

IV. Where the acceptance of a decision by the subordinate is crucial for its effective implementation, and one is not sure that an autocratic decision-making approach would be acceptable, eliminate the A_1 and A_2 approaches since neither provide an opportunity for the subordinate to participate in the decision process. By taking this course of action the risk of the subordinate rejecting the decision is minimized.

V. Where the acceptance of the decision by the subordinate is critical, it is uncertain that an autocratically imposed decision will be accepted and subordinates are likely to be in conflict over the most appropriate solution, in such circumstances eliminate the approaches A_1, A_2, and C_1. The reason for doing so is that A_1, A_2, and C_1 are approaches which generally require a

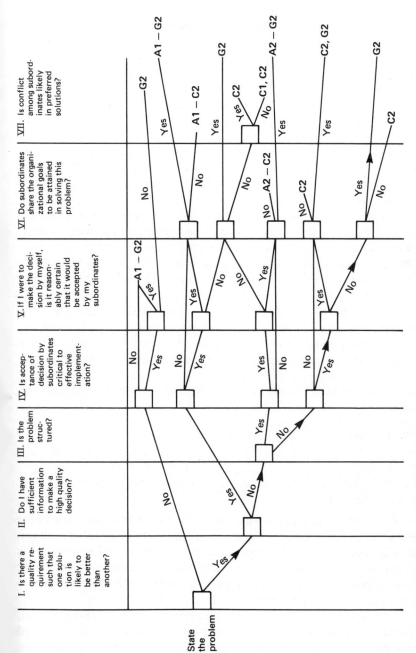

FIG. 8.5 Decision tree for group problems. Adapted from: Vroom, V. & Yetton, P. (1973) *Leadership and decision making.* Pittsburgh: University of Pittsburgh Press. P. 194.

one-to-one relationship and involve no interaction. These approaches do not provide enough opportunity for those in conflict to resolve their difficulties; as a consequence some subordinates may lack the necessary commitment to the final decision. The most appropriate approach to adopt in these circumstances is either C2 or G1 which allows those in disagreement to resolve their differences, provided they possess full knowledge of the problem.

VI. Where the quality of the decision is unimportant, and there is doubt about the acceptability of an autocratically imposed decision, then the approaches which are likely to produce a lesser degree of acceptance by subordinates—A1, A2, C1, and C2—should be eliminated. A participative approach (e.g., G2) would appear to be more suitable in these circumstances.

VII. Where acceptance of the decision by subordinates is critical, where subordinates can be trusted, and where acceptance is unlikely to be forthcoming if an autocratic approach was imposed, then eliminate the approaches A1, A2, C1, and C2. If these approaches to decision making were used, it would create the risk of a lower level of acceptance of the decision by subordinates. The approach to decision making which would appear functional in these circumstances is G2, which suggests that a high level of influence is exerted by subordinates.

Having now eliminated the inappropriate approaches to decision making, the leader is still left with more than one approach. Vroom and Yetton suggest that decision rules can be used to help with the selection of the most appropriate approach to decision making. To apply this procedure a decision tree can be used. Decision rules are presented pictorially in Fig.8.5 as a decision tree.

Before examining Fig.8.5 a brief case is introduced, which is subsequently used to follow the flow of the decision process in the figure.

An office manager is dissatisfied with having to place such heavy reliance on electric typewriters in the office and wishes to explore alternatives. He or she is not very knowledgeable about the purchase and operation of substitute equipment in the form of word processors. However, it is appreciated that word processors perform all of the normal functions of the conventional typewriter, as well as providing the user with many other facilities to alter text and to produce higher-quality copy at a faster speed.

The office manager recognizes that the secretarial staff must feel comfortable and confident using word processors, otherwise the level of productivity will fall. The office manager's relationship with the secretarial staff is good and they can identify easily with the company's goals or objectives. However, because of the calibre of the secretarial staff, and the nature of their work, they would like to have a say in any decision to replace the electric typewriters.

The problem facing the office manager and his or her staff is not clear-cut. For example, why is a word processor necessary? Is the expense justi-fied if it merely replaces a conventional typewriter? Is the expense justified if the word processor is to carry out a specific but perhaps infrequent task which is not possible on a typewriter? What about the additional costs, such as maintenance of equipment, insurance, and staff training or recruitment?

The question we can now ask is: which decision-making approach or leadership style for group problems (see Table 8.1) the office manager should use in this situation. (The letters at the end of the decision tree in Fig.8.5 denote leadership style and they correspond to those listed in Table 8.1.) On the horizontal line of Fig.8.5 is a list of questions, posed by the office manager, relevant to the problem. We can go through questions I to VI, using the information provided in the case just described, and arrive at the following answers. (Note that arrows show the flow of the decision pro-cess in the decision tree.)

I. Yes, there is a quality requirement (the office system based on word processors must function).

II. No, the leader (office manager) is not very knowledgeable about word processors.

III. No, it is not obvious how to go about the purchase, installation, and operation of an office system based on word processors.

IV. Yes, the subordinates' (secretarial staff) involvement in the mak-ing of the decision to replace the electric typewriters is crucial for the accept-ance of the decision by the subordinates.

V. No, for the reasons given in IV.

VI. Yes, the subordinates have the interests of the organization firmly in mind with regard to the efficiency of the office, and therefore identify with the goals of the organization.

In this example conflict among subordinates (VII) did not arise. Fol-lowing the arrows in Fig.8.5 you will notice that the decision-making app-roach or leadership style associated with this case is G2 (a highly participative style). Given the circumstances reported in the case, it seems to be a sensible outcome. What would be the outcome if the circumstances were slightly dif-ferent? Suppose the answer to question VI was *No*, then the recommended style is C2, in which the leader permits limited participation but takes the final decision alone. The rationale for this may be that, since the sub-ordinates do not share the organizational goals, it is wise for the leader to imprint his or her authority on the decision.

In the Vroom and Yetton prescriptive model more than one of the five decision-making approaches or leadership styles shown in Table 8.1 may be effective depending on the answers given to the questions in Fig.8.5. If time is of critical importance, the leader may use an autocratic style, but a par-ticipative style could be used when the leader feels it is preferable to spend time developing subordinates. A particular strength of the model is the identification of the factors that influence the effectiveness of the leader. These were referred to earlier as: the quality requirement in decisions, the availability of relevant information or expertise, the nature of the problem, the acceptance of the decision by the subordinates, and the commitment and motivation of subordinates.

The theory has a number of attractive features, among them the issue of the involvement of subordinates in decision making. But the research methodology of the model has been criticized. It is suggested that the technique of self-reporting used by managers in devising a decision tree may be open to socially desirable responses.[62] This would arise when they report that their leadership style was more participative than it really was because they feel it is fashionable to say so.

Path-goal Model

A path-goal theory of leadership, which is somewhat similar to the expectancy theory of motivation discussed in Chapter 2, was developed by House.[63] The main functions of the leader are, according to this theory, to assist the subordinate to attain his or her goals and to ensure that the subordinate finds the experience satisfying. The theory is concerned with explaining the relationship between the behaviour of the leader and the attitudes and expectations of the subordinate.

The description of leadership behaviour is similar in a number of respects to leadership behaviour discussed in previous sections, particularly initiating structure and consideration, and consists of four dimensions:

1. *Directive Leadership:* The leader lets subordinates know what is expected of them and provides specific guidelines, rule, and regulations, and standards and schedules of the work to be done.

2. *Supportive Leadership:* The leader is concerned about the status, needs, and well-being of subordinates, is friendly, and endeavours to make work more pleasant.

3. *Participative Leadership:* The leader goes through consultation processes with subordinates, seeking their suggestions and being considerate towards them in the decision-making process.

4. *Achievement-Oriented Leadership:* The leader sets challenging goals for subordinates and shows confidence and trust when concerned with their ability to meet exacting performance standards. The leader is also concerned with trying to improve performance.

The four dimensions of leadership behaviour are related to three dispositions of the subordinate:

1. *Satisfaction of the subordinate:* The subordinates will feel satisfied if they perceive the behaviour of the leader as being responsible for their present level of satisfaction, or as being instrumental in bringing about future satisfaction.

2. *Acceptance of the leader by the subordinate.*

3. *Expectations of the subordinate:* Subordinates expect appropriate effort will lead to effective performance, and that effective performance leads to the acquisition of acceptable rewards. The behaviour of the leader produces a motivational effect, and this increases the effort put into the job by subordinates, particularly where subordinates perceive the leader as being supportive and responsible for creating a situation in which they can satisfy their personal needs as a result of effective performance.

These dispositions of the subordinate can be favourably influenced by the leader, who uses initiating structure to clarify the path to goal achievement, and consideration to make the path easier to travel, in the following ways.

1. The leader should arouse, where appropriate, the needs of subordinates for achieving results or outcomes over which subordinates have some control.

2. The leader can ensure that subordinates are personally rewarded for attaining their goals.

3. The leader can offer coaching and direction to subordinates and therefore make it easier for subordinates to derive a rewarding experience from attaining their goals.

4. The leader can help subordinates clarify their expectations about their work experiences.

5. The leader can minimize or remove frustrating obstacles in the subordinates' path to the attainment of their goals.

6. The leader can increase the opportunities for personal satisfaction that arise from effective performance.

There are two types of situational variables that have to be accommodated in path-goal theory.[64] First, the personal characteristics of subordinates have to be considered. If subordinates feel that their behaviour influences events at work (internal locus of control) then they are more likely to be satisfied with a participative leadership style. However, if subordinates believe that their accomplishments are due to luck (external locus of control) they are more likely to be satisfied with a directive leadership style. (The internal and external loci of control are discussed in Chapter 1.) Where subordinates have a high need for affiliation they are likely to be more satisfied with a supportive leadership style, whereas a directive leadership style is more acceptable when a high need for security exists.

Second, there are a number of demands or pressures in the job environment that relate directly to both leadership style and the motivational disposition of the subordinate, and they influence the ultimate performance of the subordinate. Where jobs are highly structured and the objectives or goals set for the subordinate are clear (e.g., the processing of an application for a television licence or a road fund licence for a motor vehicle), a support- ive and participative style is likely to lead to increased satisfaction. The reason for this is that jobs are already routine and therefore little direction is necessary. By contrast, a more satisfactory arrangement for unstructured jobs would be the use of a directive style, because a directive style helps to clarify an ambiguous task for subordinates (for example, a clerk in an insur- ance office finds it difficult to handle a difficult claim and the manager ex- plains the best way to proceed).

The complexity of the task is an important situational variable. This is said to interact with the individual's desire to develop his or her knowledge and ability within the job (i.e., a need for personal growth). Not all sub- ordinates share this desire with the same degree of intensity so it is possible to find two categories of subordinate, one with a strong need and the other with a weak need for personal growth. The subordinate with a strong need for personal growth who performs a complex task (e.g., negotiating the terms of a deal to merge two companies in conditions of uncertainty) is more likely to perform better under a superior exercising a participative and achievement-orientated style. The subordinate with a strong need for per- sonal growth faced with a simple task (e.g., extracting the names of com- panies on a random basis from a directory of companies) is more likely to perform better when subjected to a supportive style.

Where the subordinate has a weak need for personal growth, and faces a complex task, then a directive style is more likely to be effective. But the same subordinate who performs a simple task is more likely to be effective with a supportive and directive leader.[65] The above relationships are depic- ted in Table 8.2.

Path-goal theory deals with specific leadership behaviour and shows how it might influence employee satisfaction and performance. It recognizes the importance of situational variables and accepts individual differences. However, studies evaluating the model have generated conflicting results. Overall, empirical evidence indicates that the theory (like many others) offers useful insights into employee satisfaction, but has problems predicting employee performance.[60]

CULTURAL FACTORS

In this section a brief illustration of management practice in both Japanese and progressive British enterprises is given. There has been much comment in recent times about the differences between Japanese management prac- tices and management practices in the Western world.

TABLE 8.2
Interaction of Leadership Style and Situational Variables in Path–Goal Theory

	Situational Variables	
Characteristics of Subordinate	*Features of the Job Environment*	*Effective Leadership Style*
Internal locus of control	—	Participative
External locus of control	—	Directive
High need for affiliation	—	Supportive
High need for security	—	Directive
—	Structured jobs	Supportive and Participative
—	Unstructured jobs	Directive
Strong need for personal growth	Complex task	Participative and Achievement-orientated
Low need for personal growth	Complex task	Directive
Strong need for personal growth	Simple task	Supportive
Low need for personal growth	Simple task	Supportive and Directive

Japanese Practices

The industrial scene in Japan is quite different from that of the U.K. and Europe. Paternalism, with lifetime employment, is ingrained in the culture and this promotes loyalty and long-term commitment. Consensus is easier to foster and this makes the attainment of common goals that much easier. There is also a tendency to work in small groups and make the best use of the creative skills of all employees, with a commitment to delegation.[66] However, the contents of a comparatively recent book, written by a Japanese journalist, convey the unacceptable face of life in manufacturing industry in Japan. Life on the car assembly line was said to consist of mindless toil, subservience, callousness and exploitation.[67]

It is said that Japanese manufacturing enterprises in Britain perform well in terms of productivity and product quality, and the following exemplify the management style and practices they adopt.[68,69]

1. Meticulous attention is given to the recruitment and training of employees, including special induction courses in the company philosophy. Managers are not encouraged to remain specialists; in fact they are trained to appreciate and understand the inter-relationship and inter-dependencies between sales, finance, production, and research and development.

2. Discipline on the shopfloor includes no smoking, no eating, no chattering, and sometimes no tea breaks. A tough line is taken on absenteeism and poor time-keeping, so as to ensure the continuity of production. Apparently the workers generally appreciate the reasons for this line of action.

3. Performance charts, showing productivity for each section, are on display. As a means of keeping machine operators interested and sufficiently motivated to monitor quality, they participate in completing the charts. These charts can form a base for the assessment of employees for promotion purposes. Employees do not receive output bonuses, because bonuses tend to be equated with hurried and low-quality production.

4. There appears to be a single-minded pursuit of product quality and for that reason the production worker is an important member of the company. The managers are expected to identify with the quality of the product and the production process. The lack of distinction between skilled and unskilled operators means that the able and committed unskilled operator can eventually move easily to a supervisory or middle manager job. It is important that an operator can have a conversation about his or her machine on equal terms with a maintenance engineer.

5. Where shifts go around the clock, 10 minutes is set aside before each of the three shifts to discuss production targets, safety, and any other current topics. There are also monthly departmental meetings, as well as small working groups, to discuss matters such as safety.

6. Demarcation lines between jobs are less conspicuous. It is claimed that flexible working agreements, whereby workers carry out a number of operations, generate greater commitment and pride in work.

7. Naturally the company places emphasis on expertise and experience, but it places a particular importance on willingness and high standards of attendance, punctuality, and flexibility. It offers in return, apart from a competitive renumeration, a sense of involvement and a virtual guarantee of no redundancy, the maxim being that the company surpluses in good trading conditions can compensate for excess capacity in bad times.

8. Workers wear company uniforms and peak caps emblazoned with the corporate logo. The classless canteen is very much in evidence. Company outings are looked upon as social activities designed to foster team spirit and communication.

9. The company environment is friendly with an open style of management and frank disclosures to the workforce. Japanese managers take plenty of time to reach decisions, they listen a lot, they empathize with employees, they develop relationships of trust and display managerial professionalism. The company tolerates the closed shop, and enters into lengthy negotiations with the trade union on manning levels and flexible working practices. The British worker, who is not attached to the idea of working as a team, may react adversely to the frequent meetings. Apparently, Japanese managers have few complaints about their British operations; their nightmare appears to be the quality of the components bought in from British industry, which are alleged to be 20% more expensive than those produced by companies in Japan.

A British Example

What management style and practices can we expect to find in a progressive British company in a service industry? According to the then Chief Executive of Marks and Spencer, a number of benefits, such as a stable workforce, ready acceptance of change, high productivity, high profits (for the benefit of shareholders, staff, and retired staff), and high staff morale, are the consequence of inspired human relations practices. It is claimed that these practices are backed up by a strong commitment to the view that it's people who matter.[70] Good human relations practices at Marks and Spencer apply not only to employees, but also to customers and suppliers.

Top management must believe in and be committed to the implementation of human relations practices, and genuine respect for the individual is crucial. Personnel problems occupy much of the time of the senior board in the company. Advice and help should be delicately given where needed. Apart from mandatory staffing regulations, which are legally binding, regulations governing staff behaviour should be kept to a minimum. When delegated powers are given to local management, they are expected to act sensibly and generously in their dealings with people. By and large this is said to happen.

Top management must know how good or bad the working conditions and amenities are. "They must eat in the employees' restaurants, see whether the food is decent and well cooked, visit the washroom and the lavatories. If they are not good enough for those in charge, they are not good enough for anyone."

Managers must not only be aware of the employees' problems, but also react to them. Topics of legitimate concern include the problems of the individual at work, his or her health, well-being and progress, the working environment and profit-sharing. The company must respect the individual's contribution and provide the necessary encouragement, backed by a full and frank two-way communication system. Managers must take subordinates into their confidence; there is very little need for secrecy. Managers must explain policies and developments clearly; and the views of their staff on proposed developments must be taken into account. People should be informed of their progress, or lack of it, and credit should be given where it is due. Poor work should be the subject of frank discussion, because this stimulates people to work better in the knowledge that they will eventually receive credit for work well done.

A policy of good human relations is said to cost time, effort, and money. The role of the personnel specialist in a store consists of identifying problems, seeking the views of staff, and responding to constructive suggestions and worthwhile criticisms. They also provide training and development programmes. Managers are asked to play an active role in their communities, and sometimes are seconded for a specified time to community projects.

Other companies in Britain with successful human relations practices include STC, United Biscuits, IBM, GEC, and Remploy.

POWER AND POLITICS

Power is a critical dimension of leadership, and power and leadership are often used with the same or similar meanings. Both terms are about the ability of an individual to control or to influence others and to get someone else to engage in some activity.[71] Power is the capacity to overcome resistance, and power that is legitimized can be viewed as authority. Those subjected to authority must take it seriously for it to be effective. But power is not only the preserve of managers, because individuals and groups with different status in organizations engage in political activity.[72] Politics in organizations can be seen in the tactics people use to get power or control of resources that can be used to achieve what they want.[60]

A senior personnel practitioner had this to say about power and politics in the sphere of management:

We can't ignore the influence of power and politics in management, and managers will need help in understanding how to use, cope with, and change the power and political systems in their organization and those of its environment. It is an excellent idea to learn the good in management, but to ignore how the devious and underhand operate is equally dangerous.[73]

Two writers on organizations recognize the prevalence of politics in organizational life. Handy describes organizations as political systems in which individuals compete for resources and influence.[74] Child maintains that many decisions in organizations are arrived at and implemented through a political process.[75] He goes on to suggest that politics is about the use of power, and the decisions made encapsulate political influence. When a decision involves a major organizational change, the political process leading up to it is likely to be intensely active. In the event of power being distributed among a number of parties in an organization, the process of arriving at a decision will incorporate much negotiation and compromise. (The decision-making process is given greater coverage in Chapter 5.)

A number of strategies are used to influence events when important issues are at stake and where extra data will not resolve the issues. These strategies assume a variety of forms, and the following are illustrative:

1. There is an element of organizational politics in the job selection process when hunches are adopted with respect to the acceptability of the candidate in the light of the prevailing culture or ethos in the organization.

2. There is an element of organizational politics in the way agendas are prepared for committee meetings, and in the way information is presented to people who have to make decisions. The political element also finds expression in the hidden assumptions upon which decisions are made.

3. Political behaviour is evident when certain groups within the organization try to obtain advantage over another person or group and in the process utilize expert knowledge.

4. Junior staff could frustrate attempts to impose unacceptable changes to their jobs by real threats of opposition to the proposed changes.[72]

In one sense power is manifest in managerial positions within an organization, but in another sense power can be seen to function between employees from different parts of the organization, and can be the outcome of negotiation and bargaining. Certain groups within organizations can be far more influential than others, and possess greater power.[72]

For example, medical doctors are the most influential group in a hospital. Research and development specialists have a crucial role to play in a pharmaceutical company where product development is essential for survival. Marketing specialists are an influential group in a company faced with highly competitive market conditions (e.g., home computers, cosmetics). Accountants exert a lot of influence in organizations facing financial problems or difficulties.

In a classic study French and Raven drew the following distinction between different types of power:

1. Reward Power: The leader is able to control rewards—e.g., pay, promotion, an attractive task—which subordinates consider to be worth striving for. However, if the leader has rewards at his or her disposal to which subordinates attach no value, then the leader has no reward power. But if the leader is astute enough to disguise the valueless rewards, he or she may still have reward power.

2. Coercive Power: If subordinates are of the view that the leader is able and willing to use penalties which they dislike—e.g., withdrawal of privileges, allocation of unattractive assignments, denial of promotion opportunities and pay increases, verbal abuse, withdrawal of friendship and emotional support—then the leader has coercive power. In this situation the penalties must be perceived by the subordinates as being significant and there must be a strong probability that they will be used if necessary. This type of power can still be found in organizations, though it should be noted that certain legislation—e.g., employment protection legislation in the U.K.—offers protection against summary dismissal of disliked employees.

3. Referent Power: This type of power can be seen when subordinates think the leader has desirable characteristics which they should imitate. It could result in an indiscriminate identification with the leader. The charismatic qualities of the leader, reflected in the respect and admiration directed at him or her, are a prominent feature of this type of leadership.

4. Legitimate Power: This type of power arises if followers believe that the leader is endowed with the right to give orders to subordinates and they are obliged to accept. In this case subordinates tend to look at a title—e.g., Director—as conferring on the leader the right to give orders.

5. Expert Power: This type of power emerges when the leader is seen by subordinates as having superior knowledge and expertise which is relevant to the tasks or activities under consideration. In practice this type of power may be confined only to narrow specialist activities and functions, though leadership based on expert power could also be reflected in the other categories of power. The leader with expert power has to be able to demonstrate the right type of ability, and he or she must be perceived as somebody with credibility, trustworthiness, and honesty as well as having access to the required information.[76]

With regard to the five bases of power, a critical factor is the subordinate's perception of leadership qualities, though it is conceivable that leaders may be able to manipulate subordinates into believing they possess qualities which they don't have. The bases of power are inter-related. For example, the use of coercive power may jeopardize the use of referent power. Likewise, a leader could use legitimate power to build up his or her referent or expert power. The bases of power could be situationally determined; this arises where different styles are used in different conditions.

It is relatively common nowadays to find computer-based systems increasing the influence of those who have access to the technology and who can understand it. So those who control the system, and those who control the information, gain power relative to other staff. The progressive computerization of information is likely to alter the patterns of influence and power of key actors or participants in organizations.[77]

NEW TECHNOLOGY AND MANAGEMENT

Back in the late 1950s it was forecasted that computers would promote centralized decision making, because computers would make it possible to collect and transmit information quickly to enable decisions to be made centrally on a better informed basis. There was also the prediction that considerable economies in staffing levels could be achieved at middle management level because computers would perform much of the information processing activities of middle managers.[78]

A decade later the impact of the computer on management was considered in a study conducted in the service industry (i.e., insurance companies) and it was argued strongly that computers were likely to increase the centralization of systems of control in organizations. This applied to clerical functions and the computer was seen to have a number of capabilities.[79]

The computer ties together and integrates areas of decision making and control that previously were relatively independent of one another. The computer monitors, corrects, and adjusts actions over a much broader area than could be achieved by any human group. And because of the pyramidal structure of business organizations, the integrative function of computing results in the centralization of control, with a wider span of control for senior managers.

This evidence, which relates to clerical functions in a service setting, is challenged by evidence from a study of the impact of the computer in a manufacturing context.[80] The use of on-site computers was associated with the decentralization of operational decisions, particularly in granting autonomy to plant managers. But it is pointed out that the physical location of the computer can influence the level of management at which decisions are made; a central location gives rise to centralization, but where computer systems are distributed throughout the organization a decentralization process develops. This accords with the current trend to use more powerful individual micro-computers, which are relatively cheap, and can be easily placed on the executive's desk. The hardware is accompanied by more sophisticated software (e.g., financial modelling).

In recent years the centralization versus decentralization debate has been somewhat muted. There is a view that computer applications over a long period are confined to routine accounting and administrative activities, and that there has been no significant changes in the levels at which management decisions are made.[81] However, other evidence would suggest that we have to be discriminating in the way we view the impact of the computer on the management process. This could mean that in certain circumstances centralization is facilitated, but equally in other situations delegation may be assisted.

With new technology in the field of information processing it is possible to communicate information quickly over a wide area. If that information is based on data input of an accurate and reliable nature, senior managers may not have to rely on middle management and lower levels for control information or its interpretation, provided the information can be transmitted from the local area of operations. For example, "the scanning of bar-coded or magnetically ticketed items in retailing establishments results in transmitting control data on the itemized sales—i.e., sales registered and outstanding stock—to the store manager and to the central buying department at the company's head office."[82]

Therefore, centralization is encouraged, particularly when current and comprehensive information is transmitted directly to senior management. However, in these circumstances one should be aware of the need to use computer programmes, if available, to integrate data and draw key analyses from it, otherwise the problem of information overload and complexity for senior managers will pose difficulties. Other influences which account for centralization are: (1) the managerial ethos of the organization, particularly where entrepreneurial or family control is evident; and (2) when production operations are fairly standardized and conditions in the organization are not complex.[81,82]

Apart from the centralization effect, information technology could be used to facilitate more effective delegation. This could be achieved in the following way:

1. Units of the organization could be linked to form a common network, whereby each unit is made more aware of what other units are doing. This promotes awareness of the wider consequences of decisions taken by a particular unit. The local unit is able to inform other units and the central unit of its intentions and obtain rapid feedback. In this way consultation is facilitated, and the local unit is made aware of the intentions of the centre with regard to intervention. The end result could be a reduction in ambiguity

and this is likely to encourage local initiatives and discourage intervention from the centre.

2. The improved analytical facilities offered by information technology—e.g., programmes for sensitivity analysis and financial modelling—can enhance the capacity of local units to make sound judgements in the decision-making process. But as mentioned earlier, the potential of information technology must be married with reliable information or data so that real benefits can be gained. Prior to the onset of the era of information technology, information processing capacity of a sophisticated nature normally resided at senior levels of the organization where specialist staff could be called upon to assist the senior managers.[82]

In what way is information technology likely to have an impact on the role of the manager? It has been suggested that the introduction of computers could lead to a situation where the manager becomes less involved in the collection of information for the purposes of dissemination, simply because other members of the organization may have access to information previously denied to them.

By reducing the tasks of managers that are connected with the monitoring of information, interpersonal contacts between managers and others—an essential feature of the traditional managerial role—may become less important.

This could result in changes in the way people perceive the role of manager.[83] Likewise, it could lead to a diminution of management control when non-managerial staff have access to comprehensive and well-structured information.[84] However, there will always be a group of managers somewhere in the organization, perhaps near the top, whose managerial control will not be undermined by the development of automated information systems; and of course there will be others who will experience an increase in their managerial or supervisory control simply because, with the aid of technology, they are better able to monitor the activities of employees—e.g., quality of work, costs, and revenue.[77]

Finally, though the computer may be viewed as a supportive tool, there have been circumstances where the implementation of computer systems fostered a negative view of the computer among managerial staff. This happened in eight organizations where managers experienced an increase in the work load and variations in the pace of work following the implementation of computer systems.[83]

SUMMARY

A number of perspectives can be found in the study of leadership. This chapter opened with a brief discussion of the trait approach to leadership, followed by the impact of personality. Leadership or management style can find expression in various forms ranging from autocratic to democratic styles. The democratic style is akin to participative leadership. Concepts such as quality circles, consideration and initiating structure, and the managerial grid were discussed in the context of participative leadership. A distinction was made between micro and macro participative leadership. The strengths and weaknesses of participative leadership were considered.

A specific application of the principles of participative leadership was illustrated with reference to production, budgeting, systems design, and safety at work.

A study of leadership would not be complete without an analysis of situational theories of leadership. These theories point to the potency of the leadership environment in determining styles of leadership. The major situational theories examined were the leadership continuum, the influence-power continuum, a contingency model of leadership effectiveness, a normative or prescriptive model of leadership style, and the path-goal theory of leadership.

To finalize the discussion of leadership and management style the importance of the management culture (in a British and a Japanese context), power and politics in organizations, and new technology were acknowledged. Influences such as these add to the complexity of leadership in modern organizations.

QUESTIONS

1. What is meant by the trait approach to leadership?

2. In what way does personality interact with leadership?

3. Identify the strengths and weaknesses of participative leadership with particular reference to the budgeting process.

4. In what way can quality circles be used to enhance standards of safety at work?

5. What scope exists in the UK for the widespread application of industrial democracy within organizations?

6. Describe any one situational theory of leadership.

7. Identify the key characteristics of the Japanese concept of managerial leadership.

8. Describe the relationship between power and leadership in organizations.

9. Examine ways in which new technology is likely to affect the process of managerial leadership in organizations.

REFERENCES

1. Bavelas, A. (1960) Leadership: man and function. *Administrative Science Quarterly, 4,* 344–360.
2. Stogdill, R.M. (1948) Personal factors associated with leadership: a review of the literature. *Journal of Psychology, 25,* 35–71.
3. Mann, R.D. (1959) A review of the relationship between personality and performance in small groups. *Psychological Bulletin, 56,* 241–270.
4. Adair, J. (1980) *Developing Tomorrow's Leaders: A University Contribution.* Inaugural Lecture, University of Surrey, 5 November.
5. Lippit, R. & White, R. (1968) Leader behaviour and member reaction in three social climates. In D. Cartwright & A. Zander (Eds.), *Group Dynamics—Research and Theory.* London: Tavistock.
6. Lowin, A. (1968) Participative decision-making: a model, literature critique and prescription for research. *Organizational Behaviour and Human Performance, 3,* 69–106.
7. Thompson, V.A. (1961) Hierarchy, specialization and organizational conflict. *Administrative Science Quarterly, 5,* 5, 485–521.
8. Coch, L. & French, J.R.P. (1948) Overcoming resistance to change. *Human Relations, 1,* 512–532.
9. Argyris, C. (1973) Personality and organization theory revisited. *Administrative Science Quarterly, 18,* 2, 141–167.
10. Wispe, L.G. & Lloyd, K.E. (1955) Some situational and psychological determinants of the desire for structured interpersonal relations. *Journal of Abnormal and Social Psychology, 51,* 57–60.
11. Tannenbaum, R. & Schmidt, W.H. (1958) How to choose a leadership pattern. *Harvard Business Review, 36,* 2, 95–101.
12. Tannenbaum, A.S. (1962) Control in organizations: individual adjustment and organizational performance. *Administrative Science Quarterly, 7,* 2, 236–257.
13. Litchfield, E.H. (1956) Notes on a general theory of administration. *Administrative Science Quarterly, 1,* 1, 3–29.
14. Fromm, E. (1942) *Fear of Freedom.* London: Routledge & Kegan Paul.
15. Tannenbaum, R. and Massarik, F. (1963) Participation by subordinates in the managerial decision-making process. In R.A. Sutermeister (Ed.), *People and Productivity.* New York: McGraw-Hill.
16. Likert, R. (1967) *The Human Organization.* New York: McGraw-Hill.
17. Likert, R. (1961) *New Patterns of Management.* New York: McGraw-Hill.
18. Bennis, W. (1966) *Changing Organizations.* New York: McGraw-Hill.
19. McGregor, D. (1960) *The Human Side of Enterprise.* New York: McGraw-Hill.
20. Miles, R.E. (1965) Human relations or human resources. *Harvard Business Review, 43,* 148–63.
21. Bavelas, A. & Strauss, G. (1970) Group dynamics and inter-group relations. In W.G. Bennis, D. Benne & R. Chin (Eds.), *The Planning of Change. (2nd Edition.)* New York: Holt.
22. Daniel, W.W. & McIntosh, N. (1972) *The Right to Manage.* London: Macdonald.
23. Hofestede, G.H. (1968) *The Game of Budget Control.* London: Tavistock.
24. Bass, B.M. & Leavitt, H. (1963) Some experiments in planning and operating. *Management Science, 4,* 574–585.
25. Milani, K. (1975) The relationship of participation in budget setting to industrial supervisor performance and attitudes: a field study. *The Accounting Review,* April, 274–284.
26. Foran, M.F. & De Coster, D.R. (1974) An experimental study of the effects of participation, authoritarianism and feedback on cognitive dissonance in a standard setting situ-

ation. *The Accounting Review, October,* 751–763.

27. Parker, L.D. (1979) Participation in budget planning—the prospects surveyed. *Accounting and Business Research, Spring,* 123–137.

28. Kenis, I. (1979) Effects of budgetary goal characteristics on managerial attitudes and performance. *The Accounting Review, October,* 707–721.

29. Merchant, K.A. (1981) The design of the corporate budgeting system: influences on managerial behaviour and performance. *The Accounting Review, October,* 813–829.

30. Bromnell, P. (1981) Participation in budgeting, locus of control and organizational effectiveness. *The Accounting Review, October,* 844–860.

31. Argyris, C. (1953) Human problems with budgets. *Harvard Business Review, 31,* 1, January/February, 97–110.

32. Schiff, M. & Lewin, A.J. (1970) The impact of people on budgets. *The Accounting Review, 45,* 2, April, 259–268.

33. Dickson, C.W. & Simmons, J.K. (1970) The behavioural side of management information systems. *Business Horizon, August,* 59–71.

34. Mumford, E. (1980) Social aspects of systems analysis. *The Computer Journal, 23,* 1, 5–7.

35. The Robens Report (1972) *Safety and Health at Work.* London: HMSO Cmmd. 5034.

36. Gibson, M. & Kidd, J. (1982) Some managerial implications of the Health and Safety at Work Act. *Employee Relations, 4,* 3, 21–26.

37. Morse, N.C. & Reimer, E. (1956) The experimental change of a major organizational variable. *Journal of Abnormal and Social Psychology, 52,* 120–129.

38. Strauss, G. (1968) Human Relations—1968 style. *Industrial Relations, 7,* 3, 262–276.

39. Crozier, M. (1964) *The Bureaucratic Phenomenon.* London: Tavistock.

40. Lind, O. (1979) Employee participation in Sweden. *Employee Relations, 1,* 1, 11–16.

41. Mulder, M. (1971) Power equalization through participation. *Administrative Science Quarterly, 16,* 1, 31–38.

42. Obradovic, J. (1975) Worker participation: who participates? *Industrial Relations, 14,* 1, 32–44.

43. Warner, M. (1975) Whither Yugoslav self-management. *Industrial Relations Journal, 6,* 1, 65–72.

44. Child, J. (1977) *Industrial Participation in Israel.* Working Paper series No. 42, University of Aston in Birmingham.

45. Salim, P. (1982) Safety Circles. *Professional Safety, April,* 18–21.

46. Collard, R. (1981) The Quality Circle in context. *Personnel Management, September,* 26–30 & 51.

47. Burpeau-Di Gregorio, M.Y. & Dickson, J.W. (1983) Experiences with Quality Circles in the South West United States. *Employee Relations, 5,* 2, 12–16.

48. Russell, S. (1983) *Quality Circles in perspective.* Occasional Paper 24, Work Research Unit, Department of Employment, February.

49. Work Research Unit, Department of Employment. (1983) *Small Group Activities, Quality Circles.* Review of a Conference organized by the Work Research Unit and sponsored by the National Economic Development Office. London, 2 March.

50. Weissenberg, P. & Kavanagh, M.J. (1972) The independence of initiating structure and consideration: a review of the evidence. *Personnel Psychology, 25,* 119–130.

51. Accident Prevention Advisory Unit, Health and Safety Executive. (1981) *Managing Safety (OP3).* London: HMSO.

52. Hersey, P. & Blanchard, K. (1982) *Management of Organizational Behaviour.* Englewood Cliffs, NJ: Prentice-Hall.

53. Blake, R.R. & Mouton, J.S. (1964) *The Managerial Grid.* Houston: Gulf Publishing.

54. Tannenbaum, R. & Schmidt, W.H.(1973) How to choose a leadership pattern. *Harvard*

Business Review, May/June, 162–180.

55. Heller, F.A. (1971) *Managerial Decision-Making: A Study of Leadership Styles and Power-sharing Among Senior Managers*. London: Tavistock.

56. Heller, F.A. & Wilpert, B. (1981) *Competence and Power in Managerial Decision-making*. Chichester: John Wiley & Sons.

57. McKenna, E.F. (1978) *The Management Style of the Chief Accountant*. Farnborough: Saxon House.

58. Fiedler, F. (1967) *Theory of Leadership Effectiveness*. New York: McGraw–Hill.

59. Graen, G., Orris, J.B. & Alvares, K.M. (1971) Contingency model of leadership effectiveness: some experimental results. *Journal of Applied Psychology, 55*, 196–201.

60. Gray, J.L. & Starke, F.A. (1984) *Organizational Behaviour: Concepts and Applications (3rd Edition)*. Columbus, Ohio: Charles E. Merrill.

61. Vroom, V.H. & Yetton, P.W. (1973) *Leadership and Decision Making*. Pittsburgh: University of Pittsburgh Press.

62. Field, R. (1979) A critique of the Vroom-Yetton model of leadership behaviour. *Academy of Management Review, 4*, 249–257.

63. House, R.J. (1971) A Path-goal theory of leader effectiveness. *Administrative Science Quarterly, 16*, 3, 321–338.

64. House, R.J. & Mitchell, T.R. (1974) Path-goal theory of leadership. *Journal of Contemporary Business, 3*, 4, 81–97.

65. Griffin, R.W. (1979) Task design determinants of effective leader behaviour. *Academy of Management Review, 4*, 215–224.

66. Newbigging, E. (1983) Business and management education in Japan: some glimpses. *International Management Development, Winter*, 9–12.

67. Kamata, S. (1983) *Japan in the Passing Lane*. London: George Allen & Unwin.

68. Eglin, R. & Barber, L. (1981) Japan's rising sun in Britain. *The Sunday Times, 6 December*, 56–57.

69. Tighe, C. (1981) A testbed for togetherness. *The Sunday Times, 6 December*, 57.

70. Sieff, Lord. (1981) It's people who matter. *The Sunday Times, 13 December*.

71. Buchanan, D.A. & Huczynski, A.A. (1985) *Organizational Behaviour—An Introductory Text*. London: Prentice-Hall International.

72. Blackler, F. & Shimmin, S. (1984) *Applying Psychology in Organizations*. London: Methuen.

73. Terry, P. (1979) Management development. *Industrial and Commercial Training, 11*, 10, 423–426.

74. Handy, C. (1983) *Understanding Organizations*. London: Penguin.

75. Child, J. (1984) *Organizations: A Guide to Problems and Practice. (2nd Edition)* London: Harper & Row.

76. French, J. & Raven, B. (1958) The bases of social power. *In D. Cartwright (Ed.), Studies in Social Power*. Ann Arbor, Michigan: Institute for Social Research.

77. Kling, R. & Scacchi, W. (1980) Computing as a social action: the social dynamics of computing in complex organizations. *Advances in Computers, 19*, 249–327.

78. Leavitt, H.J. & Whisler, T.L. (1958) Management in the 1980s. *Harvard Business Review, 36*, 41–48.

79. Whisler, T.L. (1970) *The Impact of Computers on Organizations*. New York: Praeger

80. Blau, P.M., Falbe, C.M., McKinley, W. & Tracey, P.K. (1976) Technology and organization in manufacturing. *Administrative Science Quarterly, 21*, 20–40.

81. Robey, D. (1977) Computers and the management structure. Some empirical finding re-examined. *Human Relations, 30*, 963–976.

82. Child, J. (1984) New technology and developments in management organization *Omega, 12*, 3, 211–223.

83. Eason, K.D. (1980) Computer information systems and managerial tasks. In N. Byorn-Anderson (Ed.), *The Human Side of Information Processing*. Amsterdam: North Holland.

84. Oborne, D.J. (1985) *Computers at Work—A Behavioural Approach*. Chichester: John Wiley & Sons.

9 HEALTH AND WORK

9 Health and Work

The main focus in this chapter is the relationship between conditions at work and the health and welfare of the employee. To begin with, there is an overview of the nature of work. This is followed by a comment on a selected number of hazardous and stressful conditions in the work environment. Next is a definition of stress and its incidence by occupational groups, leading to an examination of stressors normally associated with white-collar employment. The chapter concludes with an examination of some remedies for alleviating or eliminating stress.

NATURE OF WORK

Work has varied in significance over the centuries. There was a view in classical Greece and feudal Europe that many types of work were dishonorable and not well-regarded, fit only for slaves or serfs. The notion that work is sacred, and even ethically necessary, is only a few hundred years old and became prevalent with the break-up of feudalism. In fact we have moved from one extreme—a puritanical view encompassing work as a severe self-discipline—to a more permissive view of work embracing an opportunity for creativity and self-expression; though in contemporary society some people would view work as a painful activity to be endured.

A job offers a person a recognized place in a community, as well as conferring self-respect and status. It provides a standard by which others judge us. In social introductions questions are asked frequently such as, "what do you do?", although job titles can be misleading because some groups use grandiose titles. Where a job title is not considered to be particularly significant, some workers may mention the organization for which they work. A good fit between the employee's characteristics and the requirements of the job could lead to a satisfied outlook and a balanced dis-

369

position. A poor fit, on the other hand, may produce the opposite effect.

Work is generally a highly organized activity and as such provides many people with a number of benefits apart from income. It offers the opportunity to structure a significant part of our waking hours, and forces us to engage in purposeful activities; it provides us with the opportunity to associate with people outside our immediate circle of family and friends; it allows us to test and clarify our own personal impressions about our status and identity; and it can permit the attainment of personal goals whilst contributing to the achievement of organizational goals.

The work ethic is deeply ingrained in Western industrialized society, and, until very recently, in the U.K. we tolerated waste and overmanning in order to preserve employment, presumably to ensure that people felt socially useful. Political ideologies focus narrowly on work as the creator of wealth. Though one can draw a distinction between work and leisure, there are certain types of leisure activity that have a number of attributes in common with work. For some people, however, enforced leisure is not a welcome experience because it is an inadequate substitute for work. It is interesting to note that at one time to be a lady or gentleman of leisure was held in high social esteem, and this was at a time when work was morally justified. The work ethic is unlikely to be dislodged by unacceptably high levels of unemployment, but it could be subjected to a significant overhaul in these circumstances.

Modern industrial society creates conditions in which it is all too easy for people to become victims of hazardous and stressful events at work. Certain environmental hazards impinge upon our senses; for example, an intolerable level of noise could be the cause of acute discomfort and eventually lead to industrial deafness. Likewise, workers who operate typesetting machines can suffer some physical discomfort from closely watching visual display units for long periods. Certain aspects of a job, such as the work load, the level of responsibility, and the interaction with people, can create unacceptable levels of pressure as well as stress. Being without work and unemployed can equally have a debilitating effect on the psychological well-being of the individual. The remainder of this chapter is devoted to an expansion of these issues.

ENVIRONMENTAL HAZARDS

The environmental hazards, referred to in this section, impinge one way or another on the senses of both blue-collar and white-collar workers. (The senses were explained in Chapter 3 in connection with perception.) Environmental hazards are associated with the factors listed in Table 9.1.

TABLE 9.1
Examples of Environmental Hazards Affecting the Individual at Work

Class of Environmental Hazard	Example	Effect on Individual
Visual	VDUs	Eyestrain due to poor screen contrast, glare, flicker
	Office decor	Bright, distracting colours, reflections from walls and shiny surfaces causing eyestrain and mood swings
Aural (Noise)	Noisy manufacturing equipment	Inability to hear warnings, headache, buzzing in the ears, deafness
	Typewriters, Computer printers, Photocopiers	Irritation, inability to concentrate
Mechanical	Lifting heavy objects	Backstrain, ruptures, hernias, pulled muscles
	Chair design and construction	Backstrain, aching necks, shoulders and arms
Chemical	Asbestos Dust	Lung disease, bronchitis
	Solvents (e.g. degreasants)	Drowsiness, drug-type "high", possible poisoning or risk of accidents due to reduced concentration and reaction time
	Skin irritants (paints, varnishes, white spirit)	Industrial dermatitis, irritations
	Vapour (e.g. carbonless copy paper)	Headaches, drowsiness

Colour Perception

Colour vision defects are seldom treated with the seriousness they deserve. Those affected are often unaware of their abnormality until an obvious error of judgement brings it to light. The red, orange, green, and brown colours pose the greatest difficulty for those who experience some degree of defective colour perception. However, it should be noted that certain colours

TABLE 9.2
Diseases Causing Colour Vision Disturbances

Disease	Colour Vision Change
Diabetes mellitus	Blue defects
Multiple sclerosis	Red-yellow defects
Pernicious anaemia	Green defect
Addison's disease	Blue-yellow defect
Vitamin A deficiency	Most colours
Congenital jaundice	Blue and green defects
Malnutrition	All colours
Spinal cerebellar ataxia ⎫ Friedreich's ataxis ⎭	Red-green defect first then mostly green defect
Brain tumour, trauma, concussion	Red-green or blue-yellow defects
Vascular accidents (stroke)	Various
Cerebral cortex disease	Blue defect
Cortical lesions	Blue defect
Syphilis	Red-green defect, blue defect
Alcoholism and cirrhosis of the liver	Blue defect

Reproduced with the Publisher's permission.
Source: Voke, J., (1982) Colour vision problems at work. *Health and Safety at Work, January,* 27-28.

placed on certain backgrounds can be a significant problem for those with normal vision and may lead to difficulties in focusing on a range of colours simultaneously, causing headaches or fatigue. Mistaking colours can be traced to a genetic factor, and there are a number of diseases associated with colour vision defects. These are shown in Table 9.2.

Apparently tests to diagnose colour abnormalities, indicating the type and severity of both inherited and acquired defects, are now available at a modest price, but it is said that industry continues to use outdated and inferior procedures.[1] It is important to be realistic in the choice of diagnostic tests; those chosen should place the pass/fail mark at a level appropriate to the job in question. The recognition of signal colours in the form of colour vision lanterns plays an important role in examining railway, civil aviation and armed services personnel for colour vision defects. The human eye experiences difficulty accommodating a variety of colours shown simultaneously on a display, and this can result in fatigue. This is more common when one colour is at distance from another.

For example, a wiring operator may have to manipulate a small coloured cable, while at the same time attending to a colour-coded wiring diagram, perhaps several centimetres away from the cable itself. After a time the operator may find that he or she is confusing the colours of the cables and the colours on the diagram and making errors, actually mistaking one colour for another.

Since our eyes tire very quickly if forced to focus in one place for any length of time, there should be a large quantity of restful scenes in the periphery of the field of vision. This environment should consist of muted colours, restful pictures, plants, and other suitable objects.

Lighting and Glare

Lighting is also of critical importance; the aims of a good system of lighting are to facilitate performance on the job, to promote safety, and to assist in the creation of a pleasing environment. When computerized systems are introduced, they are often installed in an office environment with many of the characteristics of the conventional office. Frequently there are big windows to admit as much sunshine as possible, light and bright walls, and direct overhead lighting; the latter was useful for the conditions prevailing in the precomputerized era. So we have light streaming through the windows and bouncing off the gloss-painted walls, creating mirror images and reflections on the operators' visual display unit (VDU) screens. Similar problems are created by direct overhead lighting.

How could an office environment such as this be improved? Blinds or curtains could be put up at the windows, and walls could be covered in a more sombre coloured matt finish. The brightness of the typical VDU display supplemented by a low level of overhead lighting (100 lux or less), is just acceptable for reading the source documents used by the operator. However, it may be necessary to supplement this lighting with brighter local fully adjustable lighting. One could ensure that a VDU is not sited in such a way that the operator is seated facing an unshielded window or other source of light.[2]

Glare is something one must consider when looking at the lighting and illumination provision, because it is as troublesome as inadequate lighting. It manifests itself in many different forms; for example, reflections from a VDU screen, from a bright metal trim, from decorations on the units, and from the keys and the keyboard. Signal lamps can also cause glare when they are badly positioned; glare can also arise because of the positioning and intensity of artificial light. All these sources of glare are critical to the visual comfort of the VDU operator. To reduce glare and reflection at VDU work stations, matt surfaces are preferred and if signal lamps are provided on the unit, these should be of low intensity, glare-free and preferably out of the immediate line of sight.

Visual Fatigue. Poor lighting, due either to inadequate illumination or glare, can give rise to visual fatigue which in turn can contribute to general fatigue. The keyboard operator may also experience visual fatigue when reading poor quality source documents, such as those with illegible handwriting. Though the reverse would be true if the operator inputting the information concentrated more on legible source documents than on the screen. Other considerations to bear in mind hinge on the VDU screen itself. It is beneficial to have an image on the screen which is clear and stable, and it is important to refresh the screen image to an acceptable level because too low a refresh rate can lead to a flickering image. Such an eventuality could lead to eye strain. Attention has also been given to the spacing and colours of characters on the screen, the adjustable nature of the screen, and the extent of operator control over brightness, contrast, and positioning.

Typical symptoms of temporary eye strain or visual fatigue, resulting in strain on the small ciliary muscles of the eye that are used to focus on small objects, include in their severest form: (1) eyes that are sore and dry with an itchiness that rubbing makes worse; (2) eyesight that temporarily blurs making focusing difficult; (3) photophobia, which is an acute sensitivity to light and takes the form of a fear of bright lights; and (4) a general headache that spreads to the neck and shoulders.[3] These conditions can be aggravated by an over-heated, over-dry and smoky environment, and the overall effect is a general deterioration in the person's ability to focus and concentrate on a visual task. This could lead to increased error rates and increased accident potential in certain circumstances. Various recommendations stemming from trade unions and official organizations concentrate on the eyesight of the operator. It is suggested that the operators' eyes are tested before the start of the work, and regularly after that, and that special glasses should be provided for operators with defective vision.

VDUs and Radiation

Apparently there is no need to fear any threat from radiation emitted by VDUS. Significant improvements in the design of the cathode ray tube (CRT) and associated equipment in recent years have resulted in ionizing radiation emission from VDU terminals being almost negligible, only fractionally above the level of natural background radiation. A report prepared by the National Radiological Protection Board concluded that radiation from VDUS cannot cause physical injury to either the skin or the eyes of people working with them.[2] A similar conclusion was arrived at in a Health and Safety Executive report.[4]

Noise

Steps should be taken to protect workers from harmful exposure to noise. An example of noise that we invariably find irritating is the hum or whine of cooling fans. When the hum from a poor ventilation system is acute, it is fatiguing and hypnotic, as the author found to his personal discomfort in a hotel bedroom recently. Likewise, heavy mechanical actions and very high-frequency whining from equipment can be a source of fatigue. General architectural design should pay special attention to acoustics in places of work, because any spillover of ambient sound is irritating. Over the past few decades noise has increased at work, and it affects the attention of the worker as well as causing disturbances, stress and, inevitably, a greater proneness to accidents.

A draft directive presented to the European Commission's Advisory Committee on Health and Safety in 1980, which has now been revised, dealt with the protection of workers from harmful exposure to noise. It proposed that maximum noise levels expressed in decibels should be 70dB(A) for simple administrative workplaces and 80dB(A) for other places of work, and that a priority aim should be to reduced levels at source. Ear defenders (ear muffs and ear plugs) were looked upon as temporary exceptional measures for dealing with the problem of noise; they may not have aesthetic appeal and may prevent the worker from hearing warning alarm systems. A more appropriate set of measures would be to reduce the level of noise emitted, to install noise-absorbent material or cover the source of noise with sound-deadening hoods or screens, and to reduce the exposure time of workers to noise.

The draft directive also proposed audiometric examinations of workers where there was a risk of exposure to excessive noise, and that employers could allow for a 5db(A) increase in noise level when circumstances dictated this, but only for a short time. The reaction of British employers to the draft directive was that complying with these guidelines would be impracticable. It was felt that a noise level of 90dB(A) would be more appropriate, and that it should be recognized that the proposed guidelines would present real problems, in terms of replacement cost, for companies having factories with old and noisy machinery.[5]

The protection of hearing is also taken seriously by the Health and Safety Commission in the U.K., which has produced discussion documents on proposed regulations with regard to the protection of hearing.[6] The intention was to encourage employers to tackle noise problems by resorting to noise control engineering rather than the use of hearing protectors. Employers could only rely on the use of hearing protectors if it could be demonstrated that the adoption of noise control engineering would be prohibitively expensive and not reasonably practicable. As a means of discouraging the employer who shows an attachment to hearing protectors, exacting specifications relating to the choice of equipment and its maintenance are specified. In the discussion document it is also proposed that each company with employees exposed to continuous noise levels in excess of 90dB(A) should appoint a Noise Adviser, qualified and experienced in noise control and hearing conservation.

What is actually happening in British industry with respect to noise control? According to a survey of 200 companies in British industry the control of noise is less than adequate.[7] In 90% of the companies sampled, ear muffs and ear plugs are the only method of noise protection offered consistently.

There was a totally inadequate provision for the control of noise at source in 25% of the companies, and of all the employees in the companies sampled only 10% could be disciplined for not wearing hearing protection devices. The marking of areas where noisy machinery was located applied in only 50% of the companies. Other findings from the survey were: consultation with the union on matters connected with hearing protection only occurred in 50% of the companies; only 12% of employers gave safety representatives the noise levels of new equipment; in 57% of the companies a request by the safety representative to have a noise survey conducted was met, but only 66% of the safety representatives drawn from these companies could be present during the process of noise measurement. Finally, it was felt that the compensation received from either the state or employers as a result of industrial deafness was totally inadequate.

Inhalation of Vapour and Dust

The inhaling of certain vapours as well as asbestos and aluminium dust is a problem under continuous review. The Health and Safety Executive issued a warning to the engineering industry and allied trades not very long ago, drawing attention to the dangers of cold de-greasing solvents following reported deaths from their use.[8] Unfortunately these solvents are used in such a way that the operator may be exposed to a high concentration of vapour which can prove fatal even if the exposure is for a very short period of time. Deaths have occurred to young people working at small de-greasing tanks containing only a few inches of the solvent. Before work commences some of the solvent evaporates and forms a layer of heavy vapour. A typical piece of behaviour by the operator is to lean over the tank in order to scoop the solvent over the components, brushing the components with the solvent or swishing the components through the solvent. In the process the vapour is disturbed and the operator is likely to inhale it. Matters are made worse if the tank is in a room with still air and little ventilation; though one such death occurred in the open air. Commercial chlorinated solvents such as 1.1.1. trichloroethane, upon which de-greasers are based, are potent anaesthetics. A fairly common cause of the reported deaths is loss of consciousness followed by unobserved collapse into the vapour concentration itself as a result of falling in over the side of the de-greasing tank, or collapse in a confined space where the solvent vapour has had the chance to build up in still air.

Solvents with a pleasant odour, which give the effect of a drug-like "high" when inhaled, are also open to deliberate abuse, which can cause deaths either through poisoning by the solvent itself, or through accidents occurring because the individual is not alert and able to react quickly.

The Health and Safety Commission announced much tighter control limits—though they are not absolutely safe levels—for asbestos from January 1983. Where adequate engineering controls to meet the new limits cannot be instituted, then the workforce will be required to wear suitable protective equipment. There are likely to be a number of future measures for the control of exposure to asbestos dust, not to mention an enquiry into both the adequacy and problems of wearing suitable respiratory protective equipment and protective clothing. Other measures will include the licensing of asbestos insulation contractors, prohibiting the spraying of asbestos, prohibiting the use of asbestos in insulation, and prohibiting the import, use and marketing of crocidolite and products containing it.

Pure aluminium dust can also pose a health hazard. Aluminium as a metal is widely used both on its own and in the form of alloy in the manufacture of utensils, laboratory equipment, cable, wire, and foil; or it can be used in powder form in paints. Exposure to pure aluminium dust may produce a form of pulmonary fibrosis, the main features of which are rapidly progressive dyspnoea (i.e., difficult in breathing), cough, and weight loss. Therefore the advent of new technology in the form of the paint-spraying robot and the automation of work processes in areas such as asbestos, lead-based products, and where an atmosphere of intensive dust exists, is welcome on health grounds.

Skin Irritants

The skin is particularly vulnerable to substances in the work environment. Industrial dermatitis has tended to become more prevalent with the increase in the use of chemical-based products on construction sites.[8] Many working days are lost through this disease or disability. Substances such as brick and plaster stone dust, cement containing chromates, pitch, tar and bitumen, certain wood dusts, certain epoxy resins, paints, varnishes and stains, organic solvents, petrol, white spirit and thinners, acids, alkalis, and ionizing radiations, harm the skin in one of several ways.

Oily contaminants can block the pores and hair follicles, abrasives can remove the protective horny layer of the epidermis, and chemicals can dry up the skin's natural moisture or dissolve and remove the protective oily secretion of the skin. The end result is that the outer layers of the skin are damaged and vulnerable to contamination by particles and bacteria. The skin's natural protection is reduced further by cuts, scratches, blisters, etc., acquired from work requiring rough handling. Even though injuries may appear trivial, workers should seek first aid in these circumstances.

Allergic dermatitis occurs through hypersensitivity to specific substances (e.g., certain hardwoods or synthetic resins) which may prove harmless to many people. Once the person is sensitized to the substance he or she can never again safely handle it. Irritant dermatitis usually only attacks the areas of the skin in direct contact with the harmful substance, and it will usually respond to proper medical treatment. The preventative measures for counteracting ordinary irritant dermatitis are as follows:

1. Substitute a safer material in place of the harmful material.

2. Use no-touch techniques, i.e., gloves, mechanical aids, or remote control. There are obvious advantages in using gloves in rough handling jobs. But one has to consider what happens in the inside of the glove. Outside dirt may get in and the glove prevents perspiration evaporating into the air. As a result, the skin remains moist and soft and vulnerable to the entry of contaminants.

3. Personal Hygiene: Sometimes in order to get rid of irritant substances, such as paint, tar, oil, stains, the person resorts to using petrol or abrasives, or strong detergents, or solvents and thinners. These should be used carefully because they can be harsh on the skin and could themselves cause dermatitis, leaving the skin rough, sensitive, and liable to crack. The skin should be washed with soap and warm water and thoroughly dried, ideally applying some lanolin-based skin cream to the dried hands. The employee should avoid going to the toilet with dirty hands, so as to prevent contamination to the groin, which is a sensitive area susceptible to skin troubles.

When trying to protect the workers from certain hazards, effective protective clothing has to be considered. But it may be difficult to achieve effectiveness and at the same time to ensure that this clothing is comfortable to wear while working in some occupations. It is said that in a 24-hour period a person engaged in hard physical work can produce half a gallon of water through perspiration for every metre of skin area. That water has to evaporate off into the atmosphere or the worker becomes hot, damp, very uncomfortable, and lacking in concentration. Protective clothing that can withstand chemicals, acid, fine dust, water, or even fire might well cause the wearer to suffer from fatigue and exhaustion through a build-up of condensation. In practice the worker will probably, if at all feasible, sacrifice his or her protective clothing for the sake of comfort.

There are indications of a breakthrough in protective clothing.[8] This can be seen in protective clothing able to withstand various hazards (i.e., it acts as a barrier to water and other liquids and is completely windproof). At the same time it will permit perspiration vapour to pass freely through. So the worker can be fully protected and yet remain dry and comfortable at the job he or she is doing; as a result, one can expect more efficient job performance. Fabrics such as the new membrane will make a significant impact in the field of protective clothing. This thin material has a microporous structure with nine billion pores to the square inch. Further applications for the new fabrics are under consideration. These include outdoor welding suits, "clean

TABLE 9.3
Lifting and Carrying Loads Safely

	Carrying Distances (Range)	
	Short	Long
	0–61 cm	1.8 m
	(2 ft) ──────────────▶	(6 ft)
Max. safe weight	54.4 kg	9.0 kg
	(120 lb) ──────────────▶	(20 lb)

room" garments for the pharmaceutical and electronics industries, toxic material protection of all types, flame-retardent clothing, weather-protection suits for hostile environments and chemical splash protective clothing.

Lifting

People suffer from backaches, ruptures, hernias, and strained muscles from working in the home, garden, and in do-it-yourself building activity. Lifting heavy loads at work may then aggravate an already weakened condition. The Chartered Society of Physiotheraphy offers guidance on maximum weights for safe lifting. For example, the maximum safe weight, capable of being lifted repeatedly by an adult male, is 54.4 kg (120 lb). When walking with a load the maximum weights which can be lifted vertically, then carried over a distance, are given in Table 9.3 for a range of distances.

Maximum safe weights vary depending on the height and physique of the person. Injury to the small of the back and hernia damage as a result of lifting heavy loads are not uncommon. The expending of muscular force in the face of resistance, or supporting a heavy load without moving, consumes energy and can be painful and unacceptable. For example, the repeated grasping and lifting of smooth-surfaced heavy cartons of awkward dimensions on to high stacks in a warehouse can be uncomfortable. If employees feel a strain when lifting a load, but persist, they may hurt themselves. It is suggested that the following advice on lifting should be borne in mind:

Avoid lifting and carrying above the level of the eyes.

Avoid lifting or supporting a load in a vertical axis when the load is located any distance from the vertical axis of the body.

Provide an intermediate platform when loads are lifted on to the shoulder or lowered from the shoulder.

Look out for and eliminate features of job design that impose awkward postures.[9]

There are occasions when the consequences of lifting heavy boxes are not fully appreciated. For instance, at a particular works the sand feeding process to the foundry moulding machines was mechanized in order to increase output. The moulding boxes were not put at a suitable height for transfer to and from the machine. The increased number of heavy iron boxes to be lifted cancelled out the gains derived from the improved sand provision.

Chair Design and Posture

The right sitting position is something that should also be considered; poor chair design can contribute to a sloppy posture. A chair should be so designed that the load on the hind quarters is minimized. The chair should have proper lumbar support and allow variations in the sitting position, particularly if one person occupies it for long periods, or if many people occupy it over the working day.

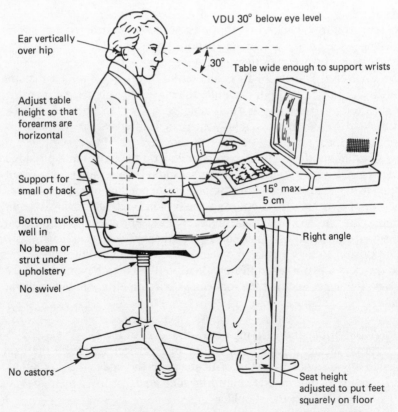

FIG. 9.1   The ideal sitting position for a computer operator. Source: Lately, P. (1982). Computing can damage your health. *Practical Computing, 5,* 126-7.

For a chair to be of the correct height the entire sole of the foot should rest on the floor, or on a foot rest, and there should be a complete centimetre between the edge of the seat and the underside of the thigh behind the knee joint. This allows the blood to circulate freely around the body. An arm rest may be considered suitable by some people, though not by others, and may be dependent on the nature of the job. The way the work is presented to the operator is also important, because bending and turning increase the load on the spine and muscles. The wrong sitting position and stressful working practices can result in aching necks, shoulders, and arms; the opportunity to stand up and stretch the limbs in these circumstances is welcome.

Given the enormous growth in computer applications for different purposes in organizations, what is the ideal sitting position for a VDU operator? The following guidelines and the diagram in Fig.9.1 provide one answer.[10]

Use a chair without castors or a seat swivel. Chairs with castors or a seat swivel provide instability and prevent your muscles from relaxing properly.

Make sure the chair has a short, flat seat that does not unduly press the knee end of the thigh.

Check that it is soft under the pelvis, and that there are no hidden beams or struts lurking under the upholstery.

Use a chair with an adjustable support for the small of the back.

Set the height of the seat so that your feet are squarely on the ground. Alternatively, provide a solid support under your feet to produce this effect.

Adjust the back rest so that when your bottom is tucked well back into the seat your ear is vertically above your hip. A little of your weight should rest vertically on the back rest.

Arrange the height of the keyboard so that when the upper arms hang vertically, your lower arms are horizontal.

Push the keyboard back from the edge of the desk until there is room to rest your wrists.

The keyboard should be flat enough so that you can operate the keys without raising the wrist from the desk or kinking it upwards.

Office Layout and Carbonless Copying Paper

Certain aspects of life in the modern office can be considered hazardous. In the open-plan office, which is often said to be more economical and functional than the smaller office, the lack of privacy and the constant disturbance and distractions have an adverse effect on some employees. The modern carbonless copying paper used in offices has been identified as a cause of mysterious symptoms which reach a peak at busy working periods.[11] The symptoms take the form of rashes, irritations to the eyes, nose and throat, headaches and drowsiness, and are caused by dust and chemical vapours created by the carbonless copying paper. This paper is coated with chemicals and tiny micro capsules containing more chemicals. When the typewriter key hits the paper, the micro capsules are crushed at that particular spot and they release their chemicals. These chemicals react with the chemicals in the coating of the paper to form permanent dyes.

Handling the paper in small quantities would not be a problem but dealing with large quantities could create dry eyes and throat and a feeling of abnormal tiredness in staff working in a confined office. This condition is aggravated by overheating and badly ventilated offices, causing what is referred to as "paper sickness". In a reported case of a businessman who suffered from paper sickness after spending only a day in a small office leafing through records kept on carbonless paper, it was found that he developed a burning sensation on his face, throat, and tongue.[11] The following day he woke up with aches in his legs. That was Saturday, but he felt much better on Sunday. On Monday, he experienced the same symptoms, having handled carbonless paper records for the morning only. Symptoms similar to the common cold—runny eyes and nose—were detected in four women who handled the carbonless paper. This was most acute in the last week of the month when the office was very busy.

The women would frequently place their hands between sheaves of carbonless paper to extract a particular sheet, and they all noticed that this caused a tingling sensation of the skin.

ORGANIZATIONAL STRESSORS

Stressful conditions have already been acknowledged in the discussion of environmental hazards. Before looking at various facets of organizational life that can generate stress, it is appropriate to be more precise in specifying what is meant by a stressful condition.

Definition of Stress
To use an analogy from physics, stress arises because of the impact of an environmental force on a physical object; the object undergoes strain and this reaction may result in temporary distortion but equally it could lead to permanent distortion.

In human terms any situation that is seen as burdensome, threatening, ambiguous, or boring is likely to induce stress. This is the type of situation that would normally strike the individual as deserving immediate attention or concern and is viewed as unfortunate and annoying. There tends to be the feeling that this situation should not exist, but because of it the person feels disappointed or annoyed and eventually is prone to anxiety, depression, anger, hostility, inadequacy and low frustration tolerance.

In other circumstances PRESSURE arises when the individual is expected to perform in a particular manner and finds it a source of discomfort and anxiety, but at the same time finds the experience a source of excitement, challenge and personal growth. It is suggested that no objective criteria is good enough to describe a situation as stressful; only the person experiencing the internal or external threat can do this.[12] Therefore the potential for stress exists when an environmental pressure is of such a magnitude as to threaten the individual's capability to cope with it in conditions where successful coping is a rewarding experience.[13]

In everyday life we rarely encounter severe stressful situations, such as prolonged lack of sleep or physical torture; instead weaker but important generators of stress such as the death of a spouse, divorce, impairment of one's faculties, loss of a job, rejection by a colleague, unrequited love, failure in examinations all play a crucial part.

But people respond differently to stressors. For example, on retirement one group of executives may feel severely depressed, another group may feel moderately sad and frustrated, and a third group may feel content and happy. For others travelling in a train is less likely to be stressful than travelling by car or aeroplane. Many of us would find it less stressful to work in difficult or dangerous conditions with people we trust than in similar conditions where we distrust others or lack confidence in ourselves.

A specialist in occupational medicine described the body's reaction to stress in the following terms.[14] The heart and breathing rates increase, blood pressure goes up, sweating increases, muscles get tense, the eyes widen, and there is heightened alertness. Tense muscles cause headaches, backaches, shoulder and back pains. Clenched hands, clenched jaws, and hunched shoulders are tell-tale signs of stress, along with frowning and fidgeting, finger tremor, and the mopping of a sweaty brow. An anxious person has "butterflies" or churning in the stomach, a dry mouth, weak legs, nausea, a thumping heart, breathlessness and a feeling of light-headedness.

Course participants at a Management College reported on symptoms of stress which they had previously experienced. These included dim or fuzzy vision, some chest pains, unusual heart beats, occasional sleep difficulties, frequent episodes of irritability, tiredness, or depression (this was by far the most frequent), and periods in which their work performance was impaired for a few days.[15] As we shall see later the effects of stress can be fatal.

We are becoming increasingly aware of the true costs of stress at work. These costs find expression in reduced quality of work, increased absenteeism, increased labour turnover, and rising medical costs. By impairing the psychological and physical well-being of employees, stress also affects the employees' family. At the level of society the effects of stress are reflected in an increase in welfare costs, an increase in socially disruptive behaviour, such as alcoholism and drug abuse, and less involvement in the community.

Stress in Different Occupations

There is a belief that some occupations are sources of greater stress than others. An analysis of mortality due to arteriosclerotic heart disease, among U.S. males by occupational classification in the age range 20–64, shows that teachers fare better than lawyers, medical practitioners, estate agents, and insurance agents.[16] However, general practitioners are more vulnerable to heart disease than are other physicians.[17]

As to suicide rates, those connected with the enforcement of law had higher mortality rates than those who administer the law. Though surprisingly those who are exposed to life-threatening situations suffer less stress than those who are not. Among medical and related personnel, practitioners with above average suicide rates are dentists and psychiatrists.[18]

Dentists are said to experience significant pressure from the demands of developing their practice. The dentist prone to stress tends to be anxiety-prone and more easily upset when confronted with excessive administrative duties and when faced with too little work because of a preoccupation with building and sustaining the practice. Dentists with raised blood pressure perceived to some extent their image as inflictors of pain. They also experienced stress from their job interfering with their personal life.[19]

It would be unwise to attribute stress, and its fatal consequences, only to professional and executive groups. There is a view that occupational stress is more likely to be found among blue-collar and routine white-collar workers.[20] This is a view shared by the Chief Medical Officer of an Insurance Company in her address to a conference on managing stress.[21] She maintained that the highest mortality rate from all causes was more likely to be found in socio-economic groups 3, 4, and 5.

In certain occupations—e.g., the police and fire service—the normal retirement age is 55. This might suggest that such occupations are stressful, and that it would be unfair to expect an employee to continue working until he or she reached the customary retirement age for most occupations (60 or 65). Of course it could also suggest that age and fitness are more critical factors for the successful operation of these services. Another occupational group in the emergency services—the ambulancemen—are said to be using the stress factor to secure a similar advantage to that enjoyed by the police and the fire service. An ambulanceman in Liverpool, who was fitted with an electro-cardiogram, experienced a significant increase in heart beat when he responded to an emergency call. The highest heart beat was recorded during two spells of stressful driving through heavy suburban and city traffic.[22]

The Fire Brigade Union has carried out a number of health studies jointly with the British Home Office, one of which included the taking of electro-cardiogram readings from a number of fire service employees to establish whether their duties made them vulnerable to cardiovascular stress likely to result in excessive heart strain and related health hazards.

In the U.S. there is research evidence suggesting that a number of factors cause stress among the police. These include low penalties imposed by the courts; distorted media publicity; an increasing number of complaints and criticisms by minority groups; lack of adequate resources; lack of public appreciation; fear and danger in the work undertaken; the fragmented nature of the work; and shiftwork. Some of these factors may very well apply to the police force in the U.K. The effects of police stress are said to be an increased incidence of alcoholism, infidelity, wife beating, child abuse, divorce, isolation, heart disease, and nervous disorders.[22]

The National Conference of Roman Catholic Priests held in Birmingham in 1984 considered the results of a survey of the clergy. Though it is recognized that many clergy lead fulfilled and happy lives, there are strong indications that a number of priests are demoralized and overburdened by pressures from both inside and outside the church. They experienced a certain amount of role ambiguity, particularly those in middle age. The survey identified two major sources of stress, one being loneliness and the other being difficulty in handling personal relationships. Once the status of the priest was that of father figure to his parish—a man set apart from his parishioners who in their eyes had no problems or feelings. Now the priest wants his parishioners to treat him as a person, and younger priests particularly are impatient for change. [23]

A survey of senior managers in 112 financial organizations conducted by MORI and reported in The Financial Times in October 1986, shortly before the Big Bang (the shake up of the financial markets) in the City of London, showed that 64% identified stress as their main health concern. The worst affected were accountants and building society managers. Presumably, the latter are feeling the effects of the cold winds of competition in the financial services market.

Those who worked in the city identified "too much work" as the biggest single factor in causing stress. Other causes mentioned were long hours, competition, pressure to perform, over-promotion, conflict between work and private life and job insecurity. The most frequently mentioned symptom of stress was a deterioration in the employee's performance. Other symptoms stated were irritability, absenteeism, problems with making decisons, difficulties with drinking, and depression.

Among the typical stressful conditions facing the manager at work are the following: too much or too little work; time pressures and deadlines to meet; having to make too many decisions; endeavouring to cope with changes that affect the job; concern about the costs in monetary and career terms of making mistakes: excessive and inconvenient working hours; highly repetitive work; the necessity to work fast; erosion of salary differentials; the prospect of redundancy or being forced into premature retirement; disparity between real authority and authority vested in the job; the feeling of

TABLE 9.4
Factors causing Stress to the Individual at Work

	Stressors	
From within Organization	*From within Individual*	*From outside Organization*
Role overload	Inbuilt inability to cope with stressful situations	Conflict between domestic life and work
Role complexity		
Role ambiguity	Dissatisfaction with career development	Fear of redundancy, unemployment, early retirement
Role conflict		
Difficult boundary roles	Aversion to shouldering responsibility for people	
Position in hierarchy	Feelings of unease in relating to others	

being trapped in a job without much chance of getting a similar or better job elsewhere; a perceived mismatch between performance on the job and the financial benefits secured; and reservations about the value of the job in contributing to the output or welfare of the organization.[24,25,26]

In practice one may find certain organizationally devised ways of alleviating pressure at work: for example, deadlines could be set at an unrealistically early date to permit a margin of error so that mistakes or shortcomings could be rectified before it is too late; decisions could be made in groups so as to share the burden of responsibility for a decision; and finally duties could be reallocated in a department when an individual is very busy and is forced to shelve certain duties. However, in practice there may be occasions when these devices are not directly at the disposal of the manager. The conditions and circumstances inside and outside the organization giving rise to stress are now discussed; these are listed in Table 9.4.

Role Pressure
Pressure generated by an organizational role can manifest itself in ways identified below.

1. Role Overload. Frequently it is said that executives put in more hours at the office than employees at a lower level in the organizational hierarchy and that they bring more work home at night. Evidence from a survey conducted by Executive Life in the U.S. suggests that one group of employees—presidents, vice-presidents, and high potential middle managers—worked between 57 and 60 hours a week. They spent 45 to 48 hours a week in the office during the day, entertained once a week and worked three nights a week, one at the office and two at home. This was the work pattern during normal times. But when on a business trip, or attending a conference, or dealing with an emergency they might put in 70 or 80 hours per week.[27]

A relationship exists between too heavy a workload—i.e., taking and making more telephone calls, more office visits to and from other people, and more meetings for a given unit of work—and heavy cigarette smoking; the latter is an important risk factor as far as coronary heart disease is concerned.[28]

Too much work can also give rise to a number of symptoms of stress, such as escapist drinking, absenteeism from work, low motivation to work, lower estimation of oneself, and unwillingness to suggest improvements to work procedures and practices.[29] Working at more than two jobs which required an excessive number of hours' work (60 plus per week) was found to be a critical contributory factor to coronary heart disease.[30] It is worth noting that the working married woman is frequently denied the opportunity to recuperate from her remunerative work, resulting in chronic fatigue.

In today's economic climate managers have responsibility for keeping costs and manning levels in check. In their role of pruning expenditure inevitably they will encounter resistance at the subordinate level, with consequences in terms of damaging relationships of trust and impairing good communications. They also have to contend with pressures from top management who naturally are concerned that policy is implemented in accordance with agreed guidelines. If there are redundancies at shopfloor level and among their colleagues in management, there is a likelihood that their workload will increase. They may also feel that they ought to be seen to be working harder.

2. Role Complexity.   Apart from too much to do, too difficult a job can equally create problems. In one study changes in the cholesterol levels of tax accountants at different times in the fiscal year were observed.[31] During the experimental period of approximately five months each accountant was visited twice monthly by the experimenter, and was closely questioned about any job-related stress he or she had experienced during the two preceding weeks. After each interview a blood sample was obtained. Serum cholesterol levels of the accountants remained fairly low during the early months of the year, but a significant increase in cholesterol was observed for approximately six weeks before the April tax deadline.

Following the tax deadline, the cholesterol levels of the accountants fell to the levels observed during January and February. It is interesting to note that there was no change in diet, which might account for the changes described above, and members of a control group (company accountants) showed no such effect. In another study blood samples were taken from medical students at times when they were under no examination pressure and then on the day or near the day of an important examination when the workload was arguably more exacting. An increase in serum cholesterol was observed in the latter situation.[32]

In a more elaborate study 100 young coronary patients were compared with a control group consisting of the same number. In 91% of the coronary patients it was noted that before the attack there was prolonged emotional strain which was associated with job responsibility. Only 20% of the control group, who were normal, suffered similar emotional strain. There was not much difference between the two groups in heredity factors, high fat diets, obesity, smoking, or lack of exercise. In most respects the young coronary patient had a history of overwork because of a strong urge to gain recognition or not to disappoint an employer, family, or others. He or she tended to be aggressive, ambitious, and operated beyond his or her normal capacity and tempo.[33] A lengthy questionnaire and interview schedule was administered to 46 coronary patients and 49 members of a control group. It was found that 50% of the patients, as opposed to 12% of the control group, reported that they worked long hours with few holidays under considerable stress and strain before falling victim to heart disease.[34] One might therefore conclude that too difficult a job can contribute to increased heart rate, tension, embarrassment, and lower self-esteem.[35]

3. Role Ambiguity.   Sometimes we overlook the importance of clearly specifying what the job requires of the individual. There are a number of circumstances in an organization when the requirements of a job are unclear as to the objectives laid down and the scope of responsibilities; as a consequence colleagues are not altogether clear about what the job entails. In such circumstances a number of undesirable consequences are likely to ensue.[36] The latter consist of a lowering of job satisfaction, self-confidence, and self-esteem, a general dissatisfaction with life and a feeling that the whole thing is futile, leading to a depressed mood, low motivation to work, an intention to quit the job, and increased blood pressure and pulse rate.[28,29]

4. Role Conflict.   If a job is arranged in such a way that the individual performing the tasks connected with the job is confused by conflicting demands—i.e., the person is sandwiched between two groups of people who expect a different kind of service or expect a service different from the one that is presently rendered—or if the person is doing things he or she does not want to do or does not think are part of his or her job description, then the seeds of conflict are sown. As conflict develops a lowering of job satisfaction is experienced, more so if the conflicting demands originate from the desks of powerful figures in the organization. In addition an increase in heart rate and feeling tense about the job is likely to materialize.[28,36] A significant relationship was found between role conflict and coronary heart disease among managerial employees in the kibbutz system in Israel; though occupations requiring excessive physical activity (e.g., agricultural workers) were associated with a lower incidence of coronary heart disease.[37]

5. Boundary Roles.   It is often suggested that one of the more stressful jobs is that performed by people occupying a boundary role, that is, when the job takes them into contact with people in other departments and outside the organization.[36] It is in this capacity, as representatives of their own department, that strain arises. The supervisor (the "man in the middle"), who performs a boundary spanning role which is vulnerable to a high degree of conflict, was found to be particularly at risk in the sense that he was seven times more likely to develop ulcers than shopfloor workers.[38]

Chief executives in Israeli state business enterprises, who perform a boundary spanning role between the organization and government bureaucracy, were said to experience conflict over objectives, decisions, and government relationships, and these were a source of stress.[39] Sometimes one finds a certain rigidity in management and worker roles where the potential for better understanding and communication is not fully realized due to a concern with outmanoeuvering one's opponent and the absence of a serious attempt to solve long-term problems. This is likely to be reflected in management and trade union relations. Managers, or for that matter industrial relations specialists, playing this type of role in a harsh economic climate could experience severe stress.

6. Responsibility for People.   Bearing responsibility for people, rather than for things—where one has to spend more time interacting with others, having to attend more meetings, and having to meet deadlines often working alone — is associated with coronary heart disease in the form of diastolic blood pressure and serum cholesterol levels.[40] This appears to be the predicament of the older executive who has assumed greater responsibility.[41] But one must concede that as one gets older considerations other than increased responsibility may play a potent force as generators of stress. For example, there may be the realization that further career advancement is not possible, that the prospect of approaching retirement is unwelcome, particularly for the individual with narrow or insignificant interests outside work, and a feeling that one is isolated within the organization.[42] Just as we identify greater responsibility as a source of stress, the same could be said of too little responsibility.

Hierarchical Level

The incidence of stress can vary depending upon the organizational level at which the manager operates. Partners in accounting firms experienced less stress and strain than other staff, with junior staff experiencing most stress.[43] Lower and middle managers are said to experience more symptoms of em-

otional and physical ill health than senior managers.[44] This is not far removed from a view which suggests that the most likely candidate for a heart
attack is not the senior executive; it is the junior executive, probably striving
for the top, or the white-collar worker surrounded by frustration.[45]

Life at different levels of the organization is viewed as both a source of
satisfaction and stress.[44] Top managers showed a tendency to be more outgoing and derived more satisfaction from managing people and putting aside
time for problems connected with the development of people. They appear
to feel pressure from a substantial amount of communication and consultation, and are satisfied when they are free from decision-making processes
based on consultation. They feel prone to pressure from bureaucratic rules
and regulations which tend to constrain their behaviour unduly, and they
feel that their present jobs, as opposed to their previous jobs, make greater
demands on their leisure and family time; this is a source of pressure because
of the time spent and the conflict with home demands. They are not very
interested in opportunities outside the company and the fact that they have
reached their career ceiling and may have to retire early poses little problem.

For middle managers, dealing with personnel problems was a source of
pressure. Using new systems or methods on a frequent basis was also a
source of pressure. Like the top manager, they also felt prone to pressure
from bureaucratic rules and regulations and the intrusion of business into
leisure and family time. Middle managers do not like to feel pushed for time.
They are more likely to feel pressure as a result of perceiving a lack of opportunity within the company at a time when new jobs are more demanding
and competition for them is severe.

In recent years the plight of the female manager has been acknowledged.[46] It is suggested that as more women are entering managerial positions they are subjected to a greater number of work-related pressures compared with their male counterparts. In addition, women in management are
often subjected to additional pressures of trying to maintain a family or a
home. However, differences between the sexes in sources and levels of occupational stress is poorly supported by the evidence at our disposal.[47,48]

It appears that making important decisions is a source of pressure for
middle managers, unlike top managers who are more likely to share important decisions.

This calls to mind a classic study which showed that making a decision
can cause ulcers in conditions when all other factors are kept constant.[27]
Two monkeys were strapped in seats facing a light and a lever, with an elec-
trified rod at their feet. One monkey had access to a dummy lever and the
other was able to control the flow of electric current by using an operational
lever (executive control). A light flashed every 20 seconds and both monkeys would get a mild electric shock unless the monkey with executive control pressed the lever. The monkey with access to the dummy lever soon

ignored it because it was totally ineffective and therefore had to rely on the other monkey to press the lever every time the light flashed. This required the monkey with executive control to act fairly quickly.

The monkey with the dummy lever remained in excellent health, but the decision-making monkey who exercised executive control died on the 23rd day, the apparent victim of an ulcer. However, contradictory evidence comes from a group of researchers at the University of Wisconsin, who exposed monkeys to a loud, irritating noise, but allowed half of them to interrupt the sound by pulling on a chain.[49] Though both groups of monkeys were exposed to the same noise, those with access to the chain showed lower levels of stress-related hormones in their blood. Being in control seemed to be an advantage in these circumstances, unlike the previous situation. Perhaps the difference in stimuli—an electric shock as opposed to a loud noise—may have been a contributory factor to the eventual outcome.

Work Relationships

There stems from the relationship between superiors, subordinates and colleagues a number of desirable and undesirable consequences. When the relationship is good it leads to the advancement of individual and organizational health. When the relationship is deficient or bad, as one finds in circumstances where distrust among staff is rampant, it can give rise to poor or inadequate inter-personal communication, leading to reduced job satisfaction and a feeling of being threatened by one's colleagues and superiors.[28,36]

Jealousy, humiliation, arguments, and reprimands all contribute to feelings of stress, and may lead to negative emotions which can be exhausting and debilitating. John Hunter, the eighteenth-century physician, who was prone to angina pectoris, once remarked that his life was in the hands of any rascal who chose to annoy or tease him. He got into an argument with a colleague who contradicted him and became very involved in a verbal encounter; he then stopped talking, left the room, and immediately dropped dead.[50] Where rivalry and office politics occur in relationships between colleagues, support from one's peers may be lacking in difficult situations with obvious repercussions.[12]

If a highly competitive atmosphere exists, sharing of problems may cease as an activity because people fear that they may not be able to stand their ground and perform adequately. In today's conditions of proposed cuts in expenditure and programmes of rationalization, quite understandably people feel anxious in the face of uncertainty as to what is going to happen next. In such conditions there is a real danger of losing a sense of belonging and identification with the organization or part of it, with obvious repercussions in terms of anxiety and stress.

The dampening influence emanating from an incompetent superior cannot be overstated. This may be reflected in a number of ways. The superior may be bankrupt technically in conditions where a deficiency in this respect is serious. He or she may be unable to focus seriously on key issues, prone to digress frequently and listen inattentively, fail to act on sensible ideas or suggestions put forward for serious consideration, and may lack the confidence to take initiatives backed up by a reasonable amount of preparation. In addition a failure to empathize with others and the lack of a modicum of charisma are limiting factors. The subordinate who expects a better calibre superior and is encumbered with the type of manager just described may suffer from some of the classical symptoms of stress.

In comparatively recent times the desirability of getting managers to adopt a participative leadership style has been advocated. It is believed that the superior who extends the hand of friendship to subordinates, who develops mutual trust, respect, and warmth with subordinates and is constructive in his or her criticisms, without playing favourites or taking advantage of subordinates, is likely to go a long way in neutralizing pressure which originates from the job.[51] It is claimed that more involvement in the decision-making process by subordinates where they get feedback on their performance and are duly recognized for their contribution, leads to higher productivity, better relationships between superiors and subordinates, more individual control and autonomy and less labour turnover, all of which are conducive to good mental health.[52]

On the other hand, lack of participation in decision making is said to promote strain and stress at work because the freedom of thought and movement enjoyed by the subordinate is restricted as a result of close supervision and low autonomy.[51] One group of researchers claims that failure to allow participation to take root was related in a significant way to a number of risks to personal health. These are poor overall physical health, escapist drinking, depressed mood, low self-esteem, low job satisfaction and satisfaction with life, low level of motivation to work, an intention to quit and absenteeism.[29]

A word of caution is called for before unequivocally endorsing the participative approach as a panacea for problems connected with management style. To use this approach successfully in managing subordinates, managers must be adept at delegating responsibilities and be able to manage effectively through an open process.[53] Otherwise, a certain level of anxiety stress, and resentment may arise because managers recognize that their actual power falls short of their formal power, and as a consequence their formal role and status is eroded. It is also conceivable that the participative approach is seen as "soft" and a waste of time partly because of the view that subordinates do not wish to get involved or participate in decision making. This eventually places a barrier in the way of doing a good job and achieving a high level of productivity. A full discussion of the participative leadership style appears in Chapter 8.

Career Development

Progression in a career is of prime importance to many executives and managers. But with fairly rapid technological, economic, and social change and development in society, uncertainty arises because of the real possibility of having to change career during one's working life. As a consequence, career development stress is likely to occur much more frequently later in life, unless executives and managers adapt their expectations to coincide with these developments. Middle age is a particularly vulnerable stage because it is then that career opportunities can decrease significantly and career progress can grind to a near halt.

In the case of men, various manifestations of the "male menopause"—considered by some to be a myth—are likely to occur.[54] These are a proneness to dwell on fears and disappointments, a feeling of being isolated, doubting one's ability to get on top of a new assignment or job, a belief that the old knowledge and skills are no longer as relevant as they once were, a realization that energy is becoming more scarce or is being channelled into family activities, and finally that one has to cope with competition from younger colleagues.

At the present time the pruning of expenditure and cutting back on staffing levels is tending to lead to a situation of more competition for the limited number of promotions within the organization. Also, with restricted career opportunities outside the organization a number of managers are likely to feel trapped because a barrier is placed in the path to the realization of their ambition and potential. In circumstances such as these frustrations develop and can be negatively directed against the organization, or the system of authority within it, or where that is not possible, against colleagues and the family.[55]

The situation can even be worse if the manager is "passed over" in the promotion stakes. Psychosomatic illness has been attributed to such an event.[56] Equally sensitive might be a situation in which a previous subordinate now becomes a person's superior.

In one sense occupational mobility has a positive aspect to it, but in another sense it may produce negative consequences. Those who are occupationally mobile (four or more job changes) and geographically mobile (two or more cross-country moves) are said to be more vulnerable to heart disease than are those who belong to stable occupational groups.[57] Some people may feel uneasy about being over-promoted, just as others would feel uneasy about being under-promoted or having reached the end of their career path.

The over-promoted manager may be grossly over-worked in order to hold down the job and at the same time may engage in behaviour designed to mask inner insecurities.[58] The person who is fully stretched, having been given responsibility exceeding his or her ability, was found to progress from minor psychological symptoms to marked psychosomatic complaints and finally to mental illness.[59] Apparently the under-promoted person, who was given responsibility below the corresponding level of his or her ability, suffered simlar complaints.

Redundancy and Unemployment

Feelings of insecurity arise because of the fear of redundancy or demotion, or the fear that one's skills are becoming obsolete, or when there is talk of early retirement. Redundancies among all staff, and executives in particular, have been increasingly common in recent years.[44] Prior to the announcement of any redundancies, rumours circulate and anxiety springs from job insecurity. If redundancy is to be selective, trust and openness suffer, leading to suspicion and perhaps severe competition. Uncertainty about the future develops and ironically the actual announcement of the redundancy programme may initially be considered a relief because people know where they stand.

But this will soon wear off and the process of instituting the redundancy programme may be equated with an exercise in removing "dead wood." Feelings of guilt and shame arise as a consequence, even though the redundant person obtains the sympathy of colleagues. Events may not take the course outlined above in the case of mass redundancies or voluntary redundancies, but it seems plausible that the process in such an eventuality would contain certain similarities to it.

Having being made redundant, the individual suffers the loss of status which accompanied the job and for some there is the danger of withdrawal due to a sense of failure. Loneliness and a feeling of isolation is not uncommon at this stage. At this time redundant employees may regard their loss as only temporary and tend to look at the new situation as if it were a long-deserved holiday. They are cushioned by a redundancy settlement and can get on with jobs needed to be done about the house.[60] In the search for another job, extreme competition is encountered and perhaps their is a feeling that a prospective employer may be unfavourably disposed to somebody who has been made redundant. With continual lack of success in securing another job comes an increasingly long period of unemployment. For the most optimistic of people this is something which erodes self-confidence and contributes to depression.

If the main wage-earner in a family—traditionally the man—suffers prolonged bouts of unemployment, these create problems of structuring time and organizing daily life, pessimism, distress, fatalism, and apathy. A spill-over to family life is likely as the individual's influence becomes less in the home.[61] This is due to his own negative view of himself as well as a negative evaluation by the family. Quite naturally this becomes a source of domestic anxiety. At a time when the wife is suffering strain from the burden o financial worries, and perhaps planning a change in lifestyle, she has also to contend with her husband's need for encouragement and emotional support. This places added strain on her. Eventually the roles may have to be reversed when the wife goes out to work and the former breadwinner stays at home, much to the relief of the wife. The children may suffer a loss of prestige among their friends and homework may suffer. The waning of the father's authority may encourage disobedience, emotional upset and anti-social behaviour.

From preliminary studies of redundancies it was shown that, when employees expected plant closures, blood pressure rose, and for those who became unemployed it continued to do so. Feelings of depression, irritation, and low self-esteem were associated with the high blood pressure. Those who found employment experienced a rapid reduction in the blood pressure level in the direction of normal. Levels of serum uric acid behaved in a similar fashion to the blood pressure as a consequence of unemployment.[62] Emotional instability was associated with increasing unemployment among unemployed engineers.[63] Eventually, the job aspirations of the unemployed could be lowered, and a lower-status job with a lower salary accepted. Where the unemployed person cannot secure another job, the individual settles for new standards and a different way of life. Social activities of all sorts are curtailed for emotional and financial reasons, and roles within the family could suffer a dramatic change.[60]

In a survey of a small group of unemployed male managerial staff in the U.K. it was concluded that, though the men passed through the shock phase on losing their jobs, none had reached the pessimism or acceptance of unemployment stage whether they had been unemployed for six months or over a year.[64] Though aware of the negative and pessimistic feelings associated with unemployment, they used conscious strategies to delay these feelings—for example, it is to be expected that it will take longer to secure a managerial or professional job; the contemporary unemployment scene makes one realize that the job situation is highly competitive, and failure to land a job is not a deficiency on one's part. Savings and redundancy payments act as a buffer against the financial hardships of unemployment, and the reduction in the stigma attached to it helps. But "bitchy" neighbours can "rub salt in the wound." There is still a reluctance to discuss unemployment.

Though the negative aspects of redundancy have been highlighted at length, it could be said that redundancy may be construed as an opportunity for somebody who has got into a rut in a job to exchange it for a better opportunity or life elsewhere. During the transitional stage, however, anxiety is still likely to prevail. Given growing executive redundancy, a pertinent question to ask is, whether managers will accept a pressurized existence with long hours at work and geographical mobility if their jobs are seen to be insecure. Perhaps the new insecurity will attract a more resilient manager with a high tolerance for ambiguity or uncertainty, or will it attract the drifter or industrial cowboy?[44]

Early Retirement

For some managers nearing retirement the call of a job with lighter responsibilities and more flexible hours is attractive, and they decide to move on.[65] Those who are compelled to retire early and those who are ill-prepared for retirement may feel dissatisfied, as would perhaps those who retire for health reasons, at least initially. There are those who retire early and find it difficult to adjust emotionally to the life of a retired person, and they can feel bored, depressed, and lonely.[44] There are others who miss the social contacts at work, and will be ill-equipped to cope with a situation in which a lot of time is spent with the spouse. However, one must not lose sight of a number of advantages attached to early retirement. These include more personal freedom, more leisure time, more time with the family and friends, and opportunities to pursue hobbies and travel, and engage in educational pursuits. These advantages would be even more attractive if the person is provided with an adequate pension and feels financially secure.

Domestic Considerations

There are a number of circumstances which originate outside the organization that can create stress. These include family problems, life crises, financial difficulties, conflict of personal beliefs with those of the organization, and family commitments competing with commitments to the organization. A topic that has attracted a fair amount of analysis and comment is the relationship between the male manager and his wife and family.[66,67] The work and home situation are interrelated since the manager has to rely on support from the home to alleviate stress originating at work and to keep him in touch with certain realities. In this way the wife's role may be seen as supportive and caring while the "thruster" husband pursues a demanding job in the knowledge that the home environment is a refuge, provided the marital relationship is not in jeopardy.

The husband may run the risk of strain and ineffectiveness if he tries to execute both the work and home roles to an adequate level. The young executive may find himself in the situation where he has to maintain a distance between his wife and the organization as he is building up his career and putting a lot of effort into the job, just at the very time his young housebound wife is also making demands on his time. By maintaining the distance between the wife and the organization he is not forced to choose between the two, at a time when he ought to involve his wife because of the need for her sympathy and understanding.[68]

It would perhaps be an oversimplification to view the relationship between the husband and his family as being strictly of the nature described above. Some wives though acting in a supportive role are bored and lonely a home and may be jealous of the husband because of his career. Others are very adept at acting as a buffer between problems arising in the home and their husband. In other situations a wife may take an outside interest and step up entertaining on behalf of her husband when the children are grown up, and may find this life absorbing and satisfying. Instead of acting in a supportive capacity a wife may be envious of the fact that the husband has insufficient time for considering her problems or achievements, and as a retaliatory measure objects to him taking work home or moving house because of the job. This could create a situation of overload during office hours and frustrated ambitions for the husband, which he is likely to resent.

There are of course relationships where the wife pursues a career, because to do so is satisfying or financially rewarding, and both husband and wife share the housework. It is when the husband expects his home comforts and does not receive them, that problems are likely to arise. Many husbands do not fully appreciate the implications for the wife of moving house as a result of changing jobs. This is even more important when the move is to a foreign country. It is almost inevitable that the mobile family is prone to developing temporary relationships, with a capacity to live for the present and turn on instant sociability and display an ability to show an indifference to the local community.[69]

From the husband's viewpoint this may be due to shortage of time and the realization that they are short-stay inhabitants. The wife may bear the brunt of the move; she has to attend to a number of matters connected with the house move; she has to create a new life in the new neighbourhood and does not have the advantage of her husband whose job status is transferred; she is expected to provide a stable environment for the children and her husband and to be in a state of readiness for the next move. In the process she may have had to sever contact with a close circle of friends or family, and this loss is very prevalent soon after the move.[70]

In the U.S. increasing divorce rates are said to be a consequence of the continuous success of the aspiring senior manager who leaves his socially unskilled wife at home.[71] Alcoholism may be a problem for some corporate wives. It is said that the ratio of female to male alcoholics in the U.S. rose from 1:5 in 1962 to 1:2 in 1973.[72] Perhaps this may be due to frustration and loneliness. Generally the plight of the wife may not be as bad as it seems because she may not encounter too many difficulties getting involved in the community, even if it is a transient one, and this involvement could act as a compensation for being somewhat isolated because of her husband's ambitions and career involvement. It is in the husband's interest to see that the wife has made a successful adjustment following the move.

Personality Factor

A number of perspectives on personality are discussed in Chapter 1. When considering the effects of stress on executives, it is wise to take into account the individual's capability or personality to withstand stressful conditions. Personality appears to be a key factor in this respect. It is suggested that patients with coronary heart disease or related diseases are emotionally unstable and introverted.[73] Employees with rigid personalities were more prone to rushing jobs assigned to them from above and to be dependent on other people. Those with flexible personalities were more likely to be influenced by others and to suffer from work overload. Introverts are said to withdraw from interpersonal relationships that produce stress and in doing so complicate matters by preventing communication and making interaction and problem solving more difficult.[36]

Friedman and Rosenman's research identifies a relationship between certain behavioural traits and a proneness to heart disease.[74] The individuals in their studies were rated on the personality factors prior to the actual medical diagnosis, and this was conducted without awareness of the behavioural traits. Those classified as Type A in behaviour were people who exhibited coronary-prone behaviour which can be expressed as follows: extreme competitiveness, striving for achievement, aggressiveness, haste, impatience, restlessness, hyperalertness, explosive speech, tenseness of facial muscles, feelings of being under pressure of time, and keenness to assume the challenge of responsibility.

A Type A person will tend to set deadlines or quotas for him or herself at work or at home at least once per week, while the opposite—Type B—will do so only occasionally. A Type A person will tend to bring work home frequently, while a Type B will rarely do so. Type A people are in general substantially involved and committed to their work and other aspects of their lives are relatively neglected. They tend to possess the following risk factors: high serum cholesterol levels, elevated beta lipoproteins, decreased blood clotting and elevated daytime excretion of norepinephrine, more incidence of acute myocardial infarction, and angina pectoris. They are also less likely to give up smoking.

The relationship between Type A behaviour and symptoms of stress is supported in a study of 236 managers in 12 different companies.[75] This showed that Type A behaviour was associated in a significant way with high blood pressure and higher cholesterol and triglyceride levels. A high percentage of the managers in each of the age groups studied were cigarette smokers and Type A managers were less interested in exercise. However, in a comparatively recent study of 384 male salaried employees in the U.S., based upon questionnaires, interviews, and physical examinations, it was found that there was no direct association between Type A behavioural patterns and risk factors connected with coronary heart disease.[76]

SUGGESTED REMEDIES FOR STRESS

Stress does not have to be viewed as a bad thing, for there is only one kind of person without conflicts—a dead one. However, too much stress is harmful and measures should be taken to tackle it with the hope of reducing it. To cope with tension or stress drugs or tranquillizers could be used, but this remedy helps the person to deal with the immediate condition or symptoms without equipping him or her to confront future stressful situations. It is suggested that to allow greater individual autonomy and participation by employees in matters that concern them is a useful approach. Where there is evidence of deficiencies in personal and interpersonal skills, techniques are available, such as sensitivity training and team building, which are designed to analyze and perfect the behavioural skills, but it is by no means conclusive that results following the use of these techniques match the expectations of those committed to their use.

One could also create an organizational environment in which people feel free and confident to say they cannot cope, where they can air their basic fears and invite help if necessary. This would require a significant shift in attitudes because to many people an admission of being a victim of stress is tantamount to acknowledging that one is unstable and incompetent. Understandably, people prefer to brush it under the carpet and remain secretive about it. However, in this context the technique of Rational Emotive Therapy (RET) might be useful.[77] RET emphasizes the rebuilding of one's thinking process about particular issues and is designed to help people who over-react to stressful situations by giving them almost complete responsibility to examine their own faulty reactions.

The assumption is that they will be able to change their emotional reactions if they modify their ideas, philosophies and attitudes about various kinds of stressors that impinge on their lives. The technique consists of a multi-pronged attack at the emotional and intellectual levels on dysfunctional ways of thinking and behaving. It tries to teach people how to treat themselves, that is, how to cope with present and future stressful conditions by recognizing that since these conditions exist they should try to cope with them as sensibly as possible, frequently trying to change them for the better by continually confronting them. A clinical psychologist, has indicated below a number of steps that the Type A person might take to change his or her habits:[78]

1. (a) Select a quiet place in your home; then sit down or lie comfortably and close your eyes. Listen to soothing instrumental music and let yourself float along with the melody. Imagine yourself in a soothing environment and allow the music to relax your muscles.

(b) In an alternate fashion tighten and relax the muscles of your hands, biceps, face, shoulders, chest, stomach, legs, and feet. Concentrate on the feeling of relaxation that follows the tightening of the muscles.

(c) As you breathe out repeat the word "one" and maintain this pattern for 10 minutes. Feel the release of tension with each breath.

If you find that you are able to relax by any one of the above methods, then use it at times when you feel stress. Take a break from the activity causing the stress and make your way to a private place and relax. Allow your mind to float away from the pressures of daily activities and remember how you felt when you relaxed at home; relive those feelings.

2. If you have mastered the technique of relaxing quickly, use imagery to neutralize the emotional reactions which arise as a consequence of the pressures you frequently encounter. First relax and then imagine yourself facing a situation that normally makes you tense—e.g., the pressure that comes about when you face a deadline. You continue to imagine this situation but at the same time you retain an awareness of relaxation. Repeat this several times, and each time imagine that you are handling the situation calmly. Should the visualization of the stress scene make you feel more tense than relaxed, terminate the exercise temporarily and repeat it until you work your way through the entire scene without feeling any tension.

3. Take active steps to control and manage your environment. For example, arrange your appointments realistically and allow enough time in between meetings so that you are not always rushing from one meeting to another. Set your priorities, if you can, in the morning of each day, and adhere to that order. Only undertake a new task when you are finished with the priority items. Learn how to cope with what others expect of you. Be frank and let them know how much effort and time you are prepared to give them and be forthcoming when you feel you cannot accept their requests. If somebody wants you to take on another task, and you feel your present workload is more than sufficient, get that person to assist you in evaluating the urgency of his or her request and then decide whether it fits among your priority items.

4. Try to avoid acting in a rushed manner, otherwise you will feel pressure. Take it easy and practise eating with slower movements, putting down your fork between bites. Slow down your steps when you walk and slow down your speech when you talk. Repeat briefly what you hear others say as you are listening to them. This will help you to understand them better and will contribute towards minimizing your impatience.

It would appear sensible to recognize differences between people, or the basis of personality and physical and mental conditions, when specifying the most appropriate techniques to use. Meditation may be effective for hypertension, but inappropriate for dealing with a peptic ulcer. In another situation psychotherapy may be suitable for treating one Type A per sonality, whereas regular exercise and vacations would suit another.

Apart from remedies based on psychotherapy and meditation, regularity of meals and their nutritional balance are of major importance in keeping fit and in raising resistance to stress. Adequate sleep and moderation in the consumption of food, drink, and drugs are also worth pursuing. Regular exercise, which can be pleasurable, at the end of the day, in the lunch break and at the weekends, can help to get rid of anger, irritation, and frustration. See the funny side of life; enthuse about things generally; put aside time for little things; encourage, pay compliments to, and praise other people when it is appropriate and proper to do so. Nurture friendships, and build a mutual support system so as to be able to discuss stresses with a trusted friend, a relative, or professional helpers. Talking through problems and putting stresses in perspective can be productive and may point in the direction of a solution. Take on hobbies which can be a source of relaxation.[14] Finally, a healthy interaction between work and the home should be promoted.

WELLNESS

As a postscript to the discussion of measures to reduce stress, it seems appropriate to acknowledge the "wellness" movement, which is proactive rather than reactive in the field of preventative health management.

As a means to promote wellness a number of organizations, particularly in the U.S., are encouraging their employees to look after their minds and bodies through more healthy life styles. Factors contributing to this development are the rising costs of health care in the U.S., often borne by companies, and the boom in physical fitness. From the company's point of view promoting good health is considered to be a wise investment.

The rationale appears to be that to stay well is less costly than to get well, to prevent illness is more sensible than to cure it, and a healthy life style enhances the chances for improved health, a longer life and quality of life.

The promotion of wellness can be viewed as a four-step process.[79]

1.   Employees are educated about health-risk factors such as poor nutrition, lack of exercise, smoking, drinking and drug abuse, and being overweight.

2.   Employees receive information about their health risk factors through life-style assessments and physical examinations.

3.   Plans are developed for employees to reduce risks through healthier life styles.

4.   Employees receive assistance from the organization to continue with the changes in their life style. This necessitates a process of monitoring and evaluation.

Wellness programmes vary in their degree of comprehensiveness. Some companies merely distribute educational material on desirable life styles, whilst others can go as far as providing an indoor track, weightlifting equipment, bicycles and workout clothes to its employees and claim consequential benefits such as reductions in absenteeism, smoking and excess weight.

An example of a wellness programme is the "Staywell" programme introduced by the Contral Data Corporation, U.S.A. in 1979. The programme consists of creating profiles of health risk, medical screening, health education and activities to change life styles. This was offered to the company's employees in San Diego and New York. Since then other sites have been included.[80] The programme is offered without charge to all the company's employees and their spouses. Participation is on a voluntary basis and all activities are provided at the place of work. The employees are allowed time off to attend an orientation session and to participate in other activites such as the health risk profile and a group interpretation meeting.

Those who sign on for the Staywell programme are weighed and measured, have their blood pressure taken and give a blood sample. Also, they complete a questionnaire on their medical outlook. The result of the physical examination and the responses on the questionnaire are used to provide a computerized health-risk profile on each person. The profile compares the individual's chronological age with his or her "risk age", and it shows how the risk can be improved if the individual changes certain behaviour. Next, those who participate in the programme are encouraged to select courses from a group of one-hour health awareness courses. These range from how to utilize the health care system to breast self-examination and substance abuse. However, the multi-session behaviour and life-style change programmes have been the most popular. These deal with specific high-risk areas such as smoking, fitness, nutrition and weight control, hypertension and stress. Specific activities to change life style and improve health are planned for each individual.

An important feature of the Staywell programme is the introduction of a follow-up programme and the use of support systems. One characteristic of the follow-up programme is the formation of employee groups consisting of individuals interested in or troubled by similar problems. Changing the culture at work and people's attitudes will be necessary for the success of the programme.

The group sessions take place at the end of each of the education and life style change courses, and for a certain period have an instructor at their disposal. Eventually group members learn to help one another to sustain the change in their behaviour, and they practice various techniques and strategies to avoid failure. Support from one's peers in the group, whether it is an exercise in reducing weight or stopping smoking, helps to persuade people to persevere with the modified behaviour. It is said that currently approximately 22,000 people, either employees of the Control Data Corporation or their spouses, participate in the Staywell programme in 14 American cities.

The Staywell programme at the Control Data Corporation is based on the following premises.[81]

Life style has a major effect on illness and life spans;

People can change their habits, with appropriate help;

The work place is the most effective place to help people change their behaviour, because people spend so much of their time there; and

Companies have a major stake in promoting a healthier life style for their employees, because of the potential benefits of reduced insurance costs, decreased absenteeism, improved productivity, and better morale.

Beneficial outcomes of wellness programmes include 50% reductions in sickness rates and absenteeism, increases in job performance and attitudes toward work, improved stamina, sounder sleep and loss of weight.[81] At the Control Data Corporation significant reductions in costs of health care have been associated with a decline in cigarette smoking, a lack of hypertension and an increase in regular exercise. A decrease in absenteeism and lost time due to illness were also associated with an increase in the number of good health habits developed in the Staywell programme. It is probably too early yet to establish whether or not "wellness" programmes are successful generally, because only a limited amount of evaluation of these programmes has so far taken place; however, there are signs of some promising results in the future.

SUMMARY

After a brief examination of the nature of work, a number of hazards in the work environment were specified. These are related to colour perception, lighting and glare, visual fatigue, noise, inhalation of vapour and dust, skin irritants, lifting, sitting position, and certain office conditions. Both blue-collar and white-collar workers can be exposed to hazardous and stressful conditions at work.

Following a definition of stress, it was suggested that occupations differ in terms of stress and risks to health. Certain stresses and strains were associated with different facets of organizational life, particularly for white-collar workers of executive rank. These covered role pressure (e.g., role overload, complexity, ambiguity, etc.), hierarchical level, work relationships, career development, redundancy and unemployment, early retirement, domestic considerations, and personality factors.

A number of remedies to counteract a stressful state were suggested. These ranged from psychotherapy and meditation to nutritional balance in intake of food, regular exercise, and a balanced personal and social existence. Finally, the concept of wellness in the context of preventative health management was introduced.

QUESTIONS

1.   What do you understand by *the nature of work*? Comment on the work ethic in conditions of high unemployment.

2.   Identify two environmental hazards and consider how they are likely to affect the welfare of the employee at work.

3.   Explain the following terms:
   (a) defective colour perception;
   (b) glare;
   (c) visual fatigue;
   (d) industrial dermatitis.

4.   Distinguish between pressure and stress in an organizational context.

5.   Identify the costs associated with stress at work.

6.   Comment on the suggestion that certain occupations are more stressful than others.

7.   With regard to role pressure, what is the difference between role-complexity and role-ambiguity?

8.   List the conditions discussed in the section of this chapter devoted to "organizational stressors," and state what you think are the two most substantial conditions contributing to executive stress in contemporary society.

9.   One of the suggested remedies for stress is Rational Emotive Therapy. Briefly explain what is involved in this technique.

10.   Explain what is meant by "wellness".

REFERENCES

1. Voke, J. (1982) Colour vision problems at work. *Health and Safety at Work, January*, 27–28.

2. Anderson, D. (1980) Eyestrain or eyewash. *Health and Safety at Work, August*, 36–39.

3. Murray-Bruce, D. (1982) Promoting the healthy banker. *Journal of the Institute of Bankers, December*, 199–200.

4. Mackay, C. (1980) *Human Factors Aspects of Visual Display Unit Operation*. London: HMSO.

5. Hamilton, M. (1981) Safety, noise and communication (A report on the proceedings of the 1981 ROSPA Conference in Harrogate). *Occupational Health, June*, 291–292.

6. Else, D. (1981) Hearing protection: who needs training? *Occupational Health, September*, 451–453.

7. British Labour Party (Research Department). (1981) *Noise at Work*, (Bargaining Report No.17). London: Labour Party Headquarters.

8. Untitled comment in the *Safety Representative. (1982) October* 1.

9. Hammond, J. (1978) *Understanding Human Engineering. An Introduction to Ergonomics*. Newton Abbot: David and Charles.

10. Lately, P. (1982) Computing can damage your health. *Practical Computing, July*, 126–127.

11. Gillie, O. (1982) Feeling tired at the office? Blame it on the copy paper. *The Sunday Times, 19 December.*

12. Lazarus, R.S. (1966) *Psychological Stress and the Coping Process*. New York: McGraw-Hill.

13. McGrath, J.E. (1976) Stress and behaviour in organizations. In M.D. Dunnett, (Ed.), *Handbook of Industrial and Organizational Psychology*. Chicago: Rand McNally.

14. Murray-Bruce, D. (1983) Promoting the healthy banker—stress. *Journal of the Institute of Bankers, April*, 62–63.

15. Melhuish, A.H. (1977) Causes and prevention of executive stress. *Occupational Health, 29*, 193–197.

16. Guralnick, L. (1963) Mortality by occupation and cause of death (Report No. 3); Mortality by industry and cause of death (Report No. 4); Mortality by occupational level and cause of death (Report No. 5) (all among men 20 to 64 years of age in USA, 1950). *Vital Statistics—Special Reports, Vol. 53*. Washington, D.C.: US Public Health Service.

17. Morris, J.N., Heady, J.A. & Barley, R.G. (1952) Coronary heart disease in medical practitioners. *British Journal of Medicine, 1*, 503–520.

18. Daubs, J. (1973) The mental health crisis in opthalmology. *American Journal of Optometry and Archives of American Academy of Optometry, 50*, 816–822.

19. Cooper, C.L., Mallinger, M. & Kahn, R. (1978) Identifying sources of occupational stress among dentists. *Journal of Occupational Psychology, 51*, 227–234.

20. Fletcher, B., Gowler, D. & Payne, R. (1979) Exploring the myth of executive stress. *Personnel Management, May*, 30–34.

21. Reynolds, M. (1980) *Executive Stress*. Unpublished paper given at conference on Managing Stress, by The Industrial Society, 18 April, in London.

22. Brooks, P. (1980) The tension of the bells. *Health and Safety at Work, October*, 47–48.

23. Longley, C. (1984) Loneliness: main cause of stress for priests. *The Times, 5 September.*

24. Sofer, V. (1970) *Men in Mid-Career*. Cambridge, UK: Cambridge University Press.

25. Kay, E. (1974) Middle management. In J. O'Toole (Ed.), *Work and the Quality of Life*. Cambridge, Mass: MIT Press.

26. Kearns, J.L. (1973) *Stress in Industry*. London: Priory Press.

27. Schoonmaker, A.N. (1969) *Anxiety and the Executive*. New York: American Management Association.

28. French, J.R.P. & Caplan, R.D. (1970) Psychosocial factors in coronary heart disease. *Industrial Medicine, 39,* 383–397.
29. Margolis, B.L., Kroes, W.H. & Quinn, R.P. (1974) Job stress: an unlisted occupational hazard. *Journal of Occupational Medicine, 16,* 654–661.
30. Russek, H.I. & Zohman, B.L. (1958) Relative significance of hereditary diet and occupational stress in CHD of young adults. *American Journal of Medical Science, 235,* 266–275.
31. Friedman, M., Rosenman, R.H. & Caroll, V. (1957) Changes in the serum cholesterol and blood clotting time of men subject to cyclic variation of occupational stress. *Circulation, 17,* 852–861.
32. Dreyfus, F. & Czaczkes, J.W. (1959) Blood cholesterol and uric acid of healthy medical students under the stress of an examination. *Archives of Internal Medicine, 103,* 708–711.
33. Russek, H.I. (1965) Stress, tobacco and coronary heart disease in North American professional groups. *Journal of the American Medical Association, 192,* 189–194.
34. Miles, H.H.W., Waldfogel, S., Barrabee, E.L. & Cobb, S. (1954) Psychosomatic study of 46 young men with coronary artery disease. *Psychosomatic Medicine, 16,* 455–477.
35. French, J.R.P. & Caplan, R.D. (1973) Organizational stress and individual strain. In A.J. Marrow (Ed.), *The Failure of Success,* New York: AMACOM, 30–66.
36. Kahn, R.L., Wolfe, D.M., Quinn, R.P., Snoek, J.D. & Rosenthal, R.A. (1964) *Organizational Stress.* New York: John Wiley & Sons.
37. Shirom, A., Eden, D., Silberwasser, S. & Kellerman, J.J. (1973) Job stress and the risk factors in coronary heart disease among occupational categories in Kibbutzim. *Social Science and Medicine, 7,* 875–892.
38. Margolis, B.L. & Kroes, W.H. (1974) Work and the health of man. In J. O'Toole (Ed.), *Work and the Quality of Life.* Cambridge, Mass: MIT Press.
39. Dornstein, M. (1977) Organisational conflict and role stress among chief executives in state business enterprises. *Journal of Occupational Psychology, 50,* 4, 253–263.
40. Wardwell, W.I., Hyman, M. & Bahnson, C.B. (1964) Stress and coronary disease in three field studies. *Journal of Chronic Diseases, 17,* 73–84.
41. Pincherle, G. (1972) Fitness for work. *Proceedings of the Royal Society of Medicine, 65,* 321–324.
42. Eaton, M.T. (1969) The mental health of the older executive. *Geriatric, 24,* 126–134.
43. Gaertner, J.F. & Ruthe, J.A. (1981) Job-related stress in public accounting. *Journal of Accountancy, June,* 68–74.
44. Cooper, C.L. (1979) *The Executive Gypsy: The Quality of Managerial Life.* London: The Macmillan Press.
45. Packard, V. (1962) *The Pyramid Climbers.* New York: McGraw-Hill.
46. Davidson, M.J. & Cooper C.L. (1981) Occupational stress in female managers—a review of the literature. *Journal of Enterprise Management, 3,* 115–138.
47. McKenna, E.F. & Ellis, A. (1981) Counterpoint to Davidson and Cooper (Occupational stress in female managers). *Journal of Enterprise Management, 3,* 139–142.
48. Reynolds, M. (1981) Counterpoint to Davidson and Cooper (Occupational stress in female managers). *Journal of Enterprise Management, 3,* 145–147.
49. Wallis, C. (1983) Stress: can we cope? *Time, 6 June,* 44–52.
50. Barnard, J.M. (1981) Stress: its effects on people at work. *Occupational Health, 7 July,* 353–361.
51. Buck, V. (1972) *Working Under Pressure.* London: Staples Press.
52. Coch, L. & French, J.R.P. (1948) Overcoming resistance to change. *Human Relations, 11,* 512–532.
53. Donaldson, J. & Gowler, D. (1975) Prerogatives, participation and managerial stress. In D. Gowler & K. Legge (Eds.), *Managerial Stress.* Epping: Gower Press.
54. Constandse, W.J. (19) A neglected personnel problem. *Personnel Journal, 51,* 129–133.

55. Culbert, S. (1974) *The Organization Trap.* New York: Basic Books.
56. Morris, J.N. (1956) Job rotation. *Journal of Business, October,* 268–273.
57. Syme, S.L., Hyman, M.M. & Enterline, P.E. (1964) Cultural mobility and the occurrence of coronary heart disease. *Journal of Health and Human Behaviour, 6,* 178–189.
58. McMurray, R.N. (1973) The executive neurosis. In R.L. Noland (Ed.), *Industrial Mental Health and Employee Counselling.* New York: Behavioural Publications.
59. Brook, A. (1973) Mental stress at work. *The Practitioner, 210,* 500–506.
60. Fagin, L.H. (1979) The experience of unemployment 1. The impact of unemployment. *New Universities Quarterly, Winter,* 48–64.
61. Jahoda, M. (1979) The impact of unemployment in the 1930s and the 1970s. *Bulletin of The British Psychological Society, 32,* 309–314.
62. Kasl, S.V. & Cobb, S. (1970) Blood pressure in men undergoing job loss. *Psychosomatic Medicine, 32,* 19–38.
63. Shanthamani, V.S. (1973) Unemployment and neuroticism. *Indian Journal of Social Work, 34,* 83–102.
64. Swinburne, P. (1981) The psychological impact of unemployment on managers and professional staff. *Journal of Occupational Psychology, 54,* 47–64.
65. Sleeper, R.D. (1975) Labour mobility over the life cycle. *British Journal of Industrial Relations, XIII,* 2.
66. Pahl, J.M. & Pahl, R.E. (1971) *Managers and Their Wives.* London: Allen Lane.
67. Handy, C. (1975) Difficulties of combining family and career. *The Times, September 22,* 16.
68. Beattie, R.T., Darlington, T.G. & Cripps, D.M. (1974) *The Management Threshold,* (BIM Paper OPNII). London: British Institute of Management.
69. Packard, V. (1975) *A Nation of Strangers.* New York: McKay.
70. Marshall, J. & Cooper C.L. (1976) *The Mobile Manager and His Wife.* Bradford: MCB Publications.
71. Immundo, L.V. (1974) Problems associated with managerial mobility. *Personnel Journal, 53,* 910.
72. Seidenberg, R. (1973) *Corporate Wives—Corporate Casualties.* New York: American Management Association.
73. Lebovits, B.Z., Shekelle, R.B. & Ostfeld, A.M. (1967) Prospective and retrospective studies of CHD. *Psychosomatic Medicine, 29,* 265–272.
74. Rosenman, R.H., Friedman, M. & Strauss, R. (1964) A predictive study of CHD. *Journal of the American Medical Association, 189,* 15–22.
75. Howard, J.H., Cunningham, D.A. & Rechnitzer, P.A. (1976) Health patterns associated with Type A behaviour: a managerial population. *Journal of Human Stress, March,* 24–31.
76. Chesney, M.A., Sevelius, G., Black, G.W., Ward, M.M., Swan, G.E. & Rosenman, R.H. (1981) Work environment, Type A behaviour and coronary heart disease risk factors. *Journal of Occupational Medicine, 23,* 531–555.
77. Ellis, A.A. (1974) *Humanistic Psychotherapy—The Rational Emotive Approach.* New York: McGraw-Hill.
78. Suinn, R.M. (1976) How to break the vicious cycle of stress. *Psychology Today, December,* 59–60.
79. Reed, R. W. (1984) Is education the key to lower health care costs? *Personnel Journal, 63,* 40–46.
80. McCann, J. F. (1981). Control Data's Staywell Programme. *Training and Development Journal, October,* 39–43.
81. Hall, D. T. & Goodale, J. G. (1986) *Human resource managment—Strategy, design and implementation.* Glenview, Illinois: Scott, Foresman and Company.

Author Index

Subject Index